DISCARD

Constitutional Debates on Freedom of Religion

CONSTITUTIONAL DEBATES ON FREEDOM OF RELIGION

A Documentary History

Edited by JOHN J. PATRICK
and GERALD P. LONG

Primary Documents in American History and Contemporary Issues

GREENWOOD PRESS
Westport, Connecticut • London

Library of Congress Cataloging-in-Publication Data

Constitutional debates on freedom of religion : a documentary history
/ edited by John J. Patrick, Gerald P. Long.
p. cm.—(Primary documents in American history and
contemporary issues, ISSN 1069-5605)
Includes bibliographical references and index.
ISBN 0-313-30140-9 (alk. paper)
1. Freedom of religion—United States—History—Sources.
I. Patrick, John J. II. Long, Gerald P. III. Series.
KF4783.C66   1999
342.73'0852—dc21   99-21819

British Library Cataloguing in Publication Data is available.

Library of Congress Catalog Card Number: 99-21819
ISBN: 0-313-30140-9
ISSN: 1069-5605

First published in 1999

Greenwood Press, 88 Post Road West, Westport, CT 06881
An imprint of Greenwood Publishing Group, Inc.
www.greenwood.com

Printed in the United States of America

The paper used in this book complies with the
Permanent Paper Standard issued by the National
Information Standards Organization (Z39.48-1984).

10 9 8 7 6 5 4 3 2 1

Contents

PART II: Religious Liberty in the Founding of the United States, 1776–1791

PART III: The Constitutional Right to Free Exercise of Religion, 1791–1991

PART IV: The Constitutional Prohibition of an Establishment of Religion, 1791–1991

PART V: Constitutional Issues on Freedom of Religion, 1991–1998

Series Foreword

This series is designed to meet the research needs of high school and college students by making available in one volume the key primary documents on a given historical event or contemporary issue. Documents include speeches and letters, congressional testimony, Supreme Court and lower court decisions, government reports, biographical accounts, position papers, statutes, and news stories.

The purpose of the series is twofold: (1) to provide substantive and background material on an event or issue through the texts of pivotal primary documents that shaped policy or law, raised controversy, or influenced the course of events, and (2) to trace the controversial aspects of the event or issue through documents that represent a variety of viewpoints. Documents for each volume have been selected by a recognized specialist in that subject with the advice of a board of other subject specialists, school librarians, and teachers.

To place the subject in historical perspective, the volume editor has prepared an introductory overview and a chronology of events. Documents are organized either chronologically or topically. The documents are full text or, if unusually long, have been excerpted by the volume editor. To facilitate understanding, each document is accompanied by an explanatory introduction. Suggestions for further reading follow the document or the chapter.

It is the hope of Greenwood Press that this series will enable students and other readers to use primary documents more easily in their research, to exercise critical thinking skills by examining the key documents in American history and public policy, and to critique the variety of viewpoints represented by this selection of documents.

Introduction

The Constitution of the United States of America, written in 1787 and ratified in 1788, includes only one reference to religion. In Article VI, there is a clause stating that "no religious Test shall ever be required as a Qualification to any Office or public Trust under the United States." This prohibition of religious requirements for eligibility for United States government offices has never been at issue in a federal court of law. And this clause of Article VI has been a generally accepted constitutional standard for religious liberty in the United States government from the founding era until today.

The First Amendment of the U.S. Constitution, proposed in 1789 and ratified in 1791, includes two clauses on religion. It says, "Congress shall make no law respecting an establishment of religion, or prohibiting the free exercise thereof." From 1791 until today, Americans generally have agreed that the "establishment clause" and the "free exercise clause" limit the power of the U.S. government in order to protect the religious liberty of individuals under the authority of the Constitution.

During the nineteenth century, the constitutional principles of free exercise of religion and prohibition of government-sanctioned religious establishments prevailed throughout the several states of the American federal union. Legally established religion, banned at the federal level of government in 1791 by the First Amendment, was abolished by the few state governments that had mandated it. But if blatant de jure or legal establishments of religion had passed from the United States, a de facto or informal type of religious establishment persisted. It involved a culturally rooted and voluntary preference among most Americans for Protestant Christianity.

The leading Protestant denominations during the nineteenth century were the Baptists, Congregationalists, Disciples of Christ, Episcopalians,

Lutherans, Methodists, Presbyterians, Quakers, and members of Reformed Christian churches. Most members of these various Protestant
Christian churches were descendants of settlers who had come to North
America from western and northern Europe during the seventeenth and
eighteenth centuries.[1] Their ancestors had founded the United States of
America, and they intended to maintain cultural dominance in their
country, especially with regard to religious traditions. So, they simultaneously and paradoxically affirmed American constitutional principles
on religious liberty and promoted generally held religious traditions
through nongovernmental organizations of civil society and informal accommodation with the local, state, and federal governments.

The famous French visitor to the United States in the 1830s, Alexis de
Tocqueville, noted positively the informal, nonlegal, yet tight tie in the
United States between the general Protestant form of Christianity and
the social/political order. In his acclaimed two-volume work, *Democracy
in America*, Tocqueville wrote:

> The sects that exist in the United States are innumerable. . . . [B]ut there is no
> country in the world where the Christian religion retains a greater influence over
> the souls of men than in America. . . .
> Religion in the United States takes no direct part in the government of society,
> but it must be regarded as the first of their political institutions; for if it does not
> impart a taste for freedom, it facilitates the use of it. Indeed, it is in this same
> point of view that the inhabitants of the United States themselves look upon
> religious belief. . . .
> Upon my arrival in the United States the religious aspect of the country was
> the first thing that struck my attention; and the longer I stayed there, the more
> I perceived the great political consequences resulting from this new state of
> things. . . . [T]hey all [the Americans] attributed the peaceful dominion of religion
> in their country to the separation of church and state.[2]

As a member of the Roman Catholic Church, Alexis de Tocqueville
was concerned about the marginal place of his co-religionists in American life, which resulted from the Protestant domination of political and
social affairs. Nonetheless, he observed with satisfaction the growing
numbers of Catholics in America due to immigration from Ireland, the
south German states, and other Catholic regions of Europe. And he predicted, presciently, that Roman Catholicism would eventually become a
significant part of the vast religious diversity that distinguished American society from the countries of Europe and elsewhere.[3]

More than fifty years after Alexis de Tocqueville visited and wrote
memorably about America, a distinguished British scholar, James Bryce,
visited the United States to inquire and report about its political and
social life. In his three-volume work, Lord Bryce, like Tocqueville, observed the indirect and informal yet close connection between Chris-

tianity and government, which persisted, paradoxically, in relative harmony with federal and state constitutional proscriptions against any establishment of religion. Lord Bryce wrote:

The whole matter may, I think, be summed up by saying that Christianity is in fact understood to be, though not the legally established religion, yet the national religion. So far from thinking their commonwealth godless, the Americans conceive that the religious character of a government consists in nothing but the religious belief of the individual citizens, and the conformity of their conduct to that belief.[4]

The unofficial and extralegal Protestant establishment, woven into the social and cultural fabric of nineteenth-century America, was challenged and changed during a period extending from the 1880s until the 1940s. During this time, there were massive waves of immigration to the United States that changed the ethnic composition of the American population. Newcomers streamed in from southern and eastern Europe, and these were mostly a non-Protestant mixture of peoples including Roman Catholics, Orthodox Christians, and Jews. During this period Roman Catholicism became, by far, the largest religious denomination in the United States, although Catholics were still collectively outnumbered by the various Protestant churches.[5] From the middle to the end of the twentieth century, the religious and ethnic diversity of the United States became enriched by significant numbers of newcomers from all regions of the world. And, of course, the religious traditions they carried to America, including Buddhism, Hinduism, and Islam, continued the expansion of religious pluralism that has distinguished the United States of America from its origins until today.

In combination with the global secular trends of modern life, the enhanced religious diversity of twentieth-century America has influenced a reconception of the so-called unofficial or de facto Protestant Christian establishment and a reinterpretation of the religion clauses of the First Amendment. After nearly 150 years of relative amity and comity, controversial cases on the relationship between religion and government began to come to the federal courts of law. This entry of religious/political issues into the legal arena has continued, with increasing momentum, from the 1940s through the 1990s.

During the second half of the twentieth century, Americans have argued sharply and heatedly about the exact meaning and correct applications of the First Amendment's clauses on religious establishment and free exercise of religion. These arguments have resulted in many U.S. Supreme Court cases and decisions, which have produced a substantial body of constitutional law on the establishment and free exercise clauses.

Supreme Court decisions in thirty-four key cases on issues of religious establishments and free exercise are treated in detail in Parts III and IV of this volume. But the Court's decisions have not ended public controversy about the relationships between church and state or religion and government. Indeed, the Court's decisions on some cases have exacerbated old tensions and generated new issues. The hot constitutional controversies of the 1990s about government and religion are treated in Part V of this volume. And the historical background to twentieth-century constitutional issues, the antecedent ideas and issues of the American colonial era and the founding era, are addressed in Parts I and II.

The documents in this volume were selected to exemplify the key ideas and issues on the interpretation of the Constitution's First Amendment clauses pertaining to establishment and free exercise of religion. The focus throughout is on the connection between the U.S. Constitution and freedom of religion in the United States. So documents from the colonial and founding eras, included in Parts I and II, were selected for their applicability to the constitutional issues decided by the U.S. Supreme Court in the twentieth century, which are treated in Parts III, IV, and V.

Alternative opinions are emphasized by inclusion of both significant concurring and dissenting opinions in the key cases presented in Parts III, IV, and V. Thus, alternative viewpoints on these constitutional issues, which continue to divide Americans, are highlighted in the decisions of the Court. Further, two federal statutes—the Equal Access Act of 1984 and the Religious Freedom Restoration Act of 1993—are included and discussed to emphasize interaction of Congress and the Supreme Court on Constitution-based issues of religion and government. The Equal Access Act continues to be controversial, but the Court has upheld it. By contrast, the Court has struck down as unconstitutional the Religious Freedom Restoration Act.

The text of this volume begins with a chronology of key events. An introductory essay presents the main themes, ideas, and issues of each part, I through V. Documents that pertain to the main themes, ideas, and issues are presented chronologically within each part. Each document is prefaced with an explanatory headnote, which includes questions to guide the reader's analysis of the primary source. At the end of each part, there is a select bibliography, including suggestions for further reading on the theories, ideas, and issues raised by the preceding documents.

Treatments of cases in this volume clearly reveal that many issues on government and religion decided by the Court in recent years have not been definitively settled. And the hot issues about separation or accommodation of religion and government are likely to continue to divide Americans. The framework within which these constitutional controversies are addressed, however, has long been settled, even as variations of opinions abound within, but not outside of, the prevailing constitutional system. The principles of liberty and order by which Americans deal peacefully, civilly, and lawfully with their severest controversies indeed are "a lustre to our country"—as James Madison, the primary author of the Constitution's First Amendment, noted long ago.[6] He urged us to preserve these valuable principles of liberty and order, which is our continuing challenge as responsible citizens of a constitutional democracy dedicated to security for certain inviolable rights of individuals, including the right to freedom of religion.

NOTES

1. Robert T. Handy, *Undermined Establishment: Church-State Relations in America, 1880–1920* (Princeton, N.J.: Princeton University Press, 1991), pp. 8–9.

2. Alexis de Tocqueville, *Democracy in America*, Volume 1 (New York: Alfred A. Knopf, 1987), pp. 303, 305, 308; the first volume of Tocqueville's two-volume work was published originally in France in 1835, and the second volume in 1840.

3. Ibid., pp. 300–302.

4. James Bryce, *The American Commonwealth*, Volume 2 (London: Macmillan, 1888), pp. 576–577.

5. Handy, pp. 162–193.

6. James Madison, *Memorial and Remonstrance Against Religious Assessments*, Article 9, 1785 (see Document 22).

Chronology of Key Events

1606   First Charter of Virginia from the English Crown gave the Virginia Company of London the authority to establish a colony in North America.

1607   First permanent English colony in America was founded at Jamestown, Virginia.

1620   Pilgrims, dissenters from the Church of England, reached North America and started a colony at Plymouth in the New England region and founded the Congregational Church in America.

1630   Puritans, dissenters from the Church of England, began the Massachusetts Bay Colony at Boston and established the Congregational Church as their official religion.

1632   The Second Lord Baltimore received a charter from the English Crown to establish the colony of Maryland in the Chesapeake Bay region of North America, which was intended to be a haven for Roman Catholic settlers.

1634   First Roman Catholic settlers, led by Leonard Calvert, sailed from England to begin the colony of Maryland.

1636   The Reverend Roger Williams, banished from Massachusetts Bay for disagreements on religion with established church authorities, founded the colony of Rhode Island as a haven for dissenters.

1637   Anne Hutchinson, charged with heresy by established church authorities and banished from Massachusetts Bay, found refuge in Rhode Island, the first English colony to offer tolerance of religious differences.

1647   The first public education law in America was passed in the Massachusetts Bay Colony to provide tax-supported elementary and secondary schools in which a major goal was to provide Christian education in support of the established church.

1649   The Toleration Act was passed in Maryland to protect the free exercise of religion by all Christians.

1654   The first Jewish settlers in North America came to Manhattan Island in the Dutch colony of New Amsterdam, which later became the English colony of New York.

1656   The first Quakers, members of a Christian denomination known as the Society of Friends, were arrested in Massachusetts Bay and punished because their religious beliefs were different from those of the established church.

1663   Roger Williams obtained a charter for the colony of Rhode Island from England's King Charles II that provided for separation of religion from government and freedom of conscience. It was the greatest guarantee of religious liberty for individuals anywhere in the world.

1682   William Penn founded the colony of Pennsylvania as a haven for members of the Society of Friends (Quakers), who were persecuted in England and the English colonies of North America. Religious liberty for all Christians was guaranteed by law, and there was no established church in the colony.

1702   The Maryland Assembly passed an act to establish the Church of England as the officially supported religion of the colony.

1715   The North Carolina Assembly enacted a law to make the Church of England the established religion of the colony, as it was in South Carolina and Virginia.

1734   A Christian revival movement, known as the Great Awakening, began in New England and spread throughout the English colonies of North America.

1776   Congress approved, on July 4, the Declaration of Independence of the thirteen United States of America.

1783   Representatives of the United States of America and the United Kingdom of Great Britain signed the Treaty of Paris, which recognized American independence and ended the war between the United States and the United Kingdom.

1786   The Virginia Statute for Religious Freedom, written by Thomas Jefferson, was passed by the state government.

1787   The Constitution of the United States of America, drafted and sent to the thirteen American states for ratification, included a provision in Article VI that banned any kind of religious oath or test as a qualification for public office.

1788   The U.S. Constitution, drafted in 1787, was ratified by the states.

1789   The Congress of the United States, established according to the Constitution, proposed twelve constitutional amendments, known as the Bill of Rights, and sent them to the states for ratification.

1790   Father John Carroll, the first Roman Catholic bishop in the United States, was consecrated, and Baltimore, Maryland, became his headquarters.

1791   Ten constitutional amendments, the American Bill of Rights, were ratified by the states; the First Amendment included two clauses on religion to prohibit any law "respecting an establishment of religion" and to protect the "free exercise" of religion.

1802   In a letter to the Baptist Association of Danbury, Connecticut, Thomas Jefferson stated his support for "building a wall of separation between church and State."

1833   The United States Supreme Court decided in *Barron v. Baltimore* that the rights of individuals in the Bill of Rights were guaranteed only against the federal government, and not the state governments. For example, the clauses on religion in the First Amendment could not be used to limit the powers of state governments. Thus, rights to religious liberty in the states were solely within the authority of each state government. Massachusetts, in 1833, was the last American state to prohibit a constitutional establishment of religion. And all the states had constitutional guarantees for free exercise of religion.

1868   The Fourteenth Amendment of the U.S. Constitution was ratified. It guaranteed certain rights of individuals against the power of state governments. In the twentieth century, provisions of this amendment were used by the United States Supreme Court to apply the First Amendment clauses on religion to the settlement of legal issues between individuals and their state governments.

1879   The U.S. Supreme Court made its first decision involving the clauses on religion in the First Amendment in the case of *Reynolds v. United States*, which pertained to a free exercise of religion issue in the federal territory of Utah.

1940   For the first time, the U.S. Supreme Court, in *Cantwell v. Connecticut*, invoked its doctrine of selective incorporation to use the due process clause of the Fourteenth Amendment to apply the First Amendment's free exercise of religion clause against a state government. Thus, a precedent was established that has been used subsequently to settle many freedom of religion cases involving state governments.

1947   For the first time, the U.S. Supreme Court, in *Everson v. Board of Education of Ewing Township* (New Jersey), asserted its authority to use the Fourteenth Amendment to apply the First Amendment's establishment clause against a state government. Thus, a precedent was set that has been used subsequently to settle many establishment of religion issues involving state governments.

1998   Statistics on religious denominations and identities in the United States reveal an extraordinary religious diversity, which is associated with constitutional guarantees of religious liberty and a solid tradition of religious toleration.

Part I

Colonial Roots of Religious Liberty, 1606–1776

In the world of the seventeenth century, when English settlers first came to America, religious and political interests were entangled. There was no separation of church and state; the very idea of it was unprecedented, even uncontemplated. In Spain and France, for example, the Catholic Church was the dominant religious institution which supported, and received support from, the civil governments of these two nation-states. Likewise, there was a symbiotic relationship between the English Crown and the Church of England. So the Cross and Crown traveled together from the imperial countries of Europe to their colonies in America.

The first permanent English colony in North America, at Jamestown, Virginia (1607), was authorized by the English Crown in 1606 (see Document 1, the First Charter of Virginia). This document set the legal terms and interests of the colonial proprietors, which included the objectives of converting the native inhabitants to the Anglican version of Christianity and blocking the spread of the Roman Catholic Church, which was supported by England's imperial rivals, France and Spain.

The English settlers were expected to govern themselves and otherwise conduct their lives in accordance with precepts of the Anglican Church. These religious rules for civil society and government were expanded and enforced more strictly after 1624, when Virginia became a royal colony under direct control of the Crown. At this point, the Anglican Church became the official or established religion of the colony. It would remain the governmentally established church in Virginia from the 1620s until the American Revolution of the 1770s.

Establishment of the Church of England in the colony of Virginia meant payment of taxes by the settlers to the colonial government for public support of the Church and its ministers. It also meant conformity to the church's laws, such as compulsory attendance at religious services and government-imposed punishments for deviant or dissenting behavior. (See Document 2 for examples of religiously based laws and punishments for violators.)

As the Jamestown settlers struggled to maintain and develop their colony, other colonists dissented against the Church of England, left their mother country to escape persecution, and sought religious liberty for themselves in North America. In 1620, 102 Pilgrims sailed on the *Mayflower* for Virginia and landed accidentally far to the north at a place they called Plymouth, New England. Before going ashore, they constituted their community by agreeing to a covenant, the Mayflower Compact, rooted in their version of Protestant Christianity:

Having undertaken for the Glory of God, and Advancement of the Christian Faith, and the Honor of our King and Country, a Voyage to plant the first Colony in the northern Parts of Virginia; Do by these Presents, solemnly and mutually, in the Presence of God and one another, covenant and combine ourselves together into a civil Body Politic, for our better Ordering and Preservation, and Furtherance of the Ends aforesaid.[1]

The Plymouth Colony grew slowly. By 1630, only about 300 settlers lived there. But in that year more than 1,000 newcomers from England settled nearby at a place they called the Massachusetts Bay Colony, where the great city of Boston would be located. This was the beginning of a great migration that by 1642 brought more than 20,000 English settlers to Massachusetts Bay.

These new arrivals in the New England region called themselves Puritans. Like the Pilgrims of nearby Plymouth, they, too, were dissenters against certain beliefs and practices of the Church of England. And like the Pilgrims, these Puritans had suffered persecution for their religious beliefs from officials of the English government and the state-supported Church of England. They sought religious liberty for themselves and their Congregational Church, which the Puritan officials established in the colony of Massachusetts Bay.

From the start, the New England Puritans viewed the civil government, the state, as closely tied to their church (see Document 3, Charter of Massachusetts Bay). All residents of the colony were required to pay taxes to support the Congregational Church and its ministers. And only members of the church could participate in the government of the colony. Further, everyone was bound to observe laws about religious beliefs and practices. Violators were punished, often severely (see Document 4, a set of laws enacted by the government of Massachusetts Bay). Finally, public schools supported by taxation of all inhabitants, members and nonmembers of the Congregational Church, were provided by law for the primary purpose of promoting the official religion of the colony (see Document 6).

During the 1630s, the Puritan way of life spread from Massachusetts Bay to new settlements that were to develop into the colonies of Connecticut and New Hampshire. By 1665, residents of Connecticut had obtained a legal charter for their colony. By 1680, New Hampshire was separated from Massachusetts Bay by royal commission and became a separate colony.

While the government and church were linked in the colonies of Puritan New England, each institution had distinct dimensions of authority recognized by law. For example, provisions of the Massachusetts Body of Liberties, enacted in 1641 and reaffirmed subsequently, required that the officials and officers of the church and civil government should be coordinated but distinct. Thus, an official of the government who was excommunicated by the church would not necessarily be forced from his civil office. (See Document 5.)

Laws of the civil governments of Puritan New England colonies established the Congregational Church as the official religion in Massachusetts, Connecticut, and New Hampshire. The seventeenth-century laws on religion protected one's freedom to be a Congregationalist, but no other religious beliefs were acceptable, and some could be punished. The typical seventeenth-century Puritan way to religious liberty is revealed by Section 95 of the Massachusetts Body of Liberties (see Document 5). It proclaims the person's freedom only to follow the Puritan way of religion; there was no freedom of religion for dissenters.

This kind of strict religious orthodoxy, however, provoked dissent. Anne Hutchinson, for example, was a devout Puritan. However, when she disagreed publicly with church authorities in Massachusetts Bay, Hutchinson was put on trial, convicted of heresy, and banished. In 1638, she went to Narragansett Bay in the colony of Rhode Island founded in 1636 by Roger Williams, a Puritan clergyman. He, too, had been banished by the government of Massachusetts for his disagreement with officials of the established church.

Roger Williams preached that there were many pathways to God, and that every person should be free to choose his own way. In line with Williams' ideas on religious liberty, his colony of Rhode Island became a sanctuary for religious dissenters, both Christians and Jews.

Williams eventually obtained a charter for the Rhode Island colony from King Charles II of England. This fundamental law of 1663 provided for separation of religion and government and freedom of conscience. It was the most extensive guarantee of religious liberty for individuals that had been achieved anywhere in the world of the seventeenth century (see Document 8).

Religious liberty had been broadly proclaimed in the 1649 Maryland

Toleration Act (see Document 7). But this act was not part of the fundamental law, the charter, of the Maryland Colony. Thus, it could be revoked at any time by legislative action of the colonial government. By contrast, the Rhode Island guarantee of freedom of conscience was part of the basic law, the charter, which gave it a higher status than that of a statute enacted by the colonial legislature. The constitutional status of the Rhode Island Charter of 1663 was shown by the fact that it remained in force long after the founding of the United States of America. This charter became the first Constitution of the State of Rhode Island and remained in effect until 1842.

The Rhode Island guarantee of religious liberty was the first time, anywhere in the world, that freedom of conscience was established as an individual right in the constitutional law of a people. This example of constitution-based religious liberty in Rhode Island was followed a short time later by William Penn, the founder of Pennsylvania. It was also a forerunner of the right to religious liberty included in the 1791 United States Bill of Rights.

William Penn was punished in England because of his religion. He belonged to the Society of Friends, usually called Quakers. Officials of the Church of England strongly objected to them. He was jailed for preaching his beliefs to an assembly of Quakers, an illegal act in London during the 1660s. While in prison, Penn wrote his great defense of religious liberty, *The Great Case of Liberty of Conscience* (see Document 9). He emphasized that religious faith coerced by the power of government was of little or no value. "Force never yet made a good Christian, or a good subject," wrote Penn, who simultaneously argued for liberty in religion and government.[2]

In 1681, King Charles II granted to William Penn the territory in North America that became the colony of Pennsylvania. This was done in payment of a debt owed by the King to Penn's father. William Penn resolved to use this vast tract of land, an area almost as large as England, to make a refuge for Quakers and other persecuted dissenters from established religions.

In consultation with Quaker leaders, Penn drafted a constitution for the colony of Pennsylvania, the 1682 Pennsylvania Frame of Government. It was by far the most democratic and liberal or free plan for government anywhere in the world at that time. In particular, it provided for the individual's right to freedom of conscience or free exercise of religion.

The right to religious liberty in the 1682 Pennsylvania Frame of Government was reinforced by a statute enacted at the end of 1682, the Great Law of Pennsylvania (see Document 10). This law guaranteed complete freedom of religion for all Christians. Rights of nonbelievers, however, were not recognized, and anti-Christian acts could be punished. Further, the government was expected to recognize the worth of Christian morality and to promote it. So, there was no separation of church and state in the modern sense of this idea. But in the seventeenth-century world, Pennsylvania was a model of a government limited by law to protect freedom of conscience and prevent official dictation or coercion of religious beliefs and practices.

In 1701, Penn granted a new Frame of Government, which reaffirmed the principles of the Great Law of 1682. A Charter of Privileges was enacted that offered a broad guarantee of religious liberty (see Document 12).

Pennsylvania became the American leader of a trend toward greater freedom of religion. Even in colonies with firmly established churches, such as the Congregational Church in the New England colonies of Massachusetts, Connecticut, and New Hampshire and the Anglican Church of Virginia, Maryland, the Carolinas, and New York, there was growing toleration for religious diversity. By the early years of the eighteenth century, the principle of religious toleration, if not full religious liberty, had taken root in England and its colonies.

The 1689 English Act of Toleration was passed by Parliament in the wake of England's Glorious Revolution, which brought enactment of the English Bill of Rights. The Act of Toleration maintained the special privileges of the Church of England as the established religion of the state. But it protected English subjects from punishment for dissent against the established church or for practicing other religions.

The principles of free choice and noncoercion by government in matters of religion that underlay the Act of Toleration were expressed eloquently and persuasively by the great English philosopher, John Locke, in his Letter Concerning Toleration (see Document 11). Locke's widely read letter expressed the same basic ideas written earlier by William Penn. But the theory and practice of religious liberty in Pennsylvania and three other American colonies—Delaware, New Jersey, and Rhode Island—went far beyond mere toleration to constitutional guarantees of religious liberty for individuals not enjoyed in England or in the other American colonies. Only in Pennsylvania, Delaware, New Jersey, and Rhode Island was there no official establishment of a single church (but not yet complete separation of church and state). And only in Pennsylvania was there both freedom and encouragement for Roman Catholics to openly and securely practice their kind of Christianity, which was severely restricted or even punished in England and its other colonies.

Under the leadership of the first and second Lord Baltimore, Catholics had founded the colony of Maryland, where they enacted legislation to protect liberty and toleration of all Christian forms of faith (see Document 7). But Maryland's Toleration Act did not survive. In 1692, the Maryland Council, dominated by Anglican Church supporters, rejected toleration and moved toward establishment of the Anglican Church. By the 1750s, the Catholics in Maryland were forced to pay double taxation and prohibited from voting or holding public offices.

The prevailing prejudice against Roman Catholics, in tandem with general toleration of other Christians that emerged during the 1690s and thereafter, was shown by legal provisions of New York and Massachusetts. The 1691 New York Act Declaring Rights and Privileges provided that "no person or Persons which profess Faith in God by Jesus Christ His only Son, shall at any time be any way molested, punished, disturbed, disquieted, or called in question for any Difference in Opinion, or matter of Religious Concernment." But Roman Catholics had no such rights or privileges. The law provided that "nothing herein mentioned or contained shall extend to give Liberty to any Persons of The Romish Religion to exercise their Manner of Worship."[3] Likewise, the 1692 Charter of Massachusetts Bay proclaimed that "there shall be a Liberty of Conscience allowed in the Worship of God to all Christians (except Papists) inhabiting or which shall inhabit or be resident within Our said Province or Territory."[4]

Despite the legal and social prejudice against Roman Catholics, Jews, and nonbelievers, the English colonies of North America exhibited the greatest religious toleration, even freedom of conscience, anywhere in the world of the eighteenth century. The colonial American understanding of religious liberty, however, did not include our contemporary acceptance of one's right not to believe in any religion. When colonial leaders proclaimed freedom of conscience, they assumed that religious liberty would be expressed within the boundaries of a Christian and Protestant political and social order. Catholics, Jews, and nonbelievers, for example, could neither vote in public elections nor hold positions in government in any of the English colonies of America.

The extraordinary degree of religious liberty in colonial America certainly was related to the rampant diversity of sects and churches. America manifested the greatest religious diversity of any place on earth. For example, in the colonies as a whole in 1740 the number of churches included: Congregationalist (Puritan), 423; Anglican, 246; Presbyterian, 160; Baptist, 96; Lutheran, 95; Dutch Reformed, 78; German Reformed, 51; and the Society of Friends (Quakers), more than 90. Furthermore, there were more than twenty Catholic churches, mostly in Pennsylvania, with a few in Maryland; small communities of Jews in New York City; Newport, Rhode Island; Philadelphia, Pennsylvania; Savannah, Georgia; and Charleston, South Carolina; and various small sects, such as Seventh-Day Adventists and Mennonites.[5]

This outstanding variety of religious beliefs and practices encouraged toleration of diversity, because there was no way to practically and facilely maintain religious homogeneity. The fact that a majority of people in colonial America were not members of any church was another factor that encouraged religious toleration. Even in New England, where religion dominated the colonial culture, "not more than one person in seven was a church member."[6] This large population outside the churches of colonial America tended to be disinterested in disputes about religious doctrines and heresy; their indifference influenced the growth of toleration. Yet another force for religious diversity and toleration was the mid-seventeenth-century religious movement known as the Great Awakening. This widespread burst of religious fervor tended to be anti-establishment, as "born-again" Christians reveled in direct, personal experience with God. The Great Awakening promoted the rise of the Baptists, especially in the southern colonies, which challenged the Anglican Church establishments.

Leaders of the established churches were often bewildered, shocked, or dismayed by the "undisciplined" religious passion of the Great Awakening and the exceptional religious diversity throughout the colonies. For example, a prominent Anglican Church leader in Pennsylvania, the Reverend Thomas Barton, wrote about the "swarm of sects" in Pennsylvania and elsewhere in America. And, like others of his kind, Reverend Barton lamented the circumstances that opposed religious uniformity in line with the Church of England (see Document 13).

By the 1770s, near the start of the American War of Independence, only the five southern colonies maintained a single established church, the Church of England: Maryland, Virginia, North Carolina, South Carolina, and Georgia. In Massachusetts, New Hampshire, Connecticut, and New York, there were general or multiple establishments of all types of Protestant Christian churches. And in four colonies, Rhode Island, Pennsylvania, Delaware, and New Jersey, there was no official established church.

There was astounding religious diversity even in the colonies with a single established church, which precluded strict government-imposed articles of faith. However, there was the requirement that all inhabitants pay taxes for support of the established church. Thus, in Virginia, Baptists and other non-Anglicans paid taxes to the colonial government for support of Anglican ministers and churches. And they could be punished for supporting their own religion.

In Massachusetts the Baptists were forced to pay taxes for support of the Congregational Church, but they had freedom to support their own religion, too. Anti-establishment Christians, such as the Baptists, protested this kind of tax-supported religion. Among the leading protesters was a Baptist minister, Isaac Backus (see Document 14). Near the start of the American Revolution, he pointed out the inconsistency of Congregational churchmen in Boston, who led protests against the English for imposing "taxation without representation" on inhabitants of Massachusetts. Yet, Backus claimed, these same persons approved taxation of Baptists by the Massachusetts government, which included no Baptists, to support the Congregational Church. According to Backus, this was tyranny no less unjust than that of the British government.

Reverend Backus pointed out that the 1692 colonial charter of Massachusetts guaranteed free exercise of religion to all Christians except Roman Catholics. Thus, he argued, it was illegal for the colonial government to tax Baptists to support the Congregational Church and to jail them for refusal to pay.

In most of the North American colonies, however, genuine religious toleration, even freedom of conscience, was the trend. By the beginning of the American Revolution in 1776, religious compulsion was weak or dying. The forces of political and social change, including the advancement of religious liberty, were accelerated by the revolution. The advocates of an unprecedented religious liberty, like Isaac Backus, were bound to prevail throughout post-revolutionary America.

NOTES

1. B. P. Poore, ed., *The Federal and State Constitutions, Colonial Charters, and Other Organic Laws of the United States*, Volume 2 (Washington, D.C., 1877), p. 931.

2. Richard Hofstadter, *America at 1750: A Social Portrait* (New York: Vintage Books, 1973), p. 196.

3. Neil H. Cogan, *The Complete Bill of Rights: The Drafts, Debates, Sources, and Origins* (New York: Oxford University Press, 1997), p. 25.

4. Ibid., p. 20.

5. Hofstadter, p. 183.

6. Ibid., p. 181.

DOCUMENT 1: First Charter of Virginia (November 20, 1606)

King James I of England issued a charter to the Virginia Company of London to legalize and establish the proprietors' enterprise to establish a colony in America. The primary purposes of colonial Virginia's founders were commercial and political, not religious. However, promotion of the Church of England was emphasized in the colony's founding charter. What does the charter say about propagation of religion? What does the document reveal about the relationship of church and state in England and its colonies abroad?

* * *

III. We greatly commending, and graciously accepting of, their desires for the furtherance of so noble a work, which may, by the providence of Almighty God, hereafter tend to the glory of his divine Majesty, in propagating of Christian religion to such people, as yet live in Darkness and miserable ignorance of the true knowledge and worship of God, and may in time bring the infidels and savages, living in those parts, to human civility, and to a settled and quiet government: Do, by these our letters Patents, graciously accept of, and agree to, their humble and well-intended desires. . . .

Source: William Walter Hening, ed., *The Statutes at Large: Being a Collection of All the Laws of Virginia*, Volume 1 (Richmond, 1809), p. 58.

DOCUMENT 2: Acts of the Virginia Colonial Government on Religion (1624 and 1630)

In 1624, the King of England abolished the London-based Virginia Company, the founding proprietor of the colony. Virginia became a royal colony directly under the Crown's authority. Laws made by the colonial legislature, the Virginia House of Burgesses, confirmed the central place of the Christian religion in public affairs. And the Church of England enjoyed exclusive support from the government of Virginia, which established it by law as the solely sanctioned religious institution of the colony. What do the laws of 1624 and 1630 say about the status and function of religion in the colony? Why and how do these laws provide for an establishment of religion?

* * *

Act of March 1624:

THAT there shall be in every plantation, where the people use to meet for the worship of God, a house or room sequestered for that purpose, and not to be for any temporal use whatsoever. . . .

That whosoever shall absent himself from divine service any Sunday without an allowable excuse shall forfeit a pound of tobacco, and he that absent himself a month shall forfeit 50 pounds of tobacco. . . .

That there be an uniformity in our church as near as may be to the canons in England; both in substance and circumstance, and that all persons yield ready obedience unto them under pain of censure. . . .

Act of March 1630:

IT *is ordered*, That all ministers residing and being, or who hereafter shall reside and be within this colony, shall conform themselves in all things according to the canons of the Church of England. And if there shall be any that, after notice given, shall refuse for to conform himself, he shall undergo such censure, as by the said canons in such cases is provided for such delinquent. And that all acts formerly made concerning ministers shall stand in force, and be duly observed and kept.

Source: William Walter Hening, ed., *The Statutes at Large: Being a Collection of All the Laws of Virginia*, Volume 1 (Richmond, 1809), pp. 122, 149.

DOCUMENT 3: Charter of Massachusetts Bay (March 4, 1629)

The Puritans, founders of the English colony of Massachusetts Bay, migrated initially to North America in 1630. They carried with them their charter from the English government, which established the Massachusetts Bay Company, a commercial association. This charter set forth rules of governance and trade. It also includes statements about the importance of religion. This charter reveals the combination of political and religious interests at the core of governance in the colony. What does this charter say about the proper relationship of religion and government? What does it say about the religious purposes of the colony?

* * *

... And, we do of our further grace, certain knowledge and mere motion give and grant to the said Governor and Company, and their successors, that it shall and may be lawful to and for the Governor or deputy Governor and such of the Assistants and Freemen of the said Company ... to make, ordain and establish all manner of wholesome and reasonable orders, laws, statutes, and ordinances, directions, and instructions ... for the directing, ruling, and disposing of all other matters and things whereby our said people inhabiting there may be so religiously, peaceably and civilly governed, as their good life and orderly conversation, may win and invite the natives of that country to the knowledge and obedience of the one true God and savior of mankind, and the Christian faith, which in our royal intention, and the adventurers free profession is the principal end of this plantation. . . .

Source: Frances N. Thorpe, ed., *The Federal and State Constitutions, Colonial Charters, and Other Organic Laws of the States, Territories, and Colonies Now or Heretofore Forming the United States of America*, Volume 3 (Washington, D.C., 1909), p. 1848.

DOCUMENT 4: Acts of the Massachusetts Colonial Government on Religion (1631, 1635, and 1638)

Laws were made by the General Court, the legislative branch of government in the Massachusetts Bay Colony, that provided for public support of the Puritans' religious institutions and practices. There was emphatic preference for the Congregational Church of the Puritans. Other religious practices were excluded from government and could even be punished by law. All members of the colony were legally required to support the established Congregational Church. What do the laws on religion of 1631, 1635, and 1638 reveal about the relationship of the government to religion in the Massachusetts Bay Colony? How did the laws require individuals to support the established church?

* * *

Act of 1631

... & to the end the body of the commons may be preserved of honest & good men, it was likewise ordered and agreed that for time to come no man shall be admitted to the freedom of this body politic, but such as are members of some of the churches within the limits of the same.

Act of 1635

Whereas complaint hath been made to this Court that diverse persons within this jurisdiction do usually absent themselves from church meetings upon the Lords day, power is therefore given to any two Assistants to hear & ensure, either by fine or imprisonment, (at their discretion) all misdemeanors of that kind committed by any inhabitant within this jurisdiction, provided they exceed not the fine of [five] shillings for one offense.

Act of 1638

This Court taking into consideration the necessity of an equal contribution to all common charges in towns, & observing that the chief occasion of the defect herein ariseth from hence, that many of those who are not freemen, nor members of any church, do take advantage thereby to withdraw their help in such voluntary contributions as are in use,—

It is therefore hearby declared, that every inhabitant in any town is liable to contribute to all charges, both in church & commonwealth, whereof he doth or may receive benefit; & withall it is also ordered, that every such inhabitant who shall not voluntarily contribute, proportionably to his ability, with other freemen of the same town, to all common charges, as well for upholding the ordinances in the churches as otherwise, shall be compelled thereto by assessment & distress to be levied by the constable, or other officer of the town, as in other cases.

Source: Nathaniel B. Shurtleff, ed., *Records of the Governor and Company of the Massachusetts Bay*, Volume 1 (Boston, 1853), pp. 87, 140, 240.

DOCUMENT 5: Massachusetts Body of Liberties (December 10, 1641)

In 1641, the Massachusetts colony adopted a bill of rights, the Massachusetts Body of Liberties, which included ninety-eight articles. It stated several fundamental civil liberties later protected in the United States Bill of Rights (1791). Four articles, presented below, dealt with religious liberty and relationships of civil government and religious authority: Numbers 58, 59, 60, and 95.

Article 95 protected the religious freedom of the officially established Congregational Church and all individuals acting in agreement with it. There was, however, no government sanctioned religious liberty for persons in dissent from the Puritan way of the Congregational Church.

Articles 58, 59, and 60 defined relationships between the authority of civil government and the officially established church. These articles provided that the civil government would have sole authority to conduct its public business and enforce the duly enacted laws of the colony. The church would have full freedom and authority within its own domain as long as it did not contradict the laws of the colony.

What does this document say about the scope and limits of religious liberty? What does it say about the relationship of civil authority to church authority? Compare statements on religious liberty in this document with the Maryland Toleration Act of 1649 (see Document 7).

* * *

58. Civil Authority hath power and liberty to see the peace, ordinances and Rules of Christ observed in every church according to his word, so it be done in a Civil and not in an Ecclesiastical way.

59. Civil Authority hath power and liberty to deal with any Church member in a way of Civil Justice, notwithstanding any Church relation, office, or interest.

60. No church censure shall degrade or depose any man from any Civil dignity, office, or Authority he shall have in the Commonwealth.

* * *

95. A declaration of the Liberties the Lord Jesus hath given to the Churches.

(a) All the people of God within this Jurisdiction who are not in a church way, and be orthodox in Judgment, and not scandalous in life, shall have full liberty to gather themselves into a Church Estate. Provided they do it in a Christian way, with due observation of the rules of Christ revealed in his word.

(b) Every Church hath full liberty to exercise all the ordinances of God, according to the rules of Scripture.

(c) Every Church hath free liberty of Election and ordination of all their officers from time to time, provided they be able pious and orthodox. . . .

Source: W. H. Whitmore, *The Colonial Laws of Massachusetts* (Boston, 1890), pp. 46, 59.

DOCUMENT 6: Massachusetts School Law (November 11, 1647)

The Puritans of Massachusetts strongly supported public education because they believed that direct knowledge of the Bible was essential to personal salvation. One had to read well enough to interpret Scripture to gain the reward of heaven. Harvard College was founded in 1636 to provide a religion-based education for the clergy and other leaders of the colony. And in 1647, the General Court made a law to establish elementary schools throughout the colony supported by public taxation. Each town of fifty families or more was required to establish a school to which all children of the town had access. Other New England colonies followed the example of Massachusetts within the next generation. What does the Massachusetts School Law show about the connections of government and religion in Massachusetts Bay?

* * *

It being one chief project of that old deluder, Satan, to keep men from the knowledge of the Scriptures, as in former times by keeping them in an unknown tongue, so in these latter times by persuading from the use of tongues, that so at least the true sense & meaning of the original might be clouded by false glosses of saint seeming deceivers, that learning may not be buried in the grave of our fathers in the church and commonwealth, the Lord assisting our endeavors,—

It is therefore ordered, that every township in this jurisdiction, after the Lord hath increased them to the number of 50 householders, shall then forthwith appoint one within their town to teach all such children as shall resort to him to write & read, whose wages shall be paid either by the parents or masters of such children, or by the inhabitants in general, by way of supply, as the major part of those that order the prudentials of the town shall appoint; provided, those that send their children be not oppressed by paying much more than they can have them taught for in other towns, & it is further ordered, that where any town shall increase to the number of 100 families or householders they shall set up a grammar school, the master thereof being able to instruct youth so far as they may be fitted for the university, provided, that if any town neglect the performance hereof above one year, that every such town shall pay 5 pounds to the next school till they shall perform this order.

Source: Nathaniel B. Shurtleff, ed., *Records of the Governor and Company of the Massachusetts Bay*, Volume 1 (Boston, 1853), p. 203.

DOCUMENT 7: Maryland Toleration Act (April 21, 1649)

George Calvert, the first Lord Baltimore, was granted a charter by King Charles I of England in 1632 to found the colony of Maryland in the Chesapeake Bay region of North America. The second Lord Baltimore and son of George Calvert, Cecilius, established the colony and became first proprietor of Maryland. From the start, George Calvert and his son wanted Maryland to be a safe haven for Catholics who suffered persecution for their religious beliefs in England and its American colonies. Under the influence of Lord Baltimore, the colonial government passed a law for the toleration of religious beliefs of all Christian settlers of Maryland. This law includes the first recorded use of the words "free exercise" with regard to religion. This phrase, "free exercise of religion," was included in the First Amendment of the U.S. Constitution, ratified in 1791 as part of the American Bill of Rights.

In 1654, after the Puritans gained control of Maryland following Cromwell's revolution in England, the 1649 Toleration Act was repealed, and both Catholics and Anglicans lost their religious freedom. In 1658, Lord Baltimore regained his authority as proprietor and restored the Toleration Act. In 1692, however, Maryland became a royal colony under direct authority of the Crown, and the Church of England was established in 1702 as the official religion of the colony. Nonetheless, Lord Baltimore's Toleration Act had become a symbol for religious liberty.

What were the main provisions of the Maryland Toleration Act? Why did it give security to Roman Catholics that they would not otherwise have had? What limits on religious diversity and freedom were set by this law?

* * *

... And whereas the enforcing of the conscience in matters of Religion hath frequently fallen out to be of dangerous Consequence in those commonwealths where it hath been practiced, And for the more quiet and peaceable government of this Province, and the better to preserve mutual Love and amity amongst the Inhabitants thereof. Be it Therefore ... enacted that no person ... whatsoever within this Province ... professing to believe in Jesus Christ, shall ... be any ways troubled, Molested or discountenanced for or in respect of his or her religion nor in the free exercise thereof ... nor any way compelled to the belief or exercise of any other Religion against his or her consent, so as they be not unfaithful to the Lord Proprietary, or molest or conspire against the civil Government. ... And that all & every p[er]son ... that shall presume Contrary to this Act ... willfully to wrong disturb trouble or molest any person ... professing to believe in Jesus Christ for or in respect of his or her religion or the free exercise thereof ... shall be compelled to pay treble damages to the party so wronged or molested, and for every such offense shall also forfeit 20 s[hillings] sterling in money or the value thereof, half thereof for the use of the Lord Proprietary ... and the other half for the use of the party so wronged. ... Or if the party so offending ... shall refuse or be unable to recompense the party so wronged, or to satisfy such fine or forfeiture, then such Offender shall be severely punished by public whipping & imprisonment during the pleasure of the Lord Proprietary ... without bail. ...

Source: William H. Browne, ed., *Archives of Maryland*, Volume 1 (Baltimore, 1883), pp. 244–247.

DOCUMENT 8: Rhode Island Charter (July 8, 1663)

King Charles II of England granted a colonial charter to Rhode Island in 1663. This "Charter of Rhode Island and Plymouth Plantation" recognized and confirmed the institutions of government that had been in effect since the 1640s, when Roger Williams, the colony's founder, established them. A central theme of this charter was religious liberty for individuals, which had been Roger Williams' purpose in founding this colony. At the beginning of the colony in 1636, Williams and the settlers agreed that the authority of government would not intrude into the private affairs of religion so that there would be "liberty of conscience" for all inhabitants of the colony.

Examine the excerpt below from the Rhode Island Charter, which pertains to religious liberty. Compare it to the Maryland Toleration Act (see Document 7).

* * *

. . . No person within the said colony, at any time hereafter, shall be any wise molested, punished, disquieted, or called in question, for any differences in opinion in matters of religion, and do not actually disturb the civil peace of our said colony; but that all and every person and persons may . . . have and enjoy his and their own judgments and consciences, in matters of religious concernments . . . ; they behaving themselves peaceably and quietly and not using this liberty to licentiousness and profaneness, nor to the civil injury or outward disturbance of others; any law . . . using or custom of this realm, to the contrary hereof, in any wise, notwithstanding. . . .

Source: B. P. Poore, ed., *The Federal and State Constitutions, Colonial Charters, and Other Organic Laws of the United States*, Volume 2 (Washington, D.C., 1877), pp. 1595–1603.

DOCUMENT 9: *The Great Case of Liberty of Conscience* (William Penn, 1670)

William Penn belonged to the Society of Friends in England, a religious denomination often called Quakers. In England and most of its American colonies, Quakers were not free to practice their religion. They were whipped, fined, jailed, or even put to death for their religious beliefs.

Penn strongly believed that everyone should have freedom of conscience in matters of religion. He expressed his ideas about religious liberty in a book published in England. A brief excerpt from this book is presented below. What arguments does William Penn put forth in favor of religious liberty? Compare Penn's ideas on religious liberty with the ideas of John Locke in his Letter Concerning Toleration (Document 11). Who expresses the broadest and strongest argument for religious liberty, Penn or Locke?

* * *

... First, by liberty of conscience, we mean not only a mere liberty of mind, in believing or disbelieving this or that principle or doctrine. But we also believe such liberty protects a visible way of worship, a way of worship we believe to be required of us by God. If we neglect this worship for fear or favor of mortal man, we sin and are in danger of divine wrath.

Second, by restraint or persecution, we do not only mean the strict requiring of us to believe this to be true or that to be false, and upon refusal to receive the penalties given in such cases. But by those terms we mean this much: any coercion, force or hindrance which prevents our meeting together to perform those religious exercises which are according to our faith and persuasion.

We wish to put the question in this way. Is it not true that persecution against persons exercising their liberty of conscience reduces the honor of God? Does it not also defile the Christian religion, violate the authority of Scripture, and go against the principles of common reason? Finally, does it not destroy the well-being of government itself?

Concerning the honor of God, we say that restraint and persecution for matters relating to conscience directly invade the divine right, and rob the Almighty of that which belongs to none but Himself. . . .

Source: William Penn, *The Great Case of Liberty of Conscience* (London, 1670), p. 1.

DOCUMENT 10: Great Law of Pennsylvania (December 7, 1682)

William Penn was determined to create a haven in America for Quakers and others persecuted for their religious beliefs. In 1681, he obtained a charter from King Charles II of England to found the colony of Pennsylvania with himself as proprietor.

Penn drafted a constitution for his colony in 1682, the Pennsylvania Frame of Government, which guaranteed the rule of law and the protection of individual rights, including the person's inviolable right to religious liberty. Soon after his arrival in Pennsylvania, William Penn met with settlers at the community of Chester and there enacted the Great Law, an elaboration upon certain provisions of the Pennsylvania Frame of Government. Chapter One of the Great Law underscored

Penn's great concern for the free exercise of religion and the separation of religion from interference by the civil government. In particular, he was adamant that the government should not attempt to define the religious beliefs of people living under its authority. Christian beliefs, however, were favored over other religious beliefs and nonbelief in God.

What provisions are made in this law for religious liberty? What limitations on religious liberty are expressed? Compare provisions for religious liberty in Penn's Great Law with those of the Maryland Toleration Act (Document 7) and the Rhode Island Charter (Document 8). Which document expresses the broadest and strongest guarantee of religious liberty?

* * *

Whereas the glory of Almighty God, and the good of mankind, is the reason and end of government, and therefore government, in itself, is a venerable ordinance of God; and forasmuch as it is principally desired and intended by the proprietary and governor, and the freemen of the province of Pennsylvania . . . to make and establish such laws as shall best preserve true Christians and civil liberty, in opposition to all unchristian, licentious, and unjust practices . . . —Be it therefore enacted, by William Penn, proprietary and governor, by and with the advice and consent of the deputies of the freemen of this province. . . .

1. . . . It is enacted by the authority aforesaid, that no person . . . who shall confess and acknowledge one Almighty God to be the creator, upholder, and ruler of the world and that professeth him or herself obliged in conscience to live peaceably and justly under the civil government, shall in anywise be molested or prejudiced for his or her conscientious persuasion or practice, nor shall he or she at any time be compelled to frequent or maintain any religious worship, place, or ministry whatever, contrary to his or her mind, but shall freely and fully enjoy his or her Christian liberty in that respect, without any interruption or reflection; and if any person shall abuse or deride any other for his or her different persuasion and practice in matter of religion, such shall be looked upon as a disturber of the peace, and be punished accordingly. But to the end that looseness, irreligion, and atheism may not creep in under pretense of conscience . . . be it further enacted . . . that according to the good example of the primitive Christians, and for the ease of the creation, every first day of the week, called the Lord's Day, people shall abstain from their common toil and labor, that whether masters, parents, children, or servants, they may the better dispose themselves to read the Scriptures of truth at home, or to frequent such meetings of religious worship abroad as may best suit their respective persuasions.

2. . . . [A]ll officers and persons commissionated and employed in the service of the government of this province, and all members and deputies elected to serve in assembly thereof, and all that have right to elect such deputies, shall be such as profess and declare they believe in Jesus Christ to be the Son of God, and Savior of the world, and that are not convicted of ill-fame, or unsober and dishonest conversation, and that are of one and twenty years of age at least. And . . . whosoever shall swear, in their conversation, by the name of God, or Christ, or Jesus, being legally convicted thereof, shall pay for every such offense five shillings, or suffer five days' imprisonment in the house of correction, at hard labor, to the behoof of the public, and be fed with bread and water only, during that time.

Source: Samuel Hazard, ed., *Annals of Pennsylvania, from the Discovery of the Delaware* (Philadelphia, 1850), pp. 619–620.

DOCUMENT 11: A Letter Concerning Toleration (John Locke, 1689)

John Locke, the great English philosopher, wrote four letters on toleration of religious diversity. The first of these letters was written in 1685 and published in 1689. It was the philosophical foundation for the English Act of Toleration of 1689, which set the legal terms of coexistence between the Church of England and dissenting Protestant denominations, such as Congregationalists, Baptists, Presbyterians, and Quakers. Roman Catholics in England, however, were not to be tolerated either in Locke's philosophy or in the Act of Toleration.

The English Act of Toleration provided for freedom of worship or free exercise of religion for those denominations included in the law. It also maintained the privileged position of one state-supported or established religion, the Church of England. Further, the English Act of Toleration excluded Christians outside the established Anglican Church from political rights, such as voting and holding public office. It did, however, protect dissenters against punishment by the government solely because of their openly expressed religious beliefs. Atheists, however, were not to be tolerated.

In general, terms of the English Act of Toleration were applied to the British colonies in America either by charters or the actions of royal governors. And the ideas on toleration expressed by John Locke were generally accepted throughout the colonies, even in the New England strongholds of the Congregational Church, which had severely punished or excluded dissenters. In most American colonies, free exercise of religion was tolerated for all Christians except Roman Catholics. In Pennsylvania, Rhode Island, Delaware, and New Jersey, however, freedom of religion exceeded by far the terms of the English Act of Toleration by disallowing any church to be established by law and providing for a much broader expression of religious diversity. But only in Pennsylvania were Catholics free to openly practice their religion.

What were John Locke's main arguments in favor of toleration of religious diversity? What limits did Locke place on religious toleration? Do you agree with his limitations on tolerance? Compare John Locke's ideas on religious diversity with the ideas of William Penn and Isaac Backus (see Documents 9 and 14).

* * *

I esteem it above all things necessary to distinguish exactly the business of civil government from that of religion, and to settle the just bounds that lie between the one and the other. If this be not done, there can be no end put to the controversies that will be always arising between those that have, or at least pretend to have, on the one side, a concernment for the interest of men's souls, and on the other side, a care of the commonwealth.

The commonwealth seems to me to be a society of men constituted only for the procuring, the preserving, and the advancing their own civil interests.

Civil interests I call life, liberty, health, and indolency of body; and the possession of outward things, such as money, lands, houses, furniture, and the like.

It is the duty of the civil magistrate, by the impartial execution of equal laws, to secure unto all the people in general, and to every one of his subjects in particular, the just possession of these things belonging to this life. . . .

Now that the whole jurisdiction of the magistrate reaches only to these civil concernments; and that all civil power, right, and dominion, is bounded and confined to the only care of promoting these things, and that it neither can or ought in any manner to be extended to the salvation of souls; these following considerations seem unto me abundantly to demonstrate.

First, because the care of souls is not committed to the civil magistrate, any more than to other men. It is not committed unto him, I say, by God; because it appears not that God has ever given any such authority to one man over another, as to compel any one to his religion. Nor can any such power be vested in the magistrate by the consent of the people; because no man can so far abandon the care of his own salvation, as blindly to leave it to the choice of any other, whether prince or subject, to prescribe to him what faith or worship he shall embrace. For no man can, if he would, conform his faith to the dictates of another. All the life and power of true religion consists in the outward and full persuasion of the mind; and faith is not faith without believing. . . .

In the second place. The care of souls cannot belong to the civil magistrate, because his power consists of an outward force; but true and saving religion consists in the inward persuasion of the mind, without which nothing can be acceptable to God. And such is the nature of the understanding, that it cannot be compelled to the belief of any thing by outward force. Confiscation of estate, imprisonment, torments, nothing of that nature can have any such efficacy as to make men change the inward judgment that they have framed of things.

It may indeed be alleged, that the magistrate may make use of arguments, and thereby draw the heterodox into the way of truth, and procure their salvation. I grant it; but this is common to him with other men. In teaching, instruction, and redressing the erroneous by reason, he may certainly do what becomes any good man to do. Magistracy does not oblige him to put off either humanity or Christianity. But it is one thing to persuade, another to command; one thing to press with arguments, another with penalties. . . .

In the third place, the care of the salvation of men's souls cannot belong to the magistrate; because, though the rigor of laws and the force of penalties were capable to convince and change men's minds, yet would not that help at all to the salvation of their souls. . . .

Let us now consider what a church is. A church then I take to be a voluntary society of men, joining themselves together of their own accord, in order to the public worshipping of God, in such a manner as they may judge acceptable to him, and effectual to the salvation of their souls.

I say it is a free and voluntary society. . . . No man by nature is bound unto any particular church or sect. . . . [However] no opinions contrary to human society, or to those moral rules which are necessary to the preservation of civil society, are to be tolerated by the magistrate. . . .

Again: That church can have no right to be tolerated by the magistrate, which is constituted upon such a bottom, that all those who enter into it, do thereby *ipso facto*, deliver themselves up to the protection and service of another prince. For by this means the magistrate would give way to the settling of a foreign jurisdiction in his own country, and suffer his own people to be listed, as it were, for soldiers against his own government. . . .

Lastly, those are not at all to be tolerated who deny the being of God. Promises, covenants, and oaths, which are the bonds of human society, can have no hold upon an atheist. The taking away of God, though but even in thought, dissolves all. Besides also, those that by their atheism undermine and destroy all religion, can have no pretense of religion whereupon to challenge the privilege of a Toleration. As for other practical opinions, though not absolutely free from all error, yet if they do not tend to establish domination over others, or civil impunity to the church in which they are taught, there can be no reason why they should not be tolerated.

Source: John Locke, *The Works of John Locke,* Volume 3 (London, 1888), pp. 5–7, 32.

DOCUMENT 12: Charter of Privileges of Pennsylvania (Granted by William Penn, October 28, 1701)

In 1701, William Penn, in consultation with members of the Pennsylvania colonial government, promulgated a new constitution to replace the 1682 Frame of Government. This 1701 Charter of Privileges continued as the constitution of Pennsylvania until the end of the colonial period. It was replaced in 1776 by the Pennsylvania State Constitution.

As in 1682, a primary concern of William Penn was the right to religious liberty. So this 1701 Charter of Privileges begins with an emphatic statement about religious liberty. This document represents a high point in colonial America of legal expression about the individual's right to religious liberty. Even so, it excluded Jews, Deists, and atheists from public office. However, the provisions of Penn's 1701 Charter of Privileges on religious liberty were great guarantees of religious liberty and a harbinger of the religious liberty in the American Constitution and the Bill of Rights (1791).

What does this document say about the latitude and limits of religious liberty? Compare it with the Massachusetts Body of Liberties (Document 5), the Maryland Toleration Act (Document 7), and the Rhode Island Charter (Document 8). Why is this document a grander statement on religious liberty than that of John Locke in his Letter Concerning Toleration (Document 11)?

* * *

FIRST.

BECAUSE no People can be truly happy, though under the greatest Enjoyment of Civil Liberties, if abridged of the Freedom of their Consciences, as to their Religious Profession and Worship: And Almighty God being the only Lord of Conscience, Father of Lights and Spirits; and the Author as well as Object of all divine Knowledge, Faith and Worship, who only doth enlighten the Minds, and persuade and convince the Understandings of People, I do hereby grant and declare, That no Person or Persons, inhabiting in this Province or Territories, who shall confess and acknowledge *One* almighty God, the Creator, Upholder and Ruler of the World; and profess him or themselves obliged to live quietly under the Civil Government, shall be in any Case molested or prejudiced, in his or their Person or Estate, because of his or their conscientious Persuasion or Practice, nor be compelled to frequent or maintain any religious Worship, Place or Ministry, contrary to his or their Mind, or to do or suffer any other Act or Thing, contrary to their religious Persuasion.

AND that all Persons who also profess to believe in Jesus Christ, the Savior of the World, shall be capable (notwithstanding their other Persuasions and Practices in Point of Conscience and Religion) to serve this Government in any Capacity, both legislatively and executively, he or they solemnly promising, when lawfully required, Allegiance to the King as Sovereign, and Fidelity to the Proprietary and Governor. . . .

* * *

VIII.

* * *

BUT because the Happiness of Mankind depends so much upon the Enjoying of Liberty of their Consciences as aforesaid, I do hereby solemnly declare, promise and grant, for me, my Heirs and Assigns, That the *First* Article of this Charter relating to Liberty of Conscience, and every Part and Clause therein, according to the true Intent and Meaning thereof, shall be kept and remain, without any Alteration, inviolably for ever.

Source: Francis N. Thorpe, ed., *The Federal and State Constitutions, Colonial Charters, and Other Organic Laws of the States, Territories, and Colonies Now or Heretofore Forming the United States of America*, Volume 5 (Washington, D.C., 1909), pp. 3080–3081.

DOCUMENT 13: Letter to the Society for the Propagation of the Gospel (The Reverend Thomas Barton, November 8, 1762)

The Reverend Thomas Barton was a missionary to North America from the Church of England. In 1751, he arrived in Pennsylvania and was amazed by the extraordinary diversity of religion in this colony. Reverend Barton had a negative view of great diversity in religious belief and practice, because his mission was to advance the numbers and influence of the Anglican Church. What evidence of religious diversity does Barton report? What is his view of the relationship of government to religious diversity in Pennsylvania?

* * *

This mission takes in the whole of Lancaster County (80 miles in length and 26 in breadth), part of Chester County and part of Berks. So the circumference of my mission alone is 200 miles. The County of Lancaster contains upwards of 40,000 souls. Of this number not more than 500 can be reckoned as belonging to the Church of England. The rest are German Lutherans, Calvinists, Mennonites, Moravians, New Born, Dunkers, Presbyterians, Seceders, New Lights, Covenanters, Mountain Men, Brownists, Independents, Papists, Quakers, Jews and so forth! Amid such a swarm of sects, all indulged and favored by the government, it is no wonder that the National Church should be borne down. At the last election for the county to choose assemblymen, sheriff, coroner, commissioners, assessors and the like, 5,000 citizens voted and yet not a single member of the Church was elected into any of these offices. . . .

Notwithstanding these and other like discouragements, I have the satisfaction to assure the Society that my people [members of the Anglican Church] have continued to give proofs of that submission and obedience to civil liberty which it is the glory of the Church of England to instill.

Source: W. S. Perry, ed., *Historical Collections Relating to the American Colonial Church*, Volume 2 (Hartford, 1871), p. 366.

DOCUMENT 14: An Appeal to the Public for Religious Liberty (The Reverend Isaac Backus, 1773)

A Baptist preacher in Massachusetts, Isaac Backus had converted to Christianity in 1741 in response to the Great Awakening movement. From 1756 until his death in 1806, Backus was pastor of the First Baptist Church in Middleborough, Massachusetts. He was the leading advocate in New England for the cause of religious liberty. In his great sermon of 1773, "An Appeal to the Public for Religious Liberty," Reverend Backus spoke against laws in Massachusetts that favored the Congregational Church and required Baptists and other non-Congregationalists to pay taxes in support of the church established by the government of the colony. He argued for separation of church from government and for the individual's freedom of conscience in matters of religious faith.

Reverend Backus invoked the mid-seventeenth-century struggle of Roger Williams against the established Congregational Church in Massachusetts. He lauded the Congregationalist majority in Massachusetts for permitting much greater freedom of conscience in the 1770s than their ancestors had done in the time of Roger Williams. Nonetheless, he argued that legal requirements of the 1770s, which forced Baptists to pay taxes to the government in support of the Congregational Church, were an offense against religious liberty.

Compare the arguments of Reverend Backus for religious liberty with those of William Penn (see Documents 9, 10, and 12). Why did Backus claim that genuine religious liberty did not exist in Massachusetts? Do you agree with him?

* * *

[This is] a brief view of how civil and ecclesiastical affairs are blended together among us, to the depriving of many of God's people of that liberty of conscience which he has given to them. . . .

But our blessed Lord & only Redeemer, has commanded us, to stand fast in the liberty wherewith he has made us free; and things appear so to us at present that we cannot see how we carefully obey this command, without refusing any active compliance with some laws about religious affairs that are laid upon us. . . .

The effects of the constitution of our country are such, that as it makes the majority of the people the test of orthodoxy, so it emboldens them to usurp God's judgment seat. . . . And though in our charter the king grants to all Protestants equal liberty of conscience: yet for above thirty years after it was received the Congregationalists made no laws to favor the consciences of any man, in this affair of taxes, but their own sect; and it is here called arbitrary power. . . .

[T]he first fathers of Massachusetts [were moved] to imprison, whip and banish men, only for denying infant baptism, and refusing to join in worship that was supported by violent methods; yet they were so much blinded as to declare, that there was this vast difference between these proceedings and the coercive measures which were taken against themselves in England. . . .

[Roger Williams opposed the actions against religious liberty of individuals of the government of Massachusetts.] How weighty are those arguments against combining church and state together. . . . [Y]et this author's [Roger Williams] appearing against such confusion, was the chief cause for which he was banished out of the Massachusetts colony. . . . And though few if any [Congregationalists in Massachusetts] will now venture openly to justify these proceedings, [they compel dissenters to pay taxes] to support a way [the Congregational Church] which at the same time they are allowed to dissent from. . . .

Our charter, as before observed, gives us equal religious liberty with other Christians: yet the [Congregationalists] being the greatest [majority] party, they soon made a perpetual law to support their own way, but did nothing of that nature to exempt our denomination [Baptists] from it. . . .

Here note, the inhabitants of our mother country [Britain] are not more of a party concerned, in imposing taxes on us without our consent, than they have been in this land [Massachusetts] who have made and executed laws, to tax us to uphold their worship [the Congregational Church]. . . .

But where each person, and each society, are equally protected from being injured by others, all enjoying equal liberty, to attend and support the worship which they believe is right . . . how happy are its effects in civil society? . . .

Thus we have laid before the public a brief view of our sentiments concerning liberty of conscience, and a little sketch of our sufferings on that account. If any can show us that we have made any mistakes, either about principles or facts, we would lie open to conviction. But we hope none will violate the forfeited article of faith so much, as to require us to yield a blind obedience to them, or to expect that spoiling of goods or imprisonment can move us to betray the cause of true liberty. . . .

Source: Isaac Backus, *An Appeal to the Public for Religious Liberty, Against the Oppressions of the Present Day* (Boston, 1773), pp. 9, 13–15, 18–19, 29, 35.

FURTHER READING

Bronner, Edwin B. *William Penn's Holy Experiment*. Philadelphia: Temple University Press, 1962.

Curry, Thomas J. *The First Freedoms: Church and State in America to the Passage of the First Amendment*. New York: Oxford University Press, 1986.

Ferguson, Robert A. *The American Enlightenment, 1750–1820*. Cambridge, Mass.: Harvard University Press, 1997, pp. 44–79.

Folsom, Franklin. *Give Me Liberty: America's Colonial Heritage*. Chicago: Rand McNally, 1974.

Frost, J. William. *A Perfect Freedom: Religious Liberty in Pennsylvania*. University Park: Pennsylvania State University Press, 1993.

Gaustad, Edwin S. "Colonial Religion and Liberty of Conscience." In *The Virginia Statute for Religious Freedom: Its Evolution and Consequences in American History*, edited by Merrill D. Peterson and Robert C. Vaughan. Cambridge, England: Cambridge University Press, 1988, pp. 23–42.

Heimert, Alan. *Religion and the American Mind: From the Great Awakening to the Revolution*. Cambridge, Mass.: Harvard University Press, 1966.

Henretta, James A., and Gregory H. Nobles. *Evolution and Revolution: American Society, 1600–1820.* Lexington, Mass.: Heath, 1987.

Hofstadter, Richard. *America at 1750: A Social Portrait.* New York: Vintage Books, 1973, pp. 180–293.

Morgan, Edmund S. *Roger Williams: The Church and the State.* New York: Harcourt, Brace and World, 1967.

Noonan, John T., Jr. *The Lustre of Our Country: The American Experience of Religious Freedom.* Berkeley: University of California Press, 1998, pp. 39–58.

Part II

Religious Liberty in the Founding of the United States, 1776–1791

On July 4, 1776, the second Continental Congress approved the Declaration of Independence that forever severed the union of thirteen American colonies from the United Kingdom of Great Britain. More than seven years later, on September 3, 1783, representatives of the United States of America and Great Britain signed the Treaty of Paris, which signified British recognition of American independence.

In their 1776 declaration, Americans announced that "Governments are instituted among Men" to secure certain "Unalienable Rights," among which are "Life, Liberty, and the Pursuit of Happiness." Most Americans of the founding era agreed that the individual's freedom of conscience or religious liberty was one of the "Unalienable Rights" that a good government should protect. But they argued robustly about the meaning of religious liberty, about who should or should not have it, and about how the government should act to protect it.

Public opinion about religious liberty and governmental actions to secure it varied within and between the different states. And in general, public conceptions of religious liberty were a bit different from the prevailing opinions in America today. For example, in the founding era the right to freedom of conscience usually was not extended to non-Christians or nonbelievers. And among Christians, Roman Catholics often faced discrimination and occasionally even persecution.

After 1776, the newly independent American states established new constitutions and declarations of rights, including statements about religious liberty and the relationships between churches and government. And each of the thirteen American states changed, some more and others less, the government-church arrangements of the colonial era. By 1786, for example, the five southern states—Maryland, Virginia, North Carolina, South Carolina, and Georgia—had all disestablished the Church of England or Episcopal Church. However, they tended to reserve complete freedom of religion only for Protestant Christians and required a religious oath to qualify for public office, which excluded non-Christians and nonbelievers. (See, for example, the articles on religion in the 1776 Maryland Declaration of Rights, Document 17.)

John Carroll, a Roman Catholic priest, was pleased by the trend toward religious toleration for all denominations of Christians, which he perceived in his own state, Maryland, and in other parts of America. In a public statement issued in 1784, he expressed the hope that "America may come to exhibit a proof to the world, that general and equal toleration, by giving a free circulation to fair arguments, is the most effectual method to bring all denominations of Christians to a unity of faith."[1]

Father Carroll wanted to encourage acceptance of Roman Catholics and to erode the discrimination against them that had persisted variously throughout the United States. So Carroll influenced the Pope and other administrative leaders of the Catholic Church in Rome to allow American Catholics to oversee their own selection of bishops and other church leaders in America (see Document 21). Thus, Carroll tried to overcome the opinion of many Protestants in America that Roman Catholics could not be loyal citizens of the United States because of their allegiance to a pope in Rome. In 1790, John Carroll became the first Roman Catholic bishop in the United States and did much to advance the cause of religious toleration in America.

From 1776 to 1786, Roman Catholics and other Christians enjoyed the greatest latitude for religious liberty in four states: Pennsylvania, Delaware, New Jersey, and Rhode Island. As in colonial times, these four states established no churches, levied no taxes to support religion, and proclaimed freedom of conscience. The Pennsylvania Constitution broadened its religious test for public office beyond Protestant Christianity to include all believers in God and the Old and New Testaments (see Document 16). And Rhode Island abolished its colonial-era law excluding Roman Catholics from public office.

The 1777 New York State Constitution guaranteed the "free exercise and enjoyment of religious profession and worship, without discrimination or preference" and prohibited the establishment of a preferred state church. However, a New York law in 1788 required an oath for government office that excluded Roman Catholics.[2]

Three New England states—Connecticut, Massachusetts, and New Hampshire—enacted constitutions and declarations of rights that provided state support for all Christian denominations and guaranteed free exercise of religion for all Christians. (See, for example, Document 18, which includes articles on religion in the 1780 Massachusetts Declaration of Rights.) Although these three New England states instituted constitutional governments that were supposed to equally and nonpreferentially support all Christian churches, the Congregational Church tended to be favored over the others, which reflected its majority status relative to such minority denominations as the Baptists and Presbyterians.

Public debates in Virginia on church-state arrangements and freedom of religion were especially acute from 1776 to 1786. The issues and arguments in Virginia generated ideas that eventually influenced other American states and pointed the way to clauses on religion in the United States Constitution.

The debates on religious liberty in Virginia began in 1776 during discussions about the state's Declaration of Rights. During deliberations on Article XVI of the Declaration of Rights, James Madison objected to the provision "that all men should enjoy the fullest toleration in the exercise of religion." Madison wanted to move beyond the tradition of religious toleration introduced by John Locke and the English Toleration Act of 1689 (see Document 11). So the twenty-five-year-old delegate from Orange County to Virginia's constitutional convention put forward these words: "All men are equally entitled to the free exercise of religion."[3]

Madison's proposal that a right to "free exercise of religion" should replace the phrase on religious toleration was approved, and his words were included in Article XVI of the Virginia Declaration of Rights (see Document 15). Thus, James Madison acted decisively in 1776 for the principle that every person has an equal right to free exercise of religion, which was a forerunner of his sponsorship of religious liberty in the First Amendment of the 1791 Bill of Rights.

In 1785, Madison was embroiled in another critical issue on religious liberty in Virginia that had consequences for the United States from the founding era until today. The controversy was about nonpreferential state support for all Christian churches or sects. Should the state government raise taxes for the specific purpose of supporting equally the various Christian denominations of the state?

Patrick Henry, Virginia's most popular politician, proposed that the General Assembly enact a tax law to provide public support equally and nonpreferentially for religious education and support of ministers of all Christian churches of the state. According to Henry's bill, each taxpayer could designate which church (Episcopal, Methodist, Baptist, etc.) would receive his tax payment. This was a significant departure from the colonial-era situation in which the Church of England was the only tax-supported religion in Virginia. Henry was not in favor of a single established or state-supported church for the state of Virginia. Instead, he proposed through his "Bill Establishing a Provision for

Teachers of the Christian Religion" a "general assessment" that would establish nonpreferentially all Christian churches in his state.

Patrick Henry spoke in the General Assembly for his bill and emphasized the following points:

- A free and stable government cannot be sustained without the support of Christian institutions.
- Public and private morality will suffer unless Christian religious institutions in the state are strong and active.
- History records the decline and fall of nations that failed to support their religious institutions.
- Christian institutions in Virginia are suffering from lack of voluntary financial support.
- Therefore, it is proper, for the good of the state, to require citizens of Virginia to pay a tax for support of ministers and their churches.

James Madison opposed Patrick Henry's arguments. He argued that the general assessment bill was an unacceptable limitation on the individual's freedom of conscience. Further, Madison argued that Henry's bill was an unacceptable state establishment of Christianity in general, even if it did not specify a single Christian church as preferred over others.

Henry's bill for nondiscriminatory tax support of all Christian churches, which would give no state preference to one Christian denomination over the others, was popular. Such luminaries as Edmund Randolph, Richard Henry Lee, and George Washington backed it. And other states were acting similarly, such as New Hampshire, Massachusetts, Connecticut, Maryland, South Carolina, and Georgia.

Madison, however, opposed Henry's bill, because he feared that any kind of tax-based support of religion was a dangerous intrusion into a personal and private matter, which should be free of entanglement with the state. To Madison, nonpreferential state support of religion was still an establishment of religion that violated his principle of separation of church and state.

Madison tried to mobilize public opinion in Virginia against Henry's bill for nonpreferential state support of the Christian religion. He wrote a fifteen-point protest, "Memorial and Remonstrance Against Religious Assessments," and circulated this petition throughout Virginia (see Document 22). Madison's "remonstrances" or protests were a compelling argument for broad religious liberty and against any kind of state-established religion, even a general and equal establishment of all Christian churches.

Members of the Virginia General Assembly saw many petitions when they met in October 1785. About 1,200 signatures were attached to pro-assessment petitions. More than 10,000 Virginians signed petitions against the general assessment bill. Most of the anti-assessment petitions either included Madison's statements or reflected them. Thus, at the outset of the autumn session of the General Assembly, the fate of the bill was sealed. It was referred to committee and never reported back to the General Assembly. Madison had won his campaign to defeat this proposal for state support of religion.

Madison quickly pushed for passage of Thomas Jefferson's bill for religious freedom, which had been introduced initially in 1779. Again, he was successful, and Jefferson's bill became law on January 16, 1786 (see Document 23). Madison wrote to Jefferson, then serving in Paris as the U.S. diplomatic representative to the French government, that the key ideas of the bill on religious freedom were enacted unchanged "and I flatter myself have in this country extinguished forever the ambitious hope of making laws for the human mind."[4]

Madison's hope, though genuine, was exaggerated, as many issues about religious liberty and freedom of conscience continued from his lifetime into our contemporary era. However, he had significantly advanced the cause for free exercise of religion and against any kind of state establishment of religion.

The ideas of Madison and Jefferson on the individual's right to freedom of religion were based on the doctrine of natural rights advanced by the English philosopher John Locke in his *Second Treatise of Government* (1689). According to this doctrine, the right to liberty, including the right to free exercise of religion, belongs equally to every person by virtue of the individual's membership in the human species. Thus, a good government may not justly deprive an individual of her or his natural rights, including the right to free exercise of religion. Rather, it is the duty of a good government to secure or protect the natural rights of individuals. Jefferson's discussions of religious liberty in *Notes on the State of Virginia* (1782) and the Virginia Statute for Religious Freedom (1786) are rooted in Locke's doctrine of natural rights (see Documents 20 and 23).

Ideas on religious liberty developed by Madison and Jefferson (see Documents 20, 22, 23, and 27) became foundations for the two clauses on religious liberty in the First Amendment to the United States Constitution, ratified in 1791. And the outcome of the Virginia controversy about general tax support for the Christian religion pointed to the eventual end of established religions in all the state constitutions in the United States.

By 1787, on the eve of the Constitutional Convention in Philadelphia that brought a new frame of government to the United States of America, the idea of a single state established church was dead. And even the idea of a multiple establishment—the nonpreferential state support of all Christian churches—was a hot issue in several states or had been rejected in others, such as Virginia in 1786. In 1802, for example, Thomas Jefferson wrote a letter to the Baptist Association of Danbury, Connecticut, in which he advocated "building a wall of separation between church and state."[5] Jefferson, serving his first term as President of the United States, offered his highly respected opinion in support of the Baptists' petition to end taxation in general support of the Christian religion in Connecticut. The General Assembly rejected the anti-tax petition. But sixteen years later, in 1818, Connecticut abolished its state government's support of religion. In 1833, Massachusetts became the last American state to overturn its establishment of religion.

The right to free exercise of religion, while generally undisputed and legally sanctioned, tended to be restricted in practice to Protestant Christians. Jefferson's Virginia Statute for Religious Freedom was exceptional in its broad claims for religious liberty. However, the United States generally exhibited more toleration and freedom of religion than existed anywhere else in the world of the 1780s.

The Northwest Ordinance, enacted by Congress in 1787 to establish law and order in the U.S. government's territories north and west of the Ohio River, exemplified the general American support for freedom of religion. Section 14, Article I of this law stated, "No person demeaning himself in a peaceable and orderly manner, shall ever be molested on account of his mode of worship, or religious sentiments, in the said territory."[6] The Northwest Ordinance of 1787 also reflected the general American opinion that religion was the foundation for public morality and civil society. It proclaimed in Section 14, Article III, "Religion, morality, and knowledge being necessary to good government and the happiness of mankind, schools and the means of education shall forever be encouraged."[7]

Delegates to the 1787 Constitutional Convention focused on the challenge of designing an effective but limited federal government for the United States. They hardly discussed rights of religious liberty, which were assumed to be the business of citizens at the state level of government. The new constitutional government would be granted no power to act with regard to religion. And one very significant limitation was specified in Article VI of the 1787 constitution, which prohibited any religious qualification for federal government officials (see Document 24).

During the nationwide debates on ratification of the 1787 Constitution, many Anti-Federalists, opponents of the proposed frame of government, objected, among other things, to this prohibition of a religious test for office. They feared that the way was open to the possibility that a non-Christian or an atheist might become President. Federalists effectively rebutted this Anti-Federalist objection to the 1787 Constitution. (See, for example, Document 25.) However, eleven of the original thirteen states required some kind of oath or religious test to qualify for public office.[8] During the nineteenth and twentieth centuries, most states either deleted or omitted from their constitutions any religious tests for public office. Maryland was the last state to have such a constitutional provision, and it was voided in 1961.[9]

During the ratification debates, Anti-Federalists scored points against the proposed 1787 Constitution by pointing to its lack of a declaration on rights or bill of rights. They feared that a powerful federal government, if not constitutionally restricted, would violate individual rights, such as free exercise of religion. In reply, James Madison and other Federalist defenders of the 1787 Constitution pointed to the great social diversity of the United States, including religious diversity, as a protection for rights, such as the free exercise of religion. Madison argued in *Federalist Papers 10* and *51* that the multiplicity of religious sects in America would prevent any one of them from dominating the others and violating their rights of religious liberty (see Document 26). A French immigrant to America, Hector St. John de Crevecoeur, also wrote that the extraordinary diversity of religious denominations in the United States was a strong force for toleration of differences. Since no sect could be a controlling majority with power to coerce the others, the different groups seemed ready to tolerate each other (see Document 19).

In order to win majority support for the 1787 Constitution at several state ratifying conventions, James Madison and other Federalists promised to support constitutional amendments on rights, including religious liberty, at the First Federal Congress in 1789. True to this promise, Madison, a representative to Congress from Virginia, proposed several constitutional amendments in a stirring speech on June 8, 1789 (see Document 27). Among his amendments were proposals for free exercise of religion and against any establishment of a "national religion."

Madison's proposed amendments on rights, including religious liberty, were discussed by members of the House of Representatives and the Senate, as called for by the Constitution. (See Documents 28 and 29 for examples of discussions on freedom of religion and religious establishments.) On September 25, 1789, a modified version of Madison's proposals on rights was approved by both houses of Congress and sent to the states for ratification, which occurred December 15, 1791. (See Document 30 for the First Amendment of the Bill of Rights.)

The two clauses on religion in the First Amendment, pertaining to free exercise of religion and no establishment of religion, have been constitutionally mandated in the United States from December 15, 1791, until today. And during the twentieth century, they have been controversial subjects of divisive public debates and landmark Supreme Court cases. In particular, arguments about the establishment of religion by government and separation of church and state, which were confronted by Virginians in 1785, are still with us. Issues raised during America's founding era about nonpreferential state support for religion have been confronted and adjudicated, but not definitively resolved.

NOTES

1. John Carroll, "An Address to the Roman Catholics of the United States of America," in John Tracy Ellis, ed., *Documents of American Catholic History* (Milwaukee: Bruce Publishing, 1962), pp. 146–147.

2. Thomas J. Curry, *The First Freedoms: Church and State in America to the Passage of the First Amendment* (New York: Oxford University Press, 1986), p. 162. Curry notes that a New York law of 1788 required all government officials to renounce all foreign authorities, "ecclesiastical as well as civil," which was aimed at excluding Roman Catholics with loyalty to their pope in Rome.

3. Lance Banning, "James Madison, the Statute for Religious Freedom, and the Crisis of Republican Convictions," in Merrill D. Peterson and Robert C. Vaughan, eds., *The Virginia Statute for Religious Freedom: Its Evolution and Consequences in American History* (Cambridge, England: Cambridge University Press, 1988), p. 111.

4. Ibid., p. 124.

5. Leonard W. Levy, *The Establishment Clause: Religion and the First Amendment* (New York: Macmillan, 1986), p. 182.

6. Bernard Schwartz, *The Great Rights of Mankind: A History of the American Bill of Rights* (Madison, Wis.: Madison House, 1992), pp. 101–103.

7. David Lowenthal, *No Liberty for License: The Forgotten Logic of the First Amendment* (Dallas: Spence Publishing, 1997), p. 193.

8. Isaac Kramnick and R. Laurence Moore, *The Godless Constitution: The Case Against Religious Correctness* (New York: W. W. Norton, 1997), pp. 29–31. Kramnick and Moore note that by 1787, the year of the Constitutional Convention, only Virginia and New York had eliminated religious tests for public office. But a New York state law still discriminated against Roman Catholics (see note 2 above).

9. *Torcaso v. Watkins*, 367 U.S. 488 (1961). In this case, the U.S. Supreme Court invalidated a part of the Maryland Constitution that required state government officeholders to profess belief in God.

DOCUMENT 15: The Virginia Declaration of Rights (June 12, 1776)

Virginia was prominent among the first group of newly independent American states to adopt a constitution. The task of constitution-making was assigned to a twenty-eight-man committee, appointed by a convention whose members were elected by Virginia's voters to govern the colony in the absence of British authority.

The constitutional committee's first achievement was a Declaration of Rights, written primarily by George Mason and submitted to the convention on May 27, 1776. It was passed unanimously on June 11, and then the convention turned its attention to drafting a plan of government, the body of the constitution, which would be placed after the document on rights. The Virginia Declaration of Rights was an extraordinary statement of the natural rights doctrine, which held that all persons, by virtue of their membership in the human species, possessed equally certain rights. Governments could not claim to be the source of these rights because they are rooted in human nature, and governments could not legitimately deprive people of them. Rather, the primary purpose of a good government was to secure these rights for people living under its authority. Among the natural rights proclaimed in this document are freedom of speech, religious liberty, and certain legal protections for persons accused of crimes. Further, the ideas of limited government and the rule of law pervaded the document.

The Virginia Declaration of Rights influenced similar statements of rights that preceded six other state constitutions, including those of Pennsylvania and Massachusetts (see Documents 16 and 18). Further, the federal Bill of Rights, adopted in 1791, was influenced by the Virginia Declaration of Rights. With regard to separation of church and state, however, Article VI of the U.S. Constitution and the First Amendment went beyond the protections for religious liberty provided by the Virginia Declaration of Rights, which did not disestablish the legally privileged Episcopal Church (formerly called the Church of England).

Articles I, II, III, and XVI of the sixteen-article Virginia Declaration of Rights are presented below. Only Article XVI pertains specifically to religion. The other three articles presented here pertain generally to the idea of individual rights and the responsibility of government to secure these rights. What does this document say in general about the rights of individuals and their relationship to government? What does Article XVI say about religious liberty? What is the relationship between the ideas in Articles I–III and the right to religious liberty in Article XVI?

* * *

A Declaration of Rights made by the Representatives of the good People of Virginia, assembled in full and free Convention, which rights to pertain to them and their posterity as the basis and foundation of government.

I. That all men are by nature equally free and independent, and have certain inherent rights, of which, when they enter into a state of society, they cannot by any compact, deprive or divest their posterity; namely, the enjoyment of life and liberty with the means of acquiring and possessing property, and pursuing and obtaining happiness and safety.

II. That all power is vested in, and consequently derived from, the people; that magistrates are their trustees and servants, and at all times amenable to them.

III. That government is, or ought to be, instituted for the common benefit, protection and security of the people, nation, or community; of all the various modes and forms of government, that is best which is capable of producing the greatest degree of happiness and safety, and is most effectually secured against the danger of maladministration; and that, when a government shall be found inadequate or contrary to these purposes, a majority of the community hath an indubitable, unalienable and indefeasible right to reform, alter or abolish it, in such manner as shall be judged most conducive to the public weal. . . .

XVI. That religion, or the duty which we owe to our Creator, and the manner of discharging it, can be directed only by reason and conviction, not by force or violence; and therefore all men are equally entitled to the free exercise of religion, according to the dictates of conscience; and that it is the duty of all to practice Christian forbearance, love and charity towards each other.

Source: Francis N. Thorpe, ed., *The Federal and State Constitutions, Colonial Charters, and Other Organic Laws of the States, Territories, and Colonies Now or Heretofore Forming the United States of America*, Volume 7 (Washington, D.C., 1909), pp. 3812–3814.

DOCUMENT 16: Articles on Religion in the Pennsylvania Declaration of Rights and Constitution (1776)

Pennsylvania quickly followed Virginia in the enactment of a Declaration of Rights and Frame of Government or Constitution to assert its newly declared status as a sovereign state within the United States of America. Like several other newly written American state constitutions, the Pennsylvania document proclaimed freedom of religion and disclaimed establishment of any church or sect. However, it strongly supported the idea of religion and religious institutions. And it prohibited non-Christians from holding public office through a mandated oath or test of religious belief. This religious test for public office was dropped in the 1790 Constitution and replaced with an oath that only required belief in God. However, this Constitution limited religious freedom to believers; atheists were excluded from constitutional protection for their beliefs.

What does the Pennsylvania Declaration of Rights say about freedom of conscience? How does it promote Christian churches or denominations? What limits does it place on freedom of religion? How are the Pennsylvania Declaration of Rights and Frame of Government similar to and different from the documents of Virginia, Maryland, and Massachusetts in treatment of religion? (See Documents 15, 17, and 18.)

* * *

From Article 2 of the Declaration of Rights

That all men have a natural and unalienable right to worship Almighty God according to the dictates of their own consciences and understandings: And that no man ought or of right can be compelled to attend any religious worship, or erect or support any place of worship, or maintain any ministry, contrary to, or against, his own free will and consent: Nor can any man, who acknowledges the being of a God, be justly deprived or abridged of any civil right as a citizen, on account of his religious sentiments or peculiar mode of religious worship: And that no authority can or ought to be vested in, or assumed by any power whatever, that shall in any case interfere with, or in any manner control, the right of conscience in the free exercise of religious worship.

From Article 10 of the Frame of Government

And each member, before he takes his seat, shall make and subscribe the following declaration, viz:

I do believe in one God, the creator and governor of the universe, the rewarder of the good and the punisher of the wicked. And I do acknowledge the Scriptures of the Old and New Testament to be given by Divine inspiration.

And no further or other religious test shall ever hereafter be required of any civil officer or magistrate in this State.

From Article 45 of the Frame of Government

Laws for the encouragement of virtue, and prevention of vice and immorality, shall be made and constantly kept in force, and provision shall be made for their due execution: And all religious societies or bodies of men heretofore united or incorporated for the advancement of religion or learning, or for other pious and charitable purposes, shall be encouraged and protected in the enjoyment of the privileges, immunities and estates which they were accustomed to enjoy, or could of right have enjoyed under the laws and former constitution of this state.

Source: Francis N. Thorpe, ed., *The Federal and State Constitutions, Colonial Charters, and Other Organic Laws of the States, Territories, and Colonies Now or Heretofore*

Forming the United States of America, Volume 5 (Washington, D.C., 1909), pp. 3082, 3085, 3100.

DOCUMENT 17: Articles on Religion in the Maryland Declaration of Rights (1776)

The Maryland Declaration of Rights was written in August 1776 and approved in November. This document included forty-two articles. Articles 33 and 35, which pertain to religion, are presented below. These articles guarantee an equal right to freedom of religion for all Christians, but not for non-Christians or nonbelievers. They also provide for taxation and public support for Christian ministers and churches. And there is a religious test for governmental office that excludes all non-Christians.

Compare the articles on religion in this document with the treatment of religious liberty in the declarations of rights and constitutions of Virginia, Pennsylvania, and Massachusetts. (See Documents 15, 16, and 18.)

* * *

XXXIII. That, as it is the duty of every man to worship God in such manner as he thinks most acceptable to him; all persons, professing the Christian religion, are equally entitled to protection in their religious liberty; wherefore no person ought by any law to be molested in his person or estate on account of his religious persuasion or profession, or for his religious practice; unless, under color of religion, any man shall disturb the good order, peace or safety of the State, or shall infringe the laws of morality, or injure others, in their natural, civil, or religious rights; nor ought any person to be compelled to frequent or maintain, or contribute, unless on contract, to maintain any particular place of worship, or any particular ministry: yet the Legislature may, in their discretion, lay a general and equal tax, for the support of the Christian religion; leaving to each individual the power of appointing the payment over the money, collected from him, to the support of any particular place of worship or minister, or for the benefit of the poor of his own denomination, or the poor in general of any particular county. . . .

XXXV. That no other test or qualification ought to be required, on admission to any office of trust or profit, than such oath of support and fidelity to this State, and such oath of office, as shall be directed by this

Convention, or the Legislature of this State, and a declaration of a belief in the Christian religion.

Source: Francis N. Thorpe, ed., *The Federal and State Constitutions, Colonial Charters, and Other Organic Laws of the States, Territories, and Colonies Now or Heretofore Forming the United States of America*, Volume 3 (Washington, D.C., 1909), pp. 1687–1688.

DOCUMENT 18: The Massachusetts Declaration of Rights (1780)

In September 1779, John Adams was elected to be a delegate to the Constitutional Convention of Massachusetts. At the convention, Adams was named to a three-man committee, with Samuel Adams and James Bowdoin, to draft a Declaration of Rights and Frame of Government or Constitution. Adams took on this task for the committee and submitted a draft of his work to the convention, which approved it with minor changes on March 2, 1780. The people of the state, voting in their town meetings, ratified the Declaration of Rights and Frame of Government on June 15, 1780, and the Constitution was implemented on October 25, 1780.

This Declaration of Rights owed much to the Virginia Declaration, as did the other original state declarations of rights. For example, as with the Virginia Declaration of Rights, this document stressed the natural rights doctrine, separation of powers, legal protections for the rights of persons accused of crimes, and the rule of law. Unlike the Virginia document, however, the Massachusetts Declaration of Rights emphatically provided for the state government's general and nonpreferential support of the Christian religion. It also provided for free exercise of religion among Christians of any sect or denomination. It did not, however, guarantee freedom of conscience for nonbelievers or non-Christians.

Articles I–III of the thirty-article Massachusetts Declaration of Rights are presented below. Article I pertains generally to the idea of rights and the state government's obligation to protect them. Articles II and III, which pertain directly to religion, assert the fundamental importance of religion to good government. Article II provides for free exercise of religion so long as it does not violate the rights of others or threaten the common good. Article III proclaims the authority of the state government to raise taxes to support nonpreferentially all Christian denominations.

What does the Massachusetts Declaration of Rights say about the state's authority and responsibility to support or promote religion? Why do these provisions constitute a state establishment of religion? What is the relationship of Article I, below, to Articles II and III?

* * *

ART. I.—ALL men are born free and equal, and have certain natural, essential, and unalienable rights; among which may be reckoned the right of enjoying and defending their lives and liberties; that of acquiring, possessing, and protecting property; in fine, that of seeking and obtaining their safety and happiness.

II.—IT is the right as well as the duty of all men in society, publicly, and at stated seasons, to worship the SUPREME BEING, the great creator and preserver of the universe. And no subject shall be hurt, molested, or restrained, in his person, liberty, or estate, for worshipping GOD in the manner and season most agreeable to the dictates of his own conscience; or for his religious profession or sentiments; provided he doth not disturb the public peace, or obstruct others in their religious worship.

III.—AS the happiness of a people, and the good order and preservation of civil government, essentially depend upon piety, religion and morality; and as these cannot be generally diffused through a community, but by the institution of the public worship of GOD, and of public instructions in piety, religion and morality: Therefore, to promote their happiness and to secure the good order and preservation of their government, the people of this Commonwealth have a right to invest their legislature with power to authorize and require, the several towns, parishes, precincts, and other bodies-politic, or religious societies, to make suitable provision, at their own expense, for the institution of the public worship of GOD, and for the support and maintenance of public Protestant teachers of piety, religion and morality, in all cases where such provision shall not be made voluntarily.

AND the people of this Commonwealth have also a right to, and do, invest their legislature with authority to enjoin upon all the subjects an attendance upon the instructions of the public teachers aforesaid, at stated times and seasons, if there be any on whose instructions they can conscientiously and conveniently attend.

PROVIDED notwithstanding, that the several towns, parishes, precincts, and other bodies-politic, or religious societies, shall, at all times, have the exclusive right of electing their public teachers, and of contracting with them for their support and maintenance.

AND all monies paid by the subject to the support of public worship, and of the public teachers aforesaid, shall, if he require it, be uniformly applied to the support of the public teacher or teachers of his own religious sect or denomination, provided there be any on whose instructions he attends: otherwise it may be paid towards the support of the teacher or teachers of the parish or precinct in which the said monies are raised.

AND every denomination of Christians, demeaning themselves peaceably, and as good subjects of the Commonwealth, shall be equally under the protection of the law: And no subordination of any one sect or denomination to another shall ever be established by law.

Source: The Journal of the Convention for Framing a Constitution of Government for the State of Massachusetts-Bay (Boston, 1832), pp. 225–249.

DOCUMENT 19: Liberty of Worship in America (Hector St. John de Crevecoeur, 1782)

In 1755, Michel Guillaume Jean de Crevecoeur traveled from the country of his birth, France, to the colony of New France (Quebec) in North America, where he served in the French army. Crevecoeur fought against the British during the French and Indian War and was wounded during the pivotal battle at the Plains of Abraham on September 13, 1759. This defeat led to the French loss of Canada to the British. Following his discharge from the French army, Crevecoeur migrated southward to the British colony of New York, where he changed his name to Hector St. John and became a farmer. He also became the celebrated author of *Letters from an American Farmer*. In one of these published letters, "What Is an American?," Crevecoeur described the distinguishing characteristics of the people in the new nation, the United States of America, that in 1776 proclaimed its independence from Great Britain.

Among the key characteristics of the Americans, according to Crevecoeur, was the propensity for freedom, especially freedom of conscience. According to Crevecoeur, religious toleration in America was based on diversity of religious beliefs and practices throughout the nation. Crevecoeur described religious liberty in America as something very different from that of the countries of Europe. According to Crevecoeur, the transplanted Frenchman, what factors in America influenced the development of religious liberty and toleration?

* * *

... The American is a new man, who acts upon new principles; he must therefore entertain new ideas, and form new opinions....

... As Christians, religion curbs them not in their opinions; the general indulgence leaves every one to think for themselves in spiritual matters; the laws inspect our actions, our thoughts are left to God. Industry, good living, selfishness, litigiousness, country politics, the pride of freemen, religious indifference, are their characteristics. . . .

As I have endeavored to show you how Europeans become Americans; it may not be disagreeable to show you likewise how the various Christian sects introduced, wear out, and how religious indifference becomes prevalent. When any considerable number of a particular sect happen to dwell contiguous to each other, they immediately erect a temple, and there worship the Divinity agreeably to their own peculiar ideas. Nobody disturbs them. If any new sect springs up in Europe it may happen that many of its professors will come and settle in America. As they bring their zeal with them, they are at liberty to make proselytes if they can, and to build a meeting and to follow the dictates of their consciences; for neither the government nor any other power interferes. If they are peaceable subjects, and are industrious, what is it to their neighbors how and in what manner they think fit to address their prayers to the Supreme Being? But if the sectaries are not settled close together, if they are mixed with other denominations, their zeal will cool for want of fuel, and will be extinguished in a little time. Then the Americans become as to religion, what they are as to country, allied to all. In them the name of Englishman, Frenchman, and European is lost, and in like manner, the strict modes of Christianity as practiced in Europe are lost also. This effect will extend itself still farther hereafter, and though this may appear to you as a strange idea, yet it is a very true one. . . .

. . . Thus all sects are mixed as well as all nations; thus religious indifference is imperceptibly disseminated from one end of the continent to the other, which is at present one of the strongest characteristics of the Americans. Where this will reach no one can tell, perhaps it may leave a vacuum fit to receive other systems. Persecution, religious pride, the love of contradiction, are the food of what the world commonly calls religion. These motives have ceased here; zeal in Europe is confined; here it evaporates in the great distance it has to travel; there it is a grain of powder enclosed, here it burns away in the open air, and consumes without effect. . . .

Source: Hector St. John de Crevecoeur, *Letters from an American Farmer* (London, 1912), pp. 44–51.

DOCUMENT 20: An Argument for Religious Liberty in *Notes on the State of Virginia* (Thomas Jefferson, 1782)

Thomas Jefferson, third President of the United States and writer of the Declaration of Independence, was the author of one book, *Notes on the State of Virginia*, which is considered an American classic. Jefferson discussed many topics in his book, including religious diversity in the United States and the individual's right to freedom of religion. Like his friend James Madison and the French immigrant Crevecoeur, Jefferson connected the fact of religious diversity in America to the trend toward toleration of religious differences. (See Documents 19 and 26.) And Jefferson argued strongly for the right to freedom of conscience and free exercise of religion. What does he say in this document about the person's right to religious liberty?

* * *

... [O]ur rulers can have no authority over ... natural rights, only as we have submitted to them. The rights of conscience we never submitted, we could not submit. We are answerable for them to our God. The legitimate powers of government extend to such acts only as are injurious to others. But it does me no injury for my neighbor to say there are twenty gods, or no God. It neither picks my pocket nor breaks my leg. ... Reason and free inquiry are the only effectual agents against error. Give a loose to them, they will support the true religion by bringing every false one to their tribunal, to the test of their investigation. They are the natural enemies of error, and of error only. ... Was the government to prescribe to us our medicine and diet, our bodies would be in such keeping as our souls are now. Thus in France the emetic was once forbidden as a medicine, the potato as an article of food. Government is just as infallible, too, when it fixes systems in physics. Galileo was sent to the Inquisition for affirming that the earth was a sphere; the government had declared it to be as flat as a trencher, and Galileo was obliged to abjure his error. This error, however, at length prevailed, the earth became a globe, and Descartes declared it was whirled round its axis by a vortex. The government in which he lives was wise enough to see that this was no question of civil jurisdiction, or we should all have been involved by authority in vortices. In fact, the vortices have been exploded, and the Newtonian principle of gravitation is now more firmly established, on the basis of reason, than it would be were the government to step in, and to make it an article of necessary faith. Reason and experiment have been indulged, and error has fled before them. It is error alone which needs the support of government. Truth can stand by itself. Subject opinions to coercion: whom will you make your inquisitors? Fallible men; men governed by bad passions, by private as well as public reasons. And why subject it to coercion? To produce uniformity. But is uniformity of opinion desirable? No more than of face and stature. ... Difference of opinion is advantageous in religion. The several sects perform the office of a *censor morum* over each other. ... Reason and persuasion are the only practicable instruments. To make way for these, free inquiry must be indulged; and how can we wish others to indulge it while we refuse it ourselves. . . .

Source: H. A. Washington, ed., *The Writings of Thomas Jefferson*, Volume 8 (Philadelphia, 1781), pp. 376–377.

DOCUMENT 21: Letter on the Selection of a Roman Catholic Bishop in the United States of America (Father John Carroll, February 27, 1785)

John Carroll was ordained a priest of the Roman Catholic Church in 1769. He studied and taught in Europe before returning in 1774 to Maryland, where he was born and raised. During the conflict between the British and their American colonies, Father Carroll sided with the American patriots. After the War of Independence, the Pope appointed him to be Superior of Catholic Missions for the United States of America.

Father Carroll was concerned about the anti-Catholic sentiment that prevailed in most parts of the United States. He wanted to reassure the Protestant majority that Catholics were good citizens and that their primary loyalty in political matters was to the United States and not to the Pope in Rome. Toward this goal, he wrote to Catholic Church officials in Rome with an important request. Father Carroll wanted the Catholic clergymen in the United States to have authority to elect their own bishop, who would be the head of the Church in their own country.

Father Carroll's request was granted, and he was consecrated the first Roman Catholic bishop in America in 1790. He founded Georgetown University in 1791 and became the first archbishop of Baltimore in 1811.

Beginning with his letter to Rome in 1785, Father Carroll did much to advance tolerance for the Roman Catholic Church in America. What reasons did he put forth in his letter to convince authorities in Rome to permit American clergy to select their own bishop? What does his letter suggest about difficulties faced by the Catholic Church in the United States?

* * *

THE MOST EMINENT CARDINAL may rest assured that the greatest evils would be borne by us rather than renounce the divine authority of the Holy See; that not only we priests who are here, but the Catholic people, seem so firm in the faith that they will never withdraw from obedience to the sovereign pontiff. The Catholic body, however, think that some favor should be granted to them by the Holy Father, necessary for their permanent enjoyment of the civil rights which they now enjoy, and to avert the dangers which they fear. From what I have said, and from the framework of public affairs here, Your Eminence must see how objectionable all foreign jurisdiction will be to them. The Catholics therefore desire that no pretext be given to the enemies of our religion to accuse us of depending unnecessarily on a foreign authority; and that some plan may be adopted by which hereafter an ecclesiastical superior may be appointed for this country in such a way as to retain absolutely the spiritual jurisdiction of the Holy See and at the same time remove all ground of objecting to us, as though we held anything hostile to the national independence. . . .

We desire, therefore, Most Eminent Cardinal, to provide in every way, that the faith in its integrity, due obedience toward the Apostolic See, and perfect union should flourish, and at the same time that whatever can with safety to religion be granted, shall be conceded to American Catholics in ecclesiastical government; in this way we hope that the distrust of Protestants now full of suspicion will be diminished, and that thus our affairs can be solidly established.

You have indicated, Most Eminent Cardinal, that it was the intention and design of His Holiness to appoint a Vicar Apostolic for these states, invested with the Episcopal character and title. While this paternal solicitude for us has filled us with great joy, it also at first inspired some fear; for we knew that heretofore American Protestants never could be induced to allow even a bishop of their own sect, when the attempt was made during the subjection of these provinces to the king of England; hence a fear arose that we would not be permitted to have one. But some months since in a convention of Protestant ministers of the Anglican, or as it is here called, the Episcopal Church, they decreed that as by authority of law they enjoyed the full exercise of their religion, they therefore had the right of appointing for themselves such ministers of holy things as the system and discipline [of] their sect required; namely bishops, priests, and deacons. This decision on their part was not censured by the Congress appointed to frame our laws. As the same liberty in the exercise of religion is granted to us, it necessarily follows that we enjoy the same right in regard to adopting laws for our government.

While the matter stands thus, the Holy Father will decide, and you, Most Eminent Cardinal, will consider whether the time is now opportune for appointing a bishop, what his qualifications should be, and how he should be nominated. On all these points, not as if seeking to obtain my own judgment, but to make this relation more ample, I shall note a few facts.

First, as regards the seasonableness of the step, it may be noted that there will be no excitement in the public mind if a bishop be appointed, as Protestants think of appointing one for themselves. Nay, they even hope to acquire some importance for their sect among the people from the Episcopal dignity. So, too, we trust that we shall not only acquire the same, but that great advantages will follow; inasmuch as this church will then be governed in that manner which Christ our Lord instituted. On the other hand, however, it occurs that as the Most Holy Father has already deigned to provide otherwise for conferring the sacrament of confirmation, there is no actual need for the appointment of a bishop until some candidates are found fitted to receive holy orders; this we hope will be the case in a few years, as you will understand, Most Eminent Cardinal, from a special relation which I propose writing. When that time comes, we shall perhaps be better able to make a suitable provision for a bishop than from our slender resources we can now do.

In the next place, if it shall seem best to His Holiness to assign a bishop to this country, will it be best to appoint a vicar apostolic or an ordinary with a see of his own? Which will conduce more to the progress of Catholicity; which will contribute most to remove Protestant jealousy of foreign jurisdiction? I know with certainty that this fear will increase if they know that an ecclesiastical superior is so appointed as to be removable from office at the pleasure of the Sacred Congregation *de Propaganda Fide*, or any other tribunal out of the country, or that he has no power to admit any priest to exercise the sacred function, unless that congregation has approved and sent him to us.

As to the method of nominating a bishop, I will say no more at present than this, that we are imploring God in His wisdom and mercy to guide the judgment of the Holy See, that if it does not seem proper to allow the priests who have labored for so many years in this vineyard of the Lord to propose to the Holy See the one whom they deem most fit, that some method will be adopted by which a bad feeling may not be excited among the people of this country, Catholic and Protestant.

Source: John G. Shea, *Life and Times of the Most Reverend John Carroll* (New York, 1888), pp. 251–256.

DOCUMENT 22: Memorial and Remonstrance Against Religious Assessments (James Madison, June 20, 1785)

James Madison of Orange County, Virginia, was a staunch supporter of the individual's rights to freedom from unjust or unnatural coercion by the state. He was particularly committed to the cause of religious liberty, and he believed separation of church and state to be a necessary condition of this fundamental freedom. So, in 1784–1785, as a member of the Virginia General Assembly, he led opposition to a bill that would have levied a state tax on Virginians "to restore and propagate the holy Christian religion" through financial support of Christian clergymen.

Madison certainly was not opposed to the needs and mission of organized religion. Rather, he believed these needs and this mission should be addressed in the private sphere of society, free of entanglement with and possible coercion by government. Madison's Memorial and Remonstrance was written to arouse statewide opposition to the proposed law on assessments to support religion, and it succeeded. The General Assembly set aside this bill in October 1785 in response to an outpouring of public opposition.

Madison presented fifteen distinct arguments against the proposed tax to support nonpreferentially all Christian denominations of the state. He argued that religion should neither be promoted nor interfered with by the government, because it was the individual's natural right freely to exercise it in accord with his or her conscience.

According to Madison, why would the proposed tax law in support of religious education have a harmful effect on the rights and liberties of individuals? Why, according to Madison, would this proposed law not be necessary for the well-being of the state government and society? Why would it even be harmful to the government and society? Why does Madison say that the proposed tax to support all Christian churches nonpreferentially would nonetheless constitute a state establishment of religion? What reasons does Madison present against an establishment of religion by the state government?

* * *

To The Honorable The General Assembly of
    The Commonwealth Of Virginia.
    A Memorial and Remonstrance.

We, the subscribers, citizens of the said Commonwealth, having taken into serious consideration, a Bill printed by order of the last Session of General Assembly, entitled "A Bill establishing a provision for Teachers of the Christian Religion," and conceiving that the same, if finally armed with the sanctions of a law, will be a dangerous abuse of power, are bound as faithful members of a free State, to remonstrate against it, and to declare the reasons by which we are determined. We remonstrate against the said Bill,

1. Because we hold it for a fundamental and undeniable truth, "that

Religion or the duty which we owe to our Creator and the Manner of discharging it, can be directed only by reason and conviction, not by force or violence." The Religion then of every man must be left to the conviction and conscience of every man; and it is the right of every man to exercise it as these may dictate. This right is in its nature an unalienable right. It is unalienable; because the opinions of men, depending only on the evidence contemplated by their own minds, cannot follow the dictates of other men: It is unalienable also; because what is here a right towards men, is a duty towards the Creator. It is the duty of every man to render to the Creator such homage, and such only, as he believes to be acceptable to him. This duty is precedent both in order of time and degree of obligation, to the claims of Civil Society. . . . We maintain therefore that in matters of Religion, no man's right is abridged by the institution of Civil Society, and that Religion is wholly exempt from its cognizance. True it is, that no other rule exists, by which any question which may divide a Society, can be ultimately determined, but the will of the majority; but it is also true, that the majority may trespass on the rights of the minority.

2. Because if religion be exempt from the authority of the Society at large, still less can it be subject to that of the Legislative Body. The latter are but the creatures and vicegerents [deputies] of the former. Their jurisdiction is both derivative and limited: it is limited with regard to the co-ordinate departments, more necessarily is it limited with regard to the constituents. The preservation of a free government requires not merely, that the metes and bounds which separate each department of power may be invariably maintained; but more especially, that neither of them be suffered to overleap the great Barrier which defends the rights of the people. The Rulers who are guilty of such an encroachment, exceed the commission from which they derive their authority, and are Tyrants. The People who submit to it are governed by laws made neither by themselves, nor by an authority derived from them, and are slaves.

3. Because, it is proper to take alarm at the first experiment on our liberties. We hold this prudent jealousy to be the first duty of citizens, and one of [the] noblest characteristics of the late Revolution. . . . Who does not see that the same authority which can establish Christianity, in exclusion of all other Religions, may establish with the same ease any particular sect of Christians, in exclusion of all other Sects? That the same authority which can force a citizen to contribute three pence only of his property for the support of any one establishment, may force him to conform to any other establishment in all cases whatsoever?

4. Because, the bill violates that equality which ought to be the basis of every law. . . . If "all men are by nature equally free and independent," all men are to be considered as entering into Society on equal conditions; as relinquishing no more, and therefore retaining no less, one than an-

other, of their natural rights. Above all are they to be considered as retaining an "*equal* title to the free exercise of Religion according to the dictates of conscience." Whilst we assert for ourselves a freedom to embrace, to profess and to observe the Religion which we believe to be of divine origin, we cannot deny an equal freedom to those whose minds have not yet yielded to the evidence which has convinced us. If this freedom be abused, it is an offense against God, not against man: To God, therefore, not to men, must an account of it be rendered. As the Bill violates equality by subjecting some to peculiar burdens; so it violates the same principle, by granting to others peculiar exemptions. . . .

5. Because the bill implies either that the Civil Magistrate is a competent Judge of Religious truth; or that he may employ Religion as an engine of Civil policy. The first is an arrogant pretension falsified by the contradictory opinions of Rulers in all ages, and throughout the world: The second an unhallowed perversion of the means of salvation.

6. Because the establishment proposed by the Bill is not requisite for the support of the Christian Religion. To say that it is, is a contradiction to the Christian Religion itself; for every page of it disavows a dependence on the powers of this world: it is a contradiction to fact; for it is known that this Religion both existed and flourished, not only without the support of human laws, but in spite of every opposition from them; and not only during the period of miraculous aid, but long after it had been left to its own evidence, and the ordinary care of Providence: Nay, it is a contradiction in terms; for a Religion not invented by human policy, must have pre-existed and been supported, before it was established by human policy. It is moreover to weaken in those who profess this Religion a pious confidence in its innate excellence, and the patronage of its Author; and to foster in those who still reject it, a suspicion that its friends are too conscious of its fallacies, to trust it to its own merits.

7. Because experience witnesseth that ecclesiastical establishments, instead of maintaining the purity and efficacy of Religion, have had a contrary operation. . . .

8. Because the establishment in question is not necessary for the Support of Civil Government. If it be urged as necessary for the support of Civil Government only as it is a means of supporting Religion, and it be not necessary for the latter purpose, it cannot be necessary for the former. . . .

9. Because the proposed establishment is a departure from that generous policy, which, offering an asylum to the persecuted and oppressed of every Nation and Religion, promised a lustre to our country, and an accession to the number of its citizens. . . .

10. Because, it will have a like tendency to banish our Citizens. The allurements presented by other situations are every day thinning their number. To superadd a fresh motive to emigration, by revoking the lib-

erty which they now enjoy, would be the same species of folly which has dishonored and depopulated flourishing kingdoms.

11. Because, it will destroy that moderation and harmony which the forbearance of our laws to intermeddle with Religion, has produced amongst its several sects. Torrents of blood have been spilt in the old world, by vain attempts of the secular arm to extinguish Religious discord, by proscribing all difference in Religious opinions. Time has at length revealed the true remedy. Every relaxation of narrow and rigorous policy, wherever it has been tried, has been found to assuage the disease. The American Theatre has exhibited proofs, that equal and complete liberty, if it does not wholly eradicate it, sufficiently destroys its malignant influence on the health and prosperity of the State. . . .

12. Because, the policy of the bill is adverse to the diffusion of the light of Christianity. The first wish of those who enjoy this precious gift, ought to be that it may be imparted to the whole race of mankind. Compare the number of those who have as yet received it with the number still remaining under the dominion of false Religions; and how small is the former! Does the policy of the Bill tend to lessen the disproportion? No; it at once discourages those who are strangers to the light of [revelation] from coming into the Region of it; and countenances, by example the nations who continue in darkness, in shutting out those who might convey it to them. Instead of leveling as far as possible, every obstacle to the victorious progress of truth, the Bill with an ignoble and unchristian timidity would circumscribe it, with a wall of defense, against the encroachments of error.

13. Because attempts to enforce by legal sanctions, acts obnoxious to so great a proportion of Citizens, tend to enervate the laws in general, and to slacken the bands of Society. If it be difficult to execute any law which is not generally deemed necessary or salutary, what must be the effect of so striking an example of impotency in the Government, on its general authority.

14. Because a measure of such singular magnitude and delicacy ought not to be imposed, without the clearest evidence that it is called for by a majority of citizens: and no satisfactory method is yet proposed by which the voice of the majority in this case may be determined, or its influence secured. . . .

15. Because, finally, "the equal right of every citizen to the free exercise of his Religion according to the dictates of conscience" is held by the same tenure with all our other rights. If we recur to its origin, it is equally the gift of nature; if we weigh its importance, it cannot be less dear to us; if we consult the Declaration of those rights which pertain to the good people of Virginia, as the "basis and foundation of government," it is enumerated with equal solemnity, or rather studied emphasis. . . .

Source: Gaillard Hunt, ed., *The Writings of James Madison*, Volume 2 (New York, 1910), pp. 183–191.

DOCUMENT 23: The Virginia Statute for Religious Freedom (Thomas Jefferson, January 16, 1786)

Thomas Jefferson, a friend and neighbor of James Madison in the piedmont region of Virginia, drafted a bill to buttress and enlarge the principle of religious liberty expressed in Section XVI of the 1776 Virginia Declaration of Rights. This proposed statute was introduced to the Virginia General Assembly in 1779, but it languished without adequate support for six years, until James Madison promoted its passage in the wake of his successful campaign against a proposed law that would have levied taxes for the nonpreferential support of the state's various Christian denominations.

Jefferson's bill became law in January 1786, and Virginia moved to the forefront of American states in the cause of religious liberty. Jefferson's statute is introduced by a preamble, Section I, and followed by a concluding statement, Section III. The preamble is a profound argument for freedom of expression, with particular emphasis on every person's inherent right to free exercise of religious belief. According to Jefferson, government should be prohibited by law from interfering with a person's natural right to freedom of expression, which is the intent of Section II, the statute. Section III states that the individual's right to religious liberty does not come from government; rather, it is a natural right of individuals, based in human nature, that supersedes the power of government.

How did Jefferson use the natural rights doctrine in Sections I and III to justify this statute? Compare Section II, the statute, with Section XVI of the Virginia Declaration of Rights (see Document 15). How did Jefferson's statute support and expand upon the protections for religious liberty expressed in the Virginia Declaration of Rights? Compare this statute with constitutional laws on religious liberty in other states during the founding era. (See Documents 16, 17, and 18.)

* * *

I. Whereas Almighty God hath created the mind free; that all attempts to influence it by temporal punishments or burthens, or by civil incapacitations, tend only to beget habits of hypocrisy and meanness, and are a departure from the plan of the Holy Author of our religion, who being Lord both of body and mind, yet chose not to propagate it by coercions on either, as was in His Almighty power to do; that the impious presumption of legislators and rulers, civil as well as ecclesiastical, who being themselves but fallible and uninspired men, have assumed dominion over the faith of others, setting up their own opinions and modes of thinking as the only true and infallible, and as such endeavoring to impose them on others, hath established and maintained false religions over the greatest part of the world, and through all time; that to compel a man to furnish contributions of money for the propagation of opinions which he disbelieves, is sinful and tyrannical; that even forcing him to support this or that teacher of his own religious persuasion, is depriving him of the comfortable liberty of giving his contributions to the particular pastor, whose morals he would make his pattern, and whose powers he feels most persuasive to righteousness, and is withdrawing from the ministry those temporary rewards, which proceeding from an approbation of their personal conduct, are an additional incitement to earnest and unremitting labors for the instruction of mankind; that our civil rights have no dependence on our religious opinions, any more than our opinions in physics or geometry; that therefore the proscribing [of] any citizen as unworthy [of] the public confidence by laying upon him an incapacity of being called to offices of trust and emolument, unless he profess or renounce this or that religious opinion, is depriving him injuriously of those privileges and advantages to which in common with his fellow-citizens he has a natural right; that it tends only to corrupt the principles of that religion it is meant to encourage, by bribing with a monopoly of worldly honors and emoluments, those who will externally profess and conform to it; that though indeed these are criminal who do not withstand such temptation, yet neither are those innocent who lay the bait in their way; that to suffer the civil magistrate to intrude his powers into the field of opinion, and to restrain the profession or propagation of principles on supposition of their ill tendency, is a dangerous fallacy, which at once destroys all religious liberty, because he being of course judge of that tendency will make his opinions the rule of judgment, and approve or condemn the sentiments of others only as they shall square with or differ from his own; that it is time enough for the rightful purposes of civil government, for its officers to interfere when principles break out into overt acts against peace and good order; and finally, that truth is great and will prevail if left to herself, that she is the proper and sufficient antagonist to error, and has nothing to fear from the conflict, unless by human interposition disarmed of her natural weapons, free argument and debate, errors ceasing to be dangerous when it is permitted freely to contradict them:

II. *Be it enacted by the General Assembly*, That no man shall be compelled to frequent or support any religious worship, place or ministry whatsoever, nor shall be enforced, restrained, molested, or burthened in his body or goods, nor shall otherwise suffer on account of his religious opinions or belief; but that all men shall be free to profess, and by argument to maintain, their opinions in matters of religion, and that the same shall in no wise diminish, enlarge, or affect their civil capacities.

III. And though we well know that this Assembly, elected by the people for the ordinary purposes of legislation only, have no power to restrain the acts of succeeding Assemblies, constituted with powers equal to our own, and that therefore to declare this act to be irrevocable would be of no effect in law; yet we are free to declare, and do declare, that the rights hereby asserted are of the natural rights of mankind, and that if any act shall be hereafter passed to repeal the present, or to narrow its operation, such act will be an infringement of natural right.

Source: W. W. Hening, ed., *Statutes at Large of Virginia*, Volume 12 (Richmond, 1836), pp. 84–86.

DOCUMENT 24: Article VI of the United States Constitution (1787)

The federal Constitutional Convention voted to approve the Constitution on September 15, 1787, signed it on September 17, and submitted it to the Continental Congress, still operating under the Articles of Confederation. This Constitution of 1787 included seven articles, which listed powers granted in the name of the people to the U.S. government, and by implication, powers reserved to the state governments. Limitations on the powers of both the U.S. government and the state governments were expressed. According to Article VI, the U.S. Constitution, plus laws and treaties enacted in conformity with it, would be the supreme law of the country which the states would be obligated to uphold. Article VI also prohibits any religious test or oath as a condition of eligibility for public office in the U.S. government. This is the only statement on religion in the 1787 Constitution. Compare the article on religion in the 1787 Constitution with the articles on religion in state constitutions and declarations of rights of the founding era. What are the similarities and differences? (See Documents 15, 16, 17, and 18.)

* * *

The Senators and Representatives before mentioned, and the Members of the several State Legislatures, and all executive and judicial Officers, both of the United States and of the several States, shall be bound by

Oath or Affirmation, to support this Constitution; but no religious Test shall ever be required as a Qualification to any Office or public Trust under the United States.

Source: Francis N. Thorpe, ed., *The Federal and State Constitutions, Colonial Charters, and Other Organic Laws of the States, Territories, and Colonies Now or Heretofore Forming the United States of America*, Volume 1 (Washington, D.C., 1909), p. 27.

DOCUMENT 25: An Argument Against a Religious Test for Public Office (Oliver Ellsworth, December 17, 1787)

Oliver Ellsworth represented Connecticut at the 1787 Constitutional Convention. During the debates on ratification of the Constitution, he wrote letters for publication to counter criticisms of the Anti-Federalists, opponents of the 1787 Constitution. The following letter argues for the clause that prohibits religious tests for public office in Article VI. This provision of Article VI was the target of criticism by Anti-Federalists, who claimed it would open the way to non-Christian or atheistic public officials, who would corrupt the public morals and civic virtue of the country. They also argued that it was antagonistic to religion. In reply, Oliver Ellsworth argued that this provision of Article VI would provide equal protection to all citizens with regard to their freedom of conscience. What does Ellsworth say in opposition to these critics of the religion clause of Article VI? What reasons does he present in favor of prohibiting religious tests for public office?

* * *

Some very worthy persons who have not had great advantages for information have objected against that clause in the Constitution which provides that no religious test shall ever be required as a qualification to any office or public trust under the United States. They have been afraid that this clause is unfavorable to religion. But, my countrymen, the sole purpose and effect of it is to exclude persecution and to secure to you the important right of religious liberty. We are almost the only people in the world who have a full enjoyment of this important right of human nature. In our country every man has a right to worship God in that way which is most agreeable to his conscience. If he be a good and peaceable person, he is liable to no penalties or incapacities on account of his religious sentiments; or, in other words, he is not subject to persecution.

But in other parts of the world it has been, and still is, far different. . . .

It was the universal opinion that one religion must be established by law; and that all who differed in their religious opinions must suffer the vengeance of persecution. In pursuance of this opinion, when popery was abolished in England and the Church of England was established in its stead, severe penalties were inflicted upon all who dissented from the established church. In the time of the civil wars, in the reign of Charles I, the Presbyterians got the upper hand and inflicted legal penalties upon all who differed from them in their sentiments respecting religious doctrines and discipline. When Charles II was restored, the Church of England was likewise restored, and the Presbyterians and other dissenters were laid under legal penalties and incapacities.

It was in this reign that a religious test was established as a qualification for office. . . .

A religious test is an act to be done or profession to be made relating to religion (such as partaking of the sacrament according to certain rites and forms, or declaring one's belief of certain doctrines) for the purpose of determining whether his religious opinions are such that he is admissible to a public office. A test in favor of any one denomination of Christians would be to the last degree absurd in the United States. If it were in favor of either Congregationalists, Presbyterians, Episcopalians, Baptists, or Quakers, it would incapacitate more than three-fourths of the American citizens for any public office and thus degrade them from the rank of freemen. There need be no argument to prove that the majority of our citizens would never submit to this indignity. . . .

If we mean to have those appointed to public offices who are sincere friends to religion, we, the people who appoint them, must take care to choose such characters, and not rely upon such cobweb barriers as test laws are.

But to come to the true principle by which this question ought to be determined: *The business of a civil government is to protect the citizen in his rights, to defend the community from hostile powers, and to promote the general welfare. Civil government has no business to meddle with the private opinions of the people.* If I demean myself as a good citizen, I am accountable not to man but to God for the religious opinions which I embrace and the manner in which I worship the Supreme Being. If such had been the universal sentiments of mankind and they had acted accordingly, persecution, the bane of truth and nurse of error, with her bloody axe and flaming brand, would never have turned so great a part of the world into a field of blood.

But while I assert the rights of religious liberty, I would not deny that the civil power has a right, in some cases, to interfere in matters of religion. It has a right to prohibit and punish gross immoralities and impieties; because the open practice of these is of evil example and detriment. . . .

Test laws are useless and ineffectual, unjust and tyrannical; therefore the Convention have done wisely in excluding this engine of persecution, and providing that no religious test shall ever be required.

Source: E. H. Scott, ed., *The Federalist and Other Constitutional Papers by Hamilton, Jay, Madison and Other Statesmen of Their Time*, Volume 2 (Chicago, 1894), pp. 582–583.

DOCUMENT 26: *The Federalist 51* (Publius [James Madison], February 6, 1788)

Alexander Hamilton planned a series of newspaper articles to advocate ratification of the 1787 Constitution and to thwart its opponents, the Anti-Federalists. He was joined by James Madison and John Jay in writing eighty-five *Federalist Papers*, each signed with a pseudonym, Publius.

In *Federalist Paper 51*, James Madison discussed the great social and religious diversity in the United States as a factor in diminishing the possibility of majority tyranny against unpopular minority groups. He contended that the greater the diversity of political interests or religious sects in a society, the lesser the likelihood that a permanent majority would form around a single interest or sect and use its power persistently and tyrannically against minorities. According to Madison, the great diversity of religious denominations or sects in America would generate countervailing forces against the possibility of a single established church that could dominate all the other churches.

Compare Madison's ideas about religious diversity and religious liberty with the views of Crevecoeur (see Document 19). Do you agree with Madison's contention that religious diversity is a force for religious liberty for minority groups?

* * *

It is of great importance in a republic, not only to guard the society against the oppression of its rulers; but to guard one part of the society against the injustice of the other part. Different interests necessarily exist in different classes of citizens. If a majority be united by a common interest, the rights of the minority will be insecure. There are but two methods of providing against this evil: The one by creating a will in the community independent of the majority, that is, of the society itself; the other by comprehending in the society so many separate descriptions of citizens, as will render an unjust combination of a majority of the whole, very improbable, if not impracticable. The first method prevails in all governments possessing an hereditary or self appointed authority. This at best is but a precarious security; because a power independent of the society may as well espouse the unjust views of the major, as the rightful interests, of the minor party, and may possibly be turned against both parties. The second method will be exemplified in the federal republic of the United States. Wilst all authority in it will be derived from and dependent on the society, the society itself will be broken into so many parts, interests and classes of citizens, that the rights of individuals or of the minority, will be in little danger from interested combinations of the majority. In a free government, the security for civil rights must be the same as that for religious rights. It consists in the one case in the multiplicity of interests, and in the other, in the multiplicity of sects. The degree of security in both cases will depend on the number of interests and sects; and this may be presumed to depend on the extent of country and number of people comprehended under the same government. This view of the subject must particularly recommend a proper federal system to all the sincere and considerate friends of republican government: Since it shows that in exact proportion as the territory of the union may be formed into more circumscribed confederacies or states, oppressive combinations of a majority will be facilitated, the best security under the republican form, for the rights of every class of citizens, will be diminished; and consequently, the stability and independence of some member of the government, the only other security, must be proportionally increased. Justice is the end of government. It is the end of civil society. It ever has been, and ever will be pursued, until it be obtained, or until liberty be lost in the pursuit. In a society under the forms of which the stronger faction can readily unite and oppress the weaker, anarchy may as truly be said to reign, as in a state of nature where the weaker individual is not secured against the violence of the stronger: And as in the latter state even the stronger individuals are prompted by the uncertainty of their condition, to submit to a government which may protect the weak as well as themselves: So in the former state, will the more powerful factions or parties be gradually induced by a like motive, to wish for a government which will protect all parties, the weaker as well as the more powerful. It can be little doubted, that if the state of Rhode Island was separated from the confederacy, and left to itself, the insecurity of rights under the popular form of government within such narrow limits, would be displayed by such reiterated oppressions of factious majorities, that some power altogether independent of the people would soon be called for by the voice of the very factions whose misrule had proved the necessity of it. In the extended republic of the United States, and among the great variety of interests, parties and sects which it embraces, a coalition of a majority of the whole society could seldom take place on any other principles than those of justice and the general good; and there being thus less danger to a minor from the will of the major party, there must be less pretext also, to provide for the security of the former, by introducing into the government a will not dependent on the latter; or in other words, a will independent of the society itself. It is no less certain than it is important notwithstanding the contrary opinions which have been entertained, that the larger the society, provided it lie within a practicable sphere, the more duly capable it will be of self government. And happily for the *republican cause*, the practicable sphere may be carried to a very great extent, by a judicious modification and mixture of the *federal principle*.

Source: Independent Journal (New York), February 6, 1788. See also Clinton Rossiter, ed., *The Federalist Papers* (New York: New American Library, 1965), pp. 323–325.

DOCUMENT 27: Speech on Rights in the U.S. House of Representatives (James Madison, June 8, 1789)

In a carefully prepared speech in the House of Representatives, James Madison of Virginia introduced proposals for a bill of rights in the U.S. Constitution. The proposals on religion were influenced by the 1776 Virginia Declaration of Rights and by the 1786 Virginia Statute for Religious Freedom. He recommended that the amendments be inserted into sections of the Constitution rather than appended to it. Roger Sherman of Connecticut, however, rallied opposition to this recommendation about placement of the amendments, and the House of Representatives decided that they should be appended to the Constitution as a separate Bill of Rights.

Item four in Madison's speech proposed constitutional guarantees against the establishment of a national religion and for the individual's right to free exercise of religion. The proposals in item four influenced the religion clauses of the First Amendment in the 1791 Bill of Rights.

Madison emphasized item five in his list of proposals on rights. If enacted, it would have guaranteed fundamental individual rights, including the right of religious liberty, against the power of state governments. This proposal was passed by the House of Representatives, but it was defeated by the Senate. So not until passage of the Fourteenth Amendment in 1868 was there a federal constitutional basis for limiting the power of state governments to protect rights to religious liberty. (See Document 33 in Part III for an example of the use of Fourteenth

Amendment provisions to guarantee rights of individuals against the power of a state government.)

Madison predicted that the federal courts would become "the guardians of these rights" in the Bill of Rights. He said in this speech that the federal judges "will be naturally led to resist every encroachment upon rights expressly stipulated for in the Constitution by the declaration of rights."

What specific guarantees of rights of individuals on religion did Madison propose to include in the Constitution? What were his reasons for proposing these amendments? What were the similarities of Madison's proposals to the Virginia Declaration of Rights and to the Virginia Statute on Religious Freedom?

* * *

... I will state my reasons why I think it proper to propose amendments, and state the amendments themselves. . . .

It cannot be a secret to the gentlemen in this House, that, notwithstanding the ratification of this system of Government by eleven of the thirteen United States, in some cases unanimously, in others by large majorities; yet still there is a great number of our constituents who are dissatisfied with it, among whom are many respectable for their talents and patriotism, and respectable for the jealousy they have for their liberty, which, though mistaken in its object is laudable in its motive. There is a great body of the people falling under this description, who at present feel much inclined to join their support to the cause of Federalism, if they were satisfied on this one point. We ought not to disregard their inclination, but, on principles of amity and moderation, conform to their wishes, and expressly declare the great rights of mankind secured under this Constitution. . . .

The amendments which have occurred to me, proper to be recommended by Congress to the State Legislatures, are these:

First. That there be prefixed to the Constitution a declaration, that all power is originally vested in, and consequently derived from, the people.

That Government is instituted and ought to be exercised for the benefit of the people; which consists in the enjoyment of life and liberty, with the right of acquiring and using property, and generally of pursuing and obtaining happiness and safety.

That the people have an indubitable, unalienable, and indefeasible right to reform or change their Government, whenever it be found adverse or inadequate to the purposes of its institution. . . .

Fourthly. That in article 1st, section 9, between clauses 3 and 4, be inserted these clauses, to wit: The civil rights of none shall be abridged on account of religious belief or worship, nor shall any national religion be established, nor shall the full and equal rights of conscience be in any manner, or on any pretext, infringed.

The people shall not be deprived or abridged of their right to speak, to write, or to publish their sentiments; and the freedom of the press, as one of the great bulwarks of liberty, shall be inviolable.

The people shall not be restrained from peaceably assembling and consulting for their common good; nor from applying to the Legislature by petitions, or remonstrances, for redress of their grievances. . . .

Fifthly. That in article 1st, section 10, between clauses 1 and 2, be inserted this clause, to wit:

No State shall violate the equal rights of conscience, or the freedom of the press, or the trial by jury in criminal cases. . . .

I wish also, in revising the constitution, we may throw into the section, which interdicts the abuse of certain powers in the state legislatures, some other provisions of equal if not greater importance than those already made. The words, "No state shall pass any bill of attainder, ex post facto law, &c." were wise and proper restrictions in the constitution. I think there is more danger of those powers being abused by the state governments than by the government of the United States. The same may be said of other powers which they possess, if not controlled by the general principle, that laws are unconstitutional which infringe the rights of the community. I should therefore wish to extend this interdiction, and add, as I have stated in the 5th resolution, that no state shall violate the equal right of conscience, freedom of the press, or trial by jury in criminal cases; because it is proper that every government should be disarmed of powers which trench upon those particular rights. I know in some of the state constitutions the power of the government is controlled by such a declaration, but others are not. I cannot see any reason against obtaining even a double security on those points; and nothing can give a more sincere proof of the attachment of those who opposed this constitution to those great and important rights, than to see them join in obtaining the security I have now proposed; because it must be admitted, on all hands, that the state governments are as liable to attack those invaluable privileges as the general government is, and therefore ought to be as cautiously guarded against. . . .

Having done what I conceived was my duty in bringing before this House the subject of amendments, and also stated such as I wish for and approve, and offered the reasons which occurred to me in their support I shall content myself, for the present, with moving "that a committee be appointed to consider of and report such amendments as ought to be proposed by Congress to the Legislatures of the States, to become, if ratified by three-fourths thereof, part of the Constitution of the United States." By agreeing to this motion, the subject may be going on in the committee, while other important business is proceeding to a conclusion in the House. I should advocate greater dispatch in the business of amendments, if I were not convinced of the absolute necessity there is of pursuing the organization of the Government; because I think we should obtain the confidence of our fellow-citizens, in proportion as we fortify the rights of the people against the encroachments of the Government.

Source: Gaillard Hunt, ed., The Writings of James Madison, Volume 5 (New York, 1910), pp. 370–389.

DOCUMENT 28: Discussion in the House of Representatives on Constitutional Guarantees of Religious Liberty (August 15, 1789)

On June 10, 1789, the House of Representatives agreed to consider James Madison's proposed constitutional amendments on rights, including rights to religious liberty. From July 21 to 28, Madison participated in a committee to study the proposed amendments and report on them to a meeting of the House of Representatives. On August 15, the House debated the part of the committee report on prohibiting the government of the United States from acting to establish a religion.

In his June 8, 1789 speech in Congress, Madison had proposed an amendment with the wording "nor shall any national religion be established." (See Document 27.) His use of the word "national" was debated in the House discussion of August 15 and was deleted. What reasons did Madison offer to defend his use of this word in regard to prohibiting an establishment of religion? Why did others oppose it? Why did Madison and others in the House agree to omit the word "national" from a proposed amendment against an establishment of religion?

There was general agreement among members of Congress that they were acting to restrict the government of the United States from interfering with the religious rights of individuals and legal practices in the several state governments with regard to rights of religious liberty. What was the opinion of Roger Sherman of Connecticut about this point?

* * *

The House again went into a Committee of the Whole on the proposed amendments to the constitution, Mr. Boudinot in the chair.

The fourth proposition being under consideration, as follows:

Article I. Section 9. Between paragraphs two and three insert "no religion shall be established by law, nor shall the equal rights of conscience be infringed."

Mr. Sylvester had some doubts of the propriety of the mode of expression used in this paragraph. He apprehended that it was liable to a construction different from what had been made by the committee. He feared it might be thought to have a tendency to abolish religion altogether.

Mr. Vining suggested the propriety of transposing the two members of the sentence.

Mr. Gerry said it would read better if it was, that no religious doctrine shall be established by law.

Mr. Sherman thought the amendment altogether unnecessary, inasmuch as Congress had no authority whatever delegated to them by the constitution to make religious establishments; he would, therefore, move to have it struck out.

Mr. Carroll—As the rights of conscience are, in their nature, of peculiar delicacy, and will little bear the gentlest touch of governmental hand; and as many sects have concurred in opinion that they are not well secured under the present constitution, he said he was much in favor of adopting the words. He thought it would tend more towards conciliating the minds of the people to the Government than almost any other amendment he had heard proposed. He would not contend with gentlemen about the phraseology, his object was to secure the substance in such a manner as to satisfy the wishes of the honest part of the community.

Mr. Madison said, he apprehended the meaning of the words to be, *that Congress should not establish a religion, and enforce the legal observation of it by law, nor compel men to worship God in any manner contrary to their conscience.* Whether the words are necessary or not, he did not mean to say, but they had been required by some of the State Conventions, who seemed to entertain an opinion that under the clause of the constitution, which gave power to Congress to make all laws necessary and proper to carry into execution the constitution, and the laws made under it, enabled them to make laws of such a nature as might infringe the rights of conscience, and establish a national religion; to prevent these effects he presumed the amendment was intended, and he thought it as well expressed as the nature of the language would admit.

Mr. Huntington said that he feared, with the gentleman first up on this subject, that the words might be taken in such latitude as to be extremely harmful to the cause of religion. He understood the amendment to mean what had been expressed by the gentleman from Virginia; but others might find it convenient to put another construction upon it.

The ministers of their congregations to the Eastward were maintained by the contributions of those who belonged to their society; the expense of building meeting-houses was contributed in the same manner. These things were regulated by by-laws. If an action was brought before a Federal Court on any of these cases, the person who had neglected to perform his engagements could not be compelled to do it; for a support of ministers, or building of places of worship might be construed into a religious establishment.

By the charter of Rhode Island, no religion could be established by law; he could give a history of the effects of such a regulation; indeed the people were now enjoying the blessed fruits of it. He hoped, therefore, the amendment would be made in such a way as to secure the rights of conscience, and a free exercise of the rights of religion, but not to patronize those who professed no religion at all.

Mr. Madison thought, if the word national was inserted before religion, it would satisfy the minds of honorable gentlemen. He believed that the people feared one sect might obtain a pre-eminence, or two combine together, and establish a religion to which they would compel others to conform. He thought if the word national was introduced, it would point the amendment directly to the object it was intended to prevent.

Mr. Livermore was not satisfied with that amendment; but he did not wish them to dwell long on the subject. He thought it would be better if it was altered, and made to read in this manner, that Congress shall make no laws touching religion, or infringing the rights of conscience.

Mr. Gerry did not like the term national, proposed by the gentleman from Virginia, and he hoped it would not be adopted by the House. It brought to his mind some observations that had taken place in the conventions at the time they were considering the present constitution. It had been insisted upon by those who were called antifederalists, that this form of Government consolidated the Union, the honorable gentleman's motion shows that he considers it in the same light. Those who were called antifederalists at that time complained that they had injustice done them by the title, because they were in favor of a Federal Government, and the others were in favor of a national one; the federalists were for ratifying the constitution as it stood, and the others not until amendments were made. Their names then ought not to have been distinguished by federalists and antifederalists, but rats and antirats.

Mr. Madison withdrew his motion, but observed that the words "no national religion shall be established by law," did not imply that the Government was a national one; the question was then taken on Mr. Livermore's motion, and passed in the affirmative, thirty-one for, and twenty against it.

Source: Joseph Gales and W. W. Seaton, eds., *The Debates and Proceedings in the Congress of the United States, Compiled from Authentic Materials*, Volume 1 (Washington, D.C., 1834), pp. 448–459.

DOCUMENT 29: Action in the Senate on Constitutional Guarantees of Religious Liberty (September 3 and 9, 1789)

On August 24, 1789, the House of Representatives voted to send several proposed amendments to the Senate for its approval, including the following one on religion: "Congress shall make no law establishing religion, or to prevent the free exercise thereof, or to infringe the rights of conscience." From September 3 to 9, the Senate considered the proposed amendment on religion. Compare the proposed amendment approved by the Senate on September 9 with the proposal submitted to it by the House of Representatives. Also, compare it with the clauses on religion in the First Amendment, ratified in 1791 (see Document 30).

* * *

September 3, 1789

On Motion, To amend the third Article, to read thus—"Congress shall make no law establishing any particular denomination of religion in preference to another, or prohibiting the free exercise thereof, nor shall the rights of conscience be infringed"—It passed. . . .

On Motion, To adopt the third Article proposed in the Resolve of the House of Representatives, amended by striking out these words—"Nor shall the rights of conscience be infringed"—It passed. . . .

September 9, 1789

[The Senate agreed] To amend Article the third, to read as follows, "Congress shall make no law establishing articles of faith or a mode of worship, or prohibiting the free exercise of religion."

Source: Linda Grant DePauw, ed., *Documentary History of the First Federal Congress of the United States of America*, Volume 1 (Baltimore, 1977), pp. 151, 166.

DOCUMENT 30: Clauses on Religion in the First Amendment of the United States Constitution (December 15, 1791)

On September 24, 1789, a joint committee of the Senate and House of Representatives agreed to the final wording of the religion clauses of the third of twelve proposed amendments to the Constitution. On September 25, these twelve amendments were approved by two-thirds of both houses of Congress and sent to the states for ratification.

On December 15, 1791, Virginia became the eleventh of the fourteen American states to ratify ten articles of the proposed Bill of Rights. (Vermont had become the fourteenth state in 1791.) Thus, three-fourths of the states had approved these ten amendments, which then became part of the U.S. Constitution.

During the process to ratify the twelve proposed amendments, two of them, Amendments I and II, were rejected. So proposed Amendment III, the one with clauses on religion, was renumbered to become the First Amendment of the Bill of Rights.

The First Amendment includes two clauses on religion. One of the religion clauses prevents the United States government from making any law pertaining to the establishment of a religion. This is the clause on separation of church and state at the federal level of government. The other religion clause prevents the federal government from prohibiting the free exercise of religion. This is the clause that limits the federal government to guarantee the individual's freedom of conscience. Compare these religion clauses to articles on religion in state constitutions and declarations of rights of the founding era. (See Documents 15, 16, 17, 18.) To what extent do the religion clauses of the First Amendment agree or disagree with the Virginia Statute for Religious Freedom written by Thomas Jefferson? (See Document 24.)

* * *

The First Amendment

Congress shall make no law respecting an establishment of religion, or prohibiting the free exercise thereof; or abridging the freedom of speech, or of the press; or the right of the people peaceably to assemble, and to petition the Government for a redress of grievances.

Source: National Archives and Records Administration, *The Bill of Rights: Milestone Documents in the National Archives* (Washington, D.C., 1986), p. 25.

FURTHER READING

Alley, Robert S., ed. *James Madison on Religious Liberty.* Buffalo, N.Y.: Prometheus Books, 1985.

Amar, Akhil Reed. *The Bill of Rights: Creation and Reconstruction.* New Haven: Yale University Press, 1998.

Gaustad, Edwin S. *Church and State in America.* New York: Oxford University Press, 1998.

Kramnick, Isaac, and R. Laurence Moore. *The Godless Constitution: The Case Against Religious Correctness.* New York: W. W. Norton, 1997.

Levy, Leonard W. *The Establishment Clause: Religion and the First Amendment.* New York: Macmillan, 1986.

Lowenthal, David. *No Liberty for License: The Forgotten Logic of the First Amendment.* Dallas: Spence Publishing, 1997.

Miller, William Lee. *The First Liberty: Religion and the American Republic.* New York: Paragon House, 1988.

Peterson, Merrill D., and Robert C. Vaughan, eds. *The Virginia Statute for Religious Freedom: Its Evolution and Consequences in American History.* Cambridge, England: Cambridge University Press, 1988.

Schwartz, Bernard. *The Great Rights of Mankind: A History of the American Bill of Rights.* Madison, Wis.: Madison House, 1992.

Part III

The Constitutional Right to Free Exercise of Religion, 1791– 1991

The Bill of Rights, ratified in 1791, provides for the "free exercise" of religion in its first article, Amendment I (see Document 30 in Part II). This constitutional provision guarantees that the government may not interfere with a person's free expression of religious beliefs. Everyone under the government's authority is free to choose or reject any religion. This freedom, however, has limits. The government may prohibit certain religious practices that would harm others or significantly disturb social order. For example, in *Reynolds v. United States* (1879), the United States Supreme Court upheld a federal law against polygamy in a federal territory. A member of the Church of Jesus Christ of Latter-Day Saints (Mormons) challenged this federal law by claiming it violated his First Amendment right to free exercise of religion. He argued that it was his religious duty to have more than one wife. The Court disagreed. However, it affirmed both the principle of free exercise of religion and the government's authority to set limits on this freedom for the public good (see Document 31).

Before the passage of the Bill of Rights in 1791, religious liberty had been protected in the declarations of rights and constitutions of twelve American states.[1] For example, the 1776 Virginia Declaration of Rights proclaimed in Article XVI that "all men are equally entitled to the free exercise of religion" (see Document 15 in Part II). This document was primarily the work of George Mason, but James Madison contributed this clause on religious liberty that was eventually to enter the American Bill of Rights. This was a bold step toward the unprecedented achievement on a national scale, anywhere in the world, of a fundamental natural right of individuals, one that today is included in human rights documents of the United Nations and in the constitutions of many countries around the world.

The Virginia Declaration of Rights was a model for similar pronouncements that were made in several other states. Article II of the Pennsylvania Declaration of Rights stated that "no authority can or ought to be vested in, or assumed by any power whatever, that shall in any case interfere with, or in any manner control, the right of conscience in the free exercise of religious worship" (see Document 16 in Part II). The Massachusetts Declaration of Rights said that "no subject shall be hurt, molested, or restrained in his person, liberty, or estate, for worshipping God in the manner and season most agreeable to the dictates of his own conscience" (see Document 18 in Part II).

The fact that most of the American states had enacted constitutional decrees to protect a person's right to free exercise of religion is significant because originally the Bill of Rights applied only to the federal government. This understanding about the scope of the Bill of Rights was confirmed by the United States Supreme Court in *Barron v. Baltimore* (1833).[2] Chief Justice John Marshall, writing for a unanimous Court, held that the various provisions of the Bill of Rights could not be used to limit the power of a state government. He argued that the original intention of the framers of the Bill of Rights was to limit only the government of the United States of America. It was understood, then, that the free exercise of religion clause of the First Amendment pertained only to limitations on the power of the federal government and not the state governments.

From 1791 until the twentieth century, only one case involving the federal government and the free exercise of religion clause came before the Supreme Court (see Document 31, *Reynolds v. United States*). And during the twentieth century, the Court's many decisions on free exercise of religion have dealt mostly with state governments.

Ratification of the Fourteenth Amendment in 1868 created an avenue by which selected provisions in the federal Bill of Rights could be invoked to limit the powers of state governments. Section I of this amendment says, "No State shall make or enforce any law which shall abridge the privileges or immunities of citizens of the United States; nor shall any State deprive any person of life, liberty, or property without due process of law; nor deny to any person within its jurisdiction the equal protection of the laws."

The Supreme Court at first seemed reluctant to use this new provision of the Constitution against the power of state governments to guarantee specific provisions of the Bill of Rights. For example, the Court refused an opportunity in the *Slaughterhouse Cases* (1873) to use the privileges and immunities clause of the Fourteenth Amendment to apply provisions of the Bill of Rights to limit the power of a state government.[3] And the Court tended to interpret the due process clause of the Fourteenth Amendment narrowly and thereby render it practically useless in protecting the rights of former slaves, whom it was primarily enacted to protect, or the rights of anyone else in the United States.

Not until 1897 did the United States Supreme Court use the due process clause of the Fourteenth Amendment to apply a provision of the federal Bill of Rights against the power of a state government. In *Chicago, Burlington and Quincy Railroad Company v. Chicago*, the Court decided that a governmental unit of the state of Illinois, the city of Chicago, had unfairly deprived a private railroad company of its right to property by taking its land for public use without providing adequate compensation.[4] The Court based its opinion on the Fourteenth Amendment in combination with the Fifth Amendment, a part of the Bill of Rights. The Fourteenth Amendment provides that no state shall "deprive any person of life, liberty, or property without due process of law." A provision of the Fifth Amendment says, "nor shall private property be taken for public use without just compensation." In effect, the Court decided that the due process clause of the Fourteenth Amendment could be used to "incorporate" or include the just compensation clause of the Fifth Amendment, and thereby a part of the Bill of Rights, previously understood only to limit the federal government, was used to restrict the power of a unit of state government.

The *Chicago, Burlington and Quincy Railroad* case was the beginning of an important new direction in the interpretation of the Constitution known as the "selective incorporation doctrine"—that is, the Court claimed that it could selectively apply provisions of the Bill of Rights, on a case-by-case basis, against the power of state governments. During the 1920s and 1930s, the First Amendment rights to freedom of speech, freedom of press, and freedom of assembly were selectively included or incorporated under the due process clause of the Fourteenth Amendment and thereby applied to the states. Not until 1940, however, was the free exercise clause of the First Amendment applied against the authority of a state government.

In *Cantwell v. Connecticut* (1940), the Court incorporated the free exercise clause of the First Amendment under the due process clause of the Fourteenth Amendment. While affirming the government's authority to regulate freedom of expression for the public good, the Court, in this case, limited a state government's authority in order to protect the freedom of a member of a minority religion, the Jehovah's Witnesses, to peacefully distribute information with the aim of winning converts (see Document 33). In *Cantwell*, the Court held that one's right to freedom of religious belief is absolute. But one's actions based on religious belief may be regulated by the government to protect the community.

In a few cases before 1940, the Court also examined state regulations that allegedly infringed upon religious liberty without invoking the incorporation doctrine. For example, in *Pierce v. Society of Sisters* (1925) the Court ruled that the state of Oregon could not require parents to send their children to public schools. The Court reasoned that the due process clause of the Fourteenth Amendment safeguards the liberty to send one's child to a qualified nonpublic school. Technically, therefore, *Pierce* was not a free exercise of religion case, but it frequently is cited as a defense of free exercise because antagonism against the Roman Catholic Church and its parochial schools was at the core of the anti–private school law passed by the government of Oregon (see Document 32).

Previously, in *Jacobson v. Massachusetts* (1905), the Supreme Court upheld a state law that authorized local officials to require the vaccination of a town's residents. The objection to the smallpox vaccination at issue in this case was founded on religious principles, but the Court confined its opinion to the more general liberty guarantee in the Fourteenth Amendment. The Supreme Court viewed the Massachusetts law as a valid use of the state's police power. Writing for the Court in *Jacobson*, Justice John Marshall Harlan argued:

[T]he liberty secured by the Constitution of the United States to every person within its jurisdiction does not impart an absolute right in each person to be, at all times and in all circumstances, wholly freed from restraint. There are manifold restraints to which every person is necessarily subject for the common good. On any other basis organized society could not exist with safety to its members. Society based on the rule that each one is a law unto himself would soon be confronted with disorder and anarchy.[5]

Justice Harlan recognized that while individual liberty, including religious freedom, is a necessary component of a democratic republic, the survival of any organized government and society required at least an equal measure of order and security. In *Jacobson*, this meant that the individual's freedom could be regulated by the constituted authorities, under sanction of the state, for the purpose of protecting the public collectively against threats to its well-being.

Before the U.S. Supreme Court was established, James Madison articulated the ever-present need to balance liberty with the power needed for order in a free society. In *The Federalist 51* (1788), he explained:

In framing a government which is to be administered by men over men, the great difficulty lies in this: You must first enable the government to control the governed; and in the next place, oblige it to control itself. A dependence on the people is no doubt the primary control on the government; but experience has taught mankind the necessity of auxiliary precautions.[6]

Structurally, the Constitution provides safeguards to control the power necessary for effective government. Separation of powers and checks and balances among three branches of government and division of powers between a federal government and several state governments serve as "auxiliary precautions" built into the Constitution designed by Madison and the other Framers. Judicial review exercised by the United States Supreme Court has been an especially important part of this constitutional machinery designed to seek a balance between the liberty of individuals, including free exercise of religion, and the power of government needed to impose restraints on freedom of expression for the maintenance of order and the public good.

This primary objective of achieving liberty with order was at the heart of the decision in *Cantwell v. Connecticut* (1940) discussed above (see also Document 33). This concern was also central to the contrasting decisions in the two "Flag Salute Cases" of the 1940s: *Minersville School District v. Gobitis* (1940) and *West Virginia State Board of Education v. Barnette* (1943). In the *Gobitis* case, the Court decided that a child could be punished with expulsion from school for refusing to abide by a local school district requirement that all students in public schools must participate in a ceremony to salute and pledge allegiance to the flag of the United States of America. The child in this case was a Jehovah's Witness who had been taught through his religion not to worship a graven image, such as the national flag. Writing for the Court, Justice Felix Frankfurter argued that an individual's right to free exercise of religion does not exempt that person "from obedience to a general law not aimed at the promotion or restriction of religious beliefs."[7] The promotion of national unity, loyalty, and order through participation of students in a patriotic exercise was viewed as a legitimate concern of a local school board.

Just three years later the court returned to the issue of a mandatory flag salute in public schools in *West Virginia State Board of Education v. Barnette* (1943). The Court reversed its decision in the *Gobitis* case. Justice Robert Jackson, writing for the majority of the Court, proclaimed that in matters of opinion, religious and otherwise, freedom from government coercion is "a fixed star in our constitutional constellation." (See Document 34.)

Now writing in dissent, Justice Frankfurter admonished the majority that he was not insensitive to the concerns of a minority group for religious freedom, because, as a person of Jewish heritage, he reminded his colleagues that he belonged to the "most vilified and persecuted minority in history." Nonetheless, in this instance Frankfurter argued that the Court was obliged to exercise judicial restraint by deferring to elected state and local government officials who, in his view, had neither prohibited nor imposed a religious belief.

The Court's ruling in *Gobitis* was overturned by the *Barnette* decision, which has prevailed as constitutional law. Thus, Justice Frankfurter's dissent, which was faithful to his majority opinion in the *Gobitis* case, has been obscured by Justice Jackson's opinion in *Barnette* (see Document 34).

One year after the *Barnette* decision, in *United States v. Ballard* (1944), the Supreme Court rejected the idea of "heresy trials" by announcing that it was not a function of government to determine the truthfulness of a religious belief (see Document 36). Rather, this particular kind of decision should be exercised by private religious institutions, not by the constitutional government of all the people. This premise has had a profound and lasting effect in combination with a 1961 Supreme Court case that examined the constitutionality of Sunday closing laws. In a dissenting opinion in *Braunfeld v. Brown* (1961), Justice William Brennan suggested that to be permissible, any governmental interference with an individual's free exercise of religion should involve a compelling state interest. Chief Justice Earl Warren, writing for the majority in *Braunfeld*, made an important addition to the ongoing attempt to balance religious liberty with the government's need to enact and enforce regulations of general applicability. Warren reasoned that neutral laws that indirectly limit an individual's free exercise of religion are acceptable, unless the government could reach the same end in a less burdensome manner (see Document 38).

In *Sherbert v. Verner* (1963), Justice Brennan had the opportunity to include his compelling state interest standard in a majority opinion. Now the same government that was to be neutral concerning the content of religious beliefs, as had been stated in *Ballard*, would be required to meet this burden of proof whenever a regulation was challenged for indirectly placing a burden upon religious liberty (see Document 39).

In a notable application of the *Sherbert* precedent, the Supreme Court ruled in *Wisconsin v. Yoder* (1972) that the state of Wisconsin did not have a compelling reason to require Amish parents to send their children to high school. As a result, one group of parents was granted a religious exemption from a law that still applied to other parents in the state (see Document 41). Ironically, one decade later, in another case involving an Amish defendant, the Court began a steady retreat from the compelling state interest standard. In *United States v. Lee* (1982) the Court held that the federal government had demonstrated a compelling reason to collect Social Security taxes from all employers, including an Amish farmer who had objected on religious grounds (see Document 43).

In 1986, with its decision in *Goldman v. Weinberger*, the Court continued to retreat from the *Sherbert* precedent by ruling that, despite a religious objection, it was not necessary for the United States Air Force to justify the general applicability of its dress code. According to the majority, the military was seen as a "specialized society" (see Document 45). Congress responded the following year by revising military regulations to permit reasonable articles of religious attire as long as there was no interference with assigned duties.

In 1990 a Supreme Court majority issued an unqualified rejection of the compelling interest standard that had been used for more than twenty-five years. In *Employment Division, Department of Human Resources of Oregon v. Smith* (1990), the Court came full circle by returning to the reasoning formulated in its first important free exercise case, *Reynolds v. United States* (1879). Justice Antonin Scalia, writing for the majority in *Smith*, argued that there is no reason for the government to demonstrate a compelling interest to apply a neutral law generally, irrespective of any indirect effect upon individual religious practices (see Document 47).

Congress responded to the *Smith* decision in 1993 with passage of the Religious Freedom Restoration Act (see Document 70 in Part V). The Supreme Court, in turn, issued its response to Congress with its decision in *City of Boerne v. Flores* (see Document 76 in Part V), which overturned the Religious Freedom Restoration Act.

The First Amendment guarantee of free exercise of religion is a fundamental right of individuals in the United States. Further, according to leading advocates for liberty, from Thomas Jefferson during the American founding era to the drafters of the Universal Declaration of Human Rights, issued by the United Nations in 1948, the right to freedom of conscience or free exercise of religion is universal; that is, it ought to be guaranteed to all human beings anywhere in the world. However, even the staunchest proponents of religious liberty recognize that in the interest of social order and the public good, there must be limits on the expression of this freedom by individuals. What are these limits? How do we decide when and how to impose them?

A basic and ongoing issue in any free society is deciding the limits of an individual's right to free exercise of religion. In the United States of America, these decisions often are made by the Supreme Court in response to cases that contending individuals have brought to it. The consequence of these cases and decisions has been maintenance of a precious human possession, the individual's right, free from coercion by government, to choose her or his religious beliefs and practices, which includes the freedom to change one's religious identity at will or to reject religion. Collectively, these decisions have established that concerning religion, individuals retain the right to be free from control by government.

NOTES

1. Bernard Schwartz, *The Great Rights of Mankind: A History of the American Bill of Rights* (Madison, Wis.: Madison House, 1992), p. 87.

2. *Barron v. Baltimore*, 7 Pet (32 U.S.) 243 (1833).

3. *Slaughterhouse Cases*, 16 Wall. (83 U.S.) 36 (1873).

4. *Chicago, Burlington and Quincy Railroad Company v. Chicago*, 166 U.S. 226 (1897).

5. *Jacobson v. Commonwealth of Massachusetts*, 197 U.S. 11 (1905).

6. Clinton Rossiter, ed., *The Federalist Papers* (New York: New American Library, 1965), p. 322.

7. *Minersville School District v. Gobitis*, 310 U.S. 586 (1940).

DOCUMENT 31: *Reynolds v. United States* (1879)

In the 1870s Utah was a territory under the supervision of the government of the United States. George Reynolds, a resident of Utah, was convicted for violating a federal statute that made bigamy punishable by a fine of up to five hundred dollars and a prison term of up to five years.

Reynolds, a Mormon, had received the permission of his church to marry more than one wife. One of the teachings of the Mormon religion, at this time, was that it was the duty of male followers to practice polygamy. Failure to do so, when circumstances would otherwise permit, could result in "damnation in the life to come."

When this issue reached the Supreme Court on appeal the justices had to decide whether the First Amendment's guarantee of the right to the free exercise of religion should exempt Reynolds from the law that made bigamy a criminal offense. The *Reynolds* case was the Court's first important evaluation of the free exercise clause, and a unanimous opinion was rendered by Chief Justice Morrison R. Waite.

Waite made a crucial distinction between religious beliefs and religious practices. The government cannot regulate privately held beliefs, but practices, including actions motivated by religious ideals, are subject to regulation for the common good. Chief Justice Waite reasoned that if religious beliefs were superior to the law of the land, every citizen would thereby become "a law unto himself." Government, therefore, "could exist only in name."

Concerning Reynolds' plea for an exemption from the statute, Waite concluded that marriage is both a "sacred obligation" and a civil contract. Any contract that produces "social relations and social obligations," he argued, can legitimately be regulated by government. The law was seen as a reasonable attempt to maintain public order which, of necessity, was applicable to all individuals, including those with sincere religious objections.

What is Chief Justice Waite's opinion of the practice of polygamy? What examples are used by Waite to illustrate his defense of government regulations that limit religious practices?

* * *

MR. CHIEF JUSTICE WAITE delivered the opinion of the Court.

* * *

I contemplate with sovereign reverence that act of the whole American people which declared that their legislature should "make no law respecting an establishment of religion or prohibiting the free exercise thereof," thus building a wall of separation between church and State. . . . Congress was deprived of all legislative power over mere opinion, but was left free to reach actions which were in violation of social duties or subversive of good order.

Polygamy has always been odious among the northern and western nations of Europe, and, until the establishment of the Mormon Church, was almost exclusively a feature of the life of Asiatic and of African people. At common law, the second marriage was always void and from the earliest history of England polygamy has been treated as an offense against society. . . .

[I]t is impossible to believe that the constitutional guaranty of religious freedom was intended to prohibit legislation in respect to this most important feature of social life. Marriage, while from its very nature a sacred obligation, is nevertheless, in most civilized nations, a civil contract, and usually regulated by law. Upon it society may be said to be built, and out of its fruits spring social relations and social obligations and duties, with which government is necessarily required to deal. In fact, according as monogamous or polygamous marriages are allowed, do we find the principles on which the government of the people, to a greater or less extent, rests. . . .

In our opinion, the statute immediately under consideration is within the legislative power of Congress. It is constitutional and valid as prescribing a rule of action for all those residing in the Territories, and in places over which the United States have exclusive control. This being so, the only question which remains is, whether those who make polygamy a part of their religion are excepted from the operation of the statute. If they are, then those who do not make polygamy a part of their religious belief may be found guilty and punished, while those who do, must be acquitted and go free. This would be introducing a new element into criminal law. Laws are made for the government of actions, and while they cannot interfere with mere religious belief and opinions, they may with practices. Suppose one believed that human sacrifices were a necessary part of religious worship, would it be seriously contended that the civil government under which he lived could not interfere to prevent a sacrifice? Or if a wife religiously believed it was her duty to burn herself upon the funeral pile of her dead husband, would it be beyond the power of the civil government to prevent her carrying her belief into practice?

So here, as a law of the organization of society under the exclusive dominion of the United States, it is provided that plural marriages shall not be allowed. Can a man excuse his practices to the contrary because of his religious belief? To permit this would be to make the professed doctrines of religious belief superior and the law of the land, and in effect to permit every citizen to become a law unto himself. Government could exist only in name under such circumstances. . . .

Source: *Reynolds v. United States*, 98 U.S. 145 (1879).

DOCUMENT 32: *Pierce v. Society of the Sisters of the Holy Names of Jesus and Mary* (1925)

The Oregon Compulsory Education Act of 1922, the product of a voters' initiative, required virtually all of the children in the state to attend public schools. The supporters of the ballot initiative, including the Ku Klux Klan, capitalized on anti-Catholicism and anti-immigration sentiment.

The Oregon law was opposed by the Society of Sisters, which operated primary and secondary schools in the state. In addition to meeting curriculum standards established by the state, these schools also provided "systematic religious instruction and moral training" according to the tenets of the Roman Catholic Church.

The law, which was also challenged by a privately owned military academy that did not engage in religious instruction, was alleged to have violated the due process clause of the Fourteenth Amendment in two distinct ways. First, it was argued that requiring public school attendance infringed upon a parent's right to direct the education and upbringing of his or her child. Second, the law was portrayed as an unreasonable threat to business and property rights.

Justice James C. McReynolds, writing for a unanimous Supreme Court, agreed that the Fourteenth Amendment had been violated in both respects. He noted that the state's authority to regulate education generally, by settling issues such as the proper curriculum standards and teacher qualifications, would remain intact. It would continue to be reasonable to require school attendance, but it would be unconstitutional to allow only public schools to operate.

Strictly speaking, this was not a free exercise of religion case. Nonetheless, it is often cited as an important precedent in support of religious liberty, since the principal beneficiaries of the decision were religious schools and the parents who elected to send their children to such schools. The case would also come to be regarded as a precedent for the protection of unenumerated rights, including the right to privacy.

According to Justice McReynolds, how is the obligation to educate children limited by the concept of liberty? In what way did this case involve property rights?

* * *

MR. JUSTICE McREYNOLDS delivered the opinion of the Court.

* * *

No question is raised concerning the power of the state reasonably to regulate all schools, to inspect, supervise, and examine them, their teachers and pupils; to require that all children of proper age attend some school, that teachers shall be of good moral character and patriotic disposition, that certain studies plainly essential to good citizenship must be taught, and that nothing be taught which is manifestly inimical to the public welfare.

The inevitable practical result of enforcing the act under consideration would be destruction of appellees' primary schools, and perhaps all other private primary schools for normal children within the state of Oregon. Appellees are engaged in a kind of undertaking not inherently harmful, but long regarded as useful and meritorious. Certainly there is nothing in the present records to indicate that they have failed to discharge their obligations to patrons, students, or the state. And there are no peculiar circumstances or present emergencies which demand extraordinary measures relative to primary education.

. . . [W]e think it entirely plain that the Act of 1922 unreasonably interferes with the liberty of parents and guardians to direct the upbringing and education of children under their control. As often heretofore pointed out, rights guaranteed by the Constitution may not be abridged by legislation which has no reasonable relation to some purpose within the competency of the state. The fundamental theory of liberty upon which all governments in this Union repose excludes any general power of the state to standardize its children by forcing them to accept instruction from public teachers only. The child is not the mere creature of the state; those who nurture him and direct his destiny have the right, coupled with the high duty, to recognize and prepare him for additional obligations.

Appellees are corporations, and therefore, it is said, they cannot claim for themselves the liberty which the 14th Amendment guarantees. Accepted in the proper sense, this is true. But they have business and property for which they claim protection. These are threatened with destruction through the unwarranted compulsion which appellants are exercising over present and prospective patrons of their schools. And this court has gone very far to protect against loss threatened by such action.

Source: Pierce v. Society of the Sisters of the Holy Names of Jesus and Mary, 268 U.S. 510 (1925).

DOCUMENT 33: *Cantwell v. Connecticut* (1940)

Newton Cantwell, a Jehovah's Witness, solicited contributions in New Haven, Connecticut, by going door to door with religious literature. His routine included playing a phonograph record which, like the pamphlets that he distributed, contained attacks on the Roman Catholic Church. Cantwell's activities led to convictions for both solicitation without a state-issued license and inciting a breach of the peace by others.

Cantwell's appeal provided the Supreme Court with an opportunity to make the landmark ruling that the First Amendment's free exercise of religion clause prohibits state governments from infringing upon religious liberty. The process of applying specific protections from the Bill of Rights to the states, via the liberty component in the Fourteenth Amendment's due process clause, is known as selective incorporation.

Justice Owen J. Roberts, writing for a unanimous Court, reasoned that the procedures established in Connecticut to obtain a license for solicitation constituted an unreasonable violation of religious liberty. Specifically, the state's practice of allowing its licensing officer to determine if the applicant was representing a bona fide religion was, essentially, an invitation to arbitrary and capricious decision making.

Justice Roberts relied upon the *Reynolds* precedent that freedom of religious belief is absolute, but actions based on religious beliefs may be regulated by the government for the protection of society. Time, place, and manner restrictions, for example, that regulate solicitation are reasonable uses of a state's police powers. The licensing procedure in question, however, was seen as an unreasonable prior restraint upon the free exercise of religion.

Concerning the breach of the peace charge, the Court noted that Cantwell's actions did not in fact provoke a violent reaction, and his message did not pose a clear and present danger to public order. Although his message was distasteful to many, the effort to subdue Cantwell was violative of his freedom of speech as well as his religious liberty.

What examples were used by Justice Roberts to show that neither freedom of speech nor freedom of religion are absolute? According to Justice Roberts, why is it important to allow differences of opinion to exist in areas such as religion and politics?

* * *

MR. JUSTICE ROBERTS delivered the opinion of the Court.

* * *

First. We hold that the statute, as construed and applied to the appellants, deprives them of their liberty without due process of law in contravention of the Fourteenth Amendment. The fundamental concept of liberty embodied in that Amendment embraces the liberties guaranteed by the First Amendment. The First Amendment declares that Congress shall make no law respecting an establishment of religion or prohibiting the free exercise thereof. The Fourteenth Amendment has rendered the legislatures of the states as incompetent as Congress to enact such laws. The constitutional inhibition of legislation on the subject of religion has a double aspect. On the one hand, it forestalls compulsion by law of the acceptance of any creed or the practice of any form of worship. Freedom of conscience and freedom to adhere to such religious organization or form of worship as the individual may choose cannot be restricted by law. On the other hand, it safeguards the free exercise of the chosen form of religion. Thus the Amendment embraces two concepts,—freedom to believe and freedom to act. The first is absolute but, in the nature of things, the second cannot be. Conduct remains subject to regulation for the protection of society. The freedom to act must have appropriate definition to preserve the enforcement of that protection. In every case the power to regulate must be so exercised as not, in attaining a permissible end, unduly to infringe the protected freedom. No one would contest the proposition that a State may not, by statute, wholly deny the right to preach or to disseminate religious views. Plainly such a previous and absolute restraint would violate the terms of the guarantee. It is equally clear that a State may by general and non-discriminatory legislation regulate the times, the places, and the manner of soliciting upon its streets, and of holding meetings thereon; and may in other respects safeguard the peace, good order and comfort of the community, without unconstitutionally invading the liberties protected by the Fourteenth Amendment. The appellants are right in their insistence that the Act in question is not such a regulation. If a certificate is procured, solicitation is permitted without restraint but, in the absence of a certificate, solicitation is altogether prohibited. . . .

Second. We hold that, in the circumstances disclosed, the conviction of Jesse Cantwell on the fifth count must be set aside. Decision as to the lawfulness of the conviction demands the weighing of two conflicting interests. The fundamental law declares the interest of the United States that the free exercise of religion be not prohibited and that freedom to communicate information and opinion be not abridged. The State of Connecticut has an obvious interest in the preservation and protection of peace and good order within her borders. We must determine whether the alleged protection of the State's interest, means to which end would, in the absence of limitation by the Federal Constitution, lie wholly within the State's discretion, has been pressed, in this instance, to a point where it has come into fatal collision with the overriding interest protected by the federal compact. . . .

The offense known as breach of the peace embraces a great variety of conduct destroying or menacing public order and tranquillity. It includes not only violent acts but acts and words likely to produce violence in others. No one would have the hardihood to suggest that the principle of freedom of speech sanctions incitement to riot or that religious liberty connotes the privilege to exhort others to physical attack upon those belonging to another sect. When clear and present danger of riot, disorder, interference with traffic upon the public streets, or other immediate threat to public safety, peace, or order, appears, the power of the State to prevent or punish is obvious. Equally obvious is it that a State may not unduly suppress free communication of views, religious or other, under the guise of conserving desirable conditions. Here we have a situation analogous to a conviction under a statute sweeping in a great variety of conduct under a general and indefinite characterization, and leaving to the executive and judicial branches too wide a discretion in its application. . . .

We find in the instant case no assault or threatening of bodily harm, no truculent bearing, no intentional discourtesy, no personal abuse. On the contrary, we find only an effort to persuade a willing listener to buy a book or to contribute money in the interest of what Cantwell, however misguided others may think him, conceived to be true religion.

In the realm of religious faith, and in that of political belief, sharp differences arise. In both fields the tenets of one many may seem the rankest error to his neighbor. To persuade others to his own point of view, the pleader, as we know, at times, resorts to exaggeration, to vilification of men who have been, or are, prominent in church or state, and even to false statement. But the people of this nation have ordained in the light of history, that, in spite of the probability of excesses and abuses, these liberties are, in the long view, essential to enlightened opinion and right conduct on the part of the citizens of a democracy....

Although the contents of the record not unnaturally aroused animosity, we think that, in the absence of a statute narrowly drawn to define and punish specific conduct as constituting a clear and present danger to a substantial interest of the State, the petitioner's communication, considered in the light of the constitutional guarantees, raised no such clear and present menace to public peace and order as to render him liable to conviction of the common law offense in question....

Source: Cantwell v. Connecticut, 310 U.S. 296 (1940).

DOCUMENT 34: *West Virginia State Board of Education v. Barnette* (1943)

Writing for an 8–1 majority in *Minersville School District v. Gobitis* (1940), Supreme Court Justice Felix Frankfurter stated that religious convictions cannot "relieve the citizen from the discharge of political responsibilities." With this decision the Court ruled that children in public schools could be compelled to salute the American flag and to recite the Pledge of Allegiance.

In January 1942, approximately one month after the attack on Pearl Harbor, the West Virginia State Board of Education adopted a resolution that required all students to participate in a daily salute and pledge of allegiance to the flag. This resolution, of course, was patterned after the *Gobitis* ruling, and it further required that any child who refused to participate in the salute would be expelled from school for insubordination. Such an expulsion would result in the child being designated a delinquent for being unlawfully absent from school and, as a result, the child's parent or guardian could be sentenced to jail.

The West Virginia regulation was challenged by a group of parents, including Walter Barnette, who were Jehovah's Witnesses. Their children had been taught that the flag was a graven image and, in accordance with this religious belief, they refused to participate in the state-mandated activity.

In 1943 *West Virginia State Board of Education v. Barnette* provided the Supreme Court with an opportunity to overturn the *Gobitis* ruling, which had been made just three years earlier. Supreme Court reversals are relatively rare, and normally it takes decades to accomplish such a change of direction. However, by 1943 two of the justices who had voted with the majority in *Gobitis* had been replaced and, in a dissent to an unrelated case, three other justices recanted, voting with the majority by stating that *Gobitis* had been "wrongly decided."

Justice Robert H. Jackson's majority opinion in *Barnette* relied first and foremost on the First Amendment's freedom of speech guarantee, but the decision is frequently cited as a precedent in the area of religious liberty. Reliance upon a broad interpretation of the freedom of speech clause meant that a narrow exemption on religious grounds would not be necessary.

Jackson's eloquent opinion was a strong defense of civil liberties. He wrote that the purpose of the Bill of Rights was to "withdraw certain subjects from the vicissitudes of political controversy" and to establish "principles to be applied by the courts." One such principle, according to Jackson, is that the use of coercion to promote patriotism is unconstitutional.

Justice Felix Frankfurter wrote a powerful dissent in *Barnette* that echoed his majority opinion in *Gobitis*. He held that the compulsory salute to the flag was a reasonable way to promote national unity and, thereby, fortify national security. Frankfurter opened his opinion with an unusual personal reference, to his own Jewish heritage, and he then advised the majority that, as a Jew, he was not insensitive to the importance of religious liberty. However, since the flag salute neither prohibited nor imposed a religious belief, Frankfurter argued that the matter was best left to the discretion of state and local school officials.

Justice Frankfurter admonished the majority that a judge's own opinion about the "wisdom or evil of a law" should be excluded from fulfilling "one's duty on the bench." Ironically, Justice Jackson, the author of the majority opinion, went on to support the philosophy of judicial restraint. In this regard Frankfurter and Jackson were allies on the Supreme Court until Jackson's death in 1954.

According to Justice Jackson, what limits should be maintained on the government's responsibility to promote national unity? What is the principle of "judicial self-restraint" that is advocated by Justice Frankfurter, and why is it important?

* * *

MR. JUSTICE JACKSON delivered the opinion of the Court.

* * *

There is no doubt that, in connection with the pledges, the flag salute is a form of utterance. Symbolism is a primitive but effective way of communicating ideas. The use of an emblem or flag to symbolize some system, idea, institution, or personality, is a short cut from mind to mind. Causes and nations, political parties, lodges and ecclesiastical groups seek to knit the loyalty of their followings to a flag or banner, a color or design. . . .

It is also to be noted that the compulsory flag salute and pledge requires affirmation of a belief and an attitude of mind. It is not clear whether the regulation contemplates that pupils forego any contrary convictions of their own and become unwilling converts to the prescribed ceremony or whether it will be acceptable if they simulate assent by words without belief and by a gesture barren of meaning. It is now a commonplace that censorship or suppression of expression of opinion is tolerated by our Constitution only when the expression presents a clear and present danger of action of a kind the State is empowered to prevent and punish. It would seem that involuntary affirmation could be commanded only on even more immediate and urgent grounds than silence. But here the power of compulsion is invoked without any allegation that remaining passive during a flag salute ritual creates a clear and present danger that would justify an effort even to muffle expression. To sustain the compulsory flag salute we are required to say that a Bill of Rights which guards the individual's right to speak his own mind, left it open to public authorities to compel him to utter what is not in his mind.

Whether the First Amendment to the Constitution will permit officials to order observance of ritual of this nature does not depend upon whether as a voluntary exercise we would think it to be good, bad or merely innocuous. Any credo of nationalism is likely to include what some disapprove or to omit what others think essential, and to give off different overtones as it takes on different accents or interpretations. If official power exists to coerce acceptance of any patriotic creed, what it shall contain cannot be decided by courts, but must be largely discretionary with the ordaining authority, whose power to prescribe would no doubt include power to amend. Hence validity of the asserted power to force an American citizen publicly to profess any statement of belief or to engage in any ceremony of assent to one, presents questions of power that must be considered independently of any idea we may have as to the utility of the ceremony in question.

Nor does the issue as we see it turn on one's possession of particular religious views or the sincerity with which they are held. While religion supplies appellees' motive for enduring the discomforts of making the issue in this case, many citizens who do not share these religious views hold such a compulsory rite to infringe constitutional liberty of the individual. It is not necessary to inquire whether non-conformist beliefs will exempt from the duty to salute unless we first find power to make the salute a legal duty. . . .

The Fourteenth Amendment, as now applied to the States, protects the citizen against the State itself and all of its creatures—Boards of Education not excepted. These have, of course, important, delicate, and highly discretionary functions, but none that they may not perform within the limits of the Bill of Rights. That they are educating the young for citizenship is reason for scrupulous protection of Constitutional freedoms of the individual, if we are not to strangle the free mind at its source and teach youth to discount important principles of our government as mere platitudes. . . .

The very purpose of a Bill of Rights was to withdraw certain subjects from the vicissitudes of political controversy, to place them beyond the reach of majorities and officials and to establish them as legal principles to be applied by the courts. One's right to life, liberty, and property, to free speech, a free press, freedom of worship and assembly, and other fundamental rights may not be submitted to vote; they depend on the outcome of no elections. . . .

National unity as an end which officials may foster by persuasion and example is not in question. The problem is whether under our Constitution compulsion as here employed is a permissible means for its achievement. . . .

If there is any fixed star in our constitutional constellation, it is that no official, high or petty, can prescribe what shall be orthodox in politics, nationalism, religion, or other matters of opinion or force citizens to confess by word or act their faith therein. If there are any circumstances which permit an exception, they do not now occur to us.

We think the action of the local authorities in compelling the flag salute and pledge transcends constitutional limitations on their power and invades the sphere of intellect and spirit which it is the purpose of the First Amendment to our Constitution to reserve from all official control. . . .

MR. JUSTICE FRANKFURTER, dissenting.

One who belongs to the most vilified and persecuted minority in history is not likely to be insensible to the freedoms guaranteed by our Constitution. Were my purely personal attitude relevant I should wholeheartedly associate myself with the general libertarian views in the Court's opinion, representing as they do the thought and action of a lifetime. But as judges we are neither Jew nor Gentile, neither Catholic nor agnostic. We owe equal attachment to the Constitution and are equally bound by our judicial obligations whether we derive our citizenship from the earliest or the latest immigrants to these shores. As a member of this Court I am not justified in writing my private notions of policy into the Constitution, no matter how deeply I may cherish them or how mischievous I may deem their disregard. The duty of a judge who must decide which of two claims before the Court shall prevail, that of a State to enact and enforce laws within its general competence or that of an individual to refuse obedience because of the demands of his conscience, is not that of the ordinary person. It can never be emphasized too much that one's own opinion about the wisdom or evil of a law should be excluded altogether when one is doing one's duty on the bench. The only opinion of our own even looking in that direction that is material is our opinion whether legislators could in reason have enacted such a law. In the light of all the circumstances, including the history of this question in this Court, it would require more daring than I possess to deny that reasonable legislators could have taken the action which is before us for review. Most unwillingly, therefore, I must differ from my brethren with regard to legislation like this. I cannot bring my mind to believe that the "liberty" secured by the Due Process Clause gives this Court authority to deny to the State of West Virginia the attainment of that which we all recognize as a legitimate legislative end, namely, the promotion of good citizenship, by employment of the means here chosen. . . .

The constitutional protection of religious freedom terminated disabilities, it did not create new privileges. It gave religious equality, not civil immunity. Its essence is freedom from conformity to law because of religious dogma. Religious loyalties may be exercised without hindrance from the state, not the state may not exercise that which except by leave of religious loyalties is within the domain of temporal power. Otherwise each individual could set up his own censor against obedience to laws conscientiously deemed for the public good by those whose business it is to make laws. . . .

The essence of the religious freedom guaranteed by our Constitution is therefore this: no religion shall either receive the state's support or incur its hostility. Religion is outside the sphere of political government. This does not mean that all matters on which religious organizations or beliefs may pronounce are outside the sphere of government. Were this so, instead of the separation of church and state, there would be the subordination of the state on any matter deemed within the sovereignty of the religious conscience. Much that is the concern of temporal authority affects the spiritual interests of men. But it is not enough to strike down a non-discriminatory law that it may hurt or offend some dissident view. It would be too easy to cite numerous prohibitions and injunctions to which laws run counter if the variant interpretations of the Bible were made the tests of obedience to law. The validity of secular laws cannot be measured by their conformity to religious doctrines. It is only in a theocratic state that ecclesiastical doctrines measure legal right or wrong. . . .

That which to the majority may seem essential for the welfare of the state may offend the consciences of a minority. But, so long as no inroads are made upon the actual exercise of religion by the minority, to deny the political power of the majority to enact laws concerned with civil matters, simply because they may offend the consciences of a minority, really means that the consciences of a minority are more sacred and more enshrined in the Constitution than the consciences of a majority. . . .

Source: West Virginia State Board of Education v. Barnette, 319 U.S. 624 (1943).

DOCUMENT 35: *Murdock v. Commonwealth of Pennsylvania* (1943)

Robert Murdock was convicted of violating a local ordinance that prohibited solicitation without a license. A fee was charged for this type of license. Murdock and other Jehovah's Witnesses distributed religious literature to solicit contributions from interested individuals. The Jehovah's Witnesses claimed that the license tax infringed upon their rights to freedom of speech, press, and religion. With a narrow 5–4 decision in the *Murdock* case, the Supreme Court agreed with this claim.

Justice William O. Douglas, in the majority opinion, stated that in the hierarchy of constitutional rights freedom of speech, press, and religion are in a "preferred position." This concept evolved from the earlier writings of Supreme Court Justices Oliver Wendell Holmes, Benjamin Cardozo, and Harlan Stone. Essentially this doctrine purports that certain rights are so fundamental to the survival of a free society that they qualify for even more protection than other rights. Eventually the idea led to the position that an alleged violation of such rights should be examined with a "strict scrutiny" by the Court.

Concerning the license tax, Douglas held that the solicitation in question was a form of religious activity that "occupies the same high estate under the First Amendment as do worship in the churches and preaching from the pulpits." The tax was ruled unconstitutional because the government cannot "impose a charge for the enjoyment of a right granted by the federal constitution."

In dissent, Justice Felix Frankfurter stressed that a religious activity is not inherently exempt from taxation, especially a nominal tax that would not inhibit the activity. Frankfurter also emphasized that the tax was not applied in a discriminatory fashion against the Jehovah's Witnesses or any other group.

Why does Justice Douglas believe that individuals who solicit religious literature should be judged differently from commercial booksellers? What standard does Justice Frankfurter present as the most effective way to determine the constitutionality of a tax measure?

* * *

MR. JUSTICE DOUGLAS delivered the opinion of the Court.

* * *

The cases present a single issue—the constitutionality of an ordinance which as construed and applied required religious colporteurs to pay a license tax as a condition to the pursuit of their activities.

The alleged justification for the exaction of this license tax is the fact that the religious literature is distributed with a solicitation of funds.

. . . Situations will arise where it will be difficult to determine whether a particular activity is religious or purely commercial. The distinction at times is vital. As we stated only the other day in Jamison v. Texas, "The state can prohibit the use of the streets for the distribution of purely commercial leaflets, even though such leaflets may have 'a civic appeal, or a moral platitude' appended. They may not prohibit the distribution of handbills in the pursuit of a clearly religious activity merely because the handbills invite the purchase of books for the improved understanding of the religion or because the handbills seek in a lawful fashion to promote the raising of funds for religious purposes." But the mere fact that the religious literature is "sold" by itinerant preachers rather than "donated" does not transform evangelism into a commercial enterprise. If it did, then the passing of the collection plate in church would make the church service a commercial project. The constitutional rights of those spreading their religious beliefs through the spoken and printed word are not to be gauged by standards governing retailers or wholesalers of books. The right to use the press for expressing one's views is not to be measured by the protection afforded commercial handbills. . . . As we have said, the problem of drawing the line between a purely commercial activity and a religious one will at times be difficult. On this record it plainly cannot be said that petitioners were engaged in a commercial rather than a religious venture. It is a distortion of the facts of record to describe their activities as the occupation of selling books and pamphlets. . . .

The power to tax the exercise of a privilege is the power to control or suppress its enjoyment. Those who can tax the exercise of this religious practice can make its exercise so costly as to deprive it of the resources necessary for its maintenance. Those who can tax the privilege of engaging in this form of missionary evangelism can close its doors to all those who do not have a full purse. Spreading religious beliefs in this ancient and honorable manner would thus be denied the needy. Those who can deprive religious groups of their colporteurs can take from them a part of the vital power of the press which has survived from the Reformation.

It is contended, however, that the fact that the license tax can suppress or control this activity is unimportant if it does not do so. But that is to disregard the nature of this tax. It is a license tax—a flat tax imposed on the exercise of a privilege granted by the Bill of Rights. A state may not impose a charge for the enjoyment of a right granted by the federal constitution.

The fact that the ordinance is "nondiscriminatory" is immaterial. The protection afforded by the First Amendment is not so restricted. A license tax certainly does not acquire constitutional validity because it classifies the privileges protected by the First Amendment along with the wares and merchandise of hucksters and peddlers and treats them all alike. Such equality in treatment does not save the ordinance. Freedom of press, freedom of speech, freedom of religion are in a preferred position. . . .

Considerable emphasis is placed on the kind of literature which petitioners were distributing—its provocative, abusive, and ill-mannered character and the assault which it makes on our established churches and the cherished faiths of many of us. . . . But those considerations are no justification for the license tax which the ordinance imposes. Plainly a community may not suppress, or the state tax, the dissemination of views because they are unpopular, annoying or distasteful. If that device were ever sanctioned, there would have been forged a ready instrument for the suppression of the faith which any minority cherishes but which does not happen to be in favor. That would be a complete repudiation of the philosophy of the Bill of Rights.

Jehovah's Witnesses are not "above the law." But the present ordinance is not directed to the problems with which the police power of the state is free to deal. It does not cover, and petitioners are not charged with breaches of the peace. They are pursuing their solicitations peacefully and quietly. . . .

MR. JUSTICE FRANKFURTER, dissenting.

* * *

It is altogether incorrect to say that the question here is whether a state can limit the free exercise of religion by imposing burdensome taxes. . . . No claim is made that the effect of these taxes, either separately or cumulatively, has been, or is likely to be, to restrict the petitioners' religious propaganda activities in any degree. Counsel expressly disclaim any such contention. They insist on absolute immunity from any kind of monetary exaction for their occupation. Their claim is that no tax, no matter how trifling, can constitutionally be laid upon the activity of distributing religious literature, regardless of the actual effect of the tax upon such activity. . . .

It cannot be said that the petitioners are constitutionally exempt from taxation merely because they may be engaged in religious activities or because such activities may constitute an exercise of a constitutional right. It will hardly be contended, for example, that a tax upon the income of a clergyman would violate the Bill of Rights, even though the tax is ultimately borne by the members of his church. A clergyman, no less than a judge, is a citizen. . . .

To say that the Constitution forbids the states to obtain the necessary revenue from the whole of a class that enjoys these benefits and facilities, when in fact no discrimination is suggested as between purveyors of printed matter and purveyors of other things, and the exaction is not claimed to be actually burdensome, is to say that the Constitution requires not that the dissemination of ideas in the interest of religion shall be free but that it shall be subsidized by the state. Such a claim offends the most important of all aspects of religious freedom in this country, namely, that of the separation of church and state.

The ultimate question in determining the constitutionality of a tax measure is—has the state given something for which it can ask a return? There can be no doubt that these petitioners, like all who use the streets, have received the benefits of government. Peace is maintained, traffic is regulated, health is safeguarded—these are only some of the many incidents of municipal administration. To secure them costs money, and a state's source of money is its taxing power. There is nothing in the Constitution which exempts persons engaged in religious activities from sharing equally in the costs of benefits to all, including themselves, provided by government. . . .

Source: *Murdock v. Commonwealth of Pennsylvania*, 319 U.S. 105 (1943).

DOCUMENT 36: *United States v. Ballard* (1944)

Edna W. Ballard and Donald Ballard were convicted of using the mail to defraud, a federal offense. The two individuals organized and promoted the "I Am" movement. They claimed to have the power to cure diseases and to act as "divine messengers" in communication with Jesus and St. Germain.

The trial court had instructed the jury not to consider whether the defendants' claims were literally true, but only if the defendants themselves believed them to be true. Had they exhibited "good faith," in other words. The Supreme Court was asked to determine if this was the correct instruction to the jury.

The Court, in a 5–4 decision, ruled that the instruction to the trial jury was correct. The importance of the Court's holding in *Ballard* was Justice Douglas' contention that it should not be the role of government to determine the accuracy of religious beliefs. Douglas argued that the First Amendment protects an individual's right to embrace religious theories "which are rank heresy to the followers of the orthodox faiths." Heresy trials, he wrote, "are foreign to our Constitution."

In one dissent Justice Robert Jackson admitted that he could see "nothing but humbug" in the defendants' claims, but he would have dismissed the indictment on the grounds that a religious belief should not be the basis of a criminal prosecution.

Chief Justice Harlan Stone also wrote in dissent, but he emphasized that freedom of religion does not afford one an "immunity from criminal prosecution for the fraudulent procurement of money by false statements." Stone, therefore, would have provided the prosecution with the opportunity to show that none of the alleged cures had in fact taken place.

According to Justice Douglas, why does the First Amendment protect religious beliefs that a majority of the people would consider to be extreme or foolish? Why does Justice Jackson contend that the Constitution places religious beliefs "beyond the reach of the prosecutor"? How is the position advanced by Chief Justice Stone different from the viewpoint expressed by Jackson?

* * *

MR. JUSTICE DOUGLAS delivered the opinion of the Court.

* * *

As we have noted, the Circuit Court of Appeals held that the question of the truth of the representations concerning respondent's religious doctrines or beliefs should have been submitted to the jury. And it remanded the case for a new trial. It may be that the Circuit Court of Appeals took that action because it did not think that the indictment could be properly construed as charging a scheme to defraud by means of other than misrepresentations of respondents' religious doctrines or beliefs. Or that court may have concluded that the withdrawal of the issue of the truth of those religious doctrines or beliefs was unwarranted because it resulted in a substantial change in the character of the crime charged. But on whichever basis that court rested its action, we do not agree that the truth or verity of respondents' religious doctrines or beliefs should have been submitted to the jury. Whatever this particular indictment might require, the First Amendment precludes such a course, as the United States seems to concede. . . . The First Amendment has a dual aspect. It not only "forestalls compulsion by law of the acceptance of any creed or the practice of any form of worship" but also "safeguards the free exercise of the chosen form of religion." (Cantwell v. State of Connecticut.)

. . . Freedom of thought, which includes freedom of religious belief, is basic in a society of free men. It embraces the right to maintain theories of life and of death and of the hereafter which are rank heresy to followers of the orthodox faiths. Heresy trials are foreign to our Constitution. Men may believe what they cannot prove. They may not be put to the proof of their religious doctrines or beliefs. Religious experiences which are as real as life to some may be incomprehensible to others.

Yet the fact that they may be beyond the ken of mortals does not mean that they can be made suspect before the law. Many take their gospel from the New Testament. But it would hardly be supposed that they could be tried before a jury charged with the duty of determining whether those teachings contained false representations. The miracles of the New Testament, the Divinity of Christ, life after death, the power of prayer are deep in the religious convictions of many. If one could be sent to jail because a jury in a hostile environment found those teachings false, little indeed would be left of religious freedom. The Fathers of the Constitution were not unaware of the varied and extreme views of religious sects, of the violence of disagreement among them, and of the lack of any one religious creed on which all men would agree. They fashioned a charter of government which envisaged the widest possible toleration of conflicting views. Man's relation to his God was made no concern of the state. He was granted the right to worship as he pleased and to answer to no man for the verity of his religious views. The religious views exposed by respondents might seem incredible, if not preposterous, to most people. But if those doctrines are subject to trial before a jury charged with finding their truth or falsity, then the same can be done with the religious beliefs of any sect. When the triers of fact undertake that task, they enter a forbidden domain. The First Amendment does not select any one group or any one type of religion for preferred treatment. It puts them all in that position. . . .

MR. CHIEF JUSTICE STONE, dissenting.

I am not prepared to say that the constitutional guaranty of freedom of religion affords immunity from criminal prosecution for the fraudulent procurement of money by false statements as to one's religious experiences. . . .

I cannot say that freedom of thought and worship includes freedom to procure money by making knowingly false statements about one's religious experiences. To go no further, if it were shown that a defendant in this case had asserted as a part of the alleged fraudulent scheme, that he had physically shaken hands with St. Germain in San Francisco on a day named, or that, as the indictment here alleges, by the exertion of his spiritual power he "had in fact cured hundreds of persons afflicted with diseases and ailments," I should not doubt that it would be open to the Government to submit to the jury proof that he had never been in San Francisco and that no such cures had ever been effected. In any event I see no occasion for making any pronouncement on this subject in the present case. . . .

MR. JUSTICE JACKSON, dissenting.

I should say the defendants have done just that for which they are indicted. If I might agree to their conviction without creating a precedent, I cheerfully would do so. I can see in their teachings nothing but humbug, untainted by any trace of truth. But that does not dispose of the constitutional question whether misrepresentation of religious experience or belief is prosecutable; it rather emphasizes the danger of such prosecutions.

The Ballard family claimed miraculous communication with the spirit world and supernatural power to heal the sick. They were brought to trial for mail fraud on an indictment which charged that their representations were false and they "well knew" they were false. The trial judge, obviously troubled, ruled that the court could not try whether the statements were untrue, but could inquire whether the defendants knew them to be untrue; and, if so, they could be convicted.

I find it difficult to reconcile this conclusion with our traditional religious freedoms.

In the first place, as a matter of either practice or philosophy I do not see how we can separate an issue as to what is believed from considerations as to what is believable. . . .

Prosecutions of this character easily could degenerate into religious persecution. I do not doubt that religious leaders may be convicted of fraud for making false representations on matters other than faith or experience, as for example if one represents that funds are being used to construct a church when in fact they are being used for personal purposes. But that is not this case, which reaches into wholly dangerous ground. When does less than full belief in a professed credo become actionable fraud if one is soliciting gifts or legacies? Such inquiries may discomfort orthodox as well as unconventional religious teachers, for even the most regular of them are sometimes accused of taking their orthodoxy with a grain of salt.

I would dismiss the indictment and have done with this business of judicially examining other people's faiths.

Source: United States v. Ballard, 322 U.S. (1944).

DOCUMENT 37: *Prince v. Commonwealth of Massachusetts* (1944)

A Massachusetts law prohibited boys under the age of twelve and girls under the age of eighteen from selling merchandise, including printed materials, in public places. An adult who knowingly assisted a minor in such an activity was subject to prosecution for a criminal offense.

Sarah Prince was arrested in Brockton, Massachusetts, after she allowed her nine-year-old niece to help her distribute religious pamphlets. Prince was the girl's legal guardian, and both individuals were Jehovah's Witnesses. Her subsequent conviction was appealed as a violation of her right to free exercise of religion.

In a 5–4 decision the Supreme Court ruled that the state law was constitutional. The majority opinion, written by Justice Wiley B. Rutledge, utilized two lines of reasoning that the Court had followed consistently since its holding in *Reynolds v. United States* in 1879 (see Document 31). First, the majority reiterated that while privately held religious beliefs are, by their very nature, free from government control, actions founded upon religious beliefs can be regulated to preserve the public order or to safeguard the rights of others. Second, neutral laws enacted in pursuit of a valid secular purpose are constitutional even though such laws may indirectly limit the religious liberty of a particular person or group.

In *Prince* Rutledge reasoned that while parents and guardians are rightfully afforded considerable latitude in the upbringing of children, child labor laws are reasonable extensions of the state's obligation to promote the health and welfare of minors. As Rutledge stated, a "state's authority over children's activities is broader than over like actions of adults."

Writing in dissent, Justice Frank Murphy argued that while child labor laws are generally reasonable, the state of Massachusetts had failed to demonstrate that the religious activity in question was a threat to the welfare of the child.

According to Justice Rutledge, when are state regulations that limit the actions of parents justified? Why does Justice Murphy contend that the state failed to adequately justify its actions in this case?

* * *

MR. JUSTICE RUTLEDGE delivered the opinion of the Court.

The case brings for review another episode in the conflict between Jehovah's Witnesses and state authority. This time Sarah Prince appeals from convictions for violating Massachusetts' child labor laws, by acts said to be a rightful exercise of her religious convictions. . . .

The rights of children to exercise their religion, and of parents to give them religious training and to encourage them in the practice of religious belief, as against preponderant sentiment and assertion of state power voicing it, have had recognition here, most recently in West Virginia State Board of Education v. Barnette. . . .

But the family itself is not beyond regulation in the public interest, as against a claim of religious liberty. (Reynolds v. United States.) And neither rights of religion nor rights of parenthood are beyond limitation. Acting to guard the general interest in youth's well being, the state may restrict the parent's control by requiring school attendance, regulating or prohibiting the child's labor, and in many other ways. Its authority is not nullified merely because the parent grounds his claim to control the child's course of conduct on religion or conscience. . . .

The state's authority over children's activities is broader than over like actions of adults. This is peculiarly true of public activities and in matters of employment. A democratic society rests, for its continuance, upon the healthy, well-rounded growth of young people into full maturity as citizens, with all that implies. It may secure this against impeding restraints and dangers within a broad range of selection. Among evils most appropriate for such action are the crippling effects of child employment, more especially in public places, and the possible harms arising from other activities subject to all the diverse influences of the street. It is too late now to doubt that legislation appropriately designed to reach such evils is within the state's police power, whether against the parent's claim to control of the child or one that religious scruples dictate contrary action. . . .

Street preaching, whether oral or by handing out literature, is not the primary use of the highway, even for adults. While for them it cannot be wholly prohibited, it can be regulated within reasonable limits in accommodation to the primary and other incidental uses. But, for obvious reasons, notwithstanding appellant's contrary view, the validity of such a prohibition applied to children not accompanied by an older person hardly would seem open to question. The case reduces itself therefore to the question whether the presence of the child's guardian puts a limit to the state's power. That fact may lessen the likelihood that some evils the legislation seeks to avert will occur. But it cannot forestall all of them. The zealous though lawful exercise of the right to engage in propagandizing the community, whether in religious, political or other matters, may and at times does create situations difficult enough for adults to cope with and wholly inappropriate for children, especially of tender years, to face. Other harmful possibilities could be stated, of emotional excitement and psychological or physical injury. Parents may be free to become martyrs themselves. But it does not follow they are free, in identical circumstances, to make martyrs of their children before they have reached the age of full and legal discretion when they can make that choice for themselves. . . .

MR. JUSTICE MURPHY, dissenting.

This attempt by the state of Massachusetts to prohibit a child from exercising her constitutional right to practice her religion on the public streets cannot, in my opinion, be sustained. . . .

Religious training and activity, whether performed by adult or child, are protected by the Fourteenth Amendment against interference by state action, except insofar as they violate reasonable regulations adopted for the protection of the public health, morals and welfare. Our problem here is whether a state, under the guise of enforcing its child labor laws, can lawfully prohibit girls under the age of eighteen and boys under the age of twelve from practicing their religious faith insofar as it involves the distribution or sale of religious tracts on the public streets. . . .

. . . [T]he human freedoms enumerated in the First Amendment and carried over into the Fourteenth Amendment are to be presumed to be invulnerable and any attempt to sweep away those freedoms is prima facie invalid. It follows that any restriction or prohibition must be justified by those who deny that the freedoms have been unlawfully invaded. The burden was therefore on the state of Massachusetts to prove the reasonableness and necessity of prohibiting children from engaging in religious activity of the type involved in this case.

The burden in this instance, however, is not met by vague references to the reasonableness underlying child labor legislation in general. . . .

The state, in my opinion, has completely failed to sustain its burden of proving the existence of any grave or immediate danger to any interest which it may lawfully protect. . . .

Source: *Prince v. Commonwealth of Massachusetts*, 321 U.S. 158 (1944).

DOCUMENT 38: *Braunfeld v. Brown* (1961)

Abraham Braunfeld, an Orthodox Jew, owned a clothing and furniture store in Philadelphia. To observe the Jewish Sabbath he regularly closed his store on Saturday. However, for economic reasons, he found that it was necessary to operate his business six days each week. As a result, Braunfeld's store was open on Sunday. In 1959, however, Pennsylvania enacted a Sunday closing law that prevented Braunfeld from operating in this manner.

Braunfeld sought a permanent injunction, challenging the law as a violation of his right to free exercise of religion. In a 6–3 decision, the Supreme Court ruled that the state law was constitutional. The majority opinion, written by Chief Justice Earl Warren, reasoned that the law did not prohibit a religious activity, it simply established a uniform day of rest. Warren was primarily following the logic applied in *Reynolds v. United States* (Document 31) and subsequent cases, that a neutral law with a valid secular purpose is constitutional. However, Warren did add the provision that such a law is acceptable despite an indirect burden upon religious observance "unless the State may accomplish its purpose by means which do not impose such a burden." There would now be pressure on state governments to explore reasonable alternatives to regulations that could incidentally infringe upon religious liberty.

In dissent, Justice William Brennan argued that there was no "compelling state interest" to require everyone to rest on the same day of the week. At the very least, Brennan suggested, individuals who in good faith observe a day of rest other than Sunday should be exempt from the law.

Justice Potter Stewart, also writing in dissent, observed that the Pennsylvania law forced Abraham Braunfeld to make "a crucial choice." For Stewart it was patently unconstitutional for the state to compel an individual to "choose between his religious faith and his economic survival."

Concerning regulations by the government, what distinction does Chief Justice Warren make between religious beliefs and actions based on religious beliefs? Why do Justices Brennan and Stewart object to Sunday closing laws?

* * *

MR. CHIEF JUSTICE WARREN announced the judgment of the Court.

* * *

Certain aspects of religious exercise cannot, in any way, be restricted or burdened by either federal or state legislation. Compulsion by law of the acceptance of any creed or the practice of any form of worship is strictly forbidden. The freedom to hold religious beliefs and opinions is absolute. . . .

However, the freedom to act, even when the action is in accord with one's religious convictions, is not totally free from legislative restrictions. . . .

Thus, in Reynolds v. United States, this Court upheld the polygamy conviction of a member of the Mormon faith despite the fact that an accepted doctrine of his church then imposed upon its male members the duty to practice polygamy. And, in Prince v. Commonwealth of Massachusetts, this court upheld a statute making it a crime for a girl under eighteen years of age to sell any newspapers, periodicals or merchandise in public places despite the fact that a child of the Jehovah's Witnesses faith believed that it was her religious duty to perform this work.

It is to be noted that, in the two cases just mentioned, the religious practices themselves conflicted with the public interest. In such cases, to make accommodation between the religious action and an exercise of state authority is a particularly delicate task, because resolution in favor of the State results in the choice to the individual of either abandoning his religious principle or facing criminal prosecution.

But, again, this is not the case before us because the statute at bar does not make unlawful any religious practices of appellants; the Sunday law simply regulates a secular activity and, as applied to appellants, operates so as to make the practice of their religious beliefs more expensive. Furthermore, the law's effect does not inconvenience all members of the Orthodox Jewish faith but only those who believe it necessary to work on Sunday. And even these are not faced with as serious a choice as forsaking their religious practices or subjecting themselves to criminal prosecution. Fully recognizing that the alternatives open to appellants and others similarly situated—retaining their present occupations and incurring economic disadvantage or engaging in some other commercial activity which does not call for either Saturday or Sunday labor—may well result in some financial sacrifice in order to observe their religious beliefs, still the option is wholly different than when the legislation attempts to make a religious practice itself unlawful.

To strike down, without the most critical scrutiny, legislation which imposes only an indirect burden on the exercise of religion, i.e., legislation which does not make unlawful the religious practice itself, would radically restrict the operating latitude of the legislature. . . .

Needless to say, when entering the area of religious freedom, we must be fully cognizant of the particular protection that the Constitution has accorded it. Abhorrence of religious persecution and intolerance is a basic part of our heritage. But we are a cosmopolitan nation made up of people of almost every conceivable religious preference. These denominations number almost three hundred. Consequently, it cannot be expected, much less required, that legislators enact no law regulating conduct that may in some way result in an economic disadvantage to some religious sects and not to others because of the special practices of the various religions. We do not believe that such an effect is an absolute test for determining whether the legislation violates the freedom of religion protected by the First Amendment.

Of course, to hold unassailable all legislation regulating conduct which imposes solely an indirect burden on the observance of religion would be a gross oversimplification. If the purpose or effect of a law is to impede the observance of one or all religions or is to discriminate invidiously between religions, that law is constitutionally invalid even though the burden may be characterized as being only indirect. But if the State regulates conduct by enacting a general law within its power, the purpose and effect of which is to advance the State's secular goals, the statute is valid despite its indirect burden on religious observance unless the State may accomplish its purpose by means which do not impose such a burden. . . .

MR. JUSTICE BRENNAN, concurring and dissenting.

I agree with THE CHIEF JUSTICE that there is no merit in appellants' establishment and equal-protection claims. I dissent, however, as to the claim that Pennsylvania has prohibited the free exercise of appellants' religion.

The Court has demonstrated the public need for a weekly surcease from worldly labor, and set forth the considerations of convenience which have led the Commonwealth of Pennsylvania to fix Sunday as the time for that respite. I would approach this case differently, from the point of view of the individuals whose liberty is—concededly—curtailed by these enactments. For the values of the First Amendment, as embodied in the Fourteenth, look primarily towards the preservation of personal liberty, rather than towards the fulfillment of collective goals. . . .

For in this case the Court seems to say, without so much as a deferential nod towards that high place which we have accorded religious freedom in the past, that any substantial state interest will justify encroachments on religious practice, at least if those encroachments are cloaked in the guise of some nonreligious public purpose. . . .

What, then, is the compelling state interest which impels the Commonwealth of Pennsylvania to impede appellants' freedom of worship? What overbalancing need is so weighty in the constitutional scale that it justifies this substantial, though indirect, limitation of appellants' freedom? It is not the desire to stamp out a practice deeply abhorred by society, such as polygamy, as in Reynolds, for the custom of resting one day a week is universally honored, as the Court has amply shown. Nor is it the State's traditional protection of children, as in Prince v. Commonwealth of Massachusetts, 1944, for appellants are reasoning and fully autonomous adults. It is not even the interest in seeing that everyone rests one day a week, for appellants' religion requires that they take such a rest. It is the mere convenience of having everyone rest on the same day. It is to defend this interest that the Court holds that a State need not follow the alternative route of granting an exemption for those who in good faith observe a day of rest other than Sunday. . . .

In fine, the Court, in my view, has exalted administrative convenience to a constitutional level high enough to justify making one religion economically disadvantageous. The Court would justify this result on the ground that the effect on religion, though substantial, is indirect. . . .

MR. JUSTICE STEWART, dissenting.

I agree with substantially all that Mr. Justice BRENNAN has written. Pennsylvania has passed a law which compels an Orthodox Jew to choose between his religious faith and his economic survival. That is a cruel choice. It is a choice which I think no State can constitutionally demand. For me this is not something that can be swept under the rug and forgotten in the interest of enforced Sunday togetherness. I think the impact of this law upon these appellants grossly violates their constitutional right to the free exercise of their religion.

Source: Braunfeld v. Brown, 366, U.S. 599 (1961).

DOCUMENT 39: *Sherbert v. Verner* (1963)

In 1959 the textile mill in South Carolina where Adell Sherbert had worked for over thirty years instituted a new policy. Employees were informed that they would now be required to work on Saturdays. This directive was especially disconcerting for Sherbert because, as a Seventh-Day Adventist, Saturday was to be observed as the Sabbath.

Subsequently, she was fired after refusing to work on Saturdays, and she was unable to secure a position with any of the other textile mills in the area because they also required employees to work on Saturday. When Sherbert applied for unemployment compensation from the state of South Carolina, she was classified ineligible after the determination was made that she had refused available work. In 1963 this dispute reached the Supreme Court.

By a 7–2 vote, the Court held that a state could not constitutionally deny unemployment compensation to a claimant who refused employment due to her religious beliefs. Sherbert, thereby, was granted an exemption from an otherwise valid law. Justice William Brennan, who wrote the majority opinion, reasoned that South Carolina had failed to demonstrate a compelling state interest that would justify a denial of benefits. The phrase "compelling state interest" would serve as an important precedent in the adjudication of free exercise cases for a number of years.

Justice John Marshall Harlan II, writing in dissent, argued that the South Carolina law had a valid secular purpose, and Sherbert had not been discriminated against due to her religious beliefs. Harlan was troubled by the majority's willingness to "carve out an exemption" due to an individual's religious convictions. In *Braunfeld v. Brown* (1961) Chief Justice Earl Warren had noted that the United States is a "cosmopolitan nation made up of people of almost every conceivable religious preference." (See Document 38.) The nation's religious pluralism made it inevitable that various laws would be challenged as violations of the free exercise clause.

Given the fact that states would now have to demonstrate a compelling state interest to universally apply a challenged statute and the earlier ruling, in *United States v. Ballard* (1944), that it was not proper for the government to attempt to determine the truthfulness of religious beliefs, it was equally inevitable that at least some individuals and groups would qualify for religious exemptions from laws that could still reasonably apply to the general public (see Document 36).

Why does Justice Brennan contend that South Carolina failed to demonstrate a compelling state interest that would justify the denial of unemployment benefits in this case? What inconsistency does Justice Harlan see in allowing exemptions based on religious convictions?

* * *

MR. JUSTICE BRENNAN delivered the opinion of the Court.

* * *

We turn first to the question whether the disqualification for benefits imposes any burden on the free exercise of appellant's religion. We think it is clear that it does.... Here not only is it apparent that appellant's declared ineligibility for benefits derives solely from the practice of her religion, but the pressure upon her to forego that practice is unmistakable. The ruling forces her to choose between following the precepts of her religion and forfeiting benefits, on the one hand, and abandoning one of the precepts of her religion in order to accept work, on the other hand. Governmental imposition of such a choice puts the same kind of burden upon the free exercise of religion as would a fine imposed against appellant for her Saturday worship....

Significantly South Carolina expressly saves the Sunday worshipper from having to make the kind of choice which we here hold infringes the Sabbatarian's religious liberty. . . .

We must next consider whether some compelling state interest enforced in the eligibility provisions of the South Carolina statute justifies the substantial infringement of appellant's First Amendment right. It is basic that no showing merely of a rational relationship to some colorable state interest would suffice. . . .

No such abuse or danger has been advanced in the present case. The appellees suggest no more than a possibility that the filing of fraudulent claims by unscrupulous claimants feigning religious objections to Saturday work might not only dilute the unemployment compensation fund but also hinder the scheduling by employers of necessary Saturday work. But that possibility is not apposite here because no such objection appears to have been made before the South Carolina Supreme Court, and we are unwilling to assess the importance of an asserted state interest without the views of the state court. Nor, if the contention had been made below, would the record appear to sustain it; there is no proof whatever to warrant such fears of malingering or deceit as those which the respondents now advance. Even if consideration of such evidence is not foreclosed by the prohibition against judicial inquiry into the truth or falsity of religious beliefs, United States v. Ballard, a question as to which we intimate no view since it is not before us—it is highly doubtful whether such evidence would be sufficient to warrant a substantial infringement of religious liberties. For even if the possibility of spurious claims did threaten to dilute the fund and disrupt the scheduling of work, it would plainly be incumbent upon the appellees to demonstrate that no alternative forms of regulation would combat such abuses without infringing First Amendment rights. . . .

In holding as we do, plainly we are not fostering the "establishment" of the Seventh-Day Adventist religion in South Carolina, for the extension of unemployment benefits to Sabbatarians in common with Sunday worshippers reflects nothing more than the governmental obligation of neutrality in the face of religious differences, and does not represent that involvement of religious with secular institutions which it is the object of the Establishment Clause to forestall. . . .

MR. JUSTICE HARLAN II, dissenting.

* * *

What the Court is holding is that if the State chooses to condition unemployment compensation on the applicant's availability for work, it is constitutionally compelled to *carve out an exception*—and to provide benefits—for those whose unavailability is due to their religious convictions. . . .

. . . [T]he implications of the present decision are far more troublesome than its apparently narrow dimensions would indicate at first glance. The meaning of today's holding, as already noted, is that the State must furnish unemployment benefits to one who is unavailable for work if the unavailability stems from the exercise of religious convictions. The State, in other words, must *single out* for financial assistance those whose behavior is religiously motivated, even though it denies such assistance to others whose identical behavior (in this case, inability to work on Saturdays) is not religiously motivated. . . .

It has been suggested that such singling out of religious conduct for special treatment may violate the constitutional limitations on state action. . . .

My own view, however, is that at least under the circumstances of this case it would be a permissible accommodation of religion for the State, if it *chose* to do so, to create an exception to its eligibility requirements for persons like the appellant. The constitutional obligation of "neutrality," is not so narrow a channel that the slightest deviation from an absolutely straight course leads to condemnation. There are too many instances in which no such course can be charted, too many areas in which the pervasive activities of the State justify some special provision for religion to prevent it from being submerged by an all-embracing secularism.

Source: Sherbert v. Verner, 374 U.S. 398 (1963).

DOCUMENT 40: *Welsh v. United States* (1970)

In 1776 a provision in the Pennsylvania Bill of Rights allowed for exemptions from military service resulting from conscientious objection to "bearing arms." In 1789 James Madison included a similar exemption in his original proposal for the Bill of Rights. More recently the Supreme Court has had to settle issues involving the intersection of individual rights and conscription.

The first major freedom of expression case decided by the Court, *Schenck v. United States* (1919), originated with an individual's opposition to conscription and America's involvement in World War I. By the 1960s, at the height of America's military presence in Vietnam, the military draft remained a source of controversy and debate.

Section 6(j) of the Universal Military Training and Service Act did provide an exemption for those who opposed military service as a result of "religious training and belief." This reference was further defined as "an individual's belief in a relation to a Supreme Being involving duties superior to those arising from any human relation, but does not include essentially political, sociological, or philosophical views or a merely personal moral code."

The Supreme Court relied upon a broad interpretation of this statutory provision in *United States v. Seeger* (1965) when it affirmed the conscientious objector status of a young man whose beliefs were not based on the teachings of an orthodox religion. The Court held that "sincere and meaningful belief which occupies in the life of its possessor a place parallel to that filled by the God of those admittedly qualifying for the exemption comes within the statutory definition."

In 1966, one year after the *Seeger* decision, Elliott Ashton Welsh II was sentenced to three years in prison for refusing to submit to induction into the military. Welsh, who crossed out the word "religious" on his conscientious objector application, characterized his beliefs as a product of his study of history and sociology. Welsh was convicted after it was ruled that there was no religious basis for his objection to military service.

In *Welsh v. United States* (1970) the Supreme Court gave an even broader interpretation to the conscientious objector standard than it had in *Seeger*. The majority opinion, by Justice Hugo L. Black, did so by including "beliefs which are purely ethical or moral in source and content" and, hence, not at all religious in the traditional sense of the word. In this context, at least, Justice Black was willing to view strongly held moral convictions on the same plane as orthodox religious beliefs.

Justice Byron R. White, writing in dissent, issued a call for judicial restraint. White asserted that the Court's obligation in statutory construction cases is to "enforce the will of Congress, not our own." In this particular case White believed that Congress had expressly denied exemptions not founded upon religious training and belief.

According to Justice Black, why should conscientious objector status be granted to individuals whose convictions are not strictly religious in a traditional sense? What is the Supreme Court's obligation in cases involving laws enacted by Congress, according to Justice White?

* * *

MR. JUSTICE BLACK announced the judgment of the Court.

* * *

In the case before us the Government seeks to distinguish our holding in *Seeger* on basically two grounds, both of which were relied upon by the Court of Appeals in affirming Welsh's conviction. First, it is stressed that Welsh was far more insistent and explicit than Seeger in denying that his views were religious. For example, in filling out their conscientious objector applications, Seeger put quotation marks around the word "religious," but Welsh struck the word "religious" entirely and later characterized his beliefs as having been formed "by reading in the fields of history and sociology." . . .

But very few registrants are fully aware of the broad scope of the word "religious" as used in 6(j), and accordingly a registrant's statement that his beliefs are nonreligious is a highly unreliable guide for those charged with administering the exemption. Welsh himself presents a case in point. Although he originally characterized his beliefs as nonreligious, he later upon reflection wrote a long and thoughtful letter to his Appeal Board in which he declared that his beliefs were "certainly religious in the ethical sense of the word."

The Government also seeks to distinguish *Seeger* on the ground that Welsh's views, unlike Seeger's, were "essentially political, sociological, or philosophical views or a merely personal moral code." As previously noted, the Government made the same argument about Seeger, and not without reason, for Seeger's views had a substantial political dimension. In this case, Welsh's conscientious objection to war was undeniably based in part on this perception of world politics. . . .

We certainly do not think that 6(j)'s exclusion of those persons with "essentially political, sociological, or philosophical views or a merely personal moral code" should be read to exclude those who hold strong beliefs about our domestic and foreign affairs or even those whose conscientious objection to participation in all wars is founded to a substantial extent upon consideration of public policy. The two groups of registrants that obviously do fall within these exclusions from the exemption are those whose beliefs are not deeply held and those whose objection to war does not rest at all upon moral, ethical, or religious principle but instead rests solely upon considerations of policy, pragmatism, or expediency. In applying 6(j)'s exclusion of those whose views are "essentially political, sociological, or philosophical" or of those who have a "merely personal moral code," it should be remembered that these exclusions are definitional and do not therefore restrict the category of persons who are conscientious objectors by "religious training and belief." Once the Selective Service System has taken the first step and determined under the standards set out here and in *Seeger* that the registrant is a "religious" conscientious objector, it follows that his views cannot be "essentially political, sociological, or philosophical." Nor can they be a "merely personal moral code." See United States v. Seeger.

Welsh stated that he "believe[d] the taking of life—anyone's life—to be morally wrong." . . . Welsh elaborated his beliefs in later communications with Selective Service officials. On the basis of these beliefs and the conclusion of the Court of Appeals that he held them "with the strength of more traditional religious convictions," we think Welsh was clearly entitled to a conscientious objector exemption. Section 6(j) requires no more. That section exempts from military service all those whose consciences, spurred by deeply held moral, ethical, or religious beliefs, would give them no rest or peace if they allowed themselves to become a part of an instrument of war. . . .

MR. JUSTICE WHITE, dissenting.

* * *

Whether or not United States v. Seeger accurately reflected the intent of Congress in providing draft exemptions for religious conscientious objectors to war, I cannot join today's construction of 6(j) extending draft exemption to those who disclaim religious objections to war and whose views about war represent a purely personal code arising not from religious training and belief as the statute requires but from readings in philosophy, history, and sociology. Our obligation in statutory construction cases is to enforce the will of Congress, not our own; and as Mr. Justice HARLAN has demonstrated, construing 6(j) to include Welsh exempts from the draft a class of persons to whom Congress has expressly denied an exemption.

For me that conclusion should end this case. Even if Welsh is quite right in asserting that exempting religious believers is an establishment of religion forbidden by the First Amendment, he nevertheless remains one of those persons whom Congress took pains not to relieve from military duty. Whether or not 6(j) is constitutional, Welsh had no First Amendment excuse for refusing to report for induction. If it is contrary to the express will of Congress to exempt Welsh, as I think it is, then there is no warrant for saving the religious exemption and the statute by redrafting it in this Court to include Welsh and all others like him. . . .

Source: Welsh v. United States, 398 U.S. 333 (1970).

DOCUMENT 41: *Wisconsin v. Yoder* (1972)

Jonas Yoder refused to send his children to school after they had completed the eighth grade. As a result, he was convicted for violating Wisconsin's compulsory school attendance law. This law required parents and guardians to send their children to school until they had at least reached the age of sixteen. Yoder, a member of the Old Order Amish religion, claimed that the law violated his right to free exercise of religion.

The state of Wisconsin defended its enforcement of the law by contending that a high school education is designed to prepare children to become self-sufficient members of the community. The state asserted that despite a parent's religious objection, it had an obligation to extend the benefits of secondary education to all children.

The Amish way of life is inseparable from their strict interpretation of the Bible. Yoder and other Amish parents who refused to comply with the law alleged that high school attendance would do irreparable harm to the development of their children by exposing them to worldly influences and values contrary to their religious beliefs. In addition, it was argued that high school attendance would remove Amish adolescents from their agrarian communities during the key stage in their development when vocational training takes place. The very survival of the Amish community was tied to this training.

The Supreme Court held in *Yoder* that while a state does have the authority to establish reasonable rules concerning education, a "balancing process" is required when otherwise reasonable mandates infringe upon fundamental rights, including the right to free exercise of religion. Consistent with the compelling state interest standard announced in *Sherbert v. Verner* (1963), the Amish were granted an exemption from the compulsory school attendance law that would still apply to other parents in Wisconsin.

Chief Justice Warren Burger, writing for the majority in *Yoder*, cautioned other groups and individuals that the Amish had developed a unique religious subculture over centuries and that few, if any, could qualify for a similar exemption. Contrary to the line of reasoning employed in *Welsh v. United States* (Document 40), Burger also asserted that beliefs that are philosophical and personal, rather than religious, do not "rise to the demands of the free exercise of religion clause." For Burger it would be impossible to maintain ordered liberty if individuals were completely free to establish their own rules of conduct.

The lone dissent in the 6–1 *Yoder* decision was by Justice William O. Douglas. He feared that an exemption would have the effect of imposing the parent's notion of religious duty upon the child. Douglas suggested that the state should have the authority to override a parent's religious objection if and when a mature Amish child elected to attend high school.

Why does Chief Justice Burger contend that there should be reasonable limits on a state's authority to establish compulsory education standards? As identified by Justice Douglas, what is the potential danger

contained in granting Amish parents an exemption from a compulsory
education law?

* * *

MR. CHIEF JUSTICE BURGER delivered the opinion of the Court.

* * *

In support of their position, respondents presented as expert witnesses
scholars on religion and education whose testimony is uncontradicted.
They expressed their opinions on the relationship of the Amish belief
concerning school attendance to the more general tenets of their religion,
and described the impact that compulsory high school attendance could
have on the continued survival of Amish communities as they exist in
the United States today. The history of the Amish sect was given in some
detail, beginning with the Swiss Anabaptists of the 16th century who
rejected institutionalized churches and sought to return to the early, simple, Christian life de-emphasizing material success, rejecting the com-
petitive spirit, and seeking to insulate themselves from the modern
world. As a result of their common heritage, Old Order Amish communities today are characterized by a fundamental belief that salvation
requires life in a church community separate and apart from the world
and worldly influence. This concept of life aloof from the world and its
values is central to their faith.

A related feature of Old Order Amish communities is their devotion
to a life in harmony with nature and the soil, as exemplified by the
simple life of the early Christian era that continued in America during
much of our early national life. Amish beliefs require members of the
community to make their living by farming or closely related activities.
Broadly speaking, the Old Order Amish religion pervades and determines the entire mode of life of its adherents. . . .

Amish objection to formal education beyond the eighth grade is firmly
grounded in these central religious concepts. They object to the high
school, and higher education generally, because the values they teach are
in marked variance with Amish values and the Amish way of life. . . .

Formal high school education beyond the eighth grade is contrary to
Amish beliefs, not only because it places Amish children in an environment hostile to Amish beliefs with increasing emphasis on competition
in class work and sports and with pressure to conform to the styles,
manners, and ways of the peer group, but also because it takes them
away from their community, physically and emotionally, during the
crucial and formative adolescent period of life. During this period, the
children must acquire Amish attitudes favoring manual work and

self-reliance and the specific skills needed to perform the adult role of an Amish farmer or housewife. They must learn to enjoy physical labor. Once a child has learned basic reading, writing, and elementary mathematics, these traits, skills, and attitudes admittedly fall within the category of those best learned through example and "doing" rather than in a classroom. And, at this time in life, the Amish child must also grow in his faith and his relationship to the Amish community if he is to be prepared to accept the heavy obligations imposed by adult baptism. In short, high school attendance with teachers who are not of the Amish faith—and may even be hostile to it—interposes a serious barrier to the integration of the Amish child into the Amish religious community. . . .

The Amish do not object to elementary education through the first eight grades as a general proposition because they agree that their children must have basic skills in the "three R's" in order to read the Bible, to be good farmers and citizens, and to be able to deal with non-Amish people when necessary in the course of daily affairs. They view such a basic education as acceptable because it does not significantly expose their children to worldly values or interfere with their development in the Amish community during the crucial adolescent period. While Amish accept compulsory elementary education generally, wherever possible they have established their own elementary schools in many respects like the small local schools of the past. In the Amish belief higher learning tends to develop values they reject as influences that alienate man from God. . . .

There is no doubt as to the power of a State, having a high responsibility for education of its citizens, to impose reasonable regulations for the control and duration of basic education. See *Pierce v. Society of Sisters*. Providing public schools ranks at the very apex of the function of a State. Yet even this paramount responsibility was, in *Pierce*, made to yield to the right of parents to provide an equivalent education in a privately operated system. . . . Thus, a State's interest in universal education, however highly we rank it, is not totally free from a balancing process when it impinges on fundamental rights and interests, such as those specifically protected by the Free Exercise Clause of the First Amendment, and the traditional interest of parents with respect to the religious upbringing of their children so long as they, in the words of *Pierce*, "prepare [them] for additional obligations." . . .

We come then to the quality of the claims of the respondents concerning the alleged encroachment of Wisconsin's compulsory school-attendance statute on their rights and the rights of their children to the free exercise of the religious beliefs they and their forebears have adhered to for almost three centuries. In evaluating those claims we must be careful to determine whether the Amish religious faith and their mode of life are, as they claim, inseparable and interdependent. A way of life, however virtuous and admirable, may not be interposed as a barrier to reasonable state regulation of education if it is based on purely secular considerations; to have the protection of the Religion Clauses, the claims must be rooted in religious belief. Although a determination of what is a "religious" belief or practice entitled to constitutional protection may present a most delicate question, the very concept of ordered liberty precludes allowing every person to make his own standards on matters of conduct in which society as a whole has important interests. . . .

. . . [W]e see that the record in this case abundantly supports the claim that the traditional way of life of the Amish is not merely a matter of personal preference, but one of deep religious conviction, shared by an organized group, and intimately related to daily living. . . .

The impact of the compulsory-attendance law on respondents' practice of the Amish religion is not only severe, but inescapable, for the Wisconsin law affirmatively compels them, under threat of criminal sanction, to perform acts undeniably at odds with fundamental tenets of their religious beliefs. . . . Nor is the impact of the compulsory-attendance law confined to grave interference with important Amish religious tenets from a subjective point of view. It carries with it precisely the kind of objective danger to the free exercise of religion that the First Amendment was designed to prevent. . . .

A regulation neutral on its face may, in its application, nonetheless offend the constitutional requirement for governmental neutrality if it unduly burdens the free exercise of religion. . . .

The State attacks respondents' position as one fostering "ignorance" from which the child must be protected by the State. No one can question the State's duty to protect children from ignorance but this argument does not square with the facts disclosed in the record. Whatever their idiosyncrasies as seen by the majority, this record strongly shows that the Amish community has been a highly successful social unit within our society, even if apart from the conventional "mainstream." Its members are productive and very law-abiding members of society. . . .

Aided by a history of three centuries as an identifiable religious sect and a long history as a successful and self-sufficient segment of American society, the Amish in this case have convincingly demonstrated the sincerity of their religious beliefs, the interrelationship of belief with their mode of life, the vital role that belief and daily conduct play in the continued survival of Old Order Amish communities and their religious organization, and the hazards presented by the State's enforcement of a statute generally valid as to others. Beyond this, they have carried the even more difficult burden of demonstrating the adequacy of their alternative mode of continuing informal vocational education in terms of precisely those overall interests that the State advances in support of its program of compulsory high school education. . . .

MR. JUSTICE DOUGLAS, dissenting in part.

I agree with the Court that the religious scruples of the Amish are opposed to the education of their children beyond the grade schools, yet I disagree with the Court's conclusion that the matter is within the dispensation of parents alone. The Court's analysis assumes that the only interests at stake in the case are those of the Amish parents on the one hand, and those of the State on the other. The difficulty with this approach is that, despite the Court's claim, the parents are seeking to vindicate not only their own free exercise claims, but also those of their high-school-age children. . . .

On this important and vital matter of education, I think the children should be entitled to be heard. While the parents, absent dissent, normally speak for the entire family, the education of the child is a matter on which the child will often have decided views. He may want to be a pianist or an astronaut or an oceanographer. To do so he will have to break from the Amish tradition.

It is the future of the student, not the future of the parents, that is imperiled by today's decision. If a parent keeps his child out of school beyond the grade school, then the child will be forever barred from entry into the new and amazing world of diversity that we have today. The child may decide that that is the preferred course, or he may rebel. It is the student's judgment, not his parents', that is essential if we are to give full meaning to what we have said about the Bill of Rights and of the right of students to be masters of their own destiny. If he is harnessed to the Amish way of life by those in authority over him and if his education is truncated, his entire life may be stunted and deformed. The child, therefore, should be given an opportunity to be heard before the State gives the exemption which we honor today. . . .

Source: Wisconsin v. Yoder, 406 U.S. 205 (1972).

DOCUMENT 42: *Heffron v. International Society for Krishna Consciousness* (1981)

The state of Minnesota enforced a regulation, known as Rule 6.05, that required any person or group intending to sell or distribute merchandise, including printed material, at the annual state fair to do so from a fixed booth. Organizational representatives were free to walk about the fairgrounds to communicate the organization's views on a face-to-face basis.

The International Society for Krishna Consciousness (ISKCON) challenged the rule as a violation of their right to freedom of speech and the free exercise of religion. The organization asserted that the rule suppressed a Krishna practice known as Sankirtan, by which followers of the religion solicit donations in public places by distributing religious literature.

The Supreme Court decided that there was a compelling state interest to maintain safety and crowd control at this event, which averaged over 1 million visitors each year. When measured in terms of the balancing test advanced in *Sherbert v. Verner* (1963), time, place, and manner restrictions, such as the one enforced in Minnesota, were seen as reasonable (see Document 39). First Amendment rights are not absolute.

Justice Byron R. White, writing for the majority in *Heffron*, emphasized that no distinctions were made regarding the content of speech, making the rule neutral. White also reasoned that while the state fair was a public forum, the sheer number of patrons each year justified the imposition of a different set of rules from those applicable to communication on a public street.

Justice William Brennan agreed that the restriction was valid when applied to the sale of literature and the solicitation of funds, but found it unconstitutional when applied to the simple distribution of religious literature. For Brennan, this activity would be no more disruptive than person-to-person proselytizing, which the rule, as written, allowed.

According to Justice White, under what conditions are time, place, and manner restrictions on various forms of communication justified? Why does Justice Brennan argue that the regulations examined in this case were overly intrusive?

* * *

JUSTICE WHITE delivered the opinion of the Court.

* * *

The State does not dispute that the oral and written dissemination of the Krishnas' religious views and doctrines is protected by the First Amendment. . . . Nor does it claim that this protection is lost because the written materials sought to be distributed are sold rather than given away or because contributions or gifts are solicited in the course of propagating the faith. . . .

It is also common ground, however, that the First Amendment does not guarantee the right to communicate one's views at all times and places or in any manner that may be desired. . . . The issue here, as it was below, is whether Rule 6.05 is a permissible restriction on the place and manner of communicating the views of the Krishna religion, more specifically, whether the Society may require the members of ISKCON who desire to practice Sankirtan at the State Fair to confine their distribution, sales, and solicitation activities to a fixed location.

A major criterion for a valid time, place and manner restriction is that the restriction "may not be based upon either the content or subject matter of speech." Rule 6.05 qualifies in this respect, since as the Supreme Court of Minnesota observed, the Rule applies evenhandedly to all who wish to distribute and sell written materials or to solicit funds. . . .

A valid time, place, and manner regulation must also "serve a significant governmental interest." Here, the principal justification asserted by the State in support of Rule 6.05 is the need to maintain the orderly movement of the crowd given the large number of exhibitors and persons attending the Fair. . . .

As a general matter, it is clear that a State's interest in protecting the "safety and convenience" of persons using a public forum is a valid governmental objective.

. . . Furthermore, consideration of a forum's special attributes is relevant to the constitutionality of a regulation since the significance of the governmental interest must be assessed in light of the characteristic nature and function of the particular forum involved. . . . This observation bears particular import in the present case since respondents make a number of analogies between the fairgrounds and city streets which have "immemorially been held in trust for the use of the public and . . . have been used for purposes of assembly, communicating thoughts between citizens, and discussing public questions." But it is clear that there are significant differences between a street and the fairgrounds. A street is continually open, often uncongested, and constitutes not only a necessary conduit in the daily affairs of a locality's citizens, but also a place where people may enjoy the open air or the company of friends and neighbors in a relaxed environment. The Minnesota Fair, as described above, is a temporary event attracting great numbers of visitors who come to the event for a short period to see and experience the host of exhibits and attractions at the Fair. The flow of the crowd and demands of safety are more pressing in the context of the Fair. As such, any comparisons to public streets are necessarily inexact. . . .

ISKCON desires to proselytize at the fair because it believes it can successfully communicate and raise funds. In its view, this can be done only by intercepting fair patrons as they move about, and if success is achieved, stopping them momentarily or for longer periods as money is given or exchanged for literature. This consequence would be multiplied many times over if Rule 6.05 could not be applied to confine such transactions by ISKCON and others to fixed locations. Indeed, the court below agreed that without Rule 6.05 there would be widespread disorder at the fairgrounds. The court also recognized that some disorder would inevitably result from exempting the Krishnas from the Rule. Obviously, there would be a much larger threat to the State's interest in crowd control if all other religious, nonreligious, and noncommercial organizations could likewise move freely about the fairgrounds distributing and selling literature and soliciting funds at will. Given these considerations, we hold that the State's interest in confining distribution, selling, and fund solicitation activities to fixed locations is sufficient to satisfy the requirement that a place or manner restriction must serve a substantial state interest. . . .

For Rule 6.05 to be valid as a place and manner restriction, it must also be sufficiently clear that alternative forums for the expression of respondents' protected speech exist despite the effects of the Rule. Rule 6.05 is not vulnerable on this ground. First, the Rule does not prevent ISKCON from practicing Sankirtan anywhere outside the fairgrounds. More importantly, the Rule has not been shown to deny that organization the right to conduct any desired activity at some point within the forum. Its members may mingle with the crowd and orally propagate their views. The organization may also arrange for a booth and distribute and sell literature and solicit funds from that location on the fairgrounds itself. . . .

JUSTICE BRENNAN, concurring in part and dissenting in part.

* * *

Accordingly, I join the judgment of the Court insofar as it upholds Rule 6.05's restriction on sales and solicitations. However, because I believe that the booth Rule is an overly intrusive means of achieving the State's interest in crowd control, and because I cannot accept the validity of the State's third asserted justification, I dissent from the Court's approval of Rule 6.05's restriction on the distribution of literature. . . .

The Minnesota State Fair is an annual 12-day festival of people and ideas. Located on permanent fairgrounds comprising approximately 125 acres, the fair attracts an average of 115,000 visitors on weekdays and 160,000 on Saturdays and Sundays. Once the fairgoers pay their admission fees, they are permitted to roam the fairgrounds at will, visiting booths, meeting friends, or just milling about. Significantly, each and every fairgoer, whether political candidate, concerned citizen, or member of a religious group, is free to give speeches, engage in face-to-face advocacy, campaign, or proselytize. No restrictions are placed on any fairgoer's right to speak at any time, at any place, or to any person. Thus, if on a given day 5,000 members of ISKCON came to the fair and paid their admission fees, all 5,000 would be permitted to wander throughout the fairgrounds, delivering speeches to whomever they wanted, about whatever they wanted. Moreover, because this right does not rest on Sankirtan or any other religious principle, it can be exercised by every political candidate, partisan advocate, and common citizen who has paid the price of admission. All share the identical right to move peripatetically and speak freely throughout the fairgrounds.

Because of Rule 6.05, however, as soon as a proselytizing member of ISKCON hands out a free copy of the Bhagavad-Gita to an interested listener, or a political candidate distributes his campaign brochure to a potential voter, he becomes subject to arrest and removal from the fairgrounds. This constitutes a significant restriction on First Amendment rights. By prohibiting distribution of literature outside the booths, the fair officials sharply limit the number of fairgoers to whom the proselytizers and candidates can communicate their messages. Only if a fairgoer affirmatively seeks out such information by approaching a booth does Rule 6.05 permit potential communicators to exercise their First Amendment rights. . . .

Source: Heffron v. International Society for Krishna Consciousness, 452 U.S. 640 (1981).

DOCUMENT 43: *United States v. Lee* (1982)

Edwin D. Lee owned a farm and a carpentry shop in Pennsylvania. Lee and the individuals who worked for him from time to time were members of the Old Order Amish religion. In violation of a federal law, Lee failed to withhold Social Security taxes from his employees or to pay the employer's share of such taxes. Lee asserted that while he had a religious obligation to provide assistance to fellow Amish, the payment of the taxes and the receipt of government benefits were violations of Amish beliefs.

Congress had provided an exemption from the payment of Social Security taxes for self-employed individuals, including the Amish, who objected for religious reasons. A federal district court, citing this regulation, ruled in Lee's favor after he claimed that the imposition of the taxes violated his right to free exercise of religion. On appeal, the dispute reached the Supreme Court.

In a unanimous decision, the Supreme Court reversed the lower court ruling. Writing for the Court, Chief Justice Warren Burger noted that the exemption provided by Congress was intended for self-employed individuals, and not for employers such as Lee who hired others to work on his farm and in his carpentry shop.

Burger, who wrote the majority opinion in *Wisconsin v. Yoder* (1972) a decade earlier, accepted the government's argument that the payment of Social Security taxes was not a realistic threat to the integrity of Amish beliefs. In *Yoder* (Document 41) compulsory high school attendance was viewed as a serious threat to the religiously oriented way of life practiced by the Amish. While the payment of the taxes would interfere with religious liberty to a certain degree, Burger held that the government had demonstrated a compelling interest to continue the collection of the taxes. In a nation where religious pluralism is a reality, Burger reasoned, some religious practices must "yield to the common good."

Burger did rely on the compelling state interest standard enunciated by the Court in *Sherbert v. Verner* (Document 39), but the *Lee* decision has been cited as the beginning of the end of the Court's reliance on the precedent. At the very least, the Court revealed a fear of a possible flood of similar objections to the payment of taxes. Burger acknowledged that "it would be difficult to accommodate the comprehensive social security system with myriad exceptions flowing from a wide variety of religious beliefs."

In a concurring opinion, Justice John Paul Stevens suggested that rather than requiring the government to demonstrate a compelling state interest, the burden should be on the individual objector to justify the need for a religious exemption from an otherwise valid law.

Concerning the rights of employees, why does Chief Justice Burger maintain that it would be improper for the government to allow employers to avoid the payment of Social Security taxes? Do you agree with Justice Stevens that in cases involving the free exercise of religion clause the burden should be on the individual to demonstrate that an exemption from a generally acceptable law is justified?

* * *

CHIEF JUSTICE BURGER delivered the opinion of the Court.

* * *

The preliminary inquiry in determining the existence of a constitutionally required exemption is whether the payment of social security taxes and the receipt of benefits interferes with the free exercise rights of the Amish. The Amish believe that there is a religiously based obligation to provide for their fellow members the kind of assistance contemplated by the social security system. Although the Government does not challenge the sincerity of this belief, the Government does contend that payment of social security taxes will not threaten the integrity of the Amish religious belief or observance. . . .

The conclusion that there is a conflict between the Amish faith and the obligations imposed by the social security system is only the beginning, however, and not the end of the inquiry. Not all burdens on religion are unconstitutional. . . . The state may justify a limitation on religious liberty by showing that it is essential to accomplish an overriding governmental interest. . . .

Because the social security system is nationwide, the governmental interest is apparent. The social security system in the United States serves the public interest by providing a comprehensive insurance system with a variety of benefits available to all participants, with costs shared by employers and employees. . . . This mandatory participation is indispensable to the fiscal vitality of the social security system. . . . Moreover, a comprehensive national social security system providing for voluntary participation would be almost a contradiction in terms and difficult, if not impossible, to administer. Thus, the Government's interest in assuring mandatory and continuous participation in and contribution to the social security system is very high.

The remaining inquiry is whether accommodating the Amish belief will unduly interfere with fulfillment of the governmental interest. In *Braunfeld v. Brown*, this Court noted that "to make accommodation between the religious action and an exercise of state authority is a particularly delicate task . . . because resolution in favor of the State results in the choice to the individual of either abandoning his religious principle or facing . . . prosecution." The difficulty in attempting to accommodate religious beliefs in the area of taxation is that "we are a cosmopolitan nation made up of people of almost every conceivable religious preference." (*Braunfeld*.) The Court has long recognized that balance must be struck between the values of the comprehensive social security system, which rests on a complex of actuarial factors, and the consequences of allowing religiously based exemptions. To maintain an organized society that guarantees religious freedom to a great variety of faiths requires that some religious practices yield to the common good. . . .

Unlike the situation presented in *Wisconsin v. Yoder*, it would be difficult to accommodate the comprehensive social security system with myriad exceptions flowing from a wide variety of religious beliefs. The obligation to pay the social security tax initially is not fundamentally different from the obligation to pay income taxes; the difference—in theory at least—is that the social security tax revenues are segregated for use only in furtherance of the statutory program. There is no principled way, however, for purposes of this case, to distinguish between general taxes and those imposed under the Social Security Act. If, for example, a religious adherent believes war is a sin, and if a certain percentage of the federal budget can be identified as devoted to war-related activities, such individuals would have a similarly valid claim to be exempt from paying that percentage of the income tax. The tax system could not function if denominations were allowed to challenge the tax system because tax payments were spent in a manner that violates their religious belief. . . .

Congress and the courts have been sensitive to the needs flowing from the Free Exercise Clause, but every person cannot be shielded from all the burdens incident to exercising every aspect of the right to practice religious beliefs. When followers of a particular sect enter into commercial activity as a matter of choice, the limits they accept on their own conduct as a matter of conscience and faith are not to be superimposed on the statutory schemes which are binding on others in that activity. Granting an exemption from social security taxes to an employer operates to impose the employer's religious faith on the employees. Congress drew a line in 1402(g), exempting the self-employed Amish but not all persons working for an Amish employer. The tax imposed on employers to support the social security system must be uniformly applicable to all, except as Congress provides explicitly otherwise. . . .

JUSTICE STEVENS, concurring in the judgment.

The clash between appellee's religious obligation and his civic obligation is irreconcilable. He must violate either an Amish belief or a federal statute. According to the Court, the religious duty must prevail unless the Government shows that enforcement of the civic duty "is essential to accomplish an overriding governmental interest." That formulation of the constitutional standard suggests that the Government always bears a heavy burden of justifying the application of neutral general laws to individual conscientious objectors. In my opinion, it is the objector who must shoulder the burden of demonstrating that there is a unique reason for allowing him a special exemption from a valid law of general applicability.

Source: United States v. Lee, 455 U.S. 252 (1982).

DOCUMENT 44: *Bob Jones University v. United States* (1983)

In 1970 the Internal Revenue Service (IRS) adopted a policy by which private schools that practiced racial discrimination would no longer be granted tax-exempt status (Revenue Ruling 71–447). In addition, a contribution to such a school would no longer be deductible as a charitable contribution.

Bob Jones University, located in Greenville, South Carolina, identified itself as an institution of learning which gave "special emphasis to the Christian religion and the ethics revealed in the Holy Scriptures."

The university was founded in 1927, and it excluded African American students until 1971. By 1975 the university had amended its policies to accept African American students, but it continued to deny admission to any applicant engaged in an interracial marriage or "known to advocate interracial marriage or dating." Due to this admissions policy, the IRS revoked the university's tax-exempt status on April 16, 1975.

Bob Jones University challenged this ruling by the IRS as an infringement upon religious liberty. It was the school's contention that the Bible forbids interracial dating and marriage. The assertion was made that the ban on interracial dating and marriage applied to all students, and the presence of a multiracial student body was presented as further proof that the university did not discriminate.

In an 8–1 decision the Supreme Court upheld the IRS decision to revoke the university's tax-exempt status. The majority opinion, written by Chief Justice Warren Burger, stipulated that an institution seeking tax-exempt status must serve a public purpose and not act contrary to established public policy. Burger reasoned that in an "unbroken line of cases" beginning with *Brown v. Board of Education* (1954) the Court had established the tenet that "racial discrimination in education violates a most fundamental national public policy." Even a sincere belief founded upon a reading of religious scripture cannot justify the granting of an exemption or the allowance of a deduction that would affect all taxpayers when that belief is in direct contradiction to what Burger called "elementary justice."

The lone dissent in this case was a call for judicial restraint. Justice William H. Rehnquist argued that there was simply no legislation to justify the policy adopted by the IRS, and he admonished his fellow justices that "regardless of our view on the propriety of Congress' failure to legislate we are not constitutionally empowered to act for it."

Why did Chief Justice Burger reject the contention made by Bob Jones University that it did not practice racial discrimination? If there is a national policy against racial discrimination, as Justice Rehnquist concedes, why does he view the action taken by the IRS as improper?

* * *

CHIEF JUSTICE BURGER delivered the opinion of the Court.

* * *

When the Government grants exemptions or allows deductions all taxpayers are affected; the very fact of the exemption or deduction for the donor means that other taxpayers can be said to be indirect and vicarious "donors." Charitable exemptions are justified on the basis that the exempt entity confers a public benefit—a benefit which the society or the community may not itself choose or be able to provide, or which supplements and advances the work of public institutions already supported by tax revenues. History buttresses logic to make clear that, to warrant exemption . . . an institution must demonstrably serve and be in harmony with the public interest. The institution's purpose must not be so at odds with the common community conscience as to undermine any public benefit that might otherwise be conferred. . . .

But there can no longer be any doubt that racial discrimination in education violates deeply and widely accepted views of elementary justice. . . .

It would be wholly incompatible with the concepts underlying tax exemption to grant the benefit of tax-exempt status to racially discriminatory educational entities. . . . Whatever may be the rationale for such private schools' policies, and however sincere the rationale may be, racial discrimination in education is contrary to public policy. . . .

Petitioner Bob Jones University, however, contends that it is not racially discriminatory. It emphasizes that it now allows all races to enroll, subject only to its restrictions on the conduct of all students, including its prohibitions of association between men and women of different races, and of interracial marriage. Although a ban on intermarriage or interracial dating applies to all races, decisions of this Court firmly establish that discrimination on the basis of racial affiliation and association is a form of racial discrimination. . . . We therefore find that the IRS properly applied Revenue Ruling 71–447 to Bob Jones University. . . .

JUSTICE REHNQUIST, dissenting.

The Court points out that there is a strong national policy in this country against racial discrimination. To the extent that the Court states that Congress in furtherance of this policy could deny tax-exempt status to educational institutions that promote racial discrimination, I readily agree. But, unlike the Court, I am convinced that Congress simply has failed to take this action and, as this Court has said over and over again, regardless of our view on the propriety of Congress' failure to legislate we are not constitutionally empowered to act for it. . . .

I have no disagreement with the Court's finding that there is a strong national policy in this country opposed to racial discrimination. I agree with the Court that Congress has the power to further this policy by denying 501(c)(3) [tax-exempt] status to organizations that practice racial discrimination. But as of yet Congress has failed to do so. Whatever the reasons for the failure, this Court should not legislate for Congress.

Source: Bob Jones University v. United States, 461 U.S. 574 (1983).

DOCUMENT 45: *Goldman v. Weinberger* (1986)

S. Simcha Goldman was an Orthodox Jew and an ordained rabbi. He was also a captain in the United States Air Force who served as a clinical psychologist at a base hospital in California. Following the dictates of his religion, Goldman wore a yarmulke while in and out of uniform. After being cited for a violation of the Air Force dress code, Goldman brought suit against the Secretary of Defense, Caspar W. Weinberger. Goldman argued that his conduct was "non-intrusive" and, therefore, the military lacked a compelling reason to require his compliance with the regulation.

In a 5–4 decision the Supreme Court held that the free exercise of religion clause did not prohibit the military from enforcing a regulation which, when applied to Goldman, would prevent him from wearing a yarmulke while on duty. The majority opinion, written by Justice William H. Rehnquist, asserted that the purpose of the military dress code was to perpetuate uniformity and discipline. Therefore, according to Rehnquist, the First Amendment does not require the military to "accommodate" practices such as the wearing of religious articles of clothing. The military had argued that an exemption for the wearing of a yarmulke would have opened the door for other claims, including those concerning "turbans, saffron robes, and dreadlocks."

Concerning Goldman's reliance upon the compelling interest standard enunciated in *Sherbert v. Verner* (Document 39), Rehnquist refused to apply the test in this case. His reasoning was founded on the idea that the military is a "specialized society" separate and apart from civilian society. In this specialized society, Rehnquist observed, the military is required to enforce regulations that are designed to "foster instinctive obedience, unity, commitment, and esprit de corps." This equation simply did not include the need to "encourage debate or tolerate protest."

Justice William Brennan saw the regulation as a denial of the constitutional rights of servicemen. Near the end of his dissent he wrote, "[W]e must hope that Congress will correct this wrong." In September 1987 Congress complied with this request by enacting a law that permitted members of the armed forces to wear religious apparel while in uniform provided that such articles of clothing were "neat and conservative" and that there would be no interference with the performance of assigned duties.

According to Justice Rehnquist, why should courts give "great deference" to military authorities concerning matters such as dress codes? Why does Justice Brennan contend that by ruling against Goldman the Court had failed to fulfill its constitutionally mandated role?

* * *

JUSTICE REHNQUIST delivered the opinion of the Court.

* * *

Our review of military regulations challenged on First Amendment grounds is far more deferential than constitutional review of similar laws or regulations designed for civilian society. The military need not encourage debate or tolerate protest to the extent that such tolerance is required of the civilian state by the First Amendment; to accomplish its mission the military must foster instinctive obedience, unity, commitment, and esprit de corps.

These aspects of military life do not, of course, render entirely nugatory in the military context the guarantees of the First Amendment. . . . In the context of the present case, when evaluating whether military needs justify a particular restriction on religiously motivated conduct, courts must give great deference to the professional judgment of military authorities concerning the relative importance of a particular military interest. . . .

The considered professional judgment of the Air Force is that the traditional outfitting of personnel in standardized uniforms encourages the subordination of personal preferences and identities in favor of the overall group mission. Uniforms encourage a sense of hierarchical unity by tending to eliminate outward individual distinctions except for those of rank. The Air Force considers them as vital during peacetime as during war because its personnel must be ready to provide an effective defense on a moment's notice; the necessary habits of discipline and unity must be developed in advance of trouble. . . .

Petitioner Goldman contends that the Free Exercise Clause of the First Amendment requires the Air Force to make an exception to its uniform dress requirements for religious apparel unless the accouterments create a "clear danger" of undermining discipline and esprit de corps. He asserts that in general, visible but "unobtrusive" apparel will not create such a danger and must therefore be accommodated. He argues that the Air Force failed to prove that a specific exception for his practice of wearing an unobtrusive yarmulke would threaten discipline. . . .

The desirability of dress regulations in the military is decided by the appropriate military officials, and they are under no constitutional mandate to abandon their considered professional judgment. Quite obviously, to the extent the regulations do not permit the wearing of religious apparel such as a yarmulke, a practice described by petitioner as silent devotion akin to prayer, military life may be more objectionable for petitioner and probably others. But the First Amendment does not require the military to accommodate such practices in the face of its view that they would detract from the uniformity sought by the dress regulations. The Air Force has drawn the line essentially between religious apparel that is visible and that which is not, and we hold that those portions of the regulations challenged here reasonably and evenhandedly regulate dress in the interest of the military's perceived need for uniformity. The First Amendment therefore does not prohibit them from being applied to petitioner even though their effect is to restrict the wearing of the headgear required by his religious beliefs. . . .

JUSTICE BRENNAN, dissenting.

Simcha Goldman invokes this Court's protection of his First Amendment right to fulfill one of the traditional religious obligations of a male Orthodox Jew—to cover his head before an omnipresent God. The Court's response to Goldman's request is to abdicate its role as principal expositor of the Constitution and protector of individual liberties in favor of credulous deference to unsupported assertions of military necessity. I dissent.

In ruling that the paramount interests of the Air Force override Dr. Goldman's free exercise claim, the Court overlooks the sincere and serious nature of his constitutional claim. It suggests that the desirability of certain dress regulations, rather than a First Amendment right, is at issue. . . . If Dr. Goldman wanted to wear a hat to keep his head warm or to cover a bald spot I would join the majority. Mere personal preferences in dress are not constitutionally protected. The First Amendment, however, restrains the Government's ability to prevent an Orthodox Jewish serviceman from, or punish him for, wearing a yarmulke.

Dr. Goldman has asserted a substantial First Amendment claim, which is entitled to meaningful review by this Court. The Court, however, evades its responsibility by eliminating, in all but name only, judicial review of military regulations that interfere with the fundamental constitutional rights of service personnel. . . .

In the present case, the Air Force asserts that its interests in discipline and uniformity would be undermined by an exception to the dress code permitting observant male Orthodox Jews to wear yarmulkes. The Court simply restates these assertions without offering any explanation how the exception Dr. Goldman requests reasonably could interfere with the Air Force's interests. Had the Court given actual consideration to Goldman's claim, it would have been compelled to decide in his favor. . . .

The contention that the discipline of the Armed Forces will be subverted if Orthodox Jews are allowed to wear yarmulkes with their uniforms surpasses belief. It lacks support in the record of this case, and the Air Force offers no basis for it as a general proposition. While the perilous slope permits the services arbitrarily to refuse exceptions requested to satisfy mere personal preferences, before the Air Force may burden free exercise rights it must advance, at the *very least*, a rational reason for doing so. . . .

Source: *Goldman v. Weinberger*, 475 U.S. 503 (1986).

DOCUMENT 46: *Lyng v. Northwest Indian Cemetery Protective Association* (1988)

In 1982 the United States Forest Service commissioned an environmental impact study on the possible construction of a road through the Chimney Rock section of the Six Rivers National Forest in California. The study recommended that the proposed road not be constructed due to potential damage to areas considered sacred by the members of three American Indian tribes. Historically, the Chimney Rock area was used for religious rituals that depended upon privacy, silence, and an undisturbed natural setting.

The Forest Service rejected this recommendation and selected a route for the so-called G-O road through the Chimney Rock area. This route, according to the Forest Service, avoided archeological sites and was removed as far as possible from the sites used for religious rituals by Native Americans.

At approximately the same time, the Forest Service adopted a management plan that would permit timber harvesting in the Chimney Rock area. However, protective zones were to be established around all religious sites identified in the study.

A group that included individual Indians who used the Chimney Rock area for religious rituals challenged the proposals. They claimed that both the construction of the G-O road and timber harvesting in the Chimney Rock area would violate their right to free exercise of religion.

In a 5–3 decision the Supreme Court ruled that both decisions by the Forest Service concerning the Six Rivers National Forest were constitutional. The majority opinion, written by Justice Sandra Day O'Connor, emphasized that the purpose of the free exercise of religion clause in the First Amendment is to limit government. The clause is written in terms of what the government cannot do to an individual, and not what an individual can "exact from the government."

Justice O'Connor, a proponent of judicial restraint, argued that the Constitution simply did not provide a remedy for people who hoped to constrict the government's right to the use of its own lands. O'Connor held that a "compelling justification" was not required because there was no tendency to coerce individuals to act contrary to their religious beliefs. She noted that the government had taken steps to minimize the impact on religious activities and, in her view, any interference with religious rituals was an incidental effect of a lawful government decision.

Writing in dissent, Justice William Brennan rejected the majority's contention that the government's prerogative as landowner took precedence over what he saw as a legitimate free exercise claim. Brennan was adamant that following the showing of a substantial and realistic threat to religious practices, the government is required to demonstrate "a compelling state interest sufficient to justify the infringement of those practices."

According to Justice O'Connor, why would it be impossible for the government to operate if it were required to satisfy the religious needs of all citizens? Why does Justice Brennan contend that both common sense and judicial precedents support the legal argument made by the Native Americans in this case?

* * *

JUSTICE O'CONNOR delivered the opinion of the Court.

* * *

The Free Exercise Clause of the First Amendment provides that "Congress shall make no law . . . prohibiting the free exercise [of religion]." It is undisputed that the Indian respondents' beliefs are sincere and that the Government's proposed actions will have severe adverse effects on the practice of their religion. Those respondents contend that the burden on their religious practices is heavy enough to violate the Free Exercise Clause unless the Government can demonstrate a compelling need to complete the G-O road or to engage in timber harvesting in the Chimney Rock area. We disagree. . . .

The crucial word in the constitutional text is "prohibit": "For the Free Exercise Clause is written in terms of what the government cannot do to the individual, not in terms of what the individual can exact from the government." (*Sherbert v. Verner*).

Whatever may be the exact line between unconstitutional prohibitions on the free exercise of religion and the legitimate conduct by government of its own affairs, the location of the line cannot depend on measuring the effects of a governmental action on a religious objector's spiritual development. The Government does not dispute, and we have no reason to doubt, that the logging and road-building projects at issue in this case could have devastating effects on traditional Indian religious practices. Those practices are intimately and inextricably bound up with the unique features of the Chimney Rock area, which is known to the Indians as the "high country." Individual practitioners use this area for personal spiritual development; some of their activities are believed to be critically important in advancing the welfare of the Tribe, and indeed, of mankind itself. The Indians use this area, as they have used it for a very long time, to conduct a wide variety of specific rituals that aim to accomplish their religious goals. According to their beliefs, the rituals would not be efficacious if conducted at other sites than the ones traditionally used, and too much disturbance of the area's natural state would clearly render any meaningful continuation of traditional practices impossible. . . .

. . . [T]he Constitution simply does not provide a principle that could justify upholding respondents' legal claims. However much we might wish that it were otherwise, government simply could not operate if it were required to satisfy every citizen's religious needs and desires. A broad range of government activities—from social welfare programs to foreign aid to conservation projects—will always be considered essential to the spiritual well-being of some citizens, often on the basis of sincerely held religious beliefs. Others will find the very same activities deeply offensive, and perhaps incompatible with their own search for spiritual fulfillment and with the tenets of their religion. The First Amendment must apply to all citizens alike, and it can give to none of them a veto over public programs that do not prohibit the free exercise of religion. The Constitution does not, and courts cannot, offer to reconcile the various competing demands on government, many of them rooted in sincere religious beliefs, that inevitably arise in so diverse a society as ours. That task, to the extent that it is feasible, is for the legislatures and other institutions. . . .

The Constitution does not permit government to discriminate against religions that treat particular physical sites as sacred, and a law prohibiting the Indian respondents from visiting the Chimney Rock area would raise a different set of constitutional questions. Whatever rights the Indians may have to the use of the area, however, those rights do not divest the Government of its right to use what is, after all, *its* land. . . .

Nothing in our opinion should be read to encourage governmental insensitivity to the religious needs of any citizen. The Government's rights to the use of its own land, for example, need not and should not discourage it from accommodating religious practices like those engaged in by the Indian respondents. . . . It is worth emphasizing, therefore, that the Government has taken numerous steps in this very case to minimize the impact that construction of the G-O road will have on the Indians' religious activities. First, the Forest Service commissioned a comprehensive study of the effects that the project would have on the cultural and religious value of the Chimney Rock area. The resulting 423-page report was so sympathetic to the Indians' interests that it has constituted the principal piece of evidence relied on by respondents throughout this litigation.

Although the Forest Service did not in the end adopt the report's recommendation that the project be abandoned, many other ameliorative measures were planned. No sites where specific rituals take place were to be disturbed. In fact, a major factor in choosing among alternative routes for the road was the relation of the various routes to religious sites: the route selected by the Regional Forester is, he noted, "the farthest removed from contemporary spiritual sites; thus, the adverse audible intrusions associated with the road would be less than all other alternatives."

JUSTICE BRENNAN, dissenting.

* * *

Because the Court today refuses even to acknowledge the constitutional injury respondents will suffer, and because this refusal essentially leaves Native Americans with absolutely no constitutional protection against perhaps the gravest threat to their religious practices, I dissent. . . .

The Court does not for a moment suggest that the interests served by the G-O road are in any way compelling, or that they outweigh the destructive effect construction of the road will have on respondent's religious practices. Instead, the Court embraces the Government's contention that its prerogative as landowner should always take precedence over a claim that a particular use of federal property infringes religious practices. Attempting to justify this rule, the Court argues that the First Amendment bars only outright prohibitions, indirect coercion, and penalties on the free exercise of religion. All other "incidental effects of government programs," it concludes, even those "which may make it more difficult to practice certain religions but which have no tendency to coerce individuals into acting contrary to their religious beliefs," simply do not give rise to constitutional concerns. . . . The land-use decision challenged here will restrain respondents from practicing their religion as surely and as completely as any of the governmental actions we have struck down in the past, and the Court's efforts simply to define away respondents' injury as nonconstitutional are both unjustified and ultimately unpersuasive. . . .

Ultimately, the Court's coercion test turns on a distinction between governmental actions that compel affirmative conduct inconsistent with religious belief, and those governmental actions that prevent conduct consistent with religious belief. In my view, such a distinction is without constitutional significance. . . .

. . . [W]e have recognized that laws that affect spiritual development by impeding the integration of children into the religious community or by increasing the expense of adherence to religious principles—in short, laws that frustrate or inhibit religious *practice*—trigger the protections of the constitutional guarantee. Both common sense and our prior cases teach us, therefore, that governmental action that makes the practice of a given faith more difficult necessarily penalizes that practice and thereby tends to prevent adherence to religious belief. The harm to the practitioners is the same regardless of the manner in which the government restrains their religious expression, and the Court's fear that an "effects" test will permit religious adherents to challenge governmental actions they merely find "offensive" in no way justifies its refusal to recognize the constitutional injury citizens suffer when governmental action not only offends but actually restrains their religious practices. . . .

I believe it appropriate, therefore, to require some showing of "centrality" before the Government can be required either to come forward with a compelling justification for its proposed use of federal land or to forego that use altogether. . . .

The Court today suggests that such an approach would place courts in the untenable position of deciding which practices and beliefs are "central" to a given faith and which are not, and invites the prospect of judges advising some religious adherents that they "misunderstand their own religious beliefs." In fact, however, courts need not undertake any such inquiries: like all other religious adherents, Native Americans would be the arbiters of which practices are central to their faith, subject only to the normal requirement that their claims be genuine and sincere. The question for the courts, then, is not whether the Native American claimants understand their own religion, but rather whether they have discharged their burden of demonstrating, as the Amish did with respect to the compulsory school law in *Yoder*, that the land-use decision poses a substantial and realistic threat of undermining or frustrating their religious practices. . . .

Source: Lyng v. Northwest Indian Cemetery Protective Association, 485 U.S. 439 (1988).

DOCUMENT 47: *Employment Division, Department of Human Resources of Oregon v. Smith* (1990)

Alfred Smith was fired from his job as a counselor at a private drug rehabilitation clinic in Oregon after it was learned that he had ingested peyote, a hallucinogenic drug. Smith, a member of the Native American Church, ingested the peyote for sacramental purposes while attending a religious ceremony. Under Oregon law, peyote was regarded as a controlled substance and, unlike a number of other states and the federal government, Oregon did not provide a religious exemption for the use of peyote.

After a ruling that he had been discharged from his job for "misconduct," the state of Oregon denied Smith's application for unemployment compensation. Smith challenged this action by the state as an infringement of his right to free exercise of religion. In a 6–3 decision the Supreme Court ruled that the state's denial of unemployment benefits was constitutional.

Justice Antonin Scalia, writing for the majority, stressed that the Court had "never held that an individual's religious beliefs excuse him from compliance with an otherwise valid law prohibiting conduct that the State is free to regulate." Unlike *Cantwell v. Connecticut* (Document 33), which combined a free exercise claim with freedom of speech, or *Wisconsin v. Yoder* (Document 41), which combined a free exercise claim with parental rights, *Smith* was not what Scalia called a "hybrid situation."

Significantly, Scalia rejected the precedent enunciated in *Sherbert v. Verner* (1963) that a compelling state interest must exist to justify even an incidental encroachment on religious liberty. Scalia returned to the philosophy behind the Court's ruling in *Reynolds v. United States* (1879) that a neutral, generally applicable law governs everyone's conduct, without regard to indirect effects on religious practices. Scalia quoted the *Reynolds* decision when he wrote that to make an individual's compliance with a law contingent upon the demonstration of a compelling state interest is to allow the individual "to become a law unto himself."

In a concurring opinion Justice Sandra Day O'Connor agreed that, given the state's interest in preventing the harm caused by the use of controlled substances, the denial of Smith's unemployment benefits was justified. O'Connor did, however, object to the abandonment of the balancing test set forth in *Sherbert* (see Document 39). She termed this departure from "well-settled First Amendment jurisprudence" unnecessary and "incompatible with our Nation's fundamental commitment to individual religious liberty."

Writing in dissent, Justice Harry A. Blackmun cited the compelling interest standard as a "settled and inviolate principle." Unlike Justice O'Connor, however, Blackmun held that the state of Oregon had failed to demonstrate that the use of peyote for religious purposes was harmful.

Why does Justice Scalia contend that the application of the compelling interest standard across the board would invite anarchy in a nation with a diversity of religious beliefs? For Justice O'Connor, what should be the essence of a free exercise of religion claim made by an individual citizen? Why does Justice Blackmun claim that the state in this case failed to show that the sacramental use of peyote in a religious ceremony is harmful?

* * *

JUSTICE SCALIA delivered the opinion of the Court.

* * *

. . . [T]he "exercise of religion" often involves not only belief and profession but the performance of (or abstention from) physical acts: assembling with others for a worship service, participating in sacramental use of bread and wine, proselytizing, abstaining from certain foods or certain modes of transportation. It would be true, we think (though no case of ours has involved the point), that a State would be "prohibiting the free exercise [of religion]" if it sought to ban such acts or abstentions only when they are engaged in for religious reasons, or only because of the religious belief that they display. It would doubtless be unconstitutional, for example, to ban the casting of "statues that are to be used for worship purposes," or to prohibit bowing down before a golden calf.

Respondents in the present case, however, seek to carry the meaning of "prohibiting the free exercise [of religion]" one large step further. They contend that their religious motivation for using peyote places them beyond the reach of a criminal law that is not specifically directed at their religious practice, and that is concededly constitutional as applied to those who use the drug for other reasons. They assert, in other words, that "prohibiting the free exercise [of religion]" includes requiring any individual to observe a generally applicable law that requires (or forbids) the performance of an act that his religious belief forbids (or requires). As a textual matter, we do not think the words must be given that meaning. . . .

We have never held that an individual's religious beliefs excuse him from compliance with an otherwise valid law prohibiting conduct that the State is free to regulate. On the contrary, the record of more than a century of our free exercise jurisprudence contradicts that proposition. . . .

The only decisions in which we have held that the First Amendment bars application of a neutral, generally applicable law to religiously motivated action have involved not the Free Exercise Clause alone, but the Free Exercise Clause in conjunction with other constitutional protections, such as freedom of speech and of the press (see *Cantwell v. Connecticut*). . . .

The present case does not present such a hybrid situation but a free exercise claim unconnected with any communicative activity or parental right. Respondents urge us to hold, quite simply, that when otherwise prohibitable conduct is accompanied by religious convictions, not only the convictions but the conduct itself must be free from governmental regulation. We have never held that, and decline to do so now. There being no contention that Oregon's drug law represents an attempt to regulate religious beliefs, the communication of religious beliefs, or the raising of one's children in those beliefs, the rule to which we have adhered ever since *Reynolds* plainly controls. . . .

Respondents argue that even though exemption from generally applicable criminal laws need not automatically be extended to religiously motivated actors, at least the claim for a religious exemption must be evaluated under the balancing test set forth in *Sherbert v. Verner*. Under the *Sherbert* test, governmental actions that substantially burden a religious practice must be justified by a compelling governmental interest. . . . We have never invalidated any governmental action on the basis of the *Sherbert* test except the denial of unemployment compensation. . . .

Even if we were inclined to breathe into *Sherbert* some life beyond the unemployment compensation field, we would not apply it to require exemptions from a generally applicable criminal law. . . .

To make an individual's obligation to obey such a law contingent upon the law's coincidence with his religious beliefs, except where the State's interest is "compelling"—permitting him, by virtue of his beliefs, "to become a law unto himself" (*Reynolds v. United States*)—contradicts both constitutional tradition and common sense. . . .

If the "compelling interest" test is to be applied at all, then, it must be applied across the board, to all actions thought to be religiously commanded. Moreover, if "compelling interest" really means what it says (and watering it down here would subvert its rigor in the other fields where it is applied), many laws will not meet the test. Any society adopting such a system would be courting anarchy, but that danger increases in direct proportion to the society's diversity of religious beliefs, and its determination to coerce or suppress none of them. . . .

Values that are protected against government interference through enshrinement in the Bill of Rights are not thereby banished from the political process. Just as a society that believes in the negative protection accorded to the press by the First Amendment is likely to enact laws that affirmatively foster the dissemination of the printed word, so also a society that believes in the negative protection accorded to religious belief can be expected to be solicitous of that value in its legislation as well. It is therefore not surprising that a number of States have made an exception to their drug laws for sacramental peyote use. . . .

But to say that a nondiscriminatory religious-practice exemption is permitted, or even that it is desirable, is not to say that it is constitutionally required, and that the appropriate occasions for its creation can be discerned by the courts. It may fairly be said that leaving accommodation to the political process will place at a relative disadvantage those religious practices that are not widely engaged in; but that unavoidable consequence of democratic government must be preferred to a system in which each conscience is a law unto itself or in which judges weigh the social importance of all laws against the centrality of all religious beliefs.

Because respondents' ingestion of peyote was prohibited under Oregon law, and because that prohibition is constitutional, Oregon may, consistent with the Free Exercise Clause, deny respondents unemployment compensation when their dismissal results from use of the drug. The decision of the Oregon Supreme Court is accordingly reversed.

JUSTICE O'CONNOR, concurring in the judgment.

Although I agree with the result the Court reaches in this case, I cannot join its opinion. In my view, today's holding dramatically departs from well-settled First Amendment jurisprudence, appears unnecessary to resolve the question presented, and is incompatible with our Nation's fundamental commitment to individual religious liberty. . . .

Because the First Amendment does not distinguish between religious belief and religious conduct, conduct motivated by sincere religious belief, like the belief itself, must be at least presumptively protected by the Free Exercise Clause.

The Court today, however, interprets the Clause to permit the government to prohibit, without justification, conduct mandated by an individual's religious beliefs, so long as that prohibition is generally applicable. But a law that prohibits certain conduct—conduct that happens to be an act of worship for someone—manifestly does prohibit that person's free exercise of his religion. A person who is barred from engaging in religiously motivated conduct is barred from freely exercising his religion.

Moreover, that person is barred from freely exercising his religion regardless of whether the law prohibits the conduct only when engaged in for religious reasons, only by members of that religion, or by all persons. It is difficult to deny that a law that prohibits religiously motivated conduct, even if the law is generally applicable, does not at least implicate First Amendment concerns. . . .

The Court attempts to support its narrow reading of the Clause by claiming that "[w]e have never held that an individual's religious beliefs excuse him from compliance with an otherwise valid law prohibiting conduct that the State is free to regulate." But as the Court later notes, as it must, in cases such as *Cantwell* and *Yoder* we have in fact interpreted the Free Exercise Clause to forbid application of a generally applicable prohibition to religiously motivated conduct. . . .

The Court endeavors to escape from our decisions in *Cantwell* and *Yoder* by labeling them "hybrid" decisions, but there is no denying that both cases expressly relied on the Free Exercise Clause, and that we have consistently regarded those cases as part of the mainstream of our free exercise jurisprudence. . . .

. . . [R]espondents invoke our traditional compelling interest test to argue that the Free Exercise Clause requires the State to grant them a limited exemption from its general criminal prohibition against the possession of peyote. The Court today, however, denies them even the opportunity to make that argument, concluding that "the sounder approach, and the approach in accord with the vast majority of our precedents, is to hold the [compelling interest] test inapplicable to" challenges to general criminal prohibitions.

In my view, however, the essence of a free exercise claim is relief from a burden imposed by government on religious practices or beliefs, whether the burden is imposed directly through laws that prohibit or compel specific religious practices, or indirectly through laws that, in effect, make abandonment of one's own religion or conformity to the religious beliefs of others the price of an equal place in the civil community. . . .

JUSTICE BLACKMUN, dissenting.

This Court over the years painstakingly has developed a consistent and exacting standard to test the constitutionality of a state statute that burdens the free exercise of religion. Such a statute may stand only if the law in general, and the State's refusal to allow a religious exemption in particular, are justified by a compelling interest that cannot be served by less restrictive means.

Until today, I thought this was a settled and inviolate principle of this Court's First Amendment jurisprudence. The majority, however, perfunctorily dismisses it as a "constitutional anomaly." As carefully detailed in Justice O'CONNOR's concurring opinion, the majority is able to arrive at this view only by mischaracterizing this Court's precedents. The Court discards leading free exercise cases such as *Cantwell v. Connecticut* and *Wisconsin v. Yoder* as "hybrid." The Court views traditional free exercise analysis as somehow inapplicable to criminal prohibitions (as opposed to conditions on the receipt of benefits), and to state laws of general applicability (as opposed, presumably, to laws that expressly single out religious practices). The Court cites cases in which, due to various exceptional circumstances, we found strict scrutiny inapposite, to hint that the Court has repudiated that standard altogether. In short, it effectuates a wholesale overturning of settled law concerning the Religion Clauses of our Constitution. One hopes that the Court is aware of the consequences, and that its result is not a product of overreaction to the serious problems the country's drug crisis has generated.

This distorted view of our precedents leads the majority to conclude that strict scrutiny of a state law burdening the free exercise of religion is a "luxury" that a well-ordered society cannot afford, and that the repression of minority religions is an "unavoidable consequence of democratic government." I do not believe the Founders thought their dearly bought freedom from religious persecution a "luxury," but an essential element of liberty—and they could not have thought religious intolerance "unavoidable," for they drafted the Religion Clauses precisely in order to avoid that intolerance. . . .

In weighing the clear interest of respondents Smith and Black (hereinafter respondents) in the free exercise of their religion against Oregon's asserted interest in enforcing its drug laws, it is important to articulate in precise terms the state interest involved. It is not the State's broad interest in fighting the critical "war on drugs" that must be weighed against respondents' claim, but the State's narrow interest in refusing to make an exception for the religious, ceremonial use of peyote. . . .

The State proclaims an interest in protecting the health and safety of its citizens from the dangers of unlawful drugs. It offers, however, no evidence that the religious use of peyote has ever harmed anyone. . . .

The carefully circumscribed ritual context in which respondents used peyote is far removed from the irresponsible and unrestricted recreational use of unlawful drugs. The Native American Church's internal restrictions on, and supervision of, its members' use of peyote substantially obviate the State's health and safety concerns. . . .

The State also seeks to support its refusal to make an exception for religious use of peyote by invoking its interest in abolishing drug trafficking. There is, however, practically no illegal traffic in peyote. . . .

For these reasons, I conclude that Oregon's interest in enforcing its drug laws against religious use of peyote is not sufficiently compelling to outweigh respondents' right to the free exercise of their religion. . . .

Source: Employment Division, Department of Human Resources of Oregon v. Smith, 495 U.S. 872 (1990).

FURTHER READING

Biskupic, Joan, and Elder Witt. *The Supreme Court and Individual Rights.* Washington, D.C.: Congressional Quarterly Books, 1997, pp. 83–110.

Eastland, Terry, ed. *Religious Liberty in the Supreme Court.* Grand Rapids, Mich.: William B. Eerdmans, 1993.

Epstein, Lee, and Thomas G. Walker. *Constitutional Law for a Changing America.* Washington, D.C.: Congressional Quarterly Books, 1998, pp. 363–387.

Goldwin, Robert A., and Art Kaufman, eds. *How Does the Constitution Protect Religious Freedom?* Washington, D.C.: American Enterprise Institute, 1987.

Hall, Kermit L., ed. *The Oxford Companion to the Supreme Court of the United States.* New York: Oxford University Press, 1992.

Hickok, Eugene W., Jr., ed. *The Bill of Rights: Original Meaning and Current Understanding.* Charlottesville: University Press of Virginia, 1991, pp. 54–81.

Lowenthal, David. *No Liberty for License: The Forgotten Logic of the First Amendment.* Dallas: Spence Publishing, 1997, pp. 245–265.

Patrick, John J. *The Young Oxford Companion to the Supreme Court of the United States.* New York: Oxford University Press, 1996.

Rossum, Ralph A., and G. Alan Tarr. *American Constitutional Law, Volume II: The Bill of Rights and Subsequent Amendments.* New York: St. Martin's Press, 1995, pp. 197–209.

Schwartz, Bernard. *The Great Rights of Mankind: A History of the American Bill of Rights.* Madison, Wis.: Madison House, 1992.

Part IV

The Constitutional Prohibition of an Establishment of Religion, 1791–1991

The First Amendment to the United States Constitution opens with the declaration that "Congress shall make no law respecting an establishment of religion." This statement is best understood as a limit on the power of government and not as a positive assertion of an individual right. There is consensus among Americans that the establishment clause prohibits the federal government from mandating a national religion. And there is widespread agreement that the government cannot constitutionally favor one religion over others. There has been sharp disagreement, however, about the permissible extent and kind of relationship between government and religion under the Constitution.

Constitutional historian Leonard W. Levy has argued that the establishment clause "separates government and religion so that we can maintain civility between believers and unbelievers as well as among the several hundred denominations, sects, and cults that thrive in our nation."[1] Levy is a strict separationist regarding church-state relationships. His opinion, though widely held by scholars and judges, has been contested seriously by accommodationists. They maintain that it is constitutionally permissible for the government to be nonpreferentially and neutrally involved with religion in some circumstances. Some, like Supreme Court Chief Justice William Rehnquist, argue that government support of religious denominations is constitutional as long as it is provided nonpreferentially and equally to all religions, not favoring one or some over others.[2]

Concerning the original intent of the establishment clause, Levy contends that most of the framers of the First Amendment probably meant that the government should not "promote, sponsor, or subsidize religion."[3] Levy's opponents, however, claim that the original intent of the framers was "no preference among sects" in recognition of widespread religious diversity in America.[4] All seem to agree that, at least, the establishment clause was intended by its authors and ratifiers to prevent "the newly created federal government from granting to any denomination the political and governmental privileges enjoyed in England by the established Anglican Church."[5] Further, it generally is understood that the First Amendment was not intended to abolish religious establishments that then or might in the future exist in the states. The establishment clause clearly, all seem to agree, was a limit only on the power of the federal government, not the states.[6] This opinion was affirmed by the U.S. Supreme Court in *Barron v. Baltimore* (1833).[7]

It was not until the ratification of the Fourteenth Amendment in 1868, with a provision that a state is prohibited from depriving a person of liberty without due process of law, that the Supreme Court had a vehicle by which to require the states to follow the dictates contained in the Bill of Rights. However, it was not until 1947, in *Everson v. Board of Education of Ewing Township* (Document 48), that the Court utilized this procedure, known as selective incorporation, to apply the establishment clause to the states. (See Part III for a discussion of the doctrine of selective incorporation of the Bill of Rights through the due process clause of the Fourteenth Amendment.)

Prior to 1947 the Supreme Court decided only two cases that involved the establishment clause, *Bradfield v. Roberts* (1899) and *Quick Bear v. Leupp* (1908). Both involved the expenditure of federal funds, but neither case produced a comprehensive analysis of the meaning of the establishment clause.

Everson stands as the seminal Supreme Court pronouncement on the meaning and scope of the establishment clause. The Court resolved the factual dispute in *Everson* by concluding that a state could provide transportation for students to and from parochial schools without violating the establishment clause. Following the "child benefit" theory first advanced in *Cochran v. Louisiana Board of Education* (1930), the majority in the 5–4 *Everson* decision reasoned that individual students and their parents, and not religious institutions, were the beneficiaries of the program. Justice Hugo L. Black, writing for the majority, asserted that since the state government had maintained its neutrality concerning religion, the reimbursement to parents for the cost of transportation was constitutional.

The practical result of *Everson* was an accommodation of religion by the government, but the rhetoric employed by Black to reach this destination constitutionalized Thomas Jefferson's concept of a "wall of separation" between church and state. (See Part II for a discussion on Jefferson's separationist metaphor.) Black offered the following analysis of the establishment clause:

The "establishment of religion" clause of the First Amendment means at least this: Neither a state nor the Federal Government can set up a church. Neither can pass laws which aid one religion, aid all religions, or prefer one religion over another. Neither can force nor influence a person to go to or to remain away from church against his will or force him to profess a belief or disbelief in any religion. No person can be punished for entertaining or professing religious beliefs or disbeliefs, for church attendance or non-attendance. No tax in any amount, large or small, can be levied to support any religious activities or institutions, whatever they may be called, or whatever form they may adopt to teach or practice religion. Neither a state nor the Federal Government can, openly or secretly, participate in the affairs of any religious organizations or groups and vice versa. In the words of Jefferson, the clause against establishment of religion by law was intended to erect "a wall of separation between church and State."[8]

The minority in *Everson* agreed with Justice Black's separationist sentiment that the wall between church and state should be "kept high and impregnable." They simply objected to the accommodationist result imposed by the majority.

The debate between separationist and accommodationist voices has dominated establishment clause jurisprudence ever since the 1947 *Everson* decision. In 1952, in *Zorach v. Clauson* (Document 49), Supreme Court Justice William O. Douglas provided the following justification for the accommodationist position:

We are a religious people whose institutions presuppose a Supreme Being. We guarantee the freedom to worship as one chooses. We make room for as wide a variety of beliefs and creeds as the spiritual needs of man deem necessary. We sponsor an attitude on the part of government that shows no partiality to any one group and that lets each flourish according to the zeal of its adherents and the appeal of its dogma. When the state encourages religious instruction or cooperates with religious authorities by adjusting the schedule of public events to sectarian needs, it follows the best of our traditions. For it then respects the religious nature of our people and accommodates the public service to their spiritual needs. To hold that it may not would be to find in the Constitution a requirement that the government show a callous indifference to religious groups.[9]

Ironically, in subsequent cases Douglas was usually allied with separationist voices on the Court. But in *Zorach* he was adamant that a failure on the part of government to accommodate the spiritual needs of the populace would be hostility to religion.

Establishment clause adjudication can be divided into three categories. First, there are cases involving religious activity in public schools. Second, there are cases concerning government aid to parochial schools. Third, there are cases originating outside the sphere of education that have raised questions regarding government neutrality in regard to religion.

Justice Sandra Day O'Connor, concurring in *Wallace v. Jaffree* (1985), said that the framers of the establishment clause did not anticipate the interaction of church and state in public schools because public education was virtually nonexistent when the First Amendment was drafted and ratified (see Document 61). In a number of cases starting with *Engel v. Vitale* in 1962 (Document 51), nonetheless, the Supreme Court has consistently held that the establishment clause prohibits state-sponsored religious activities, including prayer in public schools. Compulsory school attendance policies, the impressionability of children, and the potential for coerced compliance have been key factors in the resolution of these cases.

Despite the Court's consistency in the school prayer cases, public opinion polls have revealed a lack of support for the justices in this area. Lee Epstein and Thomas G. Walker have documented that in 1963 only 24 percent of a national sample approved of the Court's decision to prohibit organized prayer in public schools. In a total of ten surveys conducted between 1963 and 1994, public approval for the position first enunciated in *Engel* peaked at 43 percent in 1985 and then declined in subsequent polls.[10]

In addition, on numerous occasions, starting in 1966, congressional majorities have supported proposed amendments to the Constitution that have been designed to return organized prayer to public school classrooms. However, Congress has yet to pass such a proposal with a two-thirds vote, which is necessary to send an amendment to the states for possible ratification.[11]

The Supreme Court has shown a separationist inclination to exclude not only organized prayer, but also the promotion of religious doctrine from public schools. A pair of cases, one in 1948 and the other in 1952, examined released time programs that authorized religious instruction for public school students during normal school hours on a voluntary basis. The Court concluded that the establishment clause prohibits the promotion of religion in public school classrooms, but that a state could accommodate religion by allowing the instruction to simply take place off public school grounds.

The Court has held that teaching about religion or religious literature in history courses, for example, is permissible. It is not constitutionally permissible, however, to foster or inculcate articles of religious faith. While it is unconstitutional to promote religious beliefs in a public school classroom, it is constitutional to teach about religion or religious literature in a history, humanities, or literature course. For example, writing for the Court's majority in *School District of Abington Township, Pennsylvania v. Schempp* (1963), Justice Clark said that "one's education is not complete without a study of comparative religion or the history of religion and its relationship to the advancement of civilization. It certainly may be said that the Bible is worthy of study for its literary and historic qualities.'' (See Document 52.)

In 1987 the Court reaffirmed its position that a public school classroom is not an acceptable setting for teaching religious doctrine when it voided a state law that mandated equal time for the Biblical interpretation of creation whenever evolutionary theory was taught (see Document 63). By contrast, in 1990 the Court rendered an accommodationist holding when it concluded that student groups cannot be denied equal access to public school facilities during noninstructional hours for meetings that include prayer sessions and the teaching of religion (see Document 65). In this decision, the Court upheld as constitutional the Equal Access Act passed by Congress in 1984 (see Document 60).

The first Supreme Court case to consider the issue of government aid to parochial schools, the second category of cases concerning the establishment clause, was, of course, *Everson* in 1947. As in *Everson*, the child benefit theory has generally been the key to the resolution of so-called parochiaid cases since 1947. According to this theory, as long as the beneficiaries of government assistance are individual children and their parents the aid is constitutional. Conversely, any aid that goes directly to a religious school contravenes the establishment clause. As a result, the Court has sanctioned not only a reimbursement for the cost of transportation to and from parochial schools, it has approved state programs designed to provide students in sectarian schools with secular textbooks and to give parents tax deductions for parochial school tuition.

Applying the same standard, the Court has rejected efforts to provide religious schools with instructional materials and equipment, and even reimbursement for the transportation costs associated with field trips. Teacher salary reimbursements and supplements have also been viewed as unconstitutional.

In 1985, in *Aguilar v. Felton* (Document 62), the Court held that a program that had allowed public school teachers and counselors to enter parochial schools to provide remedial instruction and other services was unconstitutional. The majority in this 5–4 separationist decision reasoned that the program had created an excessive entanglement between church and state. However, in 1997, in *Agostini v. Felton* (see Document 75), an accommodationist majority in yet another 5–4 decision overruled the *Aguilar* precedent.

Outside the sphere of education, the third area of establishment clause jurisprudence, the standard of government neutrality has been pivotal. Justice Tom C. Clark, in *School District of Abington Township,*

Pennsylvania v. Schempp (1963), wrote that in the relationship between the individual and religion, "the State is firmly committed to a position of neutrality." (See Document 52.) Disputes concerning matters such as Sunday closing laws, tax exemptions for religious groups, and the recitation of a prayer to open the proceedings of a state legislature have been debated before the Supreme Court. The Court resolved each of these disputes with an accommodationist ruling. Sunday closing laws were viewed as having the secular purpose of providing a uniform day of rest, tax exemptions were regarded as necessary to prevent an excessive entanglement between church and state, and legislative prayer was validated primarily by citing historical tradition.

In 1989 the Court did conclude that the placement in a county courthouse of a religious display that included a banner proclaiming a sectarian message was unconstitutional (see Document 64). However, five years earlier the Court had allowed a similar display, a Christian nativity scene, to be included as a part of a larger display in a public park. The other objects in the display were traditional holiday items such as a Santa Claus house, reindeer figures, and a decorated tree.

In 1971, to help resolve establishment clause controversies, the Supreme Court announced a three-pronged test in *Lemon v. Kurtzman* (see Document 55). The roots of this so-called *Lemon* test can be traced back to the *Everson* and *Abington* decisions. To be considered constitutional, according to Chief Justice Warren E. Burger's majority opinion in *Lemon*, an action by the government must, first, have a secular purpose. Second, the primary effect of the action must neither advance nor inhibit religion. Third, the action must not foster an excessive government entanglement with religion. In its application of the test the Court has established that a violation of any one of its three components is sufficient to render a law or action unconstitutional.

The Court, in its frequent appropriations of the tripartite *Lemon* test since 1971, has produced both separationist and accommodationist decisions. Use of the test, however, has not been a prerequisite for the resolution of an establishment clause dispute. For example, in the legislative prayer case in 1983 Burger himself penned a majority opinion that ignored *Lemon* (see Document 59). The following year, in *Lynch v. Donnelly* (1984), Burger asserted the Court's "unwillingness to be confined to any single test or criterion."[12]

Justice O'Connor's concurring opinion in *Lynch* included her suggestion for a modification of the *Lemon* test. O'Connor argued that a "proper inquiry" under the purpose prong of *Lemon* should focus on "whether the government intends to convey a message of endorsement or disapproval of religion." For O'Connor, endorsement sends a message to nonadherents that they are "outsiders, not full members of the political community," and an accompanying message to adherents that they are "insiders, favored members of the political community."[13]

The most outspoken critic of the endorsement standard has been Justice Anthony M. Kennedy. In *Allegheny County v. American Civil Liberties Union, Greater Pittsburgh Chapter* (1989), a case in which Justice Harry A. Blackmun wrote a plurality opinion that invoked O'Connor's endorsement criterion, Kennedy denigrated the standard as being "flawed in its fundamentals and unworkable in practice." As an alternative, Kennedy argued that the determining factor in establishment clause cases should be whether or not there is evidence of coercion on the part of the government affecting religious beliefs or practices (see Document 64).

In 1985, writing in dissent in *Wallace v. Jaffree* (Document 61), Justice William H. Rehnquist advanced his own nonpreferentialist interpretation of the establishment clause. Rehnquist argued that his research of the original intent of the framers of the establishment clause, particularly James Madison, supported the contention that the clause was simply designed to prevent the establishment of a national religion as well as any governmental preference for one denomination or another. Rehnquist also asserted that the establishment clause was not intended to prohibit the federal government from providing "non-discriminatory aid" to religion. Rehnquist's defense of nonpreferentialism has been a hot issue among constitutional scholars.[14]

The *Lemon* test has survived because nonpreferentialism and the endorsement and coercion standards have failed to garner consistent support from a majority of the justices. Justice Clarence Thomas has concluded that establishment clause jurisprudence is in "hopeless disarray."[15]

On the surface there have been apparent contradictions. For example, the members of a state legislature can open a session with an organized prayer, but public school students cannot do so in their classrooms. A state can reimburse the parents of parochial school students for the cost of transportation to school, but it cannot reimburse parochial schools for the cost of field trip transportation. And a nativity scene standing alone in a courthouse is prohibited, but a similar display surrounded by reindeer and wishing wells in a park is allowed.

Below the surface, however, it is important to interject that every case argued before the Supreme Court presents a unique set of facts and circumstances. It can be misleading to contrast the Court's resolution of one case with that of another absent a careful analysis of the underlying principles contained in the justices' written opinions. In its application of tenets such as government neutrality, the Court has been relatively consistent in its adjudication of establishment clause issues.

Constitutional historian Melvin I. Urofsky has observed that "changes in personnel on the Court, or even the facts of a particular case, may turn an accommodationist minority in one decision into a majority in the next."[16] For example, six of the nine judges who decided the case of *Agostini v. Felton* in 1997 (an accommodationist decision) were not members of the Supreme Court in 1985 when *Aguilar v. Felton* was decided (a separationist decision). Both cases were decided by a single vote, and *Agostini* overturned *Aguilar*.[17]

Over five decades have passed since Justice Black, in *Everson*, called for a "high and impregnable" wall of separation between church and state. But this concept has been challenged. Chief Justice Burger, for example, insisted that while Jefferson's concept of a wall of separation was a "useful metaphor," it was not an accurate description of the practical relationship between church and state.[18] The one overriding constant in the procession of Supreme Court decisions concerning the establishment clause has been the debate between the advocates of accommodation and the supporters of the separationist position. This debate certainly will continue as new establishment clause issues confront the Supreme Court.

NOTES

1. Leonard W. Levy, *The Establishment Clause: Religion and the First Amendment* (New York: Macmillan, 1986), p. ix.

2. William H. Rehnquist, "The True Meaning of the Establishment Clause," in Robert A. Goldwin and Art Kaufman, eds., *How Does the Constitution Protect Religious Freedom?* (Washington, D.C.: American Enterprise Institute, 1987), pp. 99–113.

3. Levy, p. 121.

4. John S. Baker, Jr., "The Establishment Clause as Intended: No Preference Among Sects and Pluralism in a Large Commercial Republic," in Eugene W. Hickok, Jr., ed., *The Bill of Rights: Original Meaning and Current Understanding* (Charlottesville: University Press of Virginia, 1991), pp. 41–53.

5. Frederick Mark Gedicks, "Religion," in Kermit L. Hall, ed., *The Oxford Companion to the Supreme Court of the United States* (New York: Oxford University Press, 1992), p. 717.

6. Akhil Reed Amar, *The Bill of Rights: Creation and Reconstruction* (New Haven: Yale University Press, 1998), pp. 32–45.

7. *Barron v. Baltimore*, 7 Pet (32 U.S.) 243 (1833).

8. *Everson v. Board of Education of Ewing Township*, 330 U.S. 1 (1947).

9. *Zorach v. Clauson*, 343 U.S. 306 (1952).

10. Lee Epstein and Thomas G. Walker, *Constitutional Law for a Changing America* (Washington, D.C.: Congressional Quarterly, 1998), p. 421.

11. Joan Biskupic and Elder Witt, *The Supreme Court and Individual Rights* (Washington, D.C.: Congressional Quarterly Books, 1997), p. 99.

12. *Lynch v. Donnelly*, 465 U.S. 688 (1984).

13. Ibid.

14. Leonard Levy has strongly criticized Rehnquist's nonpreferentialist position; see *The Establishment Clause: Religion and the First Amendment*, p. 155. See also Bernard Schwartz's criticism of Rehnquist's use of history in support of nonpreferentialism, *The Great Rights of Mankind* (Madison, Wis.: Madison House, 1992), pp. 38–39. Chief Justice Rehnquist's defense of nonpreferentialism is defended by Baker, "Establishment Clause," pp. 42–45, and by James McClellan, "Hand's Writing on the Wall of Separation: The Significance of *Jaffree* in Future Cases on Religion," in Robert A. Goldwin and Art Kaufman, eds., *How Does the Constitution Protect Religious Freedom?* (Washington, D.C.: American Enterprise Institute, 1987), pp. 62–64.

15. *Rosenberger v. University of Virginia*, 515 U.S. 819 (1995).

16. Melvin I. Urofsky, "The Religion Clauses," in Kermit L. Hall, ed., *By and for the People* (Arlington Heights, Ill.: Harlan Davidson, 1991), p. 35.

17. *Aguilar v. Felton*, 473 U.S. 402 (1985) and *Agostini v. Felton*, 117 S. Ct. (1997).

18. *Lynch v. Donnelly*, 465 U.S. 688 (1984).

DOCUMENT 48: *Everson v. Board of Education of Ewing Township* (1947)

In 1941 the New Jersey legislature enacted a statute that allowed local boards of education to reimburse parents for the cost of bus transportation to and from school. Students attending both public schools and Catholic parochial schools were eligible for this program, since only schools operating for a profit were excluded by the statute.

Arch Everson, a taxpayer and resident of Ewing Township, believed that as a result of this legislation public money was being spent to support religious institutions. He therefore challenged the reimbursement program as a violation of the First Amendment's establishment clause.

This was not the first case involving the establishment clause to be decided by the United States Supreme Court, but it did produce the Court's first comprehensive analysis of the meaning of the establishment clause. A narrow 5–4 majority ruled that the New Jersey statute was not a violation of the First Amendment. The majority opinion was written by Justice Hugo L. Black. Justice Wiley B. Rutledge, joined by three other members of the Court, wrote the dissenting opinion.

The *Everson* decision was important for three reasons. First, following the doctrine of selective incorporation, the Court specifically applied the establishment clause to the states for the first time by invoking the due process clause of the Fourteenth Amendment. Second, Black, advocating a strict interpretation of the establishment clause, "constitutionalized" Thomas Jefferson's call for "a wall of separation between church and state." Third, Black set a number of standards for future interpretations of the establishment clause. In this regard Black reasoned that the establishment clause not only prohibits the states and the national government from setting up a church, it is intended to prevent government from aiding one religion or all religions. In addition, the government cannot compel individuals to either attend or not attend a church, or to profess belief or disbelief in any given religion. Similarly, people cannot be punished for their religious beliefs, or for either church attendance or nonattendance. Black also asserted that a tax should not be levied to support religious institutions or activities.

Ironically, while Justice Black employed separationist rhetoric that echoed the writings of Jefferson and James Madison, he did reach an accommodationist conclusion by ruling that the reimbursement program was constitutional. To this end he argued that the aid was secular in the sense that the primary beneficiaries of the program were individual students and their parents, not religious institutions. Black, in this regard, followed the "child benefit" theory introduced by the Court in 1930 in *Cochran v. Louisiana Board of Education.*

Black made the analogy that just as it would be irrational to cite the establishment clause as a reason to exclude religious schools from police and fire protection, facilitating transportation to and from accredited schools was simply a matter of public safety and not an effort by the state to directly aid religious institutions. Rather than being an adversary of religion, the state, according to Black, should maintain a position of neutrality.

Justice Rutledge agreed with the majority on the need for a strict separation between church and state. He proclaimed that the purpose of the establishment clause was to outlaw the use of public funds for religious purposes in any "guise, form or degree." Rutledge, however, was critical of the majority for its failure to recognize that transportation is an essential component in the operation of a school. For this reason he viewed the reimbursement program as a use of public funds in direct support of the religious schools in question.

Rutledge relied even more heavily on the words of Madison than did Black. Madison's "Memorial and Remonstrance Against Religious Assessments" (Document 22) was even added as an appendix to Rutledge's dissent. Especially important to Rutledge was Madison's admonition that the government should not utilize its power to tax as a conduit to either support or promote religion. Justice Black, after all, had stated, "No tax in any amount, large or small, can be levied to support any religious activities or institutions, whatever they may be called, or whatever form they may adopt to teach or practice religion." For Justice Rutledge this contradiction was the fatal flaw in the majority's holding in *Everson.*

Why was the debate in Virginia in 1785 over a tax assessment in support of religious education important for both Justice Black and Justice Rutledge? Is providing transportation to and from religious schools the equivalent of the police and fire protection that is provided indiscriminately by the government?

* * *

MR. JUSTICE BLACK delivered the opinion of the Court.

* * *

The New Jersey statute is challenged as a "law respecting an establishment of religion." The First Amendment, as made applicable to the states by the Fourteenth . . . commands that a state "shall make no law respecting an establishment of religion, or prohibiting the free exercise thereof. . . ."

The "establishment of religion" clause of the First Amendment means at least this: Neither a state nor the Federal Government can set up a church. Neither can pass laws which aid one religion, aid all religions, or prefer one religion over another. Neither can force nor influence a person to go to or to remain away from church against his will or force him to profess a belief or disbelief in any religion. No person can be punished for entertaining or professing religious beliefs or disbeliefs, for church attendance or non-attendance. No tax in any amount, large or small, can be levied to support any religious activities or institutions, whatever they may be called, or whatever form they may adopt to teach or practice religion. Neither a state nor the Federal Government can, openly or secretly, participate in the affairs of any religious organizations or groups and *vice versa*. In the words of Jefferson, the clause against establishment of religion by law was intended to erect "a wall of separation between church and State." . . .

Measured by these standards, we cannot say that the First Amendment prohibits New Jersey from spending tax-raised funds to pay the bus fares of parochial school pupils as a part of a general program under which it pays the fares of pupils attending public and other schools. It is undoubtedly true that children are helped to get to church schools. There is even a possibility that some of the children might not be sent to the church schools if the parents were compelled to pay their children's bus fares out of their own pockets when transportation to a public school would have been paid for by the State. The same possibility exists where the state requires a local transit company to provide reduced fares to school children including those attending parochial schools, or where a municipally owned transportation system undertakes to carry all school children free of charge. Moreover, state-paid policemen, detailed to protect children going to and from church schools from the very real hazards of traffic, would serve much the same purpose and accomplish much the same result as state provisions intended to guarantee free transportation of a kind which the state deems to be best for the school children's welfare. And parents might refuse to risk their children to the serious danger of traffic accidents going to and from parochial schools, the approaches to which were not protected by policemen. Similarly, parents might be reluctant to permit their children to attend schools which the state had cut off from such general government services as ordinary police and fire protection, connections for sewage disposal, public highways and sidewalks. Of course, cutting off church schools from these services so separate and so indisputably marked off from the religious function, would make it far more difficult for the schools to operate. But such is obviously not the purpose of the First Amendment. That Amendment requires the state to be a neutral in its relations with groups of religious believers and non-believers; it does not require the state to be their adversary. State power is no more to be used so as to handicap religions than it is to favor them. . . .

The First Amendment has erected a wall between church and state. That wall must be kept high and impregnable. We could not approve the slightest breach. New Jersey has not breached it here.

MR. JUSTICE RUTLEDGE, with whom MR. JUSTICE FRANKFURTER, MR. JUSTICE JACKSON, and MR. JUSTICE BURTON agree, dissenting.

* * *

Neither so high nor so impregnable today as yesterday is the wall raised between church and state by Virginia's great statute of religious freedom and the First Amendment, now made applicable to all the states by the Fourteenth. . . .

This case forces us to determine squarely for the first time what was "an establishment of religion" in the First Amendment's conception; and by that measure to decide whether New Jersey's action violates its command. . . .

Not simply an established church, but any law respecting an establishment of religion is forbidden. The Amendment was broadly but not loosely phrased. It is the compact and exact summation of its author's views formed during his long struggle for religious freedom. In Madison's own words characterizing Jefferson's Bill for Establishing Religious Freedom, the guaranty he put in our national charter, like the bill he piloted through the Virginia Assembly, was "a Model of technical precision, and perspicuous brevity." Madison could not have confused "church" and "religion," or "an established church" and "an establish-ment of religion."

The Amendment's purpose was not to strike merely at the official es-tablishment of a single sect, creed, or religion, outlawing only a formal relation such as had prevailed in England and some of the colonies. Necessarily it was to uproot all such relationships. But the object was broader than separating church and state in this narrow sense. It was to create a complete and permanent separation of the spheres of religious and civil authority by comprehensively forbidding every form of public aid or support for religion. . . .

Does New Jersey's action furnish support for religion by use of the taxing power? Certainly it does, if the test remains undiluted as Jefferson and Madison made it, that money taken by taxation from one is not to be used or given to support another's religious training or belief, or in-deed one's own. Today as then the furnishing of "contributions of money for the propagation of opinions which he disbelieves" is the forbidden exaction; and the prohibition is absolute for whatever measure brings that consequence and whatever amount may be sought or given to that end.

The funds used here were raised by taxation. The Court does not dis-pute, nor could it, that their use does in fact give aid and encouragement to religious instruction. It only concludes that this aid is not "support" in law. But Madison and Jefferson were concerned with aid and support in fact, not as a legal conclusion "entangled in precedents." Here parents pay money to send their children to parochial schools and funds raised by taxation are used to reimburse them. This not only helps the children to get to school and the parents to send them. It aids them in a substan-tial way to get the very thing they are sent to the particular school to secure, namely, religious training and teaching. . . .

New Jersey's action therefore exactly fits the type of exaction and the kind of evil at which Madison and Jefferson struck. Under the test they framed it cannot be said that the cost of transportation is no part of the cost of education or of the religious instruction given. That it is a sub-stantial and a necessary element is shown most plainly by the continuing and increasing demand for the state to assume it. Nor is there pretense that it relates only to the secular instruction given in religious schools or that any attempt is or could be made toward allocating proportional shares as between the secular and the religious instruction. It is precisely because the instruction is religious and relates to a particular faith, whether one or another, that parents send their children to religious schools under the *Pierce* doctrine. And the very purpose of the state's contribution is to defray the cost of conveying the pupil to the place where he will receive not simply secular, but also and primarily reli-gious, teaching and guidance. . . .

An appropriation from the public treasury to pay the cost of transportation to Sunday school, to weekday special classes at the church or parish house, or to the meetings of various young people's religious societies, such as the Y.M.C.A., the Y.W.C.A., the Y.M.H.A., the Epworth League, could not withstand the constitutional attack. This would be true, whether or not secular activities were mixed with the religious. If such an appropriation could not stand, then it is hard to see how one becomes valid for the same thing upon the more extended scale of daily instruction. Surely constitutionality does not turn on where or how often the mixed teaching occurs.

Finally, transportation, where it is needed, is as essential to education as any other element. Its cost is as much a part to the total expense, except at times in amount, as the cost of textbooks, of school lunches; of athletic equipment, of writing and other materials; indeed of all other items composing the total burden. Now as always the core of the educational process is the teacher-pupil relationship. Without this the richest equipment and facilities would go for naught. . . . Without buildings, without equipment, without library, textbooks and other materials, and without transportation to bring teacher and pupil together in such an effective teaching environment, there can be not even the skeleton of what our times require. Hardly can it be maintained that transportation is the least essential of these items, or that it does not in fact aid, encourage, sustain and support, just as they do, the very process which is its purpose to accomplish. No less essential is it, or the payment of its cost, than the very teaching in the classroom or payment of the teacher's sustenance. Many types of equipment, now considered essential, better could be done without.

For me, therefore, the feat is impossible to select so indispensable an item from the composite of total costs, and characterize it as not aiding, contributing to, promoting or sustaining the propagation of beliefs which it is the very end of all to bring about. Unless this can be maintained, and the Court does not maintain it, the aid thus given is outlawed. Payment of transportation is no more, nor is it any the less essential to education whether religious or secular, than payment for tuitions, for teachers' salaries, for buildings, equipment and necessary materials. Nor is it any the less directly related, in a school giving religious instruction, to the primary religious objective all those essential items of cost are intended to achieve. No rational line can be drawn between payment for such larger, but not more necessary, items and payment for transportation. . . .

Source: Everson v. Board of Education of Ewing Township, 330 U.S. 1 (1947).

DOCUMENT 49: *Zorach v. Clauson* (1952)

In the 1940s many local school boards across the United States initiated programs whereby public school students were released from their secular studies to receive religious instruction. One of these "released time" programs, in Champaign, Illinois, allowed religious teachers from the community to enter the public schools to teach religion to those students whose parents had voluntarily enrolled them in the program. These weekly sessions consumed from thirty to forty-five minutes of the regular school day. Students who did not receive the religious instruction remained in the public school building and worked on non-religious assignments.

In 1948, just one year after carefully examining the meaning of the establishment clause in *Everson v. Board of Education of Ewing Township* (see Document 48), the United States Supreme Court ruled on the constitutionality of this released time program. In *Illinois ex rel. Mc-Collum v. Board of Education* (1948), the Court held that the introduction of religious instruction into public school classrooms was a violation of the First Amendment's establishment clause. The vote in *McCollum* was 8–1, and the majority opinion was written by Justice Hugo L. Black.

In *Everson* Black had advocated a "high and impregnable" wall of separation between church and state. The Court's holding in *McCollum* was consistent with this separationist language. Black, in *McCollum*, argued that the released time program was "a utilization of the tax-established and tax-supported public school system to aid religious groups to spread their faith."

Four years after the *McCollum* decision, in *Zorach v. Clauson* (1952), the Supreme Court would revisit the constitutionality of released time programs. The Court's attention in *Zorach* was focused on a New York City program that allowed students to attend religion classes off public school grounds. These classes were held during regular school hours, and those students who did not participate remained in their public school buildings. Parents decided whether or not their children would receive religious instruction and, if so, which of the participating religious groups would provide that instruction. The facts in the two cases were virtually identical except that in *McCollum* the religion classes were conducted in the public schools, while in *Zorach* the instruction in question took place in neighboring churches or other buildings not associated with the public school system.

Tessim Zorach and others challenged the New York City system as a violation of the establishment clause. The Supreme Court, however, sustained the constitutionality of this released time program by a vote of six to three. Justice William O. Douglas wrote the majority opinion, while Justices Black, Frankfurter, and Jackson dissented. Black interpreted his own opinion in *McCollum* to include both classes held within a public school and, as in *Zorach*, religious instruction conducted elsewhere. Jackson viewed the New York City program as an example of the coercive power of government being used to promote religion.

Justice Douglas, by contrast, emphasized that the public schools had simply rearranged their schedules to accommodate the needs of a "religious people whose institutions presuppose a Supreme Being." By the 1970s released time programs began to fade from the American educational landscape, but the majority opinion in *Zorach* continues to receive attention due to the strong defense of accommodation as expressed by Justice Douglas.

According to Justice Douglas, how was the *McCollum* case fundamentally different from the *Zorach* case? Why did Justice Black believe that the program in New York City was a "combination" of church and state, as opposed to the separation of church and state? What was the key element in the New York City program that was cited by Justice Jackson as the essence of government coercion?

* * *

MR. JUSTICE DOUGLAS delivered the opinion of the Court.

* * *

This "released time" program involved neither religious instruction in public school classrooms nor the expenditure of public funds. All costs, including the application blanks, are paid by the religious organizations. The case is therefore unlike *McCollum v. Board of Education*, which involved a "released time" program from Illinois. In that case the classrooms were turned over to religious instructors. We accordingly held that the program violated the First Amendment which (by reason of the Fourteenth Amendment) prohibits the states from establishing religion or prohibiting its free exercise.

Appellants, who are taxpayers and residents of New York City and whose children attend its public schools, challenge the present law, contending it is in essence not different from the one involved in the *McCollum* case. Their argument, stated elaborately in various ways, reduces itself to this: the weight and influence of the school is put behind a program for religious instruction; public school teachers police it, keeping tab on students who are released; the classroom activities come to a halt while the students who are released for religious instruction are on leave; the school is a crutch on which the churches are leaning for support in their religious training; without the cooperation of the schools this "released time" program, like the one in the *McCollum* case, would be futile and in-effective. . . .

There is a suggestion that the system involves the use of coercion to get public school students into religious classrooms. There is no evidence in the record before us that supports that conclusion. The present record indeed tells us that the school authorities are neutral in this regard and do no more than release students whose parents so request. If in fact coercion were used, if it were established that any one or more teachers were using their office to persuade or force students to take the religious instruction, a wholly different case would be presented. Hence we put aside that claim of coercion both as respects the "free exercise" of religion and "an establishment of religion" within the meaning of the First Amendment.

Moreover, apart from that claim of coercion, we do not see how New York by this type of "released time" program has made a law respecting an establishment of religion within the meaning of the First Amendment. . . . There cannot be the slightest doubt that the First Amendment reflects the philosophy that Church and State should be separated. And so far as interference with the "free exercise" of religion and an "establishment" of religion are concerned, the separation must be complete and unequivocal. The First Amendment within the scope of its coverage permits no exception; the prohibition is absolute. The First Amendment, however, does not say that in every and all respects there shall be a separation of Church and State. Rather, it studiously defines the manner, the specific ways, in which there shall be no concert or union or dependency one on the other. That is the common sense of the matter. Otherwise the state and religion would be aliens to each other—hostile, suspicious, and even unfriendly. Churches could not be required to pay even property taxes. Municipalities would not be permitted to render police or fire protection to religious groups. Policemen who helped parishioners into their places of worship would violate the Constitution. Prayers in our legislative halls; the appeals to the Almighty in the messages of the Chief Executive; the proclamations making Thanksgiving Day a holiday; "so help me God" in our courtroom oaths—these and all other references to the Almighty that run through our laws, our public rituals, our ceremonies would be flouting the First Amendment. A fastidious atheist or agnostic could even object to the supplication with which the Court opens each session: "God save the United States and this Honorable Court." . . .

We are a religious people whose institutions presuppose a Supreme Being. We guarantee the freedom to worship as one chooses. We make room for as wide a variety of beliefs and creeds as the spiritual needs of man deem necessary. We sponsor an attitude on the part of government that shows no partiality to any one group and that lets each flourish according to the zeal of its adherents and the appeal of its dogma. When the state encourages religious instruction or cooperates with religious authorities by adjusting the schedule of public events to sectarian needs, it follows the best of our traditions. For it then respects the religious nature of our people and accommodates the public service to their spiritual needs. To hold that it may not would be to find in the Constitution a requirement that the government show a callous indifference to religious groups. That would be preferring those who believe in no religion over those who do believe. Government may not finance religious groups nor undertake religious instruction nor blend secular and sectarian education nor use secular institutions to force one or some religion on any person. But we find no constitutional requirement which makes it necessary for government to be hostile to religion and to throw its weight against efforts to widen the effective scope of religious influence. The government must be neutral when it comes to competition between sects. It may not thrust any sect on any person. It may not make a religious observance compulsory. It may not coerce anyone to attend church, to observe a religious holiday, or to take religious instruction. But it can close its doors or suspend its operations as to those who want to repair to their religious sanctuary for worship or instruction. No more than that is undertaken here. . . .

In the *McCollum* case the classrooms were used for religious instruction and the force of the public school was used to promote that instruction. Here, as we have said, the public schools do no more than accommodate their schedules to a program of outside religious instruction. We follow the *McCollum* case. But we cannot expand it to cover the present released time program unless separation of Church and State means that public institutions can make no adjustments of their schedules to accommodate the religious needs of the people. We cannot read into the Bill of Rights such a philosophy of hostility to religion.

MR. JUSTICE BLACK, dissenting.

Illinois ex rel. McCollum v. Board of Education, held invalid as an "establishment of religion" an Illinois system under which school children, compelled by law to go to public schools, were freed from some hours of required school work on condition that they attend special religious classes held in the school buildings. . . .

I see no significant difference between the invalid Illinois system and that of New York here sustained. Except for the use of the school buildings in Illinois, there is no difference between the systems which I consider even worthy of mention. In the New York program, as in that of Illinois, the school authorities release some of the children on the condition that they attend the religious classes, get reports on whether they attend, and hold the other children in the school building until the religious hour is over. As we attempted to make categorically clear, the *McCollum* decision would have been the same if the religious classes had not been held in the school buildings. . . . *McCollum* thus held that Illinois could not constitutionally manipulate the compelled classroom hours of its compulsory school machinery so as to channel children into sectarian classes. Yet that is exactly what the Court holds New York can do. . . .

Difficulty of decision in the hypothetical situations mentioned by the Court, but not now before us, should not confuse the issues in this case. Here the sole question is whether New York can use its compulsory education laws to help religious sects get attendants presumably too unenthusiastic to go unless moved to do so by the pressure of this state machinery. That this is the plan, purpose, design and consequence of the New York program cannot be denied. The state thus makes religious sects beneficiaries of its power to compel children to attend secular schools. Any use of such coercive power by the state to help or hinder some religious sects or to prefer all religious sects over nonbelievers or vice versa is just what I think the First Amendment forbids. In considering whether a state has entered this forbidden field the question is not whether it has entered too far but whether it has entered at all. New York is manipulating its compulsory education laws to help religious sects get pupils. This is not separation but combination of Church and State. . . .

State help to religion injects political and party prejudices into a holy field. It too often substitutes force for prayer, hate for love, and persecution for persuasion. Government should not be allowed, under cover of the soft euphemism of "co-operation," to steal into the sacred area of religious choice.

MR. JUSTICE JACKSON, dissenting.

This released time program is founded upon a use of the State's power of coercion, which, for me, determines its unconstitutionality. Stripped to its essentials, the plan has two stages: first, that the State compel each student to yield a large part of his time for public secular education; and, second, that some of it be "released" to him on condition that he devote it to sectarian religious purposes.

No one suggests that the Constitution would permit the State directly to require this "released" time to be spent "under the control of a duly constituted religious body." This program accomplishes that forbidden result by indirection. If public education were taking so much of the pupils' time as to injure the public or the students' welfare by encroach-ing upon their religious opportunity, simply shortening everyone's school day would facilitate voluntary and optional attendance at Church classes. But that suggestion is rejected upon the ground that if they are made free many students will not go to the Church. Hence, they must be deprived of freedom for this period, with Church attendance put to them as one of the two permissible ways of using it.

The greater effectiveness of this system over voluntary attendance after school hours is due to the truant officer who, if the youngster fails to go to the Church school, dogs him back to the public schoolroom. Here schooling is more or less suspended during the "released time" so the nonreligious attendants will not forge ahead of the churchgoing absen-tees. But it serves as a temporary jail for a pupil who will not go to Church. It takes more subtlety of mind than I possess to deny that this is governmental constraint in support of religion. It is as unconstitu-tional, in my view, when exerted by indirection as when exercised forth-rightly.

As one whose children, as a matter of free choice, have been sent to privately supported Church schools, I may challenge the Court's sug-gestion that opposition to this plan can only be antireligious, atheistic, or agnostic. My evangelistic brethren confuse an objection to compulsion with an objection to religion. It is possible to hold a faith with enough confidence to believe that what should be rendered to God does not need to be decided and collected by Caesar.

The day that this country ceases to be free for irreligion it will cease to be free for religion—except for the sect that can win political power. The same epithetical jurisprudence used by the Court today to beat down those who oppose pressuring children into some religion can devise as good epithets tomorrow against those who object to pressuring them into a favored religion. And, after all, if we concede to the State power and wisdom to single out "duly constituted religious" bodies as exclusive alternatives for compulsory secular instruction, it would be logical to also uphold the power and wisdom to choose the true faith among those "duly constituted." We start down a rough road when we begin to mix compulsory public education with compulsory godliness. . . .

Source: Zorach v. Clauson, 343 U.S. 306 (1952).

DOCUMENT 50: *McGowan v. Maryland* (1961)

On May 29, 1961, the United States Supreme Court announced its decision in *Braunfeld v. Brown* (see Document 38). In this case the

Court held that a Sunday closing law enacted in Pennsylvania was not a violation of the First Amendment's free exercise of religion clause. The law had been challenged by a store owner who was already closing his establishment on Saturdays due to his religious convictions. He objected to the government regulation that prevented him from operating on Sundays, claiming that it was an economic necessity to conduct business six days each week.

On the same day that the Court announced its holding in *Braunfeld* it also decided *McGowan v. Maryland*. As in *Braunfeld*, the subject was a Sunday closing law but, unlike *Braunfeld*, the *McGowan* case required the Court to determine whether or not such a law infringed upon the First Amendment's establishment of religion clause.

Margaret M. McGowan was one of seven employees of a large department store located in Anne Arundel County, Maryland. McGowan and the others had violated a section of the Maryland criminal code by selling miscellaneous items, such as floor wax and a stapler, on a Sunday. It was the appellants' contention that the purpose of the law was to recognize Sunday as the Christian Sabbath and to encourage church attendance. The Supreme Court rejected these allegations by holding that the law in question was not a violation of the establishment clause.

As in *Braunfeld*, Chief Justice Earl Warren wrote the majority opinion in *McGowan*. Warren did concede that when such laws were introduced during the nation's colonial period they did have a sectarian purpose. However, Warren asserted that in post–World War II America, Sunday closing laws were designed to provide a uniform day of rest, a secular goal. The Chief Justice reasoned that it would be improper to void a secular law simply because there was a religious component to the distant ancestor of that law. Such a ruling, in Warren's opinion, would constitute hostility to the public welfare that the contemporary law was intended to promote.

There were a number of exceptions to Maryland's Sunday closing law. For example, "essential" items such as medicine, gasoline, milk, bread, and tobacco products could legally be sold on Sundays. In addition, amusement parks were allowed to operate and sporting events could be scheduled. Retail outlets that did not employ more than one person other than the owner could also operate on Sundays. Warren argued that these exceptions, which were not religious in nature, could be cited as evidence that the state did not intend to promote religion via this statute.

The lone dissent in *McGowan v. Maryland* was offered by Justice William O. Douglas. He challenged the majority by speculating on the discord that would result if the members of a religious minority gained control of a state legislature and then replaced Sunday closing laws with Saturday closing laws. Justice Douglas also declared that Sunday closing laws were derived not from civil authority, but, instead, from the directive in the Third Commandment to "remember the Sabbath day." As a result, the law was a clear violation of the establishment clause because it was designed to "serve and satisfy the religious predispositions of our Christian communities." Obviously, Douglas had abandoned the accommodationist position that he had articulated in 1952 in *Zorach v. Clauson* (see Document 49) in favor of the separationist point of view.

Prohibitions against the sale of alcoholic beverages on Sunday continue to be quite common in the United States. However, with the growth of suburban shopping malls most communities have repealed many of these so-called blue laws that once affected the business life of the nation.

According to Chief Justice Earl Warren, why would it be detrimental to the common good to eliminate laws that coincide with the tenets of some or all religions? Why does Justice Douglas believe that the law in question infringes upon the rights of the minority?

* * *

MR. CHIEF JUSTICE WARREN delivered the opinion of the Court.

* * *

The essence of appellants' "establishment" argument is that Sunday is the Sabbath day of the predominant Christian sects; that the purpose of the enforced stoppage of labor on that day is to facilitate and encourage church attendance; that the purpose of setting Sunday as a day of universal rest is to induce people with no religion or people with marginal religious beliefs to join the predominant Christian sects; that the purpose of the atmosphere of tranquillity created by Sunday closing is to aid the conduct of church services and religious observance of the sacred day. . . .

There is no dispute that the original laws which dealt with Sunday labor were motivated by religious forces. But what we must decide is whether present Sunday legislation, having undergone extensive changes from the earliest forms, still retains its religious character. . . .

. . . [T]he "Establishment" Clause does not ban federal or state regulation of conduct whose reason or effect merely happens to coincide or harmonize with the tenets of some or all religions. In many instances, the Congress or state legislatures conclude that the general welfare of society, wholly apart from any religious considerations, demands such regulation. Thus, for temporal purposes, murder is illegal. And the fact that this agrees with the dictates of the Judaeo-Christian religions while it may disagree with others does not invalidate the regulation. So too with the questions of adultery and polygamy. . . .

In light of the evolution of our Sunday Closing Laws through the centuries, and of their more or less recent emphasis upon secular considerations, it is not difficult to discern that as presently written and administered, most of them, at least, are of a secular rather than of a religious character, and that presently they bear no relationship to establishment of religion as those words are used in the Constitution of the United States.

Throughout this century and longer, both the federal and state governments have oriented their activities very largely toward improvement of the health, safety, recreation and general well-being of our citizens. Numerous laws affecting public health, safety factors in industry, laws affecting hours and conditions of labor of women and children, weekend diversion at parks and beaches, and cultural activities of various kinds, now point the way toward the good life for all. Sunday Closing Laws, like those before us, have become part and parcel of this great governmental concern wholly apart from their original purposes or connotations. The present purpose and effect of most of them is to provide a uniform day of rest for all citizens; the fact that this day is Sunday, a day of particular significance for the dominant Christian sects, does not bar the State from achieving its secular goals. To say that the States cannot prescribe Sunday as a day of rest for these purposes solely because centuries ago such laws had their genesis in religion would give a constitutional interpretation of hostility to the public welfare rather than one of mere separation of church and State. . . .

MR. JUSTICE DOUGLAS, dissenting.

* * *

The institutions of our society are founded on the belief that there is an authority higher than the authority of the State; that there is a moral law which the state is powerless to alter; that the individual possesses rights, conferred by the Creator, which government must respect. . . .

But those who fashioned the First Amendment decided that if and when God is to be served, His service will not be motivated by coercive measures of government. "Congress shall make no law respecting an establishment of religion, or prohibiting the free exercise thereof"—such is the command of the First Amendment made applicable to the State by reason of the Due Process Clause of the Fourteenth. This means, as I understand it, that if a religious leaven is to be worked into the affairs of our people, it is to be done by individuals and groups, not by the Government. . . .

The issue of these cases would therefore be in better focus if we imagined that a state legislature, controlled by orthodox Jews and Seventh-Day Adventists, passed a law making it a crime to keep a shop open on Saturdays. Would a Baptist, Catholic, Methodist, or Presbyterian be compelled to obey that law or go to jail or pay a fine? Or suppose Moslems grew in political strength here and got a law through a state legislature making it a crime to keep a shop open on Fridays. Would the rest of us have to submit under the fear of criminal sanctions? . . .

It seems to me plain that by these laws the States compel one, under sanction of law, to refrain from work or recreation on Sunday because of the majority's religious views about that day. The state by law makes Sunday a symbol of respect or adherence. Refraining from work or recreation in deference to the majority's religious feelings about Sunday is within every person's choice. By what authority can government compel it? . . .

The State can, of course, require one day of rest a week: one day when every shop or factory is closed. Quite a few States make that requirement. Then the "day of rest" becomes purely and simply a health measure. But the Sunday laws operate differently. They force minorities to obey the majority's religious feelings of what is due and proper for a Christian community; they provide a coercive spur to the "weaker brethren," to those who are indifferent to the claims of a Sabbath through apathy or scruple. Can there be any doubt that Christians, now aligned vigorously in favor of these laws, would be as strongly opposed if they were prosecuted under a Moslem law that forbade them from engaging in secular activities on days that violated Moslem scruples?

There is an "establishment" of religion in the constitutional sense if any practice of any religious group has the sanction of law behind it. There is an interference with the "free exercise" of religion if what in conscience one can do or omit doing is required because of the religious scruples of the community. Hence I would declare each of those laws unconstitutional as applied to the complaining parties, whether or not they are members of a sect which observes as its Sabbath a day other than Sunday. . . .

Source: McGowan v. Maryland, 366 U.S. 420 (1961).

DOCUMENT 51: *Engel v. Vitale* (1962)

The New York State Board of Regents, which supervised the state's public school system, composed a prayer which was recommended to local school districts in its "Statement on Moral and Spiritual Training in the Schools." The Board of Education of Union Free School District No. 9 in New Hyde Park, New York, adopted the prayer and required that it be recited at the beginning of each school day in every classroom under its jurisdiction. Participation in this activity was voluntary in the sense that any student could remain silent or even leave the classroom when the prayer was being recited. This prayer read as follows: "Almighty God, we acknowledge our dependence upon Thee, and we beg Thy blessings upon us, our parents, our teachers and our Country."

The parents of ten students, including Steven I. Engel, challenged the school district's decision to require the recitation of a prayer that they asserted was contrary to the religious beliefs and practices of both themselves and their children. The ten petitioners were supported by the American Civil Liberties Union and, together, they claimed that the school board had acted in violation of the establishment clause contained in the First Amendment. The president of the school board was William J. Vitale.

The Court, in a 6–1 decision, held that the recitation of the prayer constituted a "religious activity" that was indeed a violation of the establishment clause, which is applicable to the states via the due process clause of the Fourteenth Amendment. Justice Hugo L. Black, writing for the majority, declared that "it is no part of the business of government to compose official prayers" to be recited by children in public schools. Black recognized that within a classroom there is "coercive pressure" to conform and, as a result, even a nondenominational prayer recited voluntarily would contradict the command of the establishment clause. Justice Black limited his opinion to state-authorized prayer in public schools, and he did not address other references to God or religion by the government such as the words "In God We Trust" on currency.

To support his opinion Justice Black relied heavily upon James Madison's "Memorial and Remonstrance Against Religious Assessments" (see Document 22). In addition to warning that religion is too personal to permit its "unhallowed perversion" by a civil government, Black invoked the words of Madison to reiterate that it is proper to "take alarm at the first experiment on our liberties."

The lone dissent to the majority's separationist holding was authored by Justice Potter Stewart. He viewed the majority opinion as a misapplication of the establishment clause. Stewart reasoned that to invalidate a voluntary moment of prayer was to deny willing students the opportunity to share in the "spiritual heritage of our Nation." To this end he quoted from the Court's accommodationist decision in *Zorach v. Clauson* (see Document 49).

Why does Justice Black contend that "a union of government and religion tends to destroy government and to degrade religion"? What hypothetical action by government does Justice Stewart recognize as an obvious violation of the establishment clause?

* * *

MR. JUSTICE BLACK delivered the opinion of the Court.

* * *

We think that by using its public school system to encourage recitation of the Regents' prayer, the State of New York has adopted a practice wholly inconsistent with the Establishment Clause. There can, of course, be no doubt that New York's program of daily classroom invocation of God's blessings as prescribed in the Regents' prayer is a religious activity. It is a solemn avowal of divine faith and supplication for the blessings of the Almighty. . . .

The petitioners contend among other things that the state laws requiring or permitting use of the Regents' prayer must be struck down as a violation of the Establishment Clause because that prayer was composed by governmental officials as a part of a governmental program to further religious beliefs. For this reason, petitioners argue, the State's use of the Regents' prayer in its public school system breaches the constitutional wall of separation between Church and State. We agree with that contention since we think that the constitutional prohibition against laws respecting an establishment of religion must at least mean that in this country it is no part of the business of government to compose official prayers for any group of the American people to recite as a part of a religious program carried on by government. . . .

There can be no doubt that New York's state prayer program officially establishes the religious beliefs embodied in the Regents' prayer. The respondent's argument to the contrary, which is largely based upon the contention that the Regents' prayer is "non-denominational" and the fact that the program, as modified and approved by state courts, does not require all pupils to recite the prayer but permits those who wish to do so to remain silent or be excused from the room, ignores the essential nature of the program's constitutional defects. Neither the fact that the prayer may be denominationally neutral nor the fact that its observance on the part of the students is voluntary can serve to free it from the limitations of the Establishment Clause, as it might from the Free Exercise Clause, of the First Amendment, both of which are operative against the States by virtue of the Fourteenth Amendment. Although these two clauses may in certain instances overlap, they forbid two quite different kinds of governmental encroachment upon religious freedom. The Establishment Clause, unlike the Free Exercise Clause, does not depend upon any showing of direct governmental compulsion and is violated by the enactment of laws which establish an official religion whether those laws operate directly to coerce nonobserving individuals or not. This is not to say, of course, that laws officially prescribing a particular form of religious worship do not involve coercion of such individuals. When the power, prestige and financial support of government is placed behind a particular religious belief, the indirect coercive pressure upon religious minorities to conform to the prevailing officially approved religion is plain. But the purposes underlying the Establishment Clause go much further than that. Its first and most immediate purpose rested on the belief that a union of government and religion tends to destroy government and to degrade religion. The history of governmentally established religion, both in England and in this country, showed that whenever government had allied itself with one particular form of religion, the inevitable result had been that it had incurred the hatred, disrespect and even contempt of those who held contrary beliefs. That same history showed that many people had lost their respect for any religion that had relied upon the support of government to spread its faith. The Establishment Clause thus stands as an expression of principle on the part of the Founders of our Constitution that religion is too personal, too sacred, too holy, to permit its "unhallowed perversion" by a civil magistrate. Another purpose of the Establishment Clause rested upon an awareness of the historical fact that governmentally established religions and religious persecutions go hand in hand. . . .

MR. JUSTICE STEWART, dissenting.

* * *

With all respect, I think the Court has misapplied a great constitutional principle. I cannot see how an "official religion" is established by letting those who want to say a prayer say it. On the contrary, I think that to deny the wish of these school children to join in reciting this prayer is to deny them the opportunity of sharing in the spiritual heritage of our Nation. . . .

At the opening of each day's Session of this Court we stand, while one of our officials invokes the protection of God. Since the days of John Marshall our Crier has said, "God save the United States and this Honorable Court." Both the Senate and the House of Representatives open their daily Sessions with prayer. Each of our Presidents, from George Washington to John F. Kennedy, has upon assuming his Office asked the protection and help of God.

The Court today says that the state and federal governments are without constitutional power to prescribe any particular form of words to be recited by any group of the American people on any subject touching religion. One of the stanzas of "The Star-Spangled Banner," made our National Anthem by Act of Congress in 1931, contains these verses:

> "Blest with victory and peace, may the heav'n rescued land
> Praise the Pow'r that hath made and preserved us a nation!
> Then conquer we must, when our cause it is just.
> And this be our motto 'In God is our Trust.' "

In 1954 Congress added a phrase to the Pledge of Allegiance to the Flag so that it now contains the words "one Nation *under God*, indivisible, with liberty and justice for all." In 1952 Congress enacted legislation calling upon the President each year to proclaim a National Day of Prayer. Since 1865 the words "IN GOD WE TRUST" have been impressed on our coins.

Countless similar examples could be listed, but there is no need to belabor the obvious. It was all summed up by this Court just ten years ago in a single sentence: "We are a religious people whose institutions presuppose a Supreme Being." *Zorach v. Clauson.*

I do not believe that this Court, or the Congress, or the President has by the actions and practices I have mentioned established an "official religion" in violation of the Constitution. And I do not believe the State of New York has done so in this case. What each has done has been to recognize and to follow the deeply entrenched and highly cherished spiritual traditions of our Nation—traditions which come down to us from those who almost two hundred years ago avowed their "firm Reliance on the Protection of Divine Providence" when they proclaimed the freedom and independence of this brave new world.

I dissent.

Source: Engel v. Vitale, 370 U.S. 421 (1962).

DOCUMENT 52: *School District of Abington Township, Pennsylvania v. Schempp* (1963)

In 1959 the Pennsylvania legislature enacted a law that required each public school day to open with the reading of at least ten verses from the Bible. This reading was to be completed without comment, and any student could be excused from the exercise upon the written request of his parent or guardian. At Abington High School, located in a suburb of Philadelphia, the ten verses were selected by a student and then read to the student body over the school's intercommunication system. The reading was followed by a recitation of the Lord's Prayer, for which students were asked to stand and repeat its words, and the pledge to the national flag.

The parents of Roger and Donna Schempp, two students at Abington High School, considered having their children excused from the Bible readings, but they feared that exercising this option would adversely affect the children's relationships with their teachers and classmates. They therefore challenged the statute that mandated Bible reading in the state's public schools as a violation of the First Amendment's establishment clause. The Schempp family attended the Unitarian Church, and both the children and their father, Edward, testified that specific religious doctrines conveyed by a literal reading of the Bible were contrary to their religious beliefs.

Before the United States Supreme Court it was argued that the purpose of the statute was to teach morality, not religion. To this end it was contended that while the Bible is undeniably a religious document, these "lessons in morality" were not only traditional, they were secular in nature. Conversely, counsel for the Schempp family asserted that it is impossible to separate the moral content of the Bible from its theological content.

The Supreme Court's holding in *Schempp* and a companion case that had originated in Baltimore, Maryland, came just one year after the Court had addressed the issue of school prayer in *Engel v. Vitale* (see Document 51). As in the *Engel* case, the participation of any given student was not compulsory. Unlike *Engel*, however, the words in question in *Schempp* had not been authored by the state.

In an 8–1 decision the Supreme Court ruled that the Pennsylvania statute was an unconstitutional violation of the establishment clause, which is applicable to the states via the Fourteenth Amendment. Justice Tom C. Clark, writing for the majority, postulated that a Bible reading was clearly a religious exercise and, as such, was in contradiction of the neutrality standard that each state is required to uphold.

Most important, Justice Clark formulated a two-part test that could be used in subsequent cases to measure the contents of a statute or action against the dictates of the establishment clause. First, according to Clark, if a law is to be regarded as constitutional it must exhibit a valid secular purpose. Second, the primary effect of the law should not be to advance or inhibit religion.

As in *Engel*, the lone dissent in *Schempp* was authored by Justice Potter Stewart. He viewed the Bible reading activity as permissible under the free exercise of religion clause which is also contained in the First Amendment. A denial of this activity, according to Stewart, would be emblematic of a hostility toward religion, and not neutrality. Justice

Clark, on the other hand, asserted that the majority in this instance is not free to impose its beliefs on religious minorities.

Why did Justice Clark view the Pennsylvania statute as unconstitutional even though participation was optional? According to Justice Stewart, what would constitute coercion on the part of the state regarding the promulgation of religious beliefs?

* * *

MR. JUSTICE CLARK delivered the opinion of the Court.

* * *

Applying the Establishment Clause principles to the cases at bar we find that the States are requiring the selection and reading at the opening of the school day of verses from the Holy Bible and the recitation of the Lord's Prayer by the students in unison. These exercises are prescribed as part of the curricular activities of students who are required by law to attend school. They are held in the school buildings under the supervision and with the participation of teachers employed in those schools. . . . We agree with the trial court's finding as to the religious character of the exercises. Given that finding, the exercises and the law requiring them are in violation of the Establishment Clause.

The conclusion follows that in both cases the laws require religious exercises and such exercises are being conducted in direct violation of the rights of the appellees and petitioners. Nor are these required exercises mitigated by the fact that individual students may absent themselves upon parental request, for that fact furnishes no defense to a claim of unconstitutionality under the Establishment Clause. See *Engel v. Vitale.* Further, it is no defense to urge that the religious practices here may be relatively minor encroachments on the First Amendment. The breach of neutrality that is today a trickling stream may all too soon become a raging torrent and, in the words of Madison, "it is proper to take alarm at the first experiment on our liberties." (Memorial and Remonstrance Against Religious Assessments.)

It is insisted that unless these religious exercises are permitted a "religion of secularism" is established in the schools. We argue of course that the State may not establish a "religion of secularism" in the sense of affirmatively opposing or showing hostility to religion, thus "preferring those who believe in no religion over those who do believe." (*Zorach v. Clauson.*) We do not agree, however, that this decision in any sense has that effect. In addition, it might well be said that one's education is not complete without a study of comparative religion or the history of religion and its relationship to the advancement of civilization. It certainly may be said that the Bible is worthy of study for its literary and historic qualities. Nothing we have said here indicates that such study of the Bible or of religion, when presented objectively as part of a secular program of education, may not be effected consistently with the First Amendment. But the exercises here do not fall into those categories. They are religious exercises, required by the States in violation of the command of the First Amendment that the Government maintain strict neutrality, neither aiding nor opposing religion.

Finally, we cannot accept that the concept of neutrality, which does not permit a State to require a religious exercise even with the consent of the majority of those affected, collides with the majority's right to free exercise of religion. While the Free Exercise Clause clearly prohibits the use of state action to deny the rights of free exercise to *anyone*, it has never meant that a majority could use the machinery of the State to practice its beliefs. . . .

MR. JUSTICE STEWART, dissenting.

* * *

The First Amendment declares that "Congress shall make no law respecting an establishment of religion, or prohibiting the free exercise thereof. . . ." It is, I think, a fallacious oversimplification to regard these two provisions of establishing a single constitutional standard of "separation of church and state," which can be mechanically applied in every case to delineate the required boundaries between government and religion. We err in the first place if we do not recognize, as a matter of history and as a matter of the imperatives of our free society, that religion and government must necessarily interact in countless ways. Secondly, the fact is that while in many contexts the Establishment Clause and the Free Exercise Clause fully complement each other, there are areas in which a doctrinaire reading of the Establishment Clause leads to irreconcilable conflict with the Free Exercise Clause. . . .

That the central value embodied in the First Amendment—and, more particularly in the guarantee of "liberty" contained in the Fourteenth— is the safeguarding of an individual's right to free exercise of his religion has been consistently recognized. . . .

It is this concept of constitutional protection embodied in our decisions which makes the cases before us such difficult ones for me. For there is involved in these cases a substantial free exercise claim on the part of those who affirmatively desire to have their children's school day open with the reading of passages from the Bible. . . .

What seems to me to be of paramount importance, then, is recognition of the fact that the claim advanced here in favor of Bible reading is sufficiently substantial to make simple reference to the constitutional phrase "establishment of religion" as inadequate an analysis of the cases before us as the ritualistic invocation of the nonconstitutional phrase "separation of church and state." What these cases compel, rather, is an analysis of just what the "neutrality" is which is required by the interplay of the Establishment and Free Exercise Clauses of the First Amendment, as imbedded in the Fourteenth. . . .

The governmental neutrality which the First and Fourteenth Amendments require in the cases before us, in other words, is the extension of evenhanded treatment to all who believe, doubt, or disbelieve—a refusal on the part of the State to weight the scales of private choice. In these cases, therefore, what is involved is not state action based on impermissible categories, but rather an attempt by the State to accommodate those differences which the existence in our society of a variety of religious beliefs makes inevitable. The Constitution requires that such efforts be struck down only if they are proven to entail the use of the secular authority of government to coerce a preference among such beliefs.

It may well be, as has been argued to us, that even the supposed benefits to be derived from noncoercive religious exercises in public schools are incommensurate with the administrative problems which they would create. The choice involved, however, is one for each local community and its school board, and not for this Court. For, as I have said, religious exercises are not constitutionally invalid if they simply reflect differences which exist in the society from which the school draws its pupils. They become constitutionally invalid only if their administration places the sanction of secular authority behind one or more particular religious or irreligious beliefs.

To be specific, it seems to be clear that certain types of exercises would present situations in which no possibility of coercion on the part of secular officials could be claimed to exist. Thus, if such exercises were held either before or after the official school day, or if the school schedule were such that participation were merely one among a number of desirable alternatives, it could hardly be contended that the exercises did anything more than to provide an opportunity for the voluntary expression of religious belief. On the other hand, a law which provided for religious exercises during the school day and which contained no excusal provision would obviously be unconstitutionally coercive upon those who did not wish to participate. And even under a law containing an excusal provision, if the exercises were held during the school day, and no equally desirable alternative were provided by the school authorities, the likelihood that children might be under at least some psychological compulsion to participate would be great. In a case such as the latter, however, I think we would err if we *assumed* such coercion in the absence of any evidence.

Viewed in this light, it seems to be clear that the records in both of the cases before us are wholly inadequate to support an informed or responsible decision. Both cases involve provisions which explicitly permit any student who wishes, to be excused from participation in the exercises. There is no evidence in either case as to whether there would exist any coercion of any kind upon a student who did not want to participate. . . .

Source: School District of Abington Township, Pennsylvania v. Schempp, 374 U.S. 203 (1963).

DOCUMENT 53: *Board of Education of Central School District No. 1 v. Allen* (1968)

In 1965 Section 701 of New York's Education Law was amended to require local school boards to purchase textbooks and to lend them without charge "to all children residing in such district who are enrolled in grades seven to twelve of a public or private school which complies with the compulsory education law." Parochial school students were eligible for this program, but only textbooks approved by public school officials could be loaned. It was therefore argued that since only secular textbooks were involved, the neutrality of the state with regard to religion would not be compromised. Supporters of the legislation also argued that the purpose of the law was to benefit all students, regardless of the type of accredited school that they attended.

Members of the school board that had jurisdiction over Rensselaer and Columbia Counties in New York viewed the legislation as a violation of the First Amendment's establishment clause, which applies to individual states via the Fourteenth Amendment. The school board members feared that if they failed to loan textbooks to parochial school students they would be removed from office by James E. Allen, Jr., New York's Commissioner of Education. Faced with the dilemma of having to comply with a law that they considered to be unconstitutional to retain their jobs, the school board decided to challenge the validity of the statute.

When this dispute reached the United States Supreme Court, in 1968, the justices relied heavily upon two precedents. In the first, *Cochran v. Louisiana Board of Education* (1930), the Court upheld the constitutionality of a law that required the state of Louisiana to provide all school children, including those in parochial schools, with textbooks paid for with public funds. Rather than being challenged as a violation of the establishment clause, however, this practice was alleged to have been contrary to the property component of the Fourteenth Amendment's due process clause.

In the second precedent, *Everson v. Board of Education of Ewing Township* (see Document 48), the Court upheld the constitutionality of a program whereby the parents of parochial school students were reimbursed by the state for the cost of bus transportation to and from school. Justice Hugo L. Black, writing for the majority in *Everson*, considered this aid to be secular in nature, and not an unconstitutional violation of the establishment clause, because the primary beneficiaries were the students and not religious institutions. This "child benefit" theory had been introduced in *Cochran*.

The Supreme Court ruled that the New York law that required local school boards to provide secular textbooks to students in religious schools was constitutional, citing the child benefit theory evident in both *Cochran* and *Everson*. Justice Byron R. White wrote the majority opinion in *Board of Education of Central School District No. 1 v. Allen* (1968), which was decided by a 6–3 vote. The decision demonstrated that an accommodationist holding could be reached by justices following the two-prong test that had been formulated in *School District of Abington Township, Pennsylvania v. Schempp* (see Document 52).

Ironically, Justice Black, who wrote the majority opinion in *Everson*, wrote in dissent in *Allen*. Justices William O. Douglas and Abe Fortas also wrote dissenting opinions in this case. Black, Douglas, and Fortas all felt that furnishing textbooks, unlike providing bus transportation, was evidence of direct state aid to religious institutions.

To square with the dictates of the establishment clause, according to the Supreme Court's *Schempp* decision, a law must exhibit a secular purpose and neither advance nor inhibit religion. Why did Justice White believe that the New York statute examined in *Allen* "passed" both prongs of this test? Why did Justice Black reject the contention that a ruling in favor of the constitutionality of the New York textbook statute would be consistent with the majority opinion that he had authored two decades earlier in *Everson*? Was Justice Douglas' contention that even a secular textbook could contain "shadings" that would continually remind parochial school students of the sectarian orientation of their education a realistic fear, and, if so, would this constitute a violation of the establishment clause? According to Justice Fortas, what was the most "vital aspect" of the New York statute?

* * *

MR. JUSTICE WHITE delivered the opinion of the Court.

* * *

Underlying these cases, and underlying also the legislative judgments that have preceded the court decisions, has been a recognition that private education has played and is playing a significant and valuable role in raising national levels of knowledge, competence, and experience. Americans care about the quality of the secular education available to their children. They have considered high quality education to be an indispensable ingredient for achieving the kind of nation, and the kind of citizenry, that they have desired to create. Considering this attitude, the continued willingness to rely on private school systems, including parochial systems, strongly suggests that a wide segment of informed opinion, legislative and otherwise, has found that those schools do an acceptable job of providing secular education to their students. This judgment is further evidence that parochial schools are performing, in addition to their sectarian function, the task of secular education.

Against this background of judgment and experience, unchallenged in the meager record before us in this case, we cannot agree with appellants either that all teaching in a sectarian school is religious or that the processes of secular and religious training are so intertwined that secular textbooks furnished to students by the public are in fact instrumental in the teaching of religion. This case comes to us after summary judgment entered on the pleadings. Nothing in this record supports the proposition that all textbooks, whether they deal with mathematics, physics, foreign languages, history, or literature, are used by the parochial schools to teach religion. No evidence has been offered about particular schools, particular courses, particular teachers, or particular books. We are unable to hold, based solely on judicial notice, that this statute results in unconstitutional involvement of the State with religious instruction or that 701, for this or the other reasons urged, is a law respecting the establishment of religion within the meaning of the First Amendment. . . .

MR. JUSTICE BLACK, dissenting.

* * *

I know of no prior opinion of this Court upon which the majority here can rightfully rely to support its holding this New York law constitutional. In saying this, I am not unmindful of the fact that the New York Court of Appeals purported to follow Everson v. Board of Education, in which this Court, in an opinion written by me, upheld a New Jersey law authorizing reimbursement to parents for the transportation of children attending sectarian schools. That law did not attempt to deny the benefit of its general terms to children of any faith going to any legally authorized school. Thus, it was treated in the same way as a general law paying the streetcar fare *of all school children*, or a law providing midday lunches for all children or all school children, or a law to provide police protection for children going to and from school, or general laws to provide police and fire protection for buildings, including, of course, churches and church school buildings as well as others.

As my Brother DOUGLAS so forcefully shows, in an argument with which I fully agree, upholding a State's power to pay bus or streetcar fares for school children cannot provide support for the validity of a state law using tax-raised funds to buy school books for a religious school. The First Amendment's bar to establishment of religion must preclude a State from using funds levied from all of its citizens to purchase books for use by sectarian schools, which, although "secular," realistically will in some way inevitably tend to propagate the religious views of the favored sect. Books are the most essential tool of education since they contain the resources of knowledge which the educational process is designed to exploit. In this sense it is not difficult to distinguish books, which are the heart of any school, from bus fares, which provide a convenient and helpful general public transportation service. With respect to the former, state financial support actively and directly assists the teaching and propagation of sectarian religious viewpoints in clear conflict with the First Amendment's establishment bar; with respect to the latter, the State merely provides a general and nondiscriminatory transportation service in no way related to substantive religious views and beliefs. . . .

I still subscribe to the belief that tax-raised funds cannot constitutionally be used to support religious schools, buy their school books, erect their buildings, pay their teachers, or pay any other of their maintenance expenses, even to the extent of one penny. The First Amendment's prohibition against governmental establishment of religion was written on the assumption that state aid to religion and religious schools generates discord, disharmony, hatred, and strife among our people, and that any government that supplies such aids is to that extent a tyranny. And I still believe that the only way to protect minority religious groups from majority groups in this country is to keep the wall of separation between church and state high and impregnable as the First and Fourteenth Amendments provide. The Court's affirmance here bodes nothing but evil to religious peace in this country.

MR. JUSTICE DOUGLAS, dissenting.

* * *

Whatever may be said of *Everson*, there is nothing ideological about a bus. There is nothing ideological about a school lunch, or a public nurse, or a scholarship. The constitutionality of such public aid to students in parochial schools turns on considerations not present in this textbook case. The textbook goes to the very heart of education in a parochial school. It is the chief, although not solitary, instrumentality for propagating a particular religious creed or faith. How can we possibly approve such state aid to a religion? . . .

Even where the treatment given to a particular topic in a school textbook is not blatantly sectarian, it will necessarily have certain shadings that will lead a parochial school to prefer one text over another. . . .

The initiative to select and requisition "the books desired" is with the parochial school. Powerful religious-political pressures will therefore be on the state agencies to provide the books that are desired.

These then are the battlegrounds where control of textbook distribution will be won or lost. Now that "secular" textbooks will pour into religious schools, we can rest assured that a contest will be on to provide those books for religious schools which the dominant religious group concludes best reflect the theocentric or other philosophy of the particular church.

The stakes are now extremely high—just as they were in the school prayer cases (see Engel v. Vitale)—to obtain approval of what is "proper." For the "proper" books will radiate the "correct" religious view not only in the parochial school but in the public school as well. . . .

MR. JUSTICE FORTAS, dissenting.

The majority opinion of the Court upholds the New York statute by ignoring a vital aspect of it. Public funds are used to buy, for students in sectarian schools, textbooks which are selected and prescribed by the sectarian schools themselves. As my Brother DOUGLAS points out, despite the transparent camouflage that the books are furnished to students, the reality is that they are selected and their use is prescribed by the sectarian authorities. The child must use the prescribed book. He cannot use a different book prescribed for use in the public schools. The State cannot choose the book to be used. It is true that the public school boards must "approve" the book selected by the sectarian authorities; but this has no real significance. . . .

This is not a "general" program. It is a specific program to use state funds to buy books prescribed by sectarian schools which, in New York, are primarily Catholic, Jewish, and Lutheran sponsored schools. It could be called a "general" program only if the school books made available to all children were precisely the same—the books selected for and used in the public schools. But this program is not one in which all children are treated alike, regardless of where they go to school. This program, in its unconstitutional features, is hand-tailored to satisfy the specific needs of sectarian schools. Children attending such schools are given *special* books—books selected by the sectarian authorities. How can this be other than the use of public money to aid those sectarian establishments? . . .

Source: Board of Education of Central School District No. 1 v. Allen, 392 U.S. 236 (1968).

DOCUMENT 54: *Walz v. Tax Commission of the City of New York* (1970)

Frederick Walz, a property owner in Richmond County, New York, sought an injunction to prevent the New York City Tax Commission from granting tax exemptions to religious organizations for properties used solely for religious worship. Walz claimed that this type of exemption required those property owners who were not exempt to make involuntary contributions to religious groups. This, according to Walz, was a violation of the First Amendment's establishment clause, which applies to the states via the due process clause of the Fourteenth Amendment.

The New York Constitution authorized property tax exemptions for religious, educational, and charitable organizations that were not operating for a profit. Historically, tax exemptions of this nature have been utilized in all of the states. This fact, however, did not deter Walz from challenging the constitutionality of the practice in New York.

Upon appeal, the dispute eventually reached the United States Supreme Court, where oral arguments were heard in November 1969. Chief Justice Earl Warren had retired from the Court in June 1969, and Court observers were interested in how establishment clause cases would be adjudicated under the leadership of his replacement, Warren E. Burger. In May 1970 these observers had an answer, as the majority opinion in *Walz* was written by the new Chief Justice.

Seven years earlier, in *School District of Abington Township, Pennsylvania v. Schempp* (see Document 52), the Supreme Court had devised a two-part test to measure the constitutionality of an alleged violation of the establishment clause. In addition to exhibiting a secular purpose, a law was expected to neither advance nor inhibit religion. Chief Justice Burger concluded that the purpose of the property tax exemption was not to establish or sponsor religion. He also interpreted the second part of the *Schempp* test to be an evaluation of legislative purpose as he concluded that the intent of the tax exemption was neither the advancement nor the inhibition of religion.

Burger, however, focused his attention on the effect of the exemption. In this regard he introduced a new standard to examine the constitutionality of alleged violations of the establishment clause. To be valid, Burger argued, a law must not produce an excessive government entanglement with religion. He conceded that such a test was one of degree, but in this particular case he concluded that the elimination of the exemption would increase the involvement of government with religion. By an 8–1 vote the practice of granting property tax exemptions to religious organizations was upheld by the Supreme Court.

Chief Justice Burger's majority opinion in *Walz*, in addition to introducing an additional standard to be applied in establishment clause cases, demonstrated that he generally favored a policy of accommodation with regard to church and state issues. He recognized that the Constitution requires the government to maintain a position of neutrality, but he also advised the public that an absolute separation of church and state was simply impossible.

The lone dissent in *Walz* was by Justice William O. Douglas. He argued that the doctrine of selective incorporation places strict constitutional restraints on the states, including adherence to the dictates of the establishment clause. For Douglas, who relied heavily upon the reasoning contained in James Madison's "Memorial and Remonstrance Against Religious Assessments" (see Document 22), the property tax exemption was simply a subsidy for religious organizations that contravened the establishment clause.

Why did Chief Justice Burger contend that a property tax exemption for religious organizations was the best possible way to maintain a separation of church and state? Why did Justice Douglas view the exemption as a subsidy that would improperly benefit religious groups?

* * *

MR. CHIEF JUSTICE BURGER delivered the opinion of the Court.

* * *

We cannot read New York's statute as attempting to establish religion; it is simply sparing the exercise of religion from the burden of property taxation levied on private profit institutions.

We find it unnecessary to justify the tax exemption on the social welfare services or "good works" that some churches perform for parishioners and others—family counseling, aid to the elderly and the infirm, and to children. Churches vary substantially in the scope of such services; programs expand or contract according to resources and need. As public-sponsored programs enlarge, private aid from the church sector may diminish. The extent of social services may vary, depending on whether the church serves an urban or rural, a rich or poor constituency.

To give emphasis to so variable an aspect of the work of religious bodies would introduce an element of governmental evaluation and standards as to the worth of particular social welfare programs, thus producing a kind of continuing day-to-day relationship which the policy of neutrality seeks to minimize. Hence, the use of a social welfare yardstick as a significant element to qualify for tax exemption could conceivably give rise to confrontations that could escalate to constitutional dimensions.

Determining that the legislative purpose of tax exemption is not aimed at establishing, sponsoring, or supporting religion does not end the inquiry, however. We must also be sure that the end result—the effect— is not an excessive government entanglement with religion. The test is inescapably one of degree. Either course, taxation of churches or exemption, occasions some degree of involvement with religion. Elimination of exemption would tend to expand the involvement of government by giving rise to tax valuation of church property, tax liens, tax foreclosures, and the direct confrontations and conflicts that follow in the train of those legal processes.

Granting tax exemptions to churches necessarily operates to afford an indirect economic benefit and also gives rise to some, but yet a lesser, involvement than taxing them. In analyzing either alternative the questions are whether the involvement is excessive, and whether it is a continuing one calling for official and continuing surveillance leading to an impermissible degree of entanglement. . . .

The grant of a tax exemption is not sponsorship since the government does not transfer part of its revenue to churches but simply abstains from demanding that the church support the state. No one has ever suggested that tax exemption has converted libraries, art galleries, or hospitals into arms of the state or put employees "on the public payroll." There is no genuine nexus between tax exemption and establishment of religion. . . . The exemption creates only a minimal and remote involvement between church and state and far less than taxation of churches. It restricts the fiscal relationship between church and state, and tends to complement and reinforce the desired separation insulating each from the other. . . .

All of the 50 States provide for tax exemption of places of worship, most of them doing so by constitutional guarantees. For so long as federal income taxes have had any potential impact on churches—over 75 years—religious organizations have been expressly exempt from the tax. Such treatment is an "aid" to churches no more and no less in principle than the real estate tax exemption granted by States. Few concepts are more deeply embedded in the fabric of our national life, beginning with pre-Revolutionary colonial times, than for the government to exercise at the very least this kind of benevolent neutrality toward churches and religious exercise generally so long as none was favored over others and none suffered interference. . . .

MR. JUSTICE DOUGLAS, dissenting.

* * *

Churches perform some functions that a State would constitutionally be empowered to perform. I refer to nonsectarian social welfare operations such as the care of orphaned children and the destitute and people who are sick. A tax exemption to agencies performing those functions would therefore be as constitutionally proper as the grant of direct subsidies to them. Under the First Amendment a State may not, however, provide worship if private groups fail to do so. . . .

That is a major difference between churches on the one hand and the rest of the nonprofit organizations on the other. Government could provide or finance operas, hospitals, historical societies, and all the rest because they represent social welfare programs within the reach of the police power. In contrast, government may not provide or finance worship because of the Establishment Clause any more than it may single out "atheistic" or "agnostic" centers or groups and create or finance them. . . .

On the record of this case, the church *qua* nonprofit, charitable organization is intertwined with the church *qua* church. A church may use the same facilities, resources, and personnel in carrying out both its secular and its sectarian activities. The two are unitary and on the present record have not been separated one from the other. The state has a public policy of encouraging private public welfare organizations, which it desires to encourage through tax exemption. Why may it not do so and include churches *qua* welfare organizations on a nondiscriminatory basis? That avoids, it is argued, a discrimination against churches and in a real sense maintains neutrality toward religion which the First Amendment was designed to foster. Welfare services, whether performed by churches or by nonreligious groups, may well serve the public welfare.

Whether a particular church seeking an exemption for its welfare work could constitutionally pass muster would depend on the special facts. The assumption is that the church is a purely private institution, promoting a sectarian cause. The creed, teaching, and beliefs of one may be undesirable or even repulsive to others. Its sectarian faith sets it apart from all others and makes it difficult to equate its constituency with the general public. The extent that its facilities are open to all may only indicate the nature of its proselytism. Yet though a church covers up its religious symbols in welfare work its welfare activities may merely be a phase of sectarian activity. I have said enough to indicate the nature of this tax exemption problem.

Direct financial aid to church or tax exemptions to the church *qua* church is not, in my view, even arguably permitted. Sectarian causes are certainly not anti-public and many would rate their own church or perhaps all churches as the highest form of welfare. The difficulty is that sectarian causes must remain in the private domain not subject to public control or subsidy. That seems to me to be the requirement of the Establishment Clause. . . .

The exemptions provided here insofar as welfare projects are concerned may have the ring of neutrality. But subsidies either through direct grant or tax exemption for sectarian causes, whether carried on by church *qua* church or by church *qua* welfare agency, must be treated differently, lest we in time allow the church *qua* church to be on the public payroll, which, I fear, is imminent. . . .

Source: Walz v. Tax Commission of the City of New York, 397 U.S. 664 (1970).

DOCUMENT 55: *Lemon v. Kurtzman, Superintendent of Public Instruction of Pennsylvania* (1971)

In 1968 the Pennsylvania legislature enacted the Nonpublic Elementary and Secondary Education Act. The legislation authorized the use of public funds to directly reimburse nonpublic schools, including parochial schools, for teachers' salaries, textbooks, and instructional materials. Teachers could only be reimbursed for the teaching of secular subjects, and textbooks and instructional materials had to be approved by the state's Superintendent of Public Instruction. In addition, participating schools were required to keep separate records of their secular and nonsecular expenses.

When the statute was enacted there were almost 1,200 nonpublic schools in Pennsylvania that were attended by over 535,000 students, more than 20 percent of the total number of pupils in the state. The vast majority of these schools were affiliated with the Roman Catholic Church. Following the passage of the bill the state spent about $5 million annually to reimburse nonpublic schools for the teaching of secular subjects.

Members of the Pennsylvania legislature who had supported the bill had expressed a concern that the state's nonpublic schools were in a crisis situation due to rapidly rising costs. Nonetheless, Alton Lemon, a Pennsylvania resident and taxpayer, challenged the constitutionality of the law. It was his contention that the use of public funds to support religious schools violated the religion clauses of the First Amendment, which apply to the states via the due process clause of the Fourteenth Amendment.

The legal challenge initiated by Alton Lemon eventually reached the

United States Supreme Court on appeal. By the time *Lemon v. Kurtzman, Superintendent of Public Instruction of Pennsylvania* was heard and decided by the Court, in 1971, it had been joined by a companion case, *Earley v. DiCenso.* This second case required the Court to examine Rhode Island's 1969 Salary Supplement Act. This law authorized the use of public funds to supplement the salaries of teachers in nonpublic schools by up to 15 percent for the teaching of secular subjects. The act stipulated that, once supplemented, the salary of a qualifying teacher was not to exceed the maximum salary paid to teachers in Rhode Island's public schools.

Teachers in parochial schools were eligible for the salary supplement, but all applicants had to agree in writing that they would not teach religion as long as they were enrolled in the program. When the law was enacted in 1969 about 95 percent of the nonpublic schools in Rhode Island were affiliated with the Roman Catholic Church. In addition, of the 250 teachers who applied for the salary supplementation, all were employed by Catholic schools. Members of the Rhode Island legislature, who had originally supported the bill that would come to sanction the use of public funds to increase the salaries of such teachers, cited a legislative finding that the quality of education available in nonpublic elementary schools had been jeopardized by the rapidly rising salaries needed to attract competent and dedicated teachers.

The Supreme Court held that the statutes of both Pennsylvania and Rhode Island were unconstitutional. Chief Justice Warren E. Burger wrote the majority opinion. The vote in *Lemon,* the Pennsylvania case, was 8–0, with Justice Thurgood Marshall not participating. Justice Byron R. White wrote a dissent in the Rhode Island case, *Earley,* which was decided by an 8–1 margin.

Chief Justice Burger observed that, far from creating a wall of separation between church and state, as Thomas Jefferson had proclaimed in his famous metaphor, the establishment clause creates "a blurred, indistinct, and variable barrier depending on all the circumstances of a particular relationship." In earlier accommodationist rulings the Court had allowed the use of public funds to provide students in parochial schools with textbooks (see Document 53) and to reimburse parents for the cost of transporting their children to and from parochial schools (see Document 48). Burger, however, viewed both of the statutes in question as laws that fostered an excessive government entanglement with religion by making religious institutions, rather than individual students or their parents, the direct beneficiaries of state aid.

Burger had introduced the excessive entanglement standard in 1970, just one year prior to *Lemon,* when he wrote the majority opinion in *Walz v. Tax Commission of the City of New York* (see Document 54).

In *Lemon* Burger clarified that the relatively new excessive entanglement test was not intended to replace the two-part test announced in *School District of Abington Township, Pennsylvania v. Schempp* (see Document 52). Rather, Burger added the excessive entanglement test to the two-part test from the *Schempp* decision to create a tripartite test to evaluate possible violations of the establishment clause.

The resulting *Lemon* test, which Burger asserted was the product of "cumulative criteria developed by the Court over many years," stipulated that to be considered constitutional a law was required to pass all three parts of the test. First, a law must have a secular purpose. Second, the primary effect of a law must neither advance nor inhibit religion. Third, a law must not foster an excessive government entanglement with religion.

Concerning the Pennsylvania and Rhode Island statutes, Burger concluded that both laws had a secular purpose, the improvement of the teaching of secular subjects in nonpublic schools. He also concluded that neither statute had the effect of either advancing or inhibiting religion. However, Burger was especially troubled by the prospect of state surveillance of a religious school's activities that would be necessary to differentiate secular expenses from sectarian expenses. He therefore concluded that the impact of such a law would be an unconstitutional entanglement between church and state.

Justice White, however, rejected the contention that the administration of the Rhode Island program produced an excessive government entanglement with religion. He also stated that there was no evidence that the Pennsylvania statute had resulted in the use of public funds for the teaching of sectarian material in secular classes.

Why did Chief Justice Burger believe that the passage of laws that authorize state aid to parochial schools will inevitably lead to divisive political battles? According to Justice White, what is the "insoluble paradox" created by the Court in its reading of the Rhode Island statute?

* * *

MR. CHIEF JUSTICE BURGER delivered the opinion of the Court.

* * *

Every analysis in this area must begin with consideration of the cumulative criteria developed by the Court over many years. Three such tests may be gleaned from our cases. First, the statute must have a secular legislative purpose; second, its principal or primary effect must be one that neither advances nor inhibits religion, *Board of Education v. Allen*

(1968); finally, the statute must not foster "an excessive government entanglement with religion." [*Walz v. Tax Commission* (1970)].

Inquiry into the legislative purposes of the Pennsylvania and Rhode Island statutes affords no basis for a conclusion that the legislative intent was to advance religion. On the contrary, the statutes themselves clearly state that they are intended to enhance the quality of the secular education in all schools covered by the compulsory attendance laws. There is no reason to believe the legislatures meant anything else. A State always has a legitimate concern for maintaining minimum standards in all schools it allows to operate. . . .

In *Allen* the Court acknowledged that secular and religious teachings were not necessarily so intertwined that secular textbooks furnished to students by the State were in fact instrumental in the teaching of religion. The legislatures of Rhode Island and Pennsylvania have concluded that secular and religious education are identifiable and separable. In the abstract we have no quarrel with this conclusion.

The two legislatures, however, have also recognized that church-related elementary and secondary schools have a significant religious mission and that a substantial portion of their activities is religiously oriented. They have therefore sought to create statutory restrictions designed to guarantee the separation between secular and religious educational functions and to ensure that State financial aid supports only the former. All these provisions are precautions taken in candid recognition that these programs approached, even if they did not intrude upon, the forbidden areas under the Religion Clauses. We need not decide whether these legislative precautions restrict the principal or primary effect of the programs to the point where they do not offend the Religion Clauses, for we conclude that the cumulative impact of the entire relationship arising under the statutes in each State involves excessive entanglement between government and religion. . . .

Our prior holdings do not call for total separation between church and state; total separation is not possible in an absolute sense. Some relationship between government and religious organizations is inevitable. . . . Judicial caveats against entanglement must recognize that the line of separation, far from being a "wall," is a blurred, indistinct, and variable barrier depending on all the circumstances of a particular relationship. . . .

In order to determine whether the government entanglement with religion is excessive, we must examine the character and purposes of the institutions that are benefited, the nature of the aid that the State provides, and the resulting relationship between the government and the religious authority. . . .

(a) Rhode Island program

The District Court made extensive findings on the grave potential for excessive entanglement that inheres in the religious character and purpose of the Roman Catholic elementary schools of Rhode Island, to date the sole beneficiaries of the Rhode Island Salary Supplement Act. . . .

The substantial religious character of these church-related schools give[s] rise to entangling church-state relationships of the kind the Religion Clauses sought to avoid. Although the District Court found that concern for religious values did not inevitably or necessarily intrude into the content of secular subjects, the considerable religious activities of these schools led the legislature to provide for careful governmental controls and surveillance by state authorities in order to ensure that state aid supports only secular education. . . .

A comprehensive, discriminating, and continuing state surveillance will inevitably be required to ensure that these restrictions are obeyed and the First Amendment otherwise respected. Unlike a book, a teacher cannot be inspected once so as to determine the extent and intent of his or her personal beliefs and subjective acceptance of the limitations imposed by the First Amendment. These prophylactic contacts will involve excessive and enduring entanglement between state and church. . . .

(b) Pennsylvania program

The Pennsylvania statute also provides state aid to church-related schools for teachers' salaries. The complaint describes an educational system that is very similar to the one existing in Rhode Island. According to the allegations, the church-related elementary and secondary schools are controlled by religious organizations, have the purpose of propagating and promoting a particular religious faith, and conduct their operations to fulfill that purpose. Since this complaint was dismissed for failure to state a claim for relief, we must accept these allegations as true for purposes of our review.

As we noted earlier, the very restrictions and surveillance necessary to ensure that teachers play a strictly nonideological role give rise to entanglements between church and state. The Pennsylvania statute, like that of Rhode Island, fosters this kind of relationship. Reimbursement is not only limited to courses offered in the public schools and materials approved by state officials, but the statute excludes "any subject matter expressing religious teaching, or the morals or forms of worship of any sect." In addition, schools seeking reimbursement must maintain accounting procedures that require the State to establish the cost of the secular as distinguished from the religious instruction.

The Pennsylvania statute, moreover, has the further defect of providing state financial aid directly to the church-related school. This factor distinguishes both *Everson* and *Allen*, for in both those cases the Court was careful to point out that state aid was provided to the student and his parents—not to the church-related school. . . .

. . . The highways of church and state relationships are not likely to be one-way streets, and the Constitution's authors sought to protect religious worship from the pervasive power of government. The history of many countries attests to the hazards of religion's intruding into the political arena or of political power intruding into the legitimate and free exercise of religious belief. . . .

MR. JUSTICE WHITE, concurring in the judgment in *Lemon v. Kurtzman, Superintendent of Public Instruction of Pennsylvania* and dissenting in *Earley v. DiCenso.*

* * *

The Court strikes down the Rhode Island statute on its face. No fault is found with the secular purpose of the program; there is no suggestion that the purpose of the program was aid to religion disguised in secular attire. Nor does the Court find that the primary effect of the program is to aid religion rather than to implement secular goals. The Court nevertheless finds that impermissible "entanglement" will result from administration of the program. . . .

The Court thus creates an insoluble paradox for the State and the parochial schools. The State cannot finance secular instruction if it permits religion to be taught in the same classroom; but if it exacts a promise that religion not be so taught—a promise the school and its teachers are quite willing and on this record able to give—and enforces it, it is then entangled in the "no entanglement" aspect of the Court's Establishment Clause jurisprudence. . . .

Source: Lemon v. Kurtzman, Superintendent of Public Instruction of Pennsylvania, 403 U.S. 602 (1971).

DOCUMENT 56: *Meek v. Pittenger* (1975)

In July 1972 the Pennsylvania legislature passed two bills concerning nonpublic schools, including church-affiliated schools. The first, Act 194, authorized the state to provide nonpublic school students with auxiliary services. Services such as speech and hearing therapy, guidance counseling, psychological testing, and remedial instruction were within the scope of this legislation. The second statute, Act 195, authorized the state to provide nonpublic schools with instructional materials and equipment. Instructional materials included items such as periodicals, maps, charts, recordings, and films. Instructional equipment included film projectors, tape recorders, and laboratory paraphernalia. Act 195 also required the state to loan secular textbooks to students attending nonpublic schools.

When these two bills were enacted, approximately one-quarter of the school children in Pennsylvania attended nonpublic schools. About 75 percent of the nonpublic schools that qualified for state aid were affiliated with a religious organization, principally the Roman Catholic Church. The legislature's stated purpose in enacting the two laws was to assure that every school child would share equitably in benefits such as textbooks, instructional materials, and auxiliary services that were provided free of charge to pupils attending public schools in the state.

In February 1973 three individuals, including Sylvia Meek, challenged the constitutionality of Acts 194 and 195. All three were Pennsylvania residents and taxpayers, and they were supported by four organizations. The organizations were the American Civil Liberties Union, the National Association for the Advancement of Colored People, the Pennsylvania Jewish Community Relations Council, and Americans United for Separation of Church and State. The plaintiffs alleged that both statutes violated the First Amendment's establishment of religion clause, which applies to the states by way of the Fourteenth Amendment's due process clause. This allegation was founded upon the plaintiffs' belief that the statutes had the effect of promoting religion by authorizing direct aid to religious institutions. The complaint listed John C. Pittenger, Pennsylvania's Secretary of Education, and other state officials as defendants.

The United States Supreme Court's decision was authored by Justice Potter Stewart. To analyze the two Pennsylvania statutes Stewart implemented the three-part test announced by the Court in 1971 in *Lemon v. Kurtzman* (see Document 55). As a result, the textbook loan program was ruled constitutional, but the provisions that authorized auxiliary services, instructional materials, and instructional equipment for religious schools were all regarded as violations of the establishment clause.

In 1968, in *Board of Education of Central School District No. 1 v. Allen* (see Document 53), the Supreme Court had validated a New York program whereby the state loaned secular textbooks to parochial school students. As in *Allen*, the Court in *Meek* reasoned that the primary beneficiaries of the textbook loan program were children and not religious institutions.

Conversely, according to Stewart, the loan of instructional materials and equipment had the primary effect of advancing religion by directly assisting sectarian schools. Such a law, following the second prong of the *Lemon* test, is to be regarded as a violation of the establishment clause. The legislature's intention to provide nonpublic schools, including religious schools, with auxiliary services was seen as a violation of the third prong of the *Lemon* test, the prohibition against excessive government entanglements with religion.

The purpose of the *Lemon* test, Stewart stated, was to provide Supreme Court justices with a set of guidelines to measure possible violations of the establishment clause. For Stewart the test did not set "precise limits" on constitutional inquiry. In *Meek* three other justices, using the standards announced in *Lemon*, wrote opinions in which they concurred in part and dissented in part with Stewart's holding. The three were Chief Justice Warren E. Burger, Justice William J. Brennan, and Justice William H. Rehnquist.

Three justices, Burger, Rehnquist, and Byron R. White, would have affirmed the district court ruling that only the loan of instructional equipment was unconstitutional. In their eyes equipment such as film projectors and tape recorders could be used for religious instruction. Burger, Rehnquist, and White also agreed with the lower court that the textbooks, materials, and services in question were "secular, neutral, and nonideological."

Three other justices, Brennan, Thurgood Marshall, and William O. Douglas, found all aspects of Acts 194 and 195 unconstitutional, including the textbook loan program. Justice Brennan, in his opinion, asserted that it was "pure fantasy to treat the textbook loan program as a loan to students."

In *Meek* the textbook loan program, on the one hand, was ruled constitutional. On the other hand, programs to provide sectarian schools with auxiliary services, instructional materials, and equipment were regarded as violations of the establishment clause. Why did the Supreme Court make these distinctions? Do you agree or disagree with the Court's reasoning?

* * *

MR. JUSTICE STEWART announced the judgment of the Court and delivered the opinion of the Court.

This case requires us to determine once again whether a state law providing assistance to nonpublic, church-related, elementary and secondary schools is constitutional under the Establishment Clause of the First Amendment, made applicable to the States by the Fourteenth Amendment. . . .

In judging the constitutionality of the various forms of assistance authorized by Acts 194 and 195, the District Court applied the three-part test that has been clearly stated, if not easily applied, by this Court in recent Establishment Clause cases.

These tests constitute a convenient, accurate distillation of this Court's efforts over the past decades to evaluate a wide range of governmental action challenged as violative of the constitutional prohibition against laws "respecting an establishment of religion," and thus provide the proper framework of analysis for the issues presented in the case before us. It is well to emphasize, however, that the tests must not be viewed as setting the precise limits to the necessary constitutional inquiry, but serve only as guidelines with which to identify instances in which the objectives of the Establishment Clause have been impaired. . . .

The District Court held that the textbook loan provisions of Act 195 are constitutionally indistinguishable from the New York textbook loan program upheld in Board of Education v. Allen. . . .

Like the New York program, the textbook provisions of Act 195 extend to all school children the benefits of Pennsylvania's well-established policy of lending textbooks free of charge to elementary and secondary schools students. As in *Allen*, Act 195 provides that the textbooks are to be lent directly to the student, not to the nonpublic school itself, although, again as in *Allen*, the administrative practice is to have student requests for the books filed initially with the nonpublic school and to have the school authorities prepare collective summaries of these requests which they forward to the appropriate public officials. Thus, the financial benefit of Pennsylvania's textbook program, like New York's, is to parents and children, not to the nonpublic schools. . . .

Although textbooks are lent only to students, Act 195 authorizes the loan of instructional material and equipment directly to qualifying nonpublic elementary and secondary schools in the Commonwealth. The appellants assert that such direct aid to Pennsylvania's nonpublic schools, including church-related institutions, constitutes an impermissible establishment of religion.

Act 195 is accompanied by legislative findings that the welfare of the Commonwealth requires that present and future generations of school children be assured ample opportunity to develop their intellectual capacities. Act 195 is intended to further that objective by extending the benefits of free educational aids to every school child in the Commonwealth, including nonpublic school students who constitute approximately one quarter of the school children in Pennsylvania. But we agree with the appellants that the direct loan of instructional material and equipment has the unconstitutional primary effect of advancing religion because of the predominantly religious character of the schools benefiting from the Act. . . .

Unlike Act 195, which provides only for the loan of teaching material and equipment, Act 194 authorizes the Secretary of Education, through the intermediate units, to supply professional staff, as well as supportive materials, equipment, and personnel, to the nonpublic schools of the Commonwealth. The "auxiliary services" authorized by Act 194—remedial and accelerated instruction, guidance counseling and testing, speech and hearing services—are provided directly to nonpublic school children with the appropriate special need. But the services are provided only on the nonpublic school premises, and only when "requested by nonpublic school representatives." . . .

. . . This potential for political entanglement, together with the administrative entanglement which would be necessary to ensure that auxiliary-services personnel remain strictly neutral and nonideological when functioning in church-related schools, compels the conclusion that Act 194 violates the constitutional prohibition against laws "respecting an establishment of religion." . . .

MR. JUSTICE BRENNAN, with whom MR. JUSTICE DOUGLAS and MR. JUSTICE MARSHALL join, concurring in part and dissenting in part.

I join in the reversal of the District Court's judgment insofar as that judgment upheld the constitutionality of Act 194 and the provisions of Act 195 respecting instructional materials and equipment, but dissent from Part III and the affirmance of the judgment upholding the constitutionality of the textbook provisions of Act 195. . . .

First, it is pure fantasy to treat the textbook program as a loan to students. . . . The Commonwealth has promulgated "Guidelines for the Administration of Acts 194 and 195" to implement the statutes. These regulations, unlike those upheld in *Allen*, constitute a much more intrusive and detailed involvement of the State and its processes into the administration of nonpublic schools. The whole business is handled by the schools and public authorities, and neither parents nor students have a say. The guidelines make crystal clear that the nonpublic school, not its pupils, is the motivating force behind the textbook loan, and that virtually the entire loan transaction is to be, and is in fact, conducted between officials of the nonpublic school, on the one hand, and officers of the State, on the other. . . .

Second, in any event, *Allen* itself made clear that, far from providing a *per se* immunity from examination of the substance of the State's program, even if the fact were, and it is not, that textbooks are loaned to the children rather than to the schools, that is only one among the factors to be weighed in determining the compatibility of the program with the Establishment Clause. And, clearly, in the context of application of the factor of political divisiveness, it is wholly irrelevant whether the loan is to the children or to the school. A divisive political potential exists because aid programs, like Act 195, are dependent on continuing annual appropriations, and Act 195's textbook loan program, even if we accepted it as a form of loans to students, involves increasingly massive sums now approaching $5,000,000 annually. It would blind reality to treat massive aid to nonpublic schools, under the guise of loans to the students, as not creating "a serious potential for divisive conflict over the issue of aid to religion." . . .

Finally, the textbook loan provisions of Act 195, even if ostensibly limiting loans to nonpublic school children, violate the Establishment Clause for reasons independent of the political-divisiveness factor. As I have said, unlike the New York statute in *Allen* which extended assistance to all students, whether attending public or nonpublic schools, Act 195 extends textbook assistance only to a special class of students, children who attend nonpublic schools which are, as the plurality notes, primarily religiously oriented. . . .

Source: Meek v. Pittenger, 421 U.S. 349 (1975).

DOCUMENT 57: *Wolman v. Walter* (1977)

Following the 1975 decision by the United States Supreme Court in *Meek v. Pittenger* (see Document 56), the Ohio legislature enacted a statute that was designed to provide various forms of aid to students in the state's nonpublic schools. In *Meek* some of the state aid was alleged to have been provided directly to students in nonpublic schools, and some of the aid went directly to the schools. The Ohio enactment specified that all of the state assistance was to go directly to the students. Specifically, the Ohio statute authorized the state to provide students in nonpublic schools with secular textbooks. In addition, standardized tests and scoring services, diagnostic speech and hearing services, and diagnostic psychological services were authorized by the law. Another section of the statute stipulated that nonpublic school students in need of specialized therapeutic, guidance, and remedial services were eligible to receive such services from public employees as long as these activities were performed in public schools, public centers, or mobile units located off the premises of the participating nonpublic schools. Instructional materials and equipment could be loaned upon the request of nonpublic school pupils or their parents and, finally, the legislation authorized the state to provide the transportation necessary to allow nonpublic school students to participate in field trips. All materials and services were to be equivalent to those materials and services utilized by the students in Ohio's public schools.

Members of the Ohio legislature who supported the bill argued that aid to students in nonpublic schools was justified because the state had a legitimate interest in protecting the health of young people by providing a fertile educational environment for all the children attending school in Ohio. In this regard it was also argued that since nonpublic schools are utilized to fulfill the state's compulsory education requirement, the state has a legitimate interest in the evaluation of both teachers and students in nonpublic schools to ensure that proper standards of instruction are maintained.

Benson A. Wolman and other individuals who were both residents and taxpayers in Ohio challenged the statute as a violation of the First Amendment's establishment of religion clause, which is applicable to the states via the Fourteenth Amendment's due process clause. The lawsuit noted that during the 1974–1975 school year 691 of Ohio's 720 chartered nonpublic schools were sectarian institutions. As a result, approximately 96 percent of the students enrolled in nonpublic schools were attending church-affiliated schools and, further, 92 percent of the students not attending public schools in Ohio were attending Catholic elementary and secondary schools.

The lawsuit targeted a number of state officials, including the State Superintendent of Public Instruction, and it alleged that the state's initial biennial appropriation to finance the multifaceted program exceeded $88 million. It was argued that this collection of programs was patently unconstitutional because state funds were being used to support religious institutions. A three-judge district court, however, ruled that the Ohio statute was constitutional in all respects. This holding was appealed to the U.S. Supreme Court.

In 1977 Justice Harry A. Blackmun delivered the opinion for a deeply divided Supreme Court. Blackmun concluded, on the one hand, that it was constitutional for the state to provide students in nonpublic schools, including religious schools, with secular textbooks, standardized tests and scoring services, diagnostic services, and therapeutic services. On the other hand, Blackmun held that it was unconstitutional for Ohio to provide the pupils in nonpublic schools with instructional materials, instructional equipment, or field trip transportation.

Blackmun utilized the three-part test devised by the Supreme Court in 1971 in *Lemon v. Kurtzman* (Document 55) to evaluate the Ohio statute and he reasoned that the enactment had a secular legislative purpose. In this case, therefore, the validity of each of the various aspects of the statute depended on whether or not the primary effect of that program either advanced religion or resulted in an excessive entanglement between church and state. This inquiry also required Blackmun to evaluate whether the principal beneficiary of the state aid was an individual student or a church-affiliated school. Under the student benefit theory announced by the Court in *Cochran v. Louisiana State*

Board of Education (1930), the former is constitutional while the latter is unconstitutional.

In response to Justice Blackmun's opinion seven of the Court's nine members concurred in part and dissented in part. Four of these seven justices issued written opinions. Justice William J. Brennan declared that the Ohio statute in its entirety was in violation of the First Amendment's prohibition against laws respecting an establishment of religion. After noting that millions of dollars were appropriated to initiate the various programs created by the legislation, he warned that "a divisive political potential of unusual magnitude inheres in the Ohio program."

More compromising than Brennan, Justice Thurgood Marshall advocated drawing a line that would permit state-funded general welfare programs to service children in sectarian schools while simultaneously prohibiting programs intended to extend publicly funded educational assistance from reaching church-affiliated schools. Such a line, for example, would allow diagnostic services while voiding the textbook loan program.

Critics of the Court's reliance upon the *Lemon* test pointed to the Court's failure to reach a solid consensus in *Wolman* as evidence that the test itself was fundamentally flawed. Justice Lewis F. Powell defended the *Lemon* test and the Court's lack of "analytical tidiness" by stating that "decisions have sought to establish principles that preserve the cherished safeguards of the Establishment clause without resort to blind absolutism."

Conversely, Justice John Paul Stevens asserted that the Court's repeated efforts to improve upon the standard announced in 1947 in *Everson v. Board of Education of Ewing Township* (see Document 48), including the *Lemon* test, had failed to accomplish the task. In *Everson* Justice Hugo L. Black had declared that "a state subsidy of sectarian schools is invalid regardless of the form it takes." Based largely on this standard Stevens stated his objection to the Court's holding that both the textbook loan program and the extension of standardized testing services to students in sectarian schools were constitutional. Stevens did, however, support the conclusion that providing these same students with diagnostic and therapeutic health services was also constitutional.

The instructional materials that Ohio planned to provide to students in nonpublic schools were secular in nature. Do you agree with Justice Blackmun's conclusion that it would be improper for the state to engage in this activity? Should a state be allowed to transport students enrolled in a sectarian school to and from field trip locations that have no religious significance? Do you favor Justice Powell's argument that the *Lemon* test provides workable guidelines for the analysis of potential violations of the establishment clause, or Justice Stevens' contention that the Supreme Court should return to the reasoning employed in the *Everson* case to examine such issues?

* * *

MR. JUSTICE BLACKMUN delivered the opinion of the Court.

* * *

II

The mode of analysis for Establishment Clause questions is defined by the three-part test that has emerged from the Court's decisions. In order to pass muster, a statute must have a secular legislative purpose, must have a principal or primary effect that neither advances nor inhibits religion, and must not foster an excessive government entanglement with religion. . . .

In the present case we have no difficulty with the first prong of this three-part test. We are satisfied that the challenged statute reflects Ohio's legitimate interest in protecting the health of its youth and in providing a fertile educational environment for all the school children of the State. As is usual in our cases, the analytical difficulty has to do with the effect and entanglement criteria. . . .

III

Textbooks

This system for the loan of textbooks to individual students bears a striking resemblance to the systems approved in *Board of Education v. Allen* (1968), and in *Meek v. Pittenger* (1975). . . . As read, the statute provides the same protections against abuse as were provided in the textbook programs under consideration in *Allen* and in *Meek*. . . .

IV

Testing and Scoring

There is no question that the State has a substantial and legitimate interest in insuring that its youth receive an adequate secular education. . . . Under the section at issue, the State provides both the schools and the school district with the means of ensuring that the minimum standards are met. The nonpublic school does not control the content of the test or its result. . . . Similarly the inability of the school to control the test eliminates the need for the supervision that gives rise to excessive entanglement. . . .

V

Diagnostic Services

We conclude that providing diagnostic services on the nonpublic school premises will not create an impermissible risk of the fostering of ideological views. It follows that there is no need for excessive surveillance, and there will not be impermissible entanglement. . . .

VI

Therapeutic Services

. . . [W]e hold that providing therapeutic and remedial services at a neutral site off the premises of the nonpublic schools will not have the impermissible effect of advancing religion. Neither will there be any excessive entanglement arising from supervision of public employees to insure that they maintain a neutral stance. It can hardly be said that the supervision of public employees performing public functions on public property creates an excessive entanglement between church and state. . . .

VII

Instructional Materials and Equipment

Although the exact nature of the material and equipment is not clearly revealed, the parties have stipulated: "It is expected that materials and equipment loaned to pupils or parents under the new law will be similar to such former materials and equipment except that to the extent that the law requires that materials and equipment capable of diversion to religious issues will not be supplied." . . .

In *Meek*, however, the Court considered the constitutional validity of a direct loan to nonpublic schools of instructional material and equipment, and, despite the apparent secular nature of the goods, held the loan impermissible. . . . Thus, even though the loan ostensibly was limited to neutral and secular instructional material and equipment, it inescapably had the primary effect of providing a direct and substantial advancement of the sectarian enterprise.

Appellees seek to avoid *Meek* by emphasizing that it involved a program of direct loans to nonpublic schools. In contrast, the material and equipment at issue under the Ohio statute are loaned to the pupil or his parent. In our view, however, it would exalt form over substance if this distinction were found to justify a result different from that in *Meek*. Before *Meek* was decided by this Court, Ohio authorized the loan of material and equipment directly to the nonpublic schools. Then, in light of *Meek*, the state legislature decided to channel the goods through the parents and pupils. Despite the technical change in legal bailee, the program in substance is the same as before: The equipment is substantially the same; it will receive the same use by the students; and it may still be stored and distributed on the nonpublic school premises. In view of the impossibility of separating the secular education function from the sectarian, the state aid inevitably flows in part in support of the religious role of the schools. . . .

VIII

Field Trips

. . . The field trips are an integral part of the educational experience, and where the teacher works within and for a sectarian institution, an unacceptable risk of fostering of religion is an inevitable by-product. . . .

IX

In summary, we hold constitutional those portions of the Ohio statute authorizing the State to provide nonpublic school pupils with books, standardized testing and scoring, diagnostic services, and therapeutic and remedial services. We hold unconstitutional those portions relating to instructional materials and equipment and field trip services.

The judgment of the District Court is therefore affirmed in part and reversed in part.

MR. JUSTICE POWELL, concurring in part, concurring in the judgment in part, and dissenting in part.

* * *

Parochial schools, quite apart from their sectarian purpose, have provided an educational alternative for millions of young Americans; they often afford wholesome competition with our public schools; and in some States they relieve substantially the tax burden incident to the operation of public schools. The State has, moreover, a legitimate interest in facilitating education of the highest quality for all children within its boundaries, whatever school their parents have chosen for them.

It is important to keep these issues in perspective. At this point in the 20th century we are quite far removed from the dangers that prompted the Framers to include the Establishment Clause in the Bill of Rights. The risk of significant religious or denominational control over our democratic processes—or even of deep political division along religious lines—is remote, and when viewed against the positive contributions of sectarian schools, any such risk seems entirely tolerable in light of the continuing oversight of this Court. Our decisions have sought to establish principles that preserve the cherished safeguard of the Establishment Clause without resort to blind absolutism. If this endeavor means a loss of some analytical tidiness, then that too is entirely tolerable. Most of the Court's decision today follows in this tradition, and I join Parts I through VI of the opinion.

With respect to Part VII, I concur only in the judgment. I am not persuaded, nor did *Meek* hold, that all loans of secular instructional material and equipment "inescapably [have] the primary effect of providing a direct and substantial advancement of the sectarian enterprise." Here the statute is expressly limited to materials incapable of diversion. Therefore the relevant question is whether the materials are such that they are "furnished for the use of individual students and at their request."

The Ohio statute includes some materials such as wall maps, charts, and other classroom paraphernalia for which the concept of a loan to individuals is a transparent fiction. A loan of these items is indistinguishable from forbidden "direct aid" to the sectarian institution itself, whoever the technical bailee. Since the provision makes no attempt to separate these instructional materials from others meaningfully lent to individuals, I agree with the Court that it cannot be sustained under our precedents. But I would find no constitutional defect in a properly limited provision lending to the individuals themselves only appropriate instructional materials and equipment similar to that customarily used in public schools.

I dissent as to Part VIII, concerning field trip transportation. The Court writes as though the statute funded the salary of the teacher who takes the students on the outing. In fact only the bus and driver are provided for the limited purpose of physical movement between the school and the secular destination of the field trip. As I find this aid indistinguishable in principle from that upheld in *Everson*, I would sustain the District Court's judgment approving this part of the Ohio statute.

MR. JUSTICE STEVENS, concurring in part and dissenting in part.

The distinction between the religious and the secular is a fundamental one. . . .

The line drawn by the Establishment Clause of the First Amendment must also have a fundamental character. It should not differentiate between direct and indirect subsidies, or between instructional materials like globes and maps on the one hand and instructional materials like textbooks on the other. For that reason, rather than the three-part test described in Part II of the plurality's opinion, I would adhere to the test enunciated for the Court by Mr. Justice Black:

"No tax in any amount, large or small, can be levied to support any religious activities or institutions, whatever they may be called, or whatever form they may adopt to teach or practice religion." (*Everson v. Board of Education.*)

Under that test, a state subsidy of sectarian schools is invalid regardless of the form it takes. The financing of buildings, field trips, instructional materials, educational tests, and school books are all equally invalid. For all give aid to the school's educational mission, which at heart is religious. On the other hand, I am not prepared to exclude the possibility that some parts of the statute before us may be administered in a constitutional manner. The State can plainly provide public health services to children attending nonpublic schools. The diagnostic and therapeutic services described in Parts V and VI of the Court's opinion may fall into this category. Although I have some misgivings on this point, I am not prepared to hold this part of the statute invalid on its face.

The Court's efforts to improve on the *Everson* test have not proved successful. "Corrosive precedents" have left us without firm principles on which to decide these cases. As this case demonstrates, the States have been encouraged to search for new ways of achieving forbidden ends. What should be a "high and impregnable" wall between church and state, has been reduced to a "blurred, indistinct, and variable barrier." . . .

Accordingly, I dissent from Parts II, III and IV of the plurality opinion.

Source: Wolman v. Walter, 443 U.S. 229 (1977).

DOCUMENT 58: *Mueller v. Allen* (1983)

In 1972 several amendments were added to New York's Education and Tax Laws. One of these amendments allowed a taxpayer to deduct a stipulated sum from his or her adjusted gross income for each child attending a nonpublic school. At the time approximately 20 percent of the students in New York, over 700,000 children, were attending nonpublic elementary and secondary schools. The vast majority of these nonpublic schools were affiliated with the Roman Catholic Church.

In 1973, however, in *Committee for Public Education & Religious Liberty v. Nyquist,* the United States Supreme Court declared that this tax relief program enacted in New York was an unconstitutional violation of the First Amendment's establishment of religion clause. The establishment clause applies to New York and all other states via the due process clause of the Fourteenth Amendment.

The majority opinion in the 6–3 *Nyquist* decision was written by Justice Lewis F. Powell. Citing the "effect prong" of the three-part test devised by the Court in 1971 in *Lemon v. Kurtzman* (see Document 55), Powell asserted that a state is required to maintain a position of neutrality that neither advances nor inhibits religion. By this standard, according to Justice Powell, the New York statute had advanced religion by providing income tax benefits for the parents of children attending predominantly parochial schools.

In 1982 a law was enacted in Minnesota that allowed taxpayers, in computing their state income tax, to deduct expenses incurred in providing tuition, textbooks, and transportation for a child who attended either elementary or secondary school. Unlike the New York statute examined in *Nyquist*, the Minnesota statute applied to children attending either a public or a nonpublic school. At the time there were approximately 500 nonpublic schools in Minnesota educating a total of over 90,000 students. About 95 percent of these pupils were enrolled in church-affiliated nonpublic schools.

The statute allowed Minnesota taxpayers to deduct up to $700 for expenses related to educating their children. A group of Minnesota taxpayers, including Van D. Mueller, claimed that the deduction, when utilized by the parents of children attending parochial schools, violated the establishment clause by providing financial assistance to those sectarian institutions. Mueller and the other taxpayers brought a legal action against Minnesota's Commissioner of Revenue, Clyde E. Allen, Jr., as well as parents who had taken the deduction for expenses related to sending their children to parochial schools. The U.S. District Court for the District of Minnesota and the Court of Appeals for the Eighth Circuit both concluded that the law was constitutional.

In 1983, one decade after the *Nyquist* ruling, the Supreme Court affirmed the constitutionality of the Minnesota tax relief program in *Mueller v. Allen*. Notwithstanding statistical data that showed that the application of the statute primarily benefited religious institutions, the majority in this 5–4 decision were greatly influenced by the fact that the deduction was available to all parents of elementary and secondary school students. Children attending public schools and nonsectarian private schools, as well as those enrolled in parochial schools, were all included in the scope of the legislation.

The majority opinion was written by Justice William H. Rehnquist, who, along with Chief Justice Warren E. Burger and Justice Byron R. White, had dissented in *Nyquist*. In *Mueller* Rehnquist, Burger, and White were joined by Justice Sandra Day O'Connor, who had joined the Court in 1981, and, ironically, by Justice Powell, author of the majority opinion in *Nyquist*.

Justice Rehnquist concluded that the Minnesota statute passed all three parts of the so-called *Lemon* test. First, according to Rehnquist, the deduction had the secular legislative purpose of ensuring that the citizens of the state were well educated. In addition, helping to assure the continued financial health of both sectarian and nonsectarian private schools was considered to be a secular purpose by Rehnquist.

Second, Rehnquist maintained that the deduction did not have the primary effect of advancing religion. Similar to deductions for medical expenses and charitable contributions, the deduction for educational expenses was available to any taxpayer, as long as he or she had a child in either an elementary or secondary school. Any aid that assisted a parochial school, it was argued, resulted from a decision made by an individual parent and, therefore, did not flow directly from the state to a sectarian institution.

Third, despite the fact that state officials would be required to validate that the textbook deduction was utilized for secular books only, Rehnquist reasoned that this requirement was not sufficient to trigger an excessive government entanglement with religion.

Writing in dissent, Justice Thurgood Marshall emphasized that the establishment clause prohibits a state from subsidizing religious education, whether it does so directly or indirectly. Marshall, who was joined by Justices William J. Brennan, Harry A. Blackmun, and John Paul Stevens, echoed the Court's admonition in *Nyquist* that the government is required to maintain a position of neutrality concerning religion.

For Justice Rehnquist, what was the crucial difference between the tax credit program examined in *Mueller v. Allen* and the one invalidated as a result of the *Nyquist* decision? Why did Justice Marshall consider the Minnesota tax relief statute to be an abrogation of the neutrality standard contained in his interpretation of the establishment clause?

* * *

JUSTICE REHNQUIST delivered the opinion of the Court.

* * *

In this case we are asked to decide whether Minnesota's tax deduction bears greater resemblance to those types of assistance to parochial schools we have approved, or to those we have struck down. . . .

The general nature of our inquiry in this area has been guided, since the decision in *Lemon v. Kurtzman*, by the "three-part" test laid down in that case. . . . While this principle is well settled, our cases have also emphasized that it provides "no more than [a] helpful signpos[t]" in dealing with Establishment Clause challenges. With this caveat in mind, we turn to the specific challenges raised against [this Minnesota statute] under the *Lemon* framework.

Little time need be spent on the question of whether the Minnesota tax deduction has a secular purpose. Under our prior decisions, governmental assistance programs have consistently survived this inquiry even when they have run afoul of other aspects of the *Lemon* framework. This reflects, at least in part, our reluctance to attribute unconstitutional motives to the States, particularly when a plausible secular purpose for the State's program may be discerned from the face of the statute. . . .

We turn therefore to the more difficult but related question whether the Minnesota statute has "the primary effect of advancing the sectarian aims of the non-public schools." In concluding that it does not, we find several features of the Minnesota tax deduction particularly significant. First, an essential feature of Minnesota's arrangement is the fact that [it] is only one among many deductions—such as those for medical expenses, and charitable contributions, available under the Minnesota tax laws. . . .

Under our prior decisions, the Minnesota Legislature's judgment that a deduction for educational expenses fairly equalizes the tax burden of its citizens and encourages desirable expenditures for educational purposes is entitled to substantial deference. . . . Most importantly, the deduction is available for educational expenses incurred by *all* parents, including those whose children attend public schools and those whose children attend nonsectarian private schools or sectarian private schools. . . .

Finally, private educational institutions, and parents paying for their children to attend these schools, make special contributions to the areas in which they operate. "Parochial schools, quite apart from their sectarian purpose, have provided an educational alternative for millions of young Americans; they often afford wholesome competition with our public schools; and in some States they relieve substantially the tax burden incident to the operation of public schools," (*Wolman v. Walter*, 1977). If parents of children in private schools choose to take special advantage of the relief provided by [the statute at issue], it is no doubt due to the fact that they bear a particularly great financial burden in educating their children. More fundamentally, whatever unequal effect may be attributed to the statutory classification can fairly be regarded as a rough return for the benefits, discussed above, provided to the State and all taxpayers by parents sending their children to parochial schools. In the light of all this, we believe it wiser to decline to engage in the type of empirical inquiry into those persons benefited by state law which petitioners urge.

Thus, we hold that the Minnesota tax deduction for educational expenses satisfied the primary effect inquiry of our Establishment Clause cases.

Turning to the third part of the *Lemon* inquiry, we have no difficulty in concluding that the Minnesota statute does not "excessively entangle" the State in religion. The only plausible source of the "comprehensive, discriminating, and continuing state surveillance," necessary to run afoul of this standard would lie in the fact that state officials must determine whether particular textbooks qualify for a deduction. In making this decision, state officials must disallow deductions taken for "instructional books and materials used in the teaching of religious tenets, doctrines or worship, the purpose of which is to inculcate such tenets, doctrines or worship." Making decisions such as this does not differ substantially from making the types of decisions approved in earlier opinions of this Court. In *Board of Education v. Allen* (1968), for example, the Court upheld the loan of secular textbooks to parents or children attending nonpublic schools; though state officials were required to determine whether particular books were or were not secular, the system was held not to violate the Establishment Clause. . . .

JUSTICE MARSHALL, dissenting.

The Establishment Clause of the First Amendment prohibits a State from subsidizing religious education, whether it does so directly or indirectly. In my view, this principle of neutrality forbids not only the tax benefits struck down in *Committee for Public Education v. Nyquist* (1973), but any tax benefit, including the tax deduction at issue here which subsidizes tuition payments to sectarian schools. I also believe that the Establishment Clause prohibits the tax deductions that Minnesota authorizes for the cost of books and other instructional materials used for sectarian purposes. . . . The Minnesota tax statute violates the Establishment Clause for precisely the same reason as the statute struck down in *Nyquist*: it has a direct and immediate effect of advancing religion. . . .

Like the law involved in *Nyquist*, the Minnesota law can be said to serve a secular purpose: promoting pluralism and diversity among the State's public and nonpublic schools. But the Establishment Clause requires more than that legislation have a secular purpose. . . .

As we recognized in *Nyquist*, direct government subsidization of parochial school tuition is impermissible because "the effect of the aid is unmistakably to provide desired financial support for nonpublic, sectarian institutions." . . . For this reason, aid to sectarian schools must be restricted to ensure that it may be not used to further the religious mission of those schools. . . .

That parents receive a reduction of their tax liability, rather than a direct reimbursement, is of no greater significance here than it was in *Nyquist*. . . .

That the Minnesota statute makes some small benefit available to all parents cannot alter the fact that the most substantial benefit provided by the statute is available only to those parents who send their children to schools that charge tuition. It is simply undeniable that the single largest expense that may be deducted under the Minnesota statute is tuition. The statute is little more than a subsidy of tuition masquerading as a subsidy of general educational expenses. The other deductible expenses are *de minimis* in comparison to tuition expenses. . . .

In my view, the lines drawn in *Nyquist* were drawn on a reasoned basis with appropriate regard for the principles of neutrality embodied by the Establishment Clause. I do not believe that the same can be said of the lines drawn by the majority today. For the first time, the Court has upheld financial support for religious schools without any reason at all to assume that the support will be restricted to the secular functions of those schools and will not be used to support religious instruction. This result is flatly at odds with the fundamental principle that a State may provide no financial support whatsoever to promote religion. . . .

Source: Mueller v. Allen, 463 U.S. 388 (1983).

DOCUMENT 59: *Marsh v. Chambers* (1983)

In 1962 the United States Supreme Court, in *Engel v. Vitale* (see Document 51), declared that the organized recitation of a prayer in a public school violates the First Amendment's establishment of religion clause. The majority's holding, in part, was based on its conclusion that children are generally impressionable and that within a classroom there is "coercive pressure" to conform. The existence of compulsory school attendance laws also had an impact on the Court's decision.

Justice William O. Douglas, concurring in *Engel*, reasoned that it was equally unconstitutional to open a legislative session with the recitation of a prayer. Two decades later the Supreme Court would formally address this issue, which had been raised by Justice Douglas in the controversial prayer in school case.

In 1981 Ernest Chambers, a member of the Nebraska legislature, challenged the constitutionality of the practice of opening each session of that body with a prayer. The prayer was delivered by a chaplain who was paid at the public's expense. Robert E. Palmer, a Presbyterian minister, had held this position for sixteen years, and he was paid $319.75 per month for each month that the legislature was in session. His prayers were described as being in the Judeo-Christian tradition.

The U.S. District Court for the District of Nebraska held that the establishment clause was not violated by the recitation of the prayer, but that it had been violated by paying the chaplain from public funds. This holding was challenged, and the court of appeals enjoined the entire chaplaincy practice after finding that it contradicted all three prongs of the tripartite test announced by the Supreme Court in 1971 in *Lemon v. Kurtzman* (see Document 55).

In 1983 the Supreme Court reversed the decision of the court of appeals. The vote in *Marsh v. Chambers* was 6–3, and the majority opinion was written by Chief Justice Warren E. Burger. Ironically, Burger, the author of the so-called *Lemon* test, based his decision entirely on historical tradition. Burger's accommodationist approach to resolving establishment clause issues without invoking the standards codified in *Lemon* had been foreshadowed in his dissenting opinion in *Committee for Public Education & Religious Liberty v. Nyquist* (1973). Burger, in *Nyquist*, wrote that the establishment clause "does not forbid governments, state or federal, to enact a program of general welfare under which benefits are distributed to private individuals, even though many of those individuals may elect to use those benefits in ways that 'aid' religious instruction or worship."

In *Marsh* Chief Justice Burger noted that not only had sessions of the Nebraska legislature opened with a prayer for over a century, sessions of Congress had opened with a prayer for approximately two centuries. In addition, the same First Congress that initiated the practice had also drafted the First Amendment. Burger, therefore, reached the conclusion that the framers of the establishment clause did not consider the chaplaincy practice to be a violation of the clause. He further asserted that it would be "incongruous" to impose a more stringent limit upon the states, by way of the Fourteenth Amendment, than the draftsmen of the First Amendment had imposed upon the national government.

Justice William J. Brennan, writing in dissent, concluded that by avoiding the dictates of the *Lemon* test the majority in *Marsh* was carving out an exception to the establishment clause rather than attempting to reshape First Amendment doctrine to accommodate Nebraska's practice of legislative prayer. Justice Brennan speculated that without an invocation of history the practice would unquestionably be regarded as unconstitutional, since even a group of law students would "nearly unanimously" recognize that legislative prayer is not consistent with the standards outlined in *Lemon v. Kurtzman*.

Concerning the majority's reliance on historical tradition, Brennan argued that the Constitution is not a static document and that in this particular case historical practice should not override the principles of neutrality and separation that are embedded in the establishment clause.

What historical traditions were cited by Chief Justice Burger as justification for upholding the practice of legislative prayer? What were the three reasons outlined by Justice Brennan for not allowing a specific historical practice to override a clear constitutional imperative to follow the dictates of the establishment of religion clause?

* * *

CHIEF JUSTICE BURGER delivered the opinion of the Court.

The opening of sessions of legislative and other deliberative public bodies with prayer is deeply embedded in the history and tradition of this country. From colonial times through the founding of the Republic and ever since, the practice of legislative prayer has coexisted with the principles of disestablishment and religious freedom. In the very court-rooms in which the United States District Judge and later three Circuit Judges heard and decided this case, the proceedings opened with an announcement that concluded, "God save the United States and this Honorable Court." The same invocation occurs at all sessions of this Court.

The tradition in many of the Colonies was, of course, linked to an established church, but the Continental Congress, beginning in 1774, adopted the traditional procedure of opening its sessions with a prayer offered by a paid chaplain. Although prayers were not offered during the Constitutional Convention, the First Congress, as one of its early items of business, adopted the policy of selecting a chaplain to open each session with prayer. . . .

On September 25, 1789, three days after Congress authorized the appointment of paid chaplains, final agreement was reached on the language of the Bill of Rights. Clearly the men who wrote the First Amendment Religion Clauses did not view paid legislative chaplains and opening prayers as a violation of that Amendment, for the practice of opening sessions with prayer has continued without interruption ever since that early session of Congress. It has also been followed consistently in most of the states, including Nebraska, where the institution of opening legislative sessions with prayer was adopted even before the State attained statehood.

Standing alone, historical patterns cannot justify contemporary violations of constitutional guarantees, but there is far more here than simply historical patterns. In this context, historical evidence sheds light not only on what the draftsmen intended the Establishment Clause to mean, but also on how they thought that Clause applied to the practice authorized by the First Congress—their actions reveal their intent. . . .

No more is Nebraska's practice of over a century, consistent with two centuries of national practice, to be cast aside. It can hardly be thought that in the same week Members of the First Congress voted to appoint and to pay a chaplain for each House and also voted to approve the draft of the First Amendment for submission to the states, they intended the Establishment Clause of the Amendment to forbid what they had just declared acceptable. In applying the First Amendment to the states through the Fourteenth Amendment, *Cantwell v. Connecticut* (1940), it would be incongruous to interpret that Clause as imposing more stringent First Amendment limits on the states than the draftsmen imposed on the Federal Government. . . .

In light of the unambiguous and unbroken history of more than 200 years, there can be no doubt that the practice of opening legislative sessions with prayer has become part of the fabric of our society. To invoke Divine guidance on the public body entrusted with making the laws is not, in these circumstances, an "establishment" of religion or a step toward establishment; it is simply a tolerable acknowledgment of beliefs widely held among the people of this country. . . .

JUSTICE BRENNAN, dissenting.

* * *

The Court makes no pretense of subjecting Nebraska's practice of legislative prayer to any of the formal "tests" that have traditionally structured our inquiry under the Establishment Clause. That it fails to do so is, in a sense, a good thing, for it simply confirms that the Court is carving out an exception to the Establishment Clause rather than reshaping Establishment Clause doctrine to accommodate legislative prayer. For my purposes, however, I must begin by demonstrating what should be obvious: that, if the Court were to judge legislative prayer through the unsentimental eye of our settled doctrine, it would have to strike it down as a clear violation of the Establishment Clause.

The most commonly cited formulation of prevailing Establishment Clause doctrine is found in *Lemon v. Kurtzman* (1971). . . .

. . . Three such tests may be gleaned from our cases. First, the statute [at issue] must have a secular legislative purpose; second, its principal or primary effect must be one that neither advances nor inhibits religion; finally, the statute must not foster "an excessive government entanglement with religion."

That the "purpose" of legislative prayer is pre-eminently religious rather than secular seems to me to be self-evident. . . .

The "primary effect" of legislative prayer is also clearly religious. . . .

Finally, there can be no doubt that the practice of legislative prayer leads to excessive "entanglement" between the State and religion. . . .

In sum, I have no doubt that, if any group of law students were asked to apply the principles of *Lemon* to the question of legislative prayer, they would nearly unanimously find the practice to be unconstitutional. . . .

Legislative prayer clearly violates the principles of neutrality and separation that are embedded within the Establishment Clause. It is contrary to the fundamental message of *Engel* and *Schempp*. It intrudes on the right to conscience by forcing some legislators either to participate in a "prayer opportunity", with which they are in basic disagreement, or to make their disagreement a matter of public comment by declining to participate. It forces all residents of the State to support a religious exercise that may be contrary to their own beliefs. It requires the State to commit itself on fundamental theological issues. It has the potential for degrading religion by allowing a religious call to worship to be intermeshed with a secular call to order. And it injects religion into the political sphere by creating the potential that each and every selection of a chaplain, or consideration of a particular prayer, or even reconsideration of the practice itself, will provoke a political battle along religious lines and ultimately alienate some religiously identified group of citizens. . . .

The argument is made occasionally that a strict separation of religion and state robs the Nation of its spiritual identity. I believe quite the contrary. It may be true that individuals cannot be "neutral" on the question of religion. But the judgment of the Establishment Clause is that neutrality by the organs of *government* on questions of religion is both possible and imperative. . . .

Source: Marsh v. Chambers, 463 U.S. 783 (1983).

DOCUMENT 60: The Equal Access Act (1984)

In July 1984, the United States Congress passed the Equal Access Act. The vote in the Senate was 88–11, and in the House of Representatives it was 377–77. There clearly was strong support in Congress for this law, which reinforces for public school students their First Amendment rights of free speech and free exercise of religion. And Congress reflected public opinion polls that showed a large majority of the American people in favor of legislation to accommodate the free exercise of religion in public schools.

The Equal Access Act specifies the conditions under which public secondary schools are required to allow student religious groups to use their facilities. If a school permits one student club or organization that is not related to the curriculum to use its facilities, then the school may be required to accommodate other noncurriculum groups that want access to its facilities to conduct meetings, including groups with religious agendas.

The Equal Access Act created a broad opening in the "wall of separation" that had blocked student religious groups from using public school facilities. This was done to buttress the constitutional right of students to free exercise of religion. But did it compromise or violate the constitutional prohibition against an establishment of religion? The

U.S. Supreme Court responded to this issue in *Board of Education of the Westside Community Schools v. Mergens* (1990). The Court decided in this case to uphold the Equal Access Act (see Document 65).

What support is provided by the Equal Access Act for the right to free exercise of religion? Does the Equal Access Act reinforce the constitutional prohibition against an establishment of religion? If so, how? Why is the Equal Access Act an example of the accommodationist position on relationships between church and state or religion and government?

* * *

(a) It shall be unlawful for any public secondary school which receives Federal financial assistance and which has a limited open forum to deny equal access or a fair opportunity to, or discriminate against, any students who wish to conduct a meeting within that limited open forum on the basis of the religious, political, philosophical, or other content of the speech at such meetings.

(b) A public secondary school has a limited open forum whenever such school grants an offering to or opportunity for one or more noncurriculum related student groups to meet on school premises during noninstructional time.

(c) Schools shall be deemed to offer a fair opportunity to students who wish to conduct a meeting within its limited open forum if such a school uniformly provides that—

    (1) the meeting is voluntary and student-initiated;

    (2) there is no sponsorship of the meeting by the school, the government, or its agents or employees;

    (3) employees or agents of the school or government are present at religious meetings only in a non-participatory capacity;

    (4) the meeting does not materially and substantially interfere with the orderly conduct of educational activities within the school; and

    (5) nonschool persons may not direct, conduct, control, or regularly attend activities of student groups.

(d) Nothing in this subchapter shall be construed to authorize the United States or any State or political subdivision thereof—

    (1) to influence the form or content of any prayer or other religious activity;

    (2) to require any person to participate in prayer or other religious activity;

    (3) to expend public funds beyond the incidental cost of providing the space for student-initiated meetings;

    (4) to compel any school agent or employee to attend a school meet-

ing if the content of the speech at the meeting is contrary to the beliefs of the agent or employee;

(5) to sanction meetings that are otherwise unlawful;

(6) to limit the rights of groups of students which are not of a specified numerical size; or

(7) to abridge the constitutional rights of any person.

(e) Notwithstanding the availability of any other remedy under the Constitution or the laws of the United States, nothing in this subchapter shall be construed to authorize the United States to deny or withhold Federal financial assistance to any school.

(f) Nothing in this subchapter shall be construed to limit the authority of the school, its agents or employees, to maintain order and discipline on school premises, to protect the well-being of students and faculty, and to assure that attendance of students at meetings is voluntary.

Source: The Congressional Record (Washington, D.C., 1984), 20 U.S.C. 4071–74. See the following World Wide Web site: http://thomas.loc.gov/

DOCUMENT 61: *Wallace v. Jaffree* (1985)

In 1978 the Alabama legislature enacted a statute that directed public school teachers to begin each school day by informing students that a moment of silence would be observed for meditation. This law, Section 16–1-20 of the Alabama Code, was replaced by a statute in 1981 that called for a daily moment of silence in public school classrooms for meditation "or voluntary prayer." This 1981 enactment was designated Section 16–1-20.1 of the Alabama Code. The following year, 1982, Alabama lawmakers authorized public school teachers to lead "willing students" in a prescribed prayer to "Almighty God . . . the Creator and Supreme Judge of the world." This third law became Section 16–1-20.2 of the Alabama Code.

Ishmael Jaffree, a resident of Mobile County, Alabama, was a self-described agnostic. He was troubled when his children reported to him that they were ridiculed and ostracized by classmates for their refusal to participate in the devotional activities that were being conducted in their classrooms. Jaffree's repeated attempts to convince school officials to stop the devotional services were not successful. In 1982 Jaffree filed a legal complaint on behalf of his children, two in the second grade and one in kindergarten. The lawsuit alleged that all three Alabama statutes were in violation of the First Amendment's establishment of religion clause, which is applicable to the states as a result of the due process clause of the Fourteenth Amendment.

The United States District Court for the Southern District of Alabama dismissed Jaffree's complaint by relying on what it termed "newly discovered historical evidence." This evidence led the district court to the conclusion that the establishment clause does not prohibit a state from establishing a religion. This decision was reversed by the U.S. Court of Appeals for the Eleventh Circuit. The dispute was then appealed to the U.S. Supreme Court, which focused its attention on the constitutionality of the 1981 statute, 16–1-20.1, which had added the words "or voluntary prayer" to the earlier mandate for a moment of silence for meditation. The Court limited its deliberations to 16–1-20.1 after the appellees decided not to question the holding that the 1978 law, 16–1-20, was constitutional, and a separate decision that the statute that authorized teachers to lead willing students in prayer, 16–1-20.2, was unconstitutional.

Once its focus was narrowed to this single legislative pronouncement, members of the Supreme Court were especially interested in the testimony that had been offered in 1981 by the sponsor of 16–1-20.1. Alabama State Senator Donald G. Holmes testified before an evidentiary hearing conducted by the district court that the bill was an "effort to return voluntary prayer to our public schools." Holmes asserted that apart from this goal he had "no other purpose in mind."

When *Wallace v. Jaffree* was decided by the Supreme Court in 1985 not a single justice contested the constitutionality of a moment of silence in public school classrooms absent any reference to prayer. However, six members of the Court viewed the addition of the three simple words "or voluntary prayer" to the original moment of silence statute enacted in Alabama as an unconstitutional endorsement of a religious activity.

Justice John Paul Stevens wrote the majority opinion in *Wallace v. Jaffree*. Relying on the test formulated by the Supreme Court in 1971 in *Lemon v. Kurtzman* (see Document 55), Stevens declared that the 1981 statute, 16–1-20.1, lacked a secular legislative purpose. This return to the *Lemon* test was significant because two years earlier the Court had resolved the establishment clause dispute in *Marsh v. Chambers* (see Document 59) without citing the *Lemon* precedent. Equally important was the reaffirmation of the emphatic pronouncement made by the Court in 1962, in *Engel v. Vitale* (see Document 51), that the First Amendment prohibits state-mandated religious activities in public schools.

Justice Sandra Day O'Connor, in a concurring opinion, asserted that while the Alabama legislature erred in its endorsement of prayer in the 1981 statute, moment of silence laws are generally constitutional. O'Connor also expressed her own preference for a modification of the *Lemon* test. She argued that it would be more effective to use the test to focus the Court's attention on whether or not the action in question was an unconstitutional endorsement of religion by the government.

Justice William H. Rehnquist, one of the three dissenting votes in *Wallace v. Jaffree,* suggested that the Court should simply scrap the tripartite *Lemon* test. Rehnquist was also sharply critical of four decades of establishment clause jurisprudence that began with the Supreme Court's invocation of Thomas Jefferson's famous "wall of separation" metaphor in 1947 in *Everson v. Board of Education* (see Document 48). Rehnquist provided his own analysis of the origin and intent of the establishment clause as well as the motives of James Madison, the primary author of the Bill of Rights. Rehnquist's conclusion was that the scope of the establishment clause should be limited to prohibiting the creation of a national religion and/or a governmental preference for a particular religion.

Rehnquist's position is known as nonpreferentialism; it would permit, as constitutional, some kinds of government support for religion as long as they are provided equally or nonpreferentially to all religious denominations. This nonpreferentialist position was an issue in Virginia in 1785, when it was advocated by Patrick Henry and opposed by James Madison (see Part II, especially Document 22). Two hundred years later, in 1985, this same issue—whether or not nonpreferentialism was an unconstitutional establishment of religion—was still a hot issue in America.

Why was Alabama's 1978 statute concerning a moment of silence in public schools ruled constitutional, but the 1981 statute ruled unconstitutional? According to Justice O'Connor, what would be the advantage of implementing an endorsement test to measure potential violations of the establishment clause? According to Justice Rehnquist, what was James Madison attempting to prevent with his original draft of what became the establishment clause in the First Amendment?

* * *

JUSTICE STEVENS delivered the opinion of the Court.

Our unanimous affirmance of the Court of Appeals' judgment . . . makes it unnecessary to comment at length on the District Court's remarkable conclusion that the Federal Constitution imposes no obstacle to Alabama's establishment of a state religion. Before analyzing the precise issue that is presented to us, it is nevertheless appropriate to recall how firmly embedded in our constitutional jurisprudence is the proposition that the several States have no greater power to restrain the individual freedoms protected by the First Amendment than does the Congress of the United States.

As is plain from its text, the First Amendment was adopted to curtail

the power of Congress to interfere with the individual's freedom to believe, to worship, and to express himself in accordance with the dictates
of his own conscience. Until the Fourteenth Amendment was added to
the Constitution, the First Amendment's restraints on the exercise of federal power simply did not apply to the States. But when the Constitution
was amended to prohibit any State from depriving any person of liberty
without due process of law, that Amendment imposed the same substantive limitations on the States' power to legislate that the First Amendment had always imposed on the Congress' power. This Court has
confirmed and endorsed this elementary proposition of law time and
time again. . . .

Just as the right to speak and the right to refrain from speaking are
complementary components of a broader concept of individual freedom
of mind, so also the individual's freedom to choose his own creed is the
counterpart of his right to refrain from accepting the creed established
by the majority. At one time it was thought that this right merely proscribed the preference of one Christian sect over another, but would not
require equal respect for the conscience of the infidel, the atheist, or the
adherent of a non-Christian faith such as Islam or Judaism. But when
the underlying principle has been examined in the crucible of litigation,
the Court has unambiguously concluded that the individual freedom of
conscience protected by the First Amendment embraces the right to select
any religious faith or none at all. This conclusion derives support not
only from the interest in respecting the individual's freedom of conscience, but also from the conviction that religious beliefs worthy of respect are the product of free and voluntary choice by the faithful, and
from recognition of the fact that the political interest in forestalling intolerance extends beyond intolerance among Christian sects—or even
intolerance among "religions"—to encompass intolerance of the disbe-
liever and the uncertain. . . . The State of Alabama, no less than the Congress of the United States, must respect that basic truth. . . .

The legislative intent to return prayer to the public schools is, of
course, quite different from merely protecting every student's right to
engage in voluntary prayer during an appropriate moment of silence
during the school day. The 1978 statute already protected that right,
containing nothing that prevented any student from engaging in voluntary prayer during a silent minute of meditation. Appellants have not
identified any secular purpose that was not fully served by 16–1-20 before the enactment of 16–1-20.1. Thus, only two conclusions are consistent with the text of 16–1-20.1: (1) the statute was enacted to convey a
message of state endorsement and promotion of prayer; or (2) the statute
was enacted for no purpose. No one suggests that the statute was nothing but a meaningless or irrational act. . . . The legislature enacted [the
statute at issue] for the sole purpose of expressing the State's endorse-

ment of prayer activities for one minute at the beginning of each school day. The addition of "or voluntary prayer" indicates that the State intended to characterize prayer as a favored practice. Such an endorsement is not consistent with the established principle that the government must pursue a course of complete neutrality toward religion. . . .

JUSTICE O'CONNOR, concurring in the judgment.

Nothing in the United States Constitution as interpreted by this Court or in the laws of the State of Alabama prohibits public school students from voluntarily praying at any time before, during, or after the school day. Alabama has facilitated voluntary silent prayers of students who are so inclined by enacting [a statute], which provides a moment of silence in appellees' schools each day. The parties to these proceedings concede the validity of this enactment. At issue in these appeals is the constitutional validity of an additional and subsequent Alabama statute, which both the District Court and the Court of Appeals concluded was enacted solely to officially encourage prayer during the moment of silence. I agree with the judgment of the Court that, in light of the findings of the courts below and the history of its enactment, [the statute at issue] violates the Establishment Clause of the First Amendment. In my view, there can be little doubt that the purpose and likely effect of this subsequent enactment is to endorse and sponsor voluntary prayer in the public schools. I write separately to identify the peculiar features of the Alabama law that render it invalid, and to explain why moment of silence laws in other States do not necessarily manifest the same infirmity. I also write to explain why neither history nor the Free Exercise Clause of the First Amendment validates the Alabama law struck down [by] the Court today. . . .

The Religion Clauses of the First Amendment, coupled with the Fourteenth Amendment's guarantee of ordered liberty, preclude both the Nation and the States from making any law respecting an establishment of religion or prohibiting the free exercise thereof. *Cantwell v. Connecticut* (1940).

. . . It once appeared that the Court had developed a workable standard by which to identify impermissible government establishments of religion. Under the now familiar *Lemon* test, statutes must have both a secular legislative purpose and a principal or primary effect that neither advances nor inhibits religion, and in addition they must not foster excessive government entanglement with religion. Despite its initial promise, the *Lemon* test has proved problematic. The required inquiry into "entanglement" has been modified and questioned, and in one case we have upheld state action against an Establishment Clause challenge without applying the *Lemon* test at all. The author of *Lemon* himself apparently questions the test's general applicability. Justice REHNQUIST today suggests that we abandon *Lemon* entirely, and in the process limit the reach of the Establishment Clause to state discrimination between sects and government designation of a particular church as a "state" or "national" one.

Perhaps because I am new to the struggle, I am not ready to abandon all aspects of the *Lemon* test. I do believe, however, that the standards announced in *Lemon* should be reexamined and refined in order to make them more useful in achieving the underlying purpose of the First Amendment. We must strive to do more than erect a constitutional "signpost," to be followed or ignored in a particular case as our predilections may dictate. Instead, our goal should be "to frame a principle for constitutional adjudication that is not only grounded in the history and language of the first amendment, but one that is also capable of consistent application to the relevant problems." Last Term, I proposed a refinement of the *Lemon* test with this goal in mind.

The *Lynch* concurrence suggested that the religious liberty protected by the Establishment Clause is infringed when the government makes adherence to religion relevant to a person's standing in the political community. Direct government action endorsing religion or a particular religious practice is invalid under this approach because it "sends a message to nonadherents that they are outsiders, not full members of the political community, and an accompanying message to adherents that they are insiders, favored members of the political community." Under this view, *Lemon's* inquiry as to the purpose and effect of a statute requires courts to examine whether government's purpose is to endorse religion and whether the statute actually conveys a message of endorsement.

The endorsement test is useful because of the analytic content it gives to the *Lemon*-mandated inquiry into legislative purpose and effect. In this country, church and state must necessarily operate within the same community. Because of this co-existence, it is inevitable that the secular interests of government and the religious interests of various sects and their adherents will frequently intersect, conflict, and combine. A statute that ostensibly promotes a secular interest often has an incidental or even a primary effect of helping or hindering a sectarian belief. Chaos would ensue if every such statute were invalid under the Establishment Clause. For example, the State could not criminalize murder for fear that it would thereby promote the Biblical command against killing. The task for the Court is to sort out those statutes and government practices whose purpose and effect go against the grain of religious liberty protected by the First Amendment.

The endorsement test does not preclude government from acknowledging religion or from taking religion into account in making law and policy. It does preclude government from conveying or attempting to convey a message that religion or a particular religious belief is favored or preferred. Such an endorsement infringes the religious liberty of the nonadherent, for "[w]hen the power, prestige and financial support of government is placed behind a particular religious belief, the indirect coercive pressure upon religious minorities to conform to the prevailing officially approved religion is plain." (*Engel v. Vitale.*) At issue today is whether state moment of silence statutes in general, and Alabama's moment of silence statute in particular, embody an impermissible endorsement of prayer in public schools. . . .

The *Engel* and *Abington* decisions are not dispositive on the constitutionality of moment of silence laws. In those cases, public school teachers and students led their classes in devotional exercises. . . .

A state-sponsored moment of silence in the public schools is different from state-sponsored vocal prayer or Bible reading. First, a moment of silence is not inherently religious. Silence, unlike prayer or Bible reading, need not be associated with a religious exercise. Second, a pupil who participates in a moment of silence need not compromise his or her beliefs. During a moment of silence, a student who objects to prayer is left to his or her own thoughts, and is not compelled to listen to the prayers or thoughts of others. For these simple reasons, a moment of silence statute does not stand or fall under the Establishment Clause according to how the Court regards vocal prayer or Bible reading. . . . It is difficult to discern a serious threat to religious liberty from a room of silent, thoughtful school children.

By mandating a moment of silence, a State does not necessarily endorse any activity that might occur during the period. . . .

Given this evidence in the record, candor requires us to admit that this Alabama statute was intended to convey a message of state encouragement and endorsement of religion. . . . It endorses the decision to pray during a moment of silence, and accordingly sponsors a religious exercise. For that reason, I concur in the judgment of the Court. . . .

JUSTICE REHNQUIST, dissenting.

Thirty-eight years ago this Court, in *Everson v. Board of Education* (1947), summarized its exegesis of Establishment Clause doctrine thus:

"In the words of Jefferson, the clause against establishment of religion by law was intended to erect 'a wall of separation between church and State.' " This language . . . quoted from Thomas Jefferson's letter to the Danbury Baptist Association the phrase "I contemplate with sovereign reverence that act of the whole American people which declared that their legislature should 'make no law respecting an establishment of religion, or prohibiting the free exercise thereof,' thus building a wall of separation between church and State."

It is impossible to build sound constitutional doctrine upon a mistaken understanding of constitutional history, but unfortunately the Establishment Clause has been expressly freighted with Jefferson's misleading metaphor for nearly 40 years. Thomas Jefferson was of course in France at the time the constitutional Amendments known as the Bill of Rights were passed by Congress and ratified by the States. His letter to the Danbury Baptist Association was a short note of courtesy, written 14 years after the Amendments were passed by Congress. He would seem to any detached observer as a less than ideal source of contemporary history as to the meaning of the Religion Clauses of the First Amendment.

Jefferson's fellow Virginian, James Madison, with whom he was joined in the battle for the enactment of the Virginia Statute of Religious Liberty of 1786, did play as large a part as anyone in the drafting of the Bill of Rights. He had two advantages over Jefferson in this regard: he was present in the United States, and he was a leading Member of the First Congress. But when we turn to the record of the proceedings in the First Congress leading up to the adoption of the Establishment Clause of the Constitution, including Madison's significant contributions thereto, we see a far different picture of its purpose than the highly simplified "wall of separation between church and State." . . .

On June 8, 1789, James Madison rose in the House of Representatives and "reminded the House that this was the day that he had heretofore named for bringing forward amendments to the Constitution." Madison's subsequent remarks in urging the House to adopt his drafts of the proposed amendments were less those of a dedicated advocate of the wisdom of such measures than those of a prudent statesman seeking the enactment of measures sought by a number of his fellow citizens which could surely do no harm and might do a great deal of good. . . .

The language Madison proposed for what ultimately became the Religion Clauses of the First Amendment was this:

"The civil rights of none shall be abridged on account of religious belief or worship, nor shall any national religion be established, nor shall the full and equal rights of conscience be in any manner, or on any pretext, infringed."

On the same day that Madison proposed them, the amendments which formed the basis for the Bill of Rights were referred by the House to a Committee of the Whole, and after several weeks' delay were then referred to a Select Committee consisting of Madison and 10 others. The Committee revised Madison's proposal regarding the establishment of religion to read:

"[N]o religion shall be established by law, nor shall the equal rights of conscience be infringed." . . .

The House refused to accept the Senate's changes in the Bill of Rights and asked for a conference; the version which emerged from the conference was that which ultimately found its way into the Constitution as a part of the First Amendment.

Congress shall make no law respecting an establishment of religion, or prohibiting the free exercise thereof.

The House and the Senate both accepted this language on successive days, and the Amendment was proposed in this form. . . .

It seems indisputable from these glimpses of Madison's thinking, as reflected by actions on the floor of the House in 1789, that he saw the Amendment as designed to prohibit the establishment of a national religion, and perhaps to prevent discrimination among sects. He did not see it as requiring neutrality on the part of government between religion and irreligion. Thus, the Court's opinion in *Everson*—while correct in bracketing Madison and Jefferson together in their exertions in their home State leading to the enactment of the Virginia Statute of Religious Liberty—is totally incorrect in suggesting that Madison carried these views onto the floor of the United States House of Representatives when he proposed the language which would ultimately become the Bill of Rights. . . .

It would seem from this evidence that the Establishment Clause of the First Amendment had acquired a well-accepted meaning: it forbade establishment of a national religion, and forbade preference among religious sects or denominations. Indeed, the first American dictionary defined the word "establishment" as "the act of establishing, founding, ratifying or ordaining," such as in "[t]he Episcopal form of religion, so called, in England." The Establishment Clause did not require government neutrality between religion and irreligion nor did it prohibit the Federal Government from providing nondiscriminatory aid to religion. There is simply no historical foundation for the proposition that the Framers intended to build the "wall of separation" that was constitutionalized in *Everson*.

Notwithstanding the absence of a historical basis for this theory of rigid separation, the wall idea might well have served as a useful albeit misguided analytical concept, had it led this Court to unified and principled results in Establishment Clause cases. The opposite, unfortunately, has been true; in the 38 years since *Everson* our Establishment Clause cases have been neither principled nor unified. Our recent opinions, many of them hopelessly divided pluralities, have with embarrassing candor conceded that the "wall of separation" is merely a "blurred, indistinct, and variable barrier," which "is not wholly accurate" and can only be "dimly perceived." . . . The "wall of separation between church and State" is a metaphor based on bad history, a metaphor which has proved useless as a guide to judging. It should be frankly and explicitly abandoned.

The Court has more recently attempted to add some mortar to *Everson's* wall through the three-part test of *Lemon v. Kurtzman*, which served at first to offer a more useful test for purposes of the Establishment Clause than did the "wall" metaphor. Generally stated, the *Lemon* test proscribes state action that has a sectarian purpose or effect, or causes an impermissible governmental entanglement with religion. . . .

The secular purpose prong has proven mercurial in application because it has never been fully defined, and we have never fully stated how the test is to operate. . . .

The entanglement test as applied in cases like *Wolman* also ignores the myriad state administrative regulations properly placed upon sectarian institutions such as curriculum, attendance, and certification requirements for sectarian schools, or fire and safety regulations for churches.

These difficulties arise because the *Lemon* test has no more grounding in the history of the First Amendment than does the wall theory upon which it rests. The three-part test represents a determined effort to craft a workable rule from a historically faulty doctrine; but the rule can only be as sound as the doctrine it attempts to service. The three-part test has simply not provided adequate standards for deciding Establishment Clause cases, as this Court has slowly come to realize. Even worse, the *Lemon* test has caused this Court to fracture into unworkable plurality opinions, depending upon how each of the three factors applies to a certain state action. The results from our school services cases show the difficulty we have encountered in making the *Lemon* test yield principled results. . . .

The true meaning of the Establishment Clause can only be seen in its history. As drafters of our Bill of Rights, the Framers inscribed the principles that control today. Any deviation from their intentions frustrates the permanence of that Charter and will only lead to the type of unprincipled decision-making that has plagued our Establishment Clause cases since *Everson*.

The Framers intended the Establishment Clause to prohibit the designation of any church as a "national" one. The Clause was also designed to stop the Federal Government from asserting a preference for one religious denomination or sect over others. Given the "incorporation" of the Establishment Clause as against the States via the Fourteenth Amendment in *Everson*, States are prohibited as well from establishing a religion or discriminating between sects. As its history abundantly shows, however, nothing in the Establishment Clause requires government to be strictly neutral between religion and irreligion, nor does that Clause prohibit Congress or the States from pursuing legitimate secular ends through nondiscriminatory sectarian means.

The Court strikes down the Alabama statute because the State wished to "characterize prayer as a favored practice." It would come as much of a shock to those who drafted the Bill of Rights as it will to a large number of thoughtful Americans today to learn that the Constitution, as construed by the majority, prohibits the Alabama Legislature from "endorsing" prayer. George Washington himself, at the request of the very Congress which passed the Bill of Rights, proclaimed a day of "public thanksgiving and prayer, to be observed by acknowledging with grateful hearts the many and signal favors of Almighty God." History must judge whether it was the Father of his Country in 1789, or a majority of the Court today, which has strayed from the meaning of the Establishment Clause.

The State surely has a secular interest in regulating the manner in which public schools are conducted. Nothing in the Establishment Clause of the First Amendment, properly understood, prohibits any such generalized "endorsement" of prayer. I would therefore reverse the judgment of the Court of Appeals.

Source: Wallace v. Jaffree, 472 U.S. 38 (1985).

DOCUMENT 62: *Aguilar v. Felton* (1985)

Title I of the Elementary and Secondary Education Act, passed by Congress in 1965, authorized the use of federal funds to help local educational institutions meet the needs of educationally deprived children from low-income families. In 1966 New York City began using Title I funds to finance a program whereby public school teachers were sent to private and religious schools to provide remedial instruction in areas such as reading and mathematics. In addition, guidance counselors, psychologists, psychiatrists, and social workers, all employed by the public school system, were assigned to various church-affiliated schools to assist students by providing clinical and guidance services.

The teachers and other professionals, who had volunteered to be sent to religious schools, had been instructed to avoid any involvement with religious activities conducted at the schools. They were supervised by field personnel who were to make at least one unannounced visit per month to the parochial schools. The classrooms used for remedial instruction were cleared of all religious symbols. The government issued the materials and equipment needed to provide instruction and other services, and these items were used only for the Title I programs. During the 1981–1982 school year over 13 percent of the students in New York City who were eligible for Title I services were enrolled in nonpublic schools. Of these, 84 percent attended schools affiliated with the Roman Catholic Church and 8 percent attended Hebrew day schools.

In 1978 six New York City taxpayers, including Betty-Louise Felton, had challenged the constitutionality of the Title I program as a violation of the First Amendment's establishment of religion clause. The United States District Court for the Eastern District of New York granted the defendants' motion for a summary judgment and dismissed the suit. This decision was reversed by the Court of Appeals for the Second Circuit.

The court of appeals, in finding the New York City program unconstitutional, cited *Meek v. Pittenger* (see Document 56) and *Wolman v. Walter* (see Document 57). Rulings by the United States Supreme Court in *Meek* (1975) and *Wolman* (1977), and other cases, were interpreted to have created an "insurmountable barrier" to the use of federal funds to send public school teachers and other professionals into religious schools for instructional, clinical, or guidance purposes.

In *Aguilar v. Felton* (1985) the Supreme Court upheld the decision by the court of appeals by a 5–4 margin. On the same day that it issued its decision in *Aguilar* the Court reached a similar conclusion in a companion case, *School District of Grand Rapids v. Ball*. Justice William J. Brennan wrote the majority opinion in *Aguilar*, and he reasoned that the New York City program required a "permanent and pervasive" state presence in sectarian schools. As a result, Brennan argued, the third prong of the test devised in 1971 in *Lemon v. Kurtzman* (see Document 55), which prohibits an excessive entanglement between church and state, had been violated.

Justice Sandra Day O'Connor, writing in dissent, questioned the utility of the entanglement standard. For O'Connor it was incongruous that any program deemed to exhibit a secular legislative purpose and not having the effect of advancing religion, the first two prongs of the so-called *Lemon* test, could subsequently be considered the source of an excessive entanglement between church and state. In this instance, Justice O'Connor viewed the cooperation between church and state as "benign," and the tragic consequence of the Court's holding in *Aguilar*, she argued, would be the denial of valuable services to students in need.

Why does Justice Brennan believe that the New York City program created an excessive entanglement between church and state? Why does Justice O'Connor believe that the risk of an excessive entanglement is exaggerated by the majority in this case?

* * *

JUSTICE BRENNAN delivered the opinion of the Court.

* * *

The principle that the state should not become too closely entangled with the church in the administration of assistance is rooted in two concerns. When the state becomes enmeshed with a given denomination in matters of religious significance, the freedom of religious belief of those who are not adherents of that denomination suffers, even when the governmental purpose underlying the involvement is largely secular. In addition, the freedom of even the adherents of the denomination is limited by the governmental intrusion into sacred matters. . . .

In *Lemon v. Kurtzman* (1971), the Court held that the supervision necessary to ensure that teachers in parochial schools were not conveying religious messages to their students would constitute the excessive entanglement of church and state. . . .

Similarly, in *Meek v. Pittenger* (1975), we invalidated a state program that offered, *inter alia*, guidance, testing, and remedial and therapeutic services performed by public employees on the premises of the parochial schools. As in *Lemon*, we observed that though a comprehensive system of supervision might conceivably prevent teachers from having the primary effect of advancing religion, such a system would inevitably lead to an unconstitutional administrative entanglement between church and state. . . .

The critical elements of the entanglement proscribed in *Lemon* and *Meek* are thus present in this case. First, as noted above, the aid is provided in a pervasively sectarian environment. Second, because assistance is provided in the form of teachers, ongoing inspection is required to ensure the absence of a religious message. In short, the scope and duration of New York City's Title I program would require a permanent and pervasive state presence in the sectarian schools receiving aid.

This pervasive monitoring by public authorities in the sectarian schools infringes precisely those Establishment Clause values at the root of the prohibition of excessive entanglement. Agents of the city must visit and inspect the religious school regularly, alert for the subtle or overt presence of religious matter in Title I classes. In addition, the religious school must obey these same agents when they make determinations as to what is and what is not a "religious symbol" and thus off limits in a Title I classroom. In short, the religious school, which has as a primary purpose the advancement and preservation of a particular religion must endure the ongoing presence of state personnel whose primary purpose is to monitor teachers and students in an attempt to guard against the infiltration of religious thought.

The administrative cooperation that is required to maintain the educational program at issue here entangles church and state in still another way that infringes interests at the heart of the Establishment Clause. Administrative personnel of the public and parochial school systems must work together in resolving matters related to schedules, classroom assignments, problems that arise in the implementation of the program, requests for additional services, and the dissemination of information regarding the program. . . .

Despite the well-intentioned efforts taken by the City of New York, the program remains constitutionally flawed owing to the nature of the aid, to the institution receiving the aid, and to the constitutional principles that they implicate—that neither the State nor Federal Government shall promote or hinder a particular faith or faith generally through the advancement of benefits or through the excessive entanglement of church and state in the administration of those benefits.

JUSTICE O'CONNOR, dissenting.

* * *

. . . [T]he Court in this litigation adheres to the three-part Establishment Clause test enunciated in *Lemon v. Kurtzman* (1971). To survive the *Lemon* test, a statute must have both a secular legislative purpose and a principal or primary effect that neither advances nor inhibits religion. Under *Lemon* and its progeny, direct state aid to parochial schools that has the purpose or effect of furthering the religious mission of the schools is unconstitutional. I agree with that principle. According to the Court, however, the New York City Title I program is defective not because of any improper purpose or effect, but rather because it fails the third part of the *Lemon* test: the Title I program allegedly fosters excessive government entanglement with religion. I disagree with the Court's analysis of entanglement, and I question the utility of entanglement as a separate Establishment Clause standard in most cases. . . .

Recognizing the weakness of any claim of an improper purpose or effect, the Court today relies entirely on the entanglement prong of *Lemon* to invalidate the New York City Title I program. The Court holds that the occasional presence of peripatetic public school teachers on parochial school grounds threatens undue entanglement of church and state because (1) the remedial instruction is afforded in a pervasively sectarian environment; (2) ongoing supervision is required to assure that the public school teachers do not attempt to inculcate religion; (3) the administrative personnel of the parochial and public school systems must work together in resolving administrative and scheduling problems; and (4) the instruction is likely to result in political divisiveness over the propriety of direct aid.

The Court concludes that this degree of supervision of public school employees by other public school employees constitutes excessive entanglement of church and state. I cannot agree. The supervision that occurs in New York City's Title I program does not differ significantly from the supervision any public school teacher receives, regardless of the location of the classroom. Justice POWELL suggests that the required supervision is extensive because the State must be *certain* that public school teachers do not inculcate religion. That reasoning would require us to close our public schools, for there is always some chance that a public school teacher will bring religion into the classroom, regardless of its location. Even if I remained confident of the usefulness of entanglement as an Establishment Clause test, I would conclude that New York City's efforts to prevent religious indoctrination in Title I classes have been adequate and have not caused excessive institutional entanglement of church and state. . . .

I adhere to the doubts about the entanglement test that were expressed in *Lynch*. It is curious indeed to base our interpretation of the Constitution on speculation as to the likelihood of a phenomenon which the parties may create merely by prosecuting a lawsuit. My reservations about the entanglement test, however, have come to encompass its institutional aspects as well. As Justice REHNQUIST has pointed out, many of the inconsistencies in our Establishment Clause decisions can be ascribed to our insistence that parochial aid programs with a valid purpose and effect may still be invalid by virtue of undue entanglement. . . .

. . . I cannot close my eyes to the fact that, over almost two decades, New York City's public school teachers have helped thousands of impoverished parochial school children to overcome educational disadvantages without once attempting to inculcate religion. Their praiseworthy efforts have not eroded and do not threaten the religious liberty assured by the Establishment Clause. The contrary judgment of the Court of Appeals should be reversed.

I respectfully dissent.

Source: Aguilar v. Felton, 473 U.S. 402 (1985).

DOCUMENT 63: *Edwards v. Aguillard* (1987)

In 1925, in one of the most infamous trials in the history of the United States, John T. Scopes was found guilty of having violated a Tennessee law that prohibited teaching evolutionary theory to students in public schools. The verdict in this so-called Monkey Trial was never reviewed by the U.S. Supreme Court, but the Court would eventually decide whether or not a state could ban the teaching of Charles Darwin's theory of evolution from public school classrooms.

In 1968, in *Epperson v. Arkansas*, a unanimous Supreme Court ruled that an Arkansas statute enacted four decades earlier and patterned after the law that precipitated the Scopes trial was contrary to the freedom of religion mandate contained in the First Amendment. Justice Abe Fortas, writing for the Court in *Epperson*, noted that the statute was probably more of a "curiosity than a vital fact of life" since there was no record in Arkansas of any prosecution under the law. Fortas reasoned that the statute was the "product of the upsurge of 'fundamentalist' religious fervor of the twenties."

Despite the practical limitations of the Arkansas statute, Fortas did seize upon the opportunity to emphasize that the government must remain neutral in matters of religious theory. He fully recognized that the law had been intended to silence the teaching of evolutionary principles due to a conflict with a particular religious doctrine, namely literal belief in the Biblical interpretation of creation as contained in the Book of Genesis.

Approximately two decades after the *Epperson* decision, in *Edwards v. Aguillard* (1987), the Supreme Court confronted Louisiana's Balanced Treatment for Creation-Science and Evolution-Science in Public School Instruction Act. This law, enacted in 1981, stipulated that public schools in the state were prohibited from teaching evolutionary theory unless the theory of "creation science" was also taught. The teaching of either theory was not required unless the other was taught. Creation science, also known as "creationism," is derived from the Biblical interpretation of the origin of life on Earth.

A group of parents, teachers, and religious leaders challenged the constitutionality of what came to be known as Louisiana's "Creationism Act." This group included Don Aguillard, an assistant principal at Acadiana High School in the state. The American Civil Liberties Union represented the plaintiffs, and it was argued that the statute was in violation of the First Amendment's establishment of religion clause. It was the state's contention that the mandate for equal time was reasonable because creationism can be supported by scientific evidence. In addition, the law's stated purpose was to protect academic freedom.

The U.S. District Court for the Eastern District of Louisiana, relying on the *Epperson* precedent, ruled that the teaching of creation science was tailored to the principles of a particular religious sect and was, therefore, unconstitutional. The Court of Appeals for the Fifth Circuit affirmed this decision. The Supreme Court, in a 7–2 decision, also considered Louisiana's Balanced Treatment Act to be a contravention of the establishment clause.

The majority opinion in *Edwards* was written by Justice William J.

Brennan. Relying upon the first prong of the tripartite test advanced in 1971 in *Lemon v. Kurtzman* (see Document 55), Brennan concluded that the statute lacked a secular legislative purpose. He reasoned that the law was simply an effort to discredit evolutionary theory by "counter-balancing" it with creationism, a bona fide religious teaching.

Justice Antonin Scalia, writing in dissent, argued that the constitutionality of a statute should not be "disposed of on the gallop" by "impugning the motives" of its supporters in the state legislature. He scornfully objected to the premise that legislation can be invalidated "on the basis of its motivation alone, without regard to its effects."

Why does Justice Brennan reject the assertion that the Louisiana statute was intended to protect academic freedom? Why does Justice Scalia contend that a statute should not be invalidated for allegedly lacking a secular purpose?

* * *

JUSTICE BRENNAN delivered the opinion of the Court.

* * *

The Establishment Clause forbids the enactment of any law "respecting an establishment of religion." The Court has applied a three-pronged test to determine whether legislation comports with the Establishment Clause. First, the legislature must have adopted the law with a secular purpose. Second, the statute's principal or primary effect must be one that neither advances nor inhibits religion. Third, the statute must not result in an excessive entanglement of government with religion. *Lemon v. Kurtzman* (1971). State action violates the Establishment Clause if it fails to satisfy any of these prongs. . . .

In this case, the purpose of the Creationism Act was to restructure the science curriculum to conform with a particular religious viewpoint. Out of many possible science subjects taught in the public schools, the legislature chose to affect the teaching of the one scientific theory that historically has been opposed by certain religious sects. As in *Epperson*, the legislature passed the Act to give preference to those religious groups which have as one of their tenets the creation of humankind by a divine creator. The "overriding fact" that confronted the Court in *Epperson* was "that Arkansas' law selects from the body of knowledge a particular segment which it proscribes for the sole reason that it is deemed to conflict with . . . a particular interpretation of the Book of Genesis by a particular religious group." Similarly, the Creationism Act is designed *either* to promote the theory of creation science which embodies a particular religious tenet by requiring that creation science be taught whenever evolution is taught *or* to prohibit the teaching of a scientific theory disfavored by certain religious sects by forbidding the teaching of evolution when creation science is not also taught. The Establishment Clause, however, "forbids *alike* the preference of a religious doctrine *or* the prohibition of theory which is deemed antagonistic to a particular dogma." Because the primary purpose of the Creationism Act is to advance a particular religious belief, the Act endorses religion in violation of the First Amendment.

The Louisiana Creationism Act advances a religious doctrine by requiring either the banishment of the theory of evolution from public school classrooms or the presentation of a religious viewpoint that rejects evolution in its entirety. The Act violates the Establishment Clause of the First Amendment because it seeks to employ the symbolic and financial support of government to achieve a religious purpose. The judgment of the Court of Appeals therefore is

Affirmed.

JUSTICE SCALIA, dissenting.

* * *

Even if I agreed with the questionable premise that legislation can be invalidated under the Establishment Clause on the basis of its motivation alone, without regard to its effects, I would still find no justification for today's decision. The Louisiana legislators who passed the "Balanced Treatment for Creation-Science and Evolution-Science Act", each of whom had sworn to support the Constitution, were well aware of the potential Establishment Clause problems and considered that aspect of the legislation with great care. After seven hearings and several months of study, resulting in substantial revision of the original proposal, they approved the Act overwhelmingly and specifically articulated the secular purpose they meant it to serve. Although the record contains abundant evidence of the sincerity of that purpose (the only issue pertinent to this case), the Court today holds, essentially on the basis of "its visceral knowledge regarding what *must* have motivated the legislators," that the members of the Louisiana Legislature knowingly violated their oaths and then lied about it. I dissent. Had requirements of the Balanced Treatment Act that are not apparent on its face been clarified by an interpretation of the Louisiana Supreme Court, or by the manner of its implementation, the Act might well be found unconstitutional; but the question of its constitutionality cannot rightly be disposed of on the gallop, by impugning the motives of its supporters. . . .

It is important to stress that the purpose forbidden by *Lemon* is the purpose to "advance religion." . . . Our cases in no way imply that the Establishment Clause forbids legislators merely to act upon their religious convictions. We surely would not strike down a law providing money to feed the hungry or shelter the homeless if it could be demonstrated that, but for the religious beliefs of the legislators, the funds would not have been approved. Also, political activism by the religiously motivated is part of our heritage. Notwithstanding the majority's implication to the contrary, we do not presume that the sole purpose of a law is to advance religion merely because it was supported strongly by organized religions or by adherents of particular faiths. To do so would deprive religious men and women of their right to participate in the political process. Today's religious activism may give us the Balanced Treatment Act, but yesterday's resulted in the abolition of slavery, and tomorrow's may bring relief for famine victims. . . . Thus, the fact that creation science coincides with the beliefs of certain religions, a fact upon which the majority relies heavily, does not itself justify invalidation of the Act. . . .

In sum, even if one concedes, for the sake of argument, that a majority of the Louisiana Legislature voted for the Balanced Treatment Act partly in order to foster (rather than merely eliminate discrimination against) Christian fundamentalist beliefs, our cases establish that that alone would not suffice to invalidate the Act, so long as there was a genuine secular purpose as well. We have, moreover, no adequate basis for disbelieving the secular purpose set forth in the Act itself, or for concluding that it is a sham enacted to conceal the legislators' violation of their oaths of office. I am astonished by the Court's unprecedented readiness to reach such a conclusion, which I can only attribute to an intellectual predisposition created by the facts and the legend of *Scopes v. State* (1927)—an instinctive reaction that any governmentally imposed requirements bearing upon the teaching of evolution must be a manifestation of Christian fundamentalist repression. In this case, however, it seems to me the Court's position is the repressive one. The people of Louisiana, including those who are Christian fundamentalists, are quite entitled, as a secular matter, to have whatever scientific evidence there may be against evolution presented in their schools, just as Mr. Scopes was entitled to present whatever scientific evidence there was for it. Perhaps what the Louisiana Legislature has done is unconstitutional because there *is* no such evidence, and the scheme they have established will amount to no more than a presentation of the Book of Genesis. But we cannot say that on the evidence before us in this summary judgment context, which includes ample uncontradicted testimony that "creation science" is a body of scientific knowledge rather than revealed belief. *Infinitely less* can we say (or should we say) that the scientific evidence for evolution is so conclusive that no one could be gullible enough to believe that there is any real scientific evidence to the contrary, so that the legislation's stated purpose must be a lie. Yet that illiberal judgment, that *Scopes*-in-reverse, is ultimately the basis on which the Court's facile rejection of the Louisiana Legislature's purpose must rest. . . .

Because I believe that the Balanced Treatment Act had a secular purpose, which is all the first component of the *Lemon* test requires, I would reverse the judgment of the Court of Appeals and remand for further consideration. . . .

Source: Edwards v. Aguillard, 482 U.S. 578 (1987).

DOCUMENT 64: *Allegheny County v. American Civil Liberties Union, Greater Pittsburgh Chapter* (1989)

Can the government maintain a religious display or allow such a display to be erected on public property without violating the establishment of religion clause contained in the First Amendment? In *Lynch v. Donnelly* (1984) the United States Supreme Court addressed this issue. The case concerned a Christian nativity scene, or creche, that was owned and maintained by the city of Pawtucket, Rhode Island. The nativity scene was annually included in a Christmas display located in a park in the city's downtown shopping district. In addition to the creche, the display included a number of other objects, such as a Santa Claus house, a Christmas tree, wishing wells, and a large banner declaring "Season's Greetings."

The Supreme Court, by a narrow 5–4 margin, held that the display was not in violation of the establishment clause. The fact that numerous secular objects surrounded the nativity scene was of crucial importance for the majority. For them the display was not intended to advocate a particular religious message; rather, it served a legitimate secular purpose by presenting the historical origins of Christmas, a national public holiday. To this end Chief Justice Warren Burger, writing for the majority, applied the three-pronged test enunciated by the Court in 1971 in *Lemon v. Kurtzman* (see Document 55). However, Burger also asserted that, in the area of establishment clause adjudication, the Court was not confined to a single test.

Burger maintained that while the concept of a wall of separation was a "useful metaphor," it was not an accurate description of the practical relationship between the government and religion. The Chief Justice declared that rather than requiring a complete separation of church and state, the Constitution "affirmatively mandates accommodation, not merely tolerance, of all religions, and forbids hostility toward any."

In 1989, five years after the *Lynch* decision, the Supreme Court re-examined the issue of locating religious displays on public property. Specifically, the Court ruled on the constitutionality of two holiday displays erected annually in Pittsburgh, Pennsylvania. The first display was a Christian nativity scene located inside the Allegheny County Courthouse. The creche had been donated by the Holy Name Society, a Roman Catholic organization, and it included a sign to that effect. The display also included a banner proclaiming "Gloria in Excelsis Deo," meaning "Glory to God in the Highest." This nativity scene, unlike the one examined in *Lynch*, stood alone. In addition, it was located near the building's grand staircase, which was described as the "most public" part of the courthouse.

The second display, located outside the City-County Building, consisted of an eighteen-foot menorah, or candelabrum, and a forty-five-foot decorated Christmas tree. The menorah was owned by a Jewish organization, Chabad, but it was stored, erected, and removed each year by the city. At the base of the Christmas tree was a sign, bearing the name of the mayor of Pittsburgh, that proclaimed the city's "salute to liberty."

Seven local residents, in conjunction with the Pittsburgh branch of the American Civil Liberties Union, filed a lawsuit charging that both displays were in violation of the establishment clause. Over four decades earlier, the Supreme Court had ruled that the establishment clause applies to state and local governments via the due process clause of the Fourteenth Amendment.

The U.S. District Court for the Western District of Pennsylvania, relying primarily on the *Lynch* precedent, denied relief by ruling in favor of the defendants. This holding, however, was reversed by the Court of Appeals for the Third Circuit. The court of appeals, invoking the tripartite *Lemon* test, ruled that both displays had the impermissible effect of endorsing religion.

The Supreme Court, by a 5–4 margin, held that the nativity scene inside the County Courthouse constituted a violation of the establishment clause. However, by a 6–3 vote, the Court ruled that the display outside the City-County Building, which featured a menorah and a Christmas tree, was constitutionally acceptable.

Three justices, including William J. Brennan and John Paul Stevens, who wrote opinions that concurred in part and dissented in part, considered both displays to be unconstitutional. Four justices, headed by Anthony M. Kennedy, who also wrote an opinion that concurred in part and dissented in part, concluded that both displays were constitutional. The deciding votes, therefore, were held by Justices Harry A. Blackmun and Sandra Day O'Connor.

Justice Blackmun delivered the opinion for the deeply divided Court in *Allegheny County v. American Civil Liberties Union, Greater Pitts-burgh Chapter* (1989), and Justice O'Connor offered a concurring opinion. For Blackmun the nativity scene had the effect of endorsing a patently Christian message. Conversely, he viewed the display with a menorah adjacent to a Christmas tree as a recognition of the secular aspects of the holiday season, as well as a tribute to the cultural diversity of those groups that celebrate the season in one fashion or another. The fact that one display was presented as a "salute to liberty" while the other included a banner with a religious declaration was also of critical importance for Justice Blackmun.

The endorsement standard utilized by Blackmun had been suggested by Justice O'Connor in her concurring opinion in *Lynch v. Donnelly*. In *Lynch* O'Connor asserted that a "proper inquiry" under the purpose prong of *Lemon* focuses on "whether the government intends to convey a message of endorsement or disapproval of religion."

Justice Kennedy, in his opinion, questioned the validity of O'Connor's endorsement test. He was also critical of Blackmun for allowing a principle originally articulated in a concurring opinion to take precedence over the majority opinion advanced in the very same case, *Lynch v. Donnelly*. Concerning the finding that the creche display was unconstitutional, Kennedy argued that such a conclusion reflected "an unjustified hostility toward religion."

If both a nativity scene and a menorah are essentially religious symbols, why does Justice Blackmun regard one display as constitutional and the other unconstitutional? Why does Justice O'Connor feel that the endorsement test captures the "essential command" of the establishment clause? Why does Justice Kennedy regard the endorsement test as "flawed in its fundamentals and unworkable in practice"? Why does Justice Brennan focus on the issue of government neutrality?

* * *

JUSTICE BLACKMUN delivered the opinion of the Court.

* * *

Precisely because of the religious diversity that is our national heritage, the Founders added to the Constitution a Bill of Rights, the very first words of which declare: "Congress shall make no law respecting an establishment of religion, or prohibiting the free exercise thereof. . . ." Perhaps in the early days of the Republic these words were understood to protect only the diversity within Christianity, but today they are recognized as guaranteeing religious liberty and equality to "the infidel, the atheist, or the adherent of a non-Christian faith such as Islam or Judaism." It is settled law that no government official in this Nation may violate these fundamental constitutional rights regarding matters of conscience. . . .

In *Lemon v. Kurtzman*, the Court sought to refine these principles by focusing on three "tests" for determining whether a government practice violates the Establishment Clause. Under the *Lemon* analysis, a statute or practice which touches upon religion, if it is to be permissible under the Establishment Clause, must have a secular purpose; it must neither advance nor inhibit religion in its principal or primary effect; and it must not foster an excessive entanglement with religion. This trilogy of tests has been applied regularly in the Court's later Establishment Clause cases.

Our subsequent decisions further have refined the definition of governmental action that unconstitutionally advances religion. In recent years, we have paid particularly close attention to whether the challenged governmental practice either has the purpose or effect of "endorsing" religion, a concern that has long had a place in our Establishment Clause jurisprudence. . . .

Of course, the word "endorsement" is not self-defining. Rather, it derives its meaning from other words that this Court has found useful over the years in interpreting the Establishment Clause. Thus, it has been noted that the prohibition against governmental endorsement of religion "preclude[s] government from conveying or attempting to convey a message that religion or a particular religious belief is *favored or preferred*." . . . Moreover, the term "endorsement" is closely linked to the term "promotion," and this Court long since has held that government "may not . . . promote one religion or religious theory against another or even against the militant opposite," *Epperson v. Arkansas* (1968). . . .

We have had occasion in the past to apply Establishment Clause principles to the government's display of objects with religious significance. In *Stone v. Graham* (1980), we held that the display of a copy of the Ten Commandments on the walls of public classrooms violates the Establishment Clause. Closer to the facts of this litigation is *Lynch v. Donnelly*, in which we considered whether the city of Pawtucket, R. I., had violated the Establishment Clause by including a creche in its annual Christmas display, located in a private park within the downtown shopping district. By a 5-to-4 decision in that difficult case, the Court upheld inclusion of the creche in the Pawtucket display, holding, *inter alia*, that the inclusion of the creche did not have the impermissible effect of advancing or promoting religion. . . .

Although Justice O'CONNOR joined the majority opinion in *Lynch*, she wrote a concurrence that differs in significant respects from the majority opinion. The main difference is that the concurrence provides a sound analytical framework for evaluating governmental use of religious symbols.

First and foremost, the concurrence squarely rejects any notion that this Court will tolerate some government endorsement of religion. Rather, the concurrence recognizes any endorsement of religion as "invalid," because it "sends a message to nonadherents that they are outsiders, not full members of the political community, and an accompanying message to adherents that they are insiders, favored members of the political community."

Second, the concurrence articulates a method for determining whether the government's use of an object with religious meaning has the effect of endorsing religion. The effect of the display depends upon the message that the government's practice communicates: the question is "what viewers may fairly understand to be the purpose of the display." That inquiry, of necessity, turns upon the context in which the contested object appears. . . .

We turn first to the county's creche display. There is no doubt, of course, that the creche itself is capable of communicating a religious message. Indeed, the creche in this lawsuit uses words, as well as the picture of the Nativity scene, to make its religious meaning unmistakably clear. "Glory to God in the Highest!" says the angel in the creche—Glory to God because of the birth of Jesus. This praise to God in Christian terms is indisputably religious—indeed sectarian—just as it is when said in the Gospel or in a church service.

Under the Court's holding in *Lynch*, the effect of a creche display turns on its setting. Here, unlike in *Lynch*, nothing in the context of the display detracts from the creche's religious message. . . .

In sum, *Lynch* teaches that government may celebrate Christmas in some manner and form, but not in a way that endorses Christian doctrine. Here, Allegheny County has transgressed this line. It has chosen to celebrate Christmas in a way that has the effect of endorsing a patently Christian message: Glory to God for the birth of Jesus Christ. Under *Lynch*, and the rest of our cases, nothing more is required to demonstrate a violation of the Establishment Clause. The display of the creche in this context, therefore, must be permanently enjoined. . . .

The display of the Chanukah menorah in front of the City-County Building may well present a closer constitutional question. The menorah, one must recognize, is a religious symbol: it serves to commemorate the miracle of the oil as described in the Talmud. But the menorah's message is not exclusively religious. The menorah is the primary visual symbol for a holiday that, like Christmas, has both religious and secular dimensions.

Moreover, the menorah here stands next to a Christmas tree and a sign saluting liberty. While no challenge has been made here to the display of the tree and the sign, their presence is obviously relevant in determining the effect of the menorah's display. The necessary result of placing a menorah next to a Christmas tree is to create an "overall holiday setting" that represents both Christmas and Chanukah—two holidays, not one.

The mere fact that Pittsburgh displays symbols of both Christmas and Chanukah does not end the constitutional inquiry. If the city celebrates both Christmas and Chanukah as religious holidays, then it violates the Establishment Clause. The simultaneous endorsement of Judaism and Christianity is no less constitutionally infirm than the endorsement of Christianity alone.

Conversely, if the city celebrates both Christmas and Chanukah as secular holidays, then its conduct is beyond the reach of the Establishment Clause. Because government may celebrate Christmas as a secular holiday, it follows that government may also acknowledge Chanukah as a secular holiday. Simply put, it would be a form of discrimination against Jews to allow Pittsburgh to celebrate Christmas as a cultural tradition while simultaneously disallowing the city's acknowledgment of Chanukah as a contemporaneous cultural tradition.

Accordingly, the relevant question for Establishment Clause purposes is whether the combined display of the tree, the sign, and the menorah has the effect of endorsing both Christian and Jewish faiths, or rather simply recognizes that both Christmas and Chanukah are part of the same winter-holiday season, which has attained a secular status in our society. Of the two interpretations of this particular display, the latter seems far more plausible and is also in line with *Lynch*.

The mayor's sign further diminishes the possibility that the tree and the menorah will be interpreted as a dual endorsement of Christianity and Judaism. The sign states that during the holiday season the city salutes liberty. Moreover, the sign draws upon the theme of light, common to both Chanukah and Christmas as winter festivals, and links that theme with this Nation's legacy of freedom, which allows an American to celebrate the holiday season in whatever way he wishes, religiously or otherwise. While no sign can disclaim an overwhelming message of endorsement, an "explanatory plaque" may confirm that in particular contexts the government's association with a religious symbol does not represent the government's sponsorship of religious beliefs. Here, the mayor's sign serves to confirm what the context already reveals: that the display of the menorah is not an endorsement of religious faith but simply a recognition of cultural diversity. . . .

JUSTICE O'CONNOR, concurring in part and concurring in the judgment.

* * *

In my concurrence in *Lynch*, I suggested a clarification of our Establishment Clause doctrine to reinforce the concept that the Establishment Clause "prohibits government from making adherence to a religion relevant in any way to a person's standing in the political community." The government violates this prohibition if it endorses or disapproves of religion. . . .

For the reasons stated in the Court's opinion in these cases, I agree that the creche displayed on the Grand Staircase of the Allegheny County Courthouse, the seat of county government, conveys a message to nonadherents of Christianity that they are not full members of the political community, and a corresponding message to Christians that they are favored members of the political community. In contrast to the creche in *Lynch*, which was displayed in a private park in the city's commercial district as part of a broader display of traditional secular symbols of the holiday season, this creche stands alone in the county courthouse. . . .

Under the endorsement test, the "history and ubiquity" of a practice is relevant not because it creates an "artificial exception" from that test. On the contrary, the "history and ubiquity" of a practice is relevant because it provides part of the context in which a reasonable observer evaluates whether a challenged governmental practice conveys a message of endorsement of religion. It is the combination of the long-standing existence of practices such as opening legislative sessions with legislative prayers or opening Court sessions with "God save the United States and this honorable Court," as well as their nonsectarian nature, that leads me to the conclusion that those particular practices, despite their religious roots, do not convey a message of endorsement of particular religious beliefs. . . .

Contrary to Justice KENNEDY's assertions, neither the endorsement test nor its application in these cases reflects "an unjustified hostility toward religion." Instead, the endorsement standard recognizes that the religious liberty so precious to the citizens who make up our diverse country is protected, not impeded, when government avoids endorsing religion or favoring particular beliefs over others. Clearly, the government can *acknowledge* the role of religion in our society in numerous ways that do not amount to an endorsement. Moreover, the government can *accommodate* religion by lifting government-imposed burdens on religion. . . .

JUSTICE KENNEDY, concurring in the judgment in part and dissenting in part.

The majority holds that the County of Allegheny violated the Establishment Clause by displaying a creche in the county courthouse, because the "principal or primary effect" of the display is to advance religion within the meaning of *Lemon v. Kurtzman* (1971). This view of the Establishment Clause reflects an unjustified hostility toward religion, a hostility inconsistent with our history and our precedents, and I dissent from this holding. The creche display is constitutional, and, for the same reasons, the display of a menorah by the city of Pittsburgh is permissible as well. . . .

If *Lynch* is still good law—and until today it was—the judgment below cannot stand. I accept and indeed approve both the holding and the reasoning of Chief Justice Burger's opinion in *Lynch*, and so I must dissent from the judgment that the creche display is unconstitutional. On the same reasoning, I agree that the menorah display is constitutional.

The majority invalidates display of the creche, not because it disagrees with the interpretation of *Lynch* applied above, but because it chooses to discard the reasoning of the *Lynch* majority opinion in favor of Justice O'CONNOR's concurring opinion in that case. It has never been my understanding that a concurring opinion "suggest[ing] a clarification of our . . . doctrine," could take precedence over an opinion joined in its entirety by five Members of the Court. As a general rule, the principle of *stare decisis* directs us to adhere not only to the holdings of our prior cases, but also to their explications of the governing rules of law. Since the majority does not state its intent to overrule *Lynch*, I find its refusal to apply the reasoning of that decision quite confusing. . . .

. . . Although a scattering of our cases have used "endorsement" as another word for "preference" or *"imprimatur,"* the endorsement test applied by the majority had its genesis in Justice O'CONNOR's concurring opinion in *Lynch*.

. . . I submit that the endorsement test is flawed in its fundamentals and unworkable in practice. The uncritical adoption of this standard is every bit as troubling as the bizarre result it produces in the cases before us. . . .

If the endorsement test, applied without artificial exceptions for historical practice, reached results consistent with history, my objections to it would have less force. But, as I understand that test, the touchstone of an Establishment Clause violation is whether nonadherents would be made to feel like "outsiders" by government recognition or accommodation of religion. Few of our traditional practices recognizing the part religion plays in our society can withstand scrutiny under a faithful application of this formula.

Some examples suffice to make plain my concerns. Since the Founding of our Republic, American Presidents have issued Thanksgiving Proclamations establishing a national day of celebration and prayer. The first such proclamation was issued by President Washington at the request of the First Congress, and "recommend[ed] and assign[ed]" a day "to be devoted by the people of these States to the service of that great and glorious Being who is the beneficent author of all the good that was, that is, or that will be," so that "we may then unite in most humbly offering our prayers and supplications to the great Lord and Ruler of Nations, and beseech Him to . . . promote the knowledge and practice of true religion and virtue. . . ." Most of President Washington's successors have followed suit, and the forthrightly religious nature of these proclamations has not waned with the years. President Franklin D. Roosevelt went so far as to "suggest a nationwide reading of the Holy Scriptures during the period from Thanksgiving Day to Christmas" so that "we may bear more earnest witness to our gratitude to Almighty God." It requires little imagination to conclude that these proclamations would cause nonadherents to feel excluded, yet they have been a part of our national heritage from the beginning.

The Executive has not been the only Branch of our Government to recognize the central role of religion in our society. The fact that this Court opens its sessions with the request that "God save the United States and this honorable Court" has been noted elsewhere. The Legislature has gone much further, not only employing legislative chaplains, but also setting aside a special prayer room in the Capitol for use by Members of the House and Senate. The room is decorated with a large stained glass panel that depicts President Washington kneeling in prayer; around him is etched the first verse of the 16th Psalm: "Preserve me, O God, for in Thee do I put my trust." Beneath the panel is a rostrum on which a Bible is placed; next to the rostrum is an American Flag. Some endorsement is inherent in these reasonable accommodations, yet the Establishment Clause does not forbid them. . . .

The approach adopted by the majority contradicts important values embodied in the Clause. Obsessive, implacable resistance to all but the most carefully scripted and secularized forms of accommodation requires this Court to act as a censor, issuing national decrees as to what is orthodox and what is not. What is orthodox, in this context, means what is secular; the only Christmas the State can acknowledge is one in which references to religion have been held to a minimum. The Court thus lends its assistance to an Orwellian rewriting of history as many understand it. I can conceive of no judicial function more antithetical to the First Amendment. . . .

JUSTICE BRENNAN, concurring in part and dissenting in part.

I have previously explained at some length my views on the relationship between the Establishment Clause and government-sponsored celebrations of the Christmas holiday. I continue to believe that the display of an object that "retains a specifically Christian [or other] religious meaning," is incompatible with the separation of church and state demanded by our Constitution. I therefore agree with the Court that Allegheny County's display of a creche at the county courthouse signals an endorsement of the Christian faith in violation of the Establishment Clause. . . . I cannot agree, however, that the city's display of a 45-foot Christmas tree and an 18-foot Chanukah menorah at the entrance to the building housing the mayor's office shows no favoritism towards Christianity, Judaism, or both. Indeed, I should have thought that the answer as to the first display supplied the answer to the second. . . .

Justice BLACKMUN, in his acceptance of the city's message of "diversity," and, even more so, Justice O'CONNOR, in her approval of the "message of pluralism and freedom to choose one's own beliefs," appear to believe that, where seasonal displays are concerned, more is better. Whereas a display might be constitutionally problematic if it showcased the holiday of just one religion, those problems vaporize as soon as more than one religion is included. I know of no principle under the Establishment Clause, however, that permits us to conclude that governmental promotion of religion is acceptable so long as one religion is not favored. We have, on the contrary, interpreted that Clause to require neutrality, not just among religions, but between religion and nonreligion. . . .

Source: Allegheny County v. American Civil Liberties Union, Greater Pittsburgh Chapter, 492 U.S. 573 (1989).

DOCUMENT 65: *Board of Education of the Westside Community Schools v. Mergens* (1990)

In 1981, in *Widmar v. Vincent,* the United States Supreme Court ruled that whenever the facilities of a state university are available to registered student organizations, university officials cannot exclude a bona fide student group solely because the purpose of that group's meeting is to express ideas that are religious in nature. The Court held that "equal access" to public facilities cannot be the product of content-based restrictions that are imposed arbitrarily.

In 1984 Congress extended the *Widmar* precedent to public secondary schools receiving federal financial assistance by passing the Equal Access Act (see Document 60). The law stipulated, first, that whenever a public high school permits at least one noncurriculum-related student group to meet on school premises during noninstructional time, it thereby creates a "limited open forum." Second, whenever such a forum is created, equal access to school facilities cannot be denied to a student group due to the religious, political, or philosophical content of their speech.

The Equal Access Act was qualified by the proviso that its intention was not to limit the authority of school officials to maintain order and discipline on school premises. Any meeting that focused on religious, political, or philosophical content was to be voluntary and student-initiated. In addition, the presence of school officials was to be simply custodial and, thus, nonparticipatory.

In 1985 a group of students at Westside High School in Omaha, Nebraska, attempted to form a Christian club at the school. The stated purpose of the group, which included Bridget Mergens, was to provide students with an opportunity to read and discuss the Bible, and to pray together. Membership was to be voluntary and open to all students. The students' proposal was later amended to include the attendance of a faculty member in a nonparticipatory, custodial capacity. School officials denied the request by Mergens and the other pupils on the grounds that the presence of such a club in a public school would constitute a violation of the establishment of religion clause. This clause, located in the First Amendment, applies to the states via the due process clause of the Fourteenth Amendment.

The students sought relief in the U.S. District Court for the District of Nebraska, where they alleged that the school officials had violated the Equal Access Act. They supported this claim by documenting that the high school had approximately thirty student clubs, including a number of noncurriculum-related groups. It was the students' contention that the presence of organizations such as the chess club, photography club, and scuba diving club meant that the school had created a limited open forum. If correct, Westside High School, a recipient of federal funds, was thereby obligated to follow the dictates of the Equal Access Act. The students alleged that their rights to freedom of speech, assembly, association, and free exercise of religion had also been abrogated.

The district court denied relief, accepting the school system's contention that all of the clubs in question were curriculum-related. This decision, however, was reversed by the U.S. Court of Appeals for the Eighth Circuit. Unlike the district court, the court of appeals rejected the assertion that all of the clubs were curriculum-related, and they reasoned that to allow school officials to act upon such a faulty claim would be to render the Equal Access Act meaningless.

The Supreme Court, in *Board of Education of the Westside Community Schools v. Mergens* (1990), affirmed the ruling by the court of appeals. Justice Sandra Day O'Connor delivered the opinion of the Court. After interpreting "noncurriculum related" to mean that which is not directly related to the body of courses offered at a particular school, O'Connor proclaimed that it was the intention of Congress to provide a "low threshold" for triggering the requirements of the Equal Access Act. Concerning the constitutionality of the act, Justice O'Connor reasoned that high school students are mature enough to understand that a public school that simply permits student speech on a nondiscriminatory basis is not simultaneously endorsing that speech.

Justice Anthony Kennedy offered a concurring opinion, but he rejected the validity of O'Connor's endorsement standard. Kennedy argued that the purpose of the establishment clause, in addition to prohibiting the creation of a state religion, is to prevent the government from using coercion to influence an individual's religious practices.

Justice Thurgood Marshall, also concurring, warned that toleration could be interpreted as an endorsement. He agreed that the Equal Access Act, as applied to the situation at Westside High School, was constitutional, but he suggested further steps to prevent the appearance that the school was endorsing the goals of the religious club.

The lone dissent in *Mergens* was offered by Justice John Paul Stevens. He rejected the claim that a limited open forum had been created by outlining the key differences between the university examined in *Widmar* and the high school attended by Bridget Mergens.

According to Justice O'Connor, what balance must public schools maintain regarding the establishment clause on the one hand, and the free speech and free exercise of religion clauses on the other hand? Why does Justice Kennedy object to the use of O'Connor's endorsement test to help resolve establishment clause disputes? According to Justice Marshall, what steps could be taken at Westside High School to help ensure that its toleration of religious speech is not seen as an endorsement of such speech? Why does Justice Stevens contend that a limited open forum had not been created at the high school despite the presence of clubs not directly related to the curriculum? Why is the Court's decision in this case an example of support for the accommodationist position on relationships between government and religion?

* * *

JUSTICE O'CONNOR delivered the opinion of the Court.

* * *

Petitioners contend that even if Westside has created a limited open forum within the meaning of the Act, its denial of official recognition to the proposed Christian club must nevertheless stand because the Act violates the Establishment Clause of the First Amendment, as applied to the States through the Fourteenth Amendment. Specifically, petitioners maintain that because the school's recognized student activities are an integral part of its educational mission, official recognition of respondents' proposed club would effectively incorporate religious activities into the school's official program, endorse participation in the religious club, and provide the club with an official platform to proselytize other students.

We disagree. In *Widmar*, we applied the three-part *Lemon* test to hold that an "equal access" policy, at the university level, does not violate the Establishment Clause. . . .

We think the logic of *Widmar* applies with equal force to the Equal Access Act. As an initial matter, the Act's prohibition of discrimination on the basis of "political, philosophical, or other" speech as well as religious speech is a sufficient basis for meeting the secular purpose prong of the *Lemon* test. . . .

Petitioners' principal contention is that the Act has the primary effect of advancing religion. Specifically, petitioners urge that, because the student religious meetings are held under school aegis, and because the State's compulsory attendance laws bring the students together (and thereby provide a ready-made audience for student evangelists), an objective observer in the position of a secondary school student will perceive official school support for such religious meetings. . . .

We disagree. First, although we have invalidated the use of public funds to pay for teaching state-required subjects at parochial schools, in part because of the risk of creating "a crucial symbolic link between government and religion, thereby enlisting—at least in the eyes of impressionable youngsters—the powers of government to the support of the religious denomination operating the school," *School Dist. of Grand Rapids v. Ball* (1985), there is a crucial difference between *government* speech endorsing religion, which the Establishment Clause forbids, and *private* speech endorsing religion, which the Free Speech and Free Exercise Clauses protect. We think that secondary school students are mature enough and are likely to understand that a school does not endorse or support student speech that it merely permits on a nondiscriminatory basis. . . .

Second, we note that the Act expressly limits participation by school officials at meetings of student religious groups, and that any such meetings must be held during "noninstructional time." The Act therefore avoids the problems of "the students' emulation of teachers as role models" and "mandatory attendance requirements." To be sure, the possibility of *student* peer pressure remains, but there is little if any risk of official state endorsement or coercion where no formal classroom activities are involved and no school officials actively participate. Moreover, petitioners' fear of a mistaken inference of endorsement is largely self-imposed, because the school itself has control over any impressions it gives its students. To the extent a school makes clear that its recognition of respondents' proposed club is not an endorsement of the views of the club's participants, students will reasonably understand that the schools' official recognition of the club evinces neutrality toward, rather than endorsement of, religious speech.

Third, the broad spectrum of officially recognized student clubs at Westside, and the fact that Westside students are free to initiate and organize additional student clubs, counteract any possible message of official endorsement of or preference for religion or a particular religious belief. Although a school may not itself lead or direct a religious club, a school that permits a student-initiated and student-led religious club to meet after school, just as it permits any other student group to do, does not convey a message of state approval or endorsement of the particular religion. Under the Act, a school with a limited open forum may not lawfully deny access to a Jewish students' club, a Young Democrats club, or a philosophy club devoted to the study of Nietzsche. To the extent that a religious club is merely one of many different student-initiated voluntary clubs, students should perceive no message of government endorsement of religion. Thus, we conclude that the Act does not, at least on its face and as applied to Westside, have the primary effect of advancing religion.

Petitioners' final argument is that by complying with the Act's requirements, the school risks excessive entanglement between government and religion. The proposed club, petitioners urge, would be required to have a faculty sponsor who would be charged with actively directing the activities of the group, guiding its leaders, and ensuring balance in the presentation of controversial ideas. Petitioners claim that this influence over the club's religious program would entangle the government in day-to-day surveillance of religion of the type forbidden by the Establishment Clause.

Under the Act, however, faculty monitors may not participate in any religious meetings, and nonschool persons may not direct, control, or regularly attend activities of student groups. Moreover, the Act prohibits school "sponsorship" of any religious meetings, which means that school officials may not promote, lead, or participate in any such meeting. Although the Act permits "[t]he assignment of a teacher, administrator, or other school employee to a meeting for custodial purposes," such custodial oversight of the student-initiated religious group, merely to ensure order and good behavior, does not impermissibly entangle government in the day-to-day surveillance or administration of religious activities. Indeed, as the Court noted in *Widmar*, a denial of equal access to religious speech might well create greater entanglement problems in the form of invasive monitoring to prevent religious speech at meetings at which such speech might occur.

Accordingly, we hold that the Equal Access Act does not on its face contravene the Establishment Clause. Because we hold that petitioners have violated the Act, we do not decide respondents' claims under the

Free Speech and Free Exercise Clauses. For the foregoing reasons, the judgment of the Court of Appeals is affirmed.

JUSTICE KENNEDY, concurring in part and concurring in the judgment.

* * *

I agree with the plurality that a school complying with the statute by satisfying the criteria . . . does not violate the Establishment Clause. The accommodation of religion mandated by the Act is a neutral one, and in the context of this case it suffices to inquire whether the Act violates either one of two principles. The first is that the government cannot "give direct benefits to religion in such a degree that it in fact 'establishes a [state] religion or religious faith, or tends to do so.' " Any incidental benefits that accompany official recognition of a religious club under the criteria set forth in the [statute] do not lead to the establishment of religion under this standard. The second principle controlling the case now before us, in my view, is that the government cannot coerce any student to participate in a religious activity. The Act is consistent with this standard as well. Nothing on the face of the Act or in the facts of the case as here presented demonstrates that enforcement of the statute will result in the coercion of any student to participate in a religious activity. The Act does not authorize school authorities to require, or even to encourage, students to become members of a religious club or to attend a club's meetings, the meetings take place while school is not in session, and the Act does not compel any school employee to participate in, or to attend, a club's meetings or activities.

The plurality uses a different test, one which asks whether school officials, by complying with the Act, have endorsed religion. It is true that when government gives impermissible assistance to a religion it can be said to have "endorsed" religion; but endorsement cannot be the test. The word endorsement has insufficient content to be dispositive. And for reasons I have explained elsewhere, its literal application may result in neutrality in name but hostility in fact when the question is the government's proper relation to those who express some religious preference.

I should think it inevitable that a public high school "endorses" a religious club, in a commonsense use of the term, if the club happens to be one of many activities that the school permits students to choose in order to further the development of their intellect and character in an extracurricular setting. But no constitutional violation occurs if the school's action is based upon a recognition of the fact that membership in a religious club is one of many permissible ways for a student to further his or her own personal enrichment. The inquiry with respect to coercion must be whether the government imposes pressure upon a student to participate in a religious activity. This inquiry, of course, must be undertaken with sensitivity to the special circumstances that exist in a secondary school where the line between voluntary and coerced participation may be difficult to draw. No such coercion, however, has been shown to exist as a necessary result of this statute, either on its face or as respondents seek to invoke it on the facts of this case. . . .

JUSTICE MARSHALL concurring in the judgment.

* * *

I agree with the majority that "noncurriculum" must be construed broadly to "prohibit schools from discriminating on the basis of the content of a student group's speech." As the majority demonstrates, such a construction "is consistent with Congress' intent to provide a low threshold for triggering the Act's requirements." In this respect, the Act as construed by the majority simply codifies in statute what is already constitutionally mandated: schools may not discriminate among student-initiated groups that seek access to school facilities for expressive purposes not directly related to the school's curriculum.

The Act's low threshold for triggering equal access, however, raises serious Establishment Clause concerns where secondary schools with fora that differ substantially from the forum in *Widmar* are required to grant access to student religious groups. Indeed, as applied in the present case, the Act mandates a religious group's access to a forum that is dedicated to promoting fundamental values and citizenship as defined by the school. The Establishment Clause does not forbid the operation of the Act in such circumstances, but it does require schools to change their relationship to their fora so as to disassociate themselves effectively from religious clubs' speech. Thus, although I agree with the plurality that the Act as applied to Westside *could* withstand Establishment Clause scrutiny, I write separately to emphasize the steps Westside must take to avoid appearing to endorse the Christian club's goals. The plurality's Establishment Clause analysis pays inadequate attention to the differences between this case and *Widmar* and dismisses too lightly the distinctive pressures created by Westside's highly structured environment.

This case involves the intersection of two First Amendment guarantees—the Free Speech Clause and the Establishment Clause. We have long regarded free and open debate over matters of controversy as necessary to the functioning of our constitutional system. That the Constitution requires toleration of speech over its suppression is no less true in our Nation's schools. . . .

But the Constitution also demands that the State not take action that has the primary effect of advancing religion. The introduction of religious speech into the public schools reveals the tension between these two constitutional commitments, because the failure of a school to stand apart from religious speech can convey a message that the school endorses rather than merely tolerates that speech. . . .

Westside thus must do more than merely prohibit faculty members from actively participating in the Christian club's meetings. It must fully disassociate itself from the club's religious speech and avoid appearing to sponsor or endorse the club's goals. It could, for example, entirely discontinue encouraging student participation in clubs and clarify that the clubs are not instrumentally related to the school's overall mission. Or, if the school sought to continue its general endorsement of those student clubs that did not engage in controversial speech, it could do so if it also affirmatively disclaimed any endorsement of the Christian club.

The inclusion of the Christian club in the type of forum presently established at Westside, without more, will not assure government neutrality toward religion. Rather, because the school endorses the extracurricular program as part of its educational mission, the inclusion of the Christian club in that program will convey to students the school-sanctioned message that involvement in religion develops "citizenship, wholesome attitudes, good human relations, knowledge and skills." We need not question the value of that message to affirm that it is not the place of schools to issue it. Accordingly, schools such as Westside must be responsive not only to the broad terms of the Act's coverage, but also to this Court's mandate that they effectively disassociate themselves from the religious speech that now may become commonplace in their facilities.

JUSTICE STEVENS, dissenting.

The dictionary is a necessary, and sometimes sufficient, aid to the judge confronted with the task of construing an opaque Act of Congress. In a case like this, however, I believe we must probe more deeply to avoid a patently bizarre result. Can Congress really have intended to issue an order to every public high school in the Nation stating, in substance, that if you sponsor a chess club, a scuba diving club, or a French club—without having formal classes in those subjects—you must also open your doors to every religious, political, or social organization, no matter how controversial or distasteful its views may be? I think not. A fair review of the legislative history of the Equal Access Act discloses that Congress intended to recognize a much narrower forum than the Court has legislated into existence today. . . .

The forum at Westside is considerably different from that which existed at the University of Missouri. In *Widmar*, we held that the university had created "a generally open forum." Over 100 officially recognized student groups routinely participated in that forum. They included groups whose activities not only were unrelated to any specific courses, but also were a kind that a state university could not properly sponsor or endorse. . . .

The Court's opinion in *Widmar* left open the question whether its holding would apply to a public high school that had established a similar public forum. That question has now been answered in the affirmative by the District Court, the Court of Appeals, and by this Court. . . .

. . . What the Court of Appeals failed to recognize, however, is the critical difference between the university forum in *Widmar* and the high school forum involved in this case. None of the clubs at the high school are even arguably controversial or partisan.

Nor would it be wise to ignore this difference. High school students may be adult enough to distinguish between those organizations that are sponsored by the school and those which lack school sponsorship even though they participate in a forum that the school does sponsor. But high school students are also young enough that open fora may be less suitable for them than for college students. . . . We would do no honor to Westside's administrators or the Congress by assuming that either treated casually the differences between high school and college students when formulating the policy and the statute at issue here.

For these reasons, I believe that the distinctions between Westside's program and the University of Missouri's program suggest what is the best understanding of the Act: An extracurricular student organization is "noncurriculum related" if it has as its purpose (or as part of its purpose) the advocacy of partisan theological, political, or ethical views. A school that admits at least one such club has apparently made the judgment that students are better off if the student community is permitted to, and perhaps even encouraged to, compete along ideological lines. This pedagogical strategy may be defensible or even desirable. But it is wrong to presume that Congress endorsed that strategy—and dictated its nationwide adoption—simply because it approved the application of *Widmar* to high schools. And it seems absurd to presume that Westside has invoked the same strategy by recognizing clubs like the Swimming Timing Team and Subsurfers which, though they may not correspond directly to anything in Westside's course offerings, are no more controversial than a grilled cheese sandwich.

Accordingly, as I would construe the Act, a high school could properly sponsor a French club, a chess club, or a scuba diving club simply because their activities are fully consistent with the school's curricular mission. It would not matter whether formal courses in any of those subjects—or in directly related subjects—were being offered as long as faculty encouragement of student participation in such groups would be consistent with both the school's obligation of neutrality and its legitimate pedagogical concerns. Nothing in *Widmar* implies that the existence of a French club, for example, would create a constitutional obligation to allow student members of the Ku Klux Klan or the Communist Party to have access to school facilities. More importantly, nothing in that case suggests that the constitutional issue should turn on whether French is being taught in a formal course while the club is functioning.

Conversely, if a high school decides to allow political groups to use its facilities, it plainly cannot discriminate among controversial groups because it agrees with the positions of some and disagrees with the ideas advocated by others. Again, the fact that the history of the Republican Party might be taught in a political science course could not justify a decision to allow the young Republicans to form a club while denying Communists, white supremacists, or Christian Scientists the same privilege. In my judgment, the political activities of the young Republicans are "noncurriculum related" for reasons that have nothing to do with the content of the political science course. The statutory definition of what is "noncurriculum related" should depend on the constitutional concern that motivated our decision in *Widmar*. . . .

The plurality focuses upon whether the Act might run afoul of the Establishment Clause because of the danger that some students will mistakenly believe that the student-initiated religious clubs are sponsored by the school. I believe that the plurality's construction of the statute obliges it to answer a further question: whether the Act violates the Establishment Clause by authorizing religious organizations to meet on high school grounds even when the high school's teachers and administrators deem it unwise to admit controversial or partisan organizations of any kind.

Under the plurality's interpretation of the Act, Congress has imposed a difficult choice on public high schools receiving federal financial assistance. If such a school continues to allow students to participate in such familiar and innocuous activities as a school chess or scuba diving club, it must also allow religious groups to make use of school facilities. Indeed, it is hard to see how a cheerleading squad or a pep club, among the most common student groups in American high schools, could avoid being "noncurriculum related" under the majority's test. The Act, as construed by the majority, comes perilously close to an outright command to allow organized prayer, and perhaps the kind of religious ceremonies involved in *Widmar*, on school premises. . . .

Source: Board of Education of the Westside Community Schools v. Mergens, 496 U.S. 226 (1990).

FURTHER READING

Alley, Robert S. *School Prayer: The Court, the Congress, and the First Amendment.* Amherst, N.Y.: Prometheus Books, 1994.

Epstein, Lee, and Thomas G. Walker. *Constitutional Law for a Changing America.* Washington, D.C.: Congressional Quarterly Books, 1998, pp. 388–433.

Hall, Kermit L., ed. *The Oxford Companion to the Supreme Court of the United States.* New York: Oxford University Press, 1992.

Hickok, Eugene W., Jr., ed. *The Bill of Rights: Original Meaning and Current Understanding.* Charlottesville: University Press of Virginia, 1991, pp. 41–53.

Howard, A. E. Dick. "The Supreme Court and the Serpentine Wall." In Merrill D. Peterson and Robert C. Vaughan, eds., *The Virginia Statute for Religious Freedom: Its Evolution and Consequences in American History.* Cambridge, England: Cambridge University Press, 1988, pp. 313–350.

Levy, Leonard W. *The Establishment Clause: Religion and the First Amendment.* New York: Macmillan, 1986.

Lowenthal, David. *No Liberty for License: The Forgotten Logic of the First Amendment.* Dallas: Spence Publishing, 1997, pp. 179–244.

McWhirter, Darien A. *The Separation of Church and State.* Phoenix: Oryx Press, 1994.

Patrick, John J. *The Young Oxford Companion to the Supreme Court of the United States.* New York: Oxford University Press, 1996.

Rossum, Ralph A., and G. Alan Tarr. *American Constitutional Law, Volume II: The Bill of Rights and Subsequent Amendments.* New York: St. Martin's Press, 1995.

Part V

Constitutional Issues on Freedom of Religion, 1991–1998

In 1998 an exhibit on the history of religious freedom in America was created by the Library of Congress. A paper that accompanied the exhibit downplayed Thomas Jefferson's call for a "wall of separation" between church and state. In response, over twenty scholars issued a joint statement that was critical of this interpretation of the famous metaphor that Jefferson had included in a letter that he wrote in 1802.[1] More than two centuries after the ratification of the Bill of Rights, in 1791, this controversy indicates that the First Amendment clauses on religion continue to spark intense debates over the meaning of free exercise of religion and no establishment of religion.

Concerning the free exercise clause, the United States Supreme Court triggered an interesting chain of events in 1990 with its holding in *Employment Division, Department of Human Resources of Oregon v. Smith* (Document 47). Prior to the *Smith* decision, for more than twenty-five years, the Court followed the precedent that it had enunciated in 1963 in *Sherbert v. Verner* (see Document 39). In *Sherbert* the majority stated that, when challenged, any action by the government that burdens an individual's free exercise of religion is only justified upon the demonstration of a compelling governmental interest. Also, according to *Sherbert*, such laws should be implemented in the least restrictive manner possible. In *Smith*, however, the Court rejected the *Sherbert* precedent by holding that the free exercise clause was not intended to release an individual from the obligation to comply with a valid and neutral law of general applicability.

The Court fortified the line of legal reasoning introduced in *Smith* three years later, in *Church of the Lukumi Babalu Aye, Inc. v. City of Hialeah* (1993) (Document 68), by holding that an ordinance that failed to satisfy the neutrality standard was an unconstitutional infringement upon the free exercise of religion. The Court reached this conclusion unanimously, but three of the justices expressed the viewpoint that *Smith* had been wrongly decided. Nonetheless, the majority decision was seen as an affirmation of the *Smith* standard.

Following the *Smith* decision, various religious groups pressured Congress to restore the compelling interest and least restrictive means tests. In 1993 Congress did so by enacting the Religious Freedom Restoration Act (see Document 70). In addition to limiting the authority of the national government to interfere with religious practices, the law also applied to state and local government officials. President Clinton praised the legislation, which he asserted would hold the government "to a very high level of proof before it interferes with someone's free exercise of religion."[2]

The constitutionality of the Religious Freedom Restoration Act was soon challenged, and in 1997, less than four years after its enactment, the law was ruled unconstitutional by the Supreme Court. In *City of Boerne v. Flores* (see Document 76) the Court concluded that by enacting the law Congress had violated two fundamental principles of American government: federalism and the separation of powers. Concerning the former, Justice Anthony M. Kennedy's majority opinion emphasized that while the power to enforce the provisions of the Fourteenth Amendment rests with Congress, this power is strictly remedial. Therefore, according to Kennedy, any suggestion that Congress has the power to decree the substance of the Fourteenth Amendment's restrictions on the states is not consistent with the design of the amendment. Regarding the latter, Kennedy stated that the "power to interpret the Constitution in a case or controversy remains in the Judiciary."

Writing in dissent, Justice Sandra Day O'Connor presented a historical analysis of the concept of religious liberty that concluded with yet another call for a reexamination of the *Smith* precedent. O'Connor asserted that the free exercise clause "requires government to justify any substantial burden on religiously motivated conduct by a compelling state interest and to impose that burden only by means narrowly tailored to achieve that interest."

Concerning the establishment clause, the two dominant issues between 1991 and 1998 were organized prayer in public schools and government aid to religious schools. In 1992, in *Lee v. Weisman* (see Document 66), the Supreme Court reaffirmed the position that a state-sponsored prayer session in a public school is unconstitutional. This stance had originally been articulated three decades earlier in *Engel v. Vitale* (1962) (see Document 51). The decision in *Lee v. Weisman*, a case that began with the recitation of a prayer at a public school's graduation ceremony, did spark a national debate. However, a middle ground on the issue remained elusive as groups such as the American

Civil Liberties Union (ACLU) and Pat Robertson's American Center for Law and Justice (ACLJ) argued opposing points of view to the public and in courtrooms across the nation.

In 1995 President Clinton addressed the issue of religion in the nation's public schools (see Document 74), and one newspaper described his statement as an effort to "cut through the confusion that has surrounded the issue for more than 30 years."[3] The President emphasized that while the establishment clause prohibits public school officials from mandating prayer sessions or providing religious instruction, students are generally free to pray privately.

Thomas Oliphant, in an editorial, characterized Clinton's position as a reasoned approach to an issue that has been dominated by a "helium-polluted shouting match" between liberals and conservatives.[4] Conversely, in a letter published by the New York Times on July 19, 1995, Nadine Strossen of the ACLU observed that while the President's address included references to the improper suppression of individual religious expression by public school officials, it failed to mention "the widespread incidents in which officials have wrongly promoted, sponsored and endorsed religious expression in the schools."[5]

In 1998 the U.S. House of Representatives considered a proposal to amend the Constitution to allow organized prayer in public schools. This proposal, sponsored by Representative Ernest Istook of Oklahoma, was also intended to allow religious symbols on public property as well as the use of tax revenue to support religious activities. Editorials in both the New York Times and USA Today warned that this so-called "Religious Freedom Amendment" would actually produce religious tyranny.[6] The proposal was supported by a majority of the members of the House, 224 to 203. This vote was, however, far short of the two-thirds majority that is required in both houses of Congress to send a proposed amendment to the states for possible ratification.

Regarding public aid to religious schools, the Supreme Court made a noteworthy separationist decision in 1994 in Board of Education of Kiryas Joel Village School District v. Grumet (see Document 71) that invalidated what had been called "religious gerrymandering." Generally, however, in recent years the Court has favored a policy of accommodation in this area of constitutional law. For example, in 1997 a 5–4 majority in Agostini v. Felton (see Document 75) overturned a decision made twelve years earlier that had barred public school employees from providing disadvantaged students in parochial schools with remedial education services.

The fact that the majority in Agostini relied upon the often maligned test introduced in 1971 in Lemon v. Kurtzman (see Document 55) to evaluate establishment clause claims added to the importance of the decision. Prior to writing for the majority in Agostini, Justice O'Connor had argued for a modification of the tripartite *Lemon* test to focus attention on whether the governmental action in question constituted an endorsement of religion. One could argue, however, that since the majority in the case overturned by *Agostini* had depended upon a strict application of the *Lemon* test, O'Connor had little choice but to follow suit in her opinion. More revealing was that in applying the same test to virtually identical circumstances, the Court reached an accommodationist conclusion in 1997 in contrast to the separationist verdict in 1985. Of course the personnel of the Court had changed significantly in the intervening twelve years.

By 1998 the most controversial issue concerning public aid for religious schools was the use of tax revenue to subsidize the cost of tuition to attend a religious school. In 1973, in *Committee for Public Education v. Nyquist*, the Supreme Court held that a New York program that extended tuition reimbursement grants to the parents of children attending nonpublic schools, including religious schools, was unconstitutional. The majority regarded the program as an unacceptable advancement of religion. However, in 1983, in *Mueller v. Allen* (see Document 58), the Court sanctioned a Minnesota program that allowed tax deductions for educational expenses incurred by the parents of children attending religious schools. Justice William Rehnquist, writing for the majority in *Mueller*, argued that the program served a secular purpose by "ensuring the State's citizenry is well educated." Rehnquist also stated that since religious schools relieve the public school system of serving an even greater number of students, there is a strong public interest in the continued financial health of such nonpublic schools.

In June 1998 the Wisconsin Supreme Court upheld the constitutionality of a voucher program established in the city of Milwaukee. Under this program a child from a low-income family in Milwaukee could qualify for a voucher worth $4,900 to attend a nonpublic school, including a religious school. When this decision was rendered in Wisconsin, it was reported that similar voucher programs were being reviewed by courts in four other states: Arizona, Maine, Ohio, and Vermont.[7]

The Wisconsin decision was appealed to the U.S. Supreme Court, but in November 1998 the Court voted not to hear the appeal. As a result the Wisconsin ruling was allowed to stand, but a precedent on the constitutionality of voucher programs that is applicable to the entire nation will require a full hearing in the U.S. Supreme Court. The likelihood that the Court will attempt to resolve the voucher issue increases as more states institute voucher programs akin to the one in Wisconsin and the four states listed above.[8]

The Supreme Court is unlikely to be swayed by public opinion, but a Gallup poll published in 1998 revealed that Americans are deeply divided on the voucher issue. For example, while a very slim majority of those surveyed supported the use of public funds to help pay the cost of tuition to private and parochial schools, the percentage of those who answered in the affirmative fell significantly when the word "voucher" was used to elicit a response.[9]

Other than a resolution to the voucher issue, two key questions could be addressed by the Supreme Court during the next few years. First, will the Court continue to favor a policy of accommodation, or will changes in the membership of the Court produce a majority that is more inclined to render separationist holdings? Second, will the *Lemon* test continue to be the yardstick by which establishment clause controversies are measured? Currently it appears to be less likely that the Court will usher in a return to the compelling state interest standard in free exercise cases, but such reversals do occur from time to time. The only certainty is that religious liberty is of such importance to so many Americans that whenever one issue appears to be resolved, another equally perplexing matter almost always arises in the arena of public discourse.

NOTES

1. Carl Hartman, "Jefferson's Stance on Religion Fuels Debate," *USA Today*, July 31, 1998.

2. Peter Steinfels, "New Law Protects Religious Practices," *New York Times*, November 17, 1993.

3. Tony Mauro and Bill Nichols, "Middle Ground on School Prayer," *USA Today*, July 13, 1995.

4. Thomas Oliphant, "Searching for Hallowed Ground in School Prayer Debate," *Boston Globe*, July 16, 1995.

5. Nadine Strossen, "Letter to the Editor," *New York Times*, July 19, 1995.

6. "The Religious Tyranny Amendment," *New York Times*, March 15, 1998; "Amendment Deprives Faithful of Protections," *USA Today*, June 4, 1998.

7. Ethan Bonner, "Wisconsin Court Backs Vouchers in Church Schools," *The New York Times*, June 11, 1998.

8. Neil A. Lewis, "School Vouchers Survive as Justices Sidestep a Debate," *New York Times*, November 10, 1998.

9. Tamara Henry, "Majority Backs Public Money for Private Schools," *USA Today*, August 26, 1998.

DOCUMENT 66: *Lee v. Weisman* (1992)

When Daniel Weisman attended the graduation of his daughter, Merith, from Nathan Bishop Middle School in Providence, Rhode Island, in 1986, a Baptist minister offered an invocation which thanked Jesus

Christ for the students' accomplishments. Weisman, a follower of the Jewish religion, complained to school officials. Nonetheless, an invocation and benediction were included in the school's scheduled graduation ceremonies in 1989, when Weisman's younger daughter, Deborah, was one of the prospective graduates.

Hoping to avoid controversy, the school's principal, Robert E. Lee, did contact a local rabbi to offer the prayers. Lee also provided the rabbi with a pamphlet prepared by the National Conference of Christians and Jews on the subject of public prayers. The principal, consistent with the guidelines contained in the pamphlet, advised the rabbi that the invocation and benediction should be nonsectarian.

Weisman, however, sought a temporary restraining order from the United States District Court for the District of Rhode Island to prohibit school officials from including either an invocation or benediction in the graduation ceremony. This motion was denied on the grounds that there was insufficient time to consider it before the scheduled graduation. During the month that followed the ceremony Weisman filed an amended complaint that sought a permanent injunction to prevent any public school official in Providence from inviting a member of the clergy to deliver a prayer at a graduation ceremony.

The District Court, citing *Lemon v. Kurtzman* (see Document 55), held that the inclusion of a prayer in a public school graduation exercise was a violation of the First Amendment's establishment of religion clause, which applies to the states via the Fourteenth Amendment. This ruling was subsequently affirmed by the U.S. Court of Appeals for the First Circuit.

Once appealed to the U.S. Supreme Court, *Lee v. Weisman*, by raising the volatile issue of state-sponsored prayer in public schools, drew considerable attention. The petitioner, Principal Robert E. Lee, was supported by the administration of President George Bush. In their *amicus curiae* brief the representatives of President Bush also asked the Court to reconsider the usefulness of the tripartite *Lemon* test.

The Supreme Court, in a 5–4 decision, held that the establishment clause does prohibit state-sponsored prayer at a public school's graduation ceremony. Justice Anthony M. Kennedy delivered the opinion of the Court. Despite what Kennedy viewed as a good faith effort to ensure that the prayers were nonsectarian, he concluded that since student attendance was obligatory, any effort to include a prayer at the ceremony would constitute indirect coercion by the school officials. Kennedy distinguished the public school setting, which compels the attendance of impressionable children, from the one reviewed in 1983 in *Marsh v. Chambers* (see Document 59). In *Marsh* the Court had voted to allow an organized prayer to open the session of a state legislature. Kennedy also reasoned that the abundance of precedents regarding organized prayer in public schools made any reconsideration of the *Lemon* test unnecessary.

Justice Harry A. Blackmun, concurring, argued that while evidence of coercion is sufficient to demonstrate an establishment clause violation, it is not necessary to conclude that a law or action is unconstitutional. Blackmun, rather, measured the constitutionality of the graduation prayer in question by invoking the endorsement standard that had originally been suggested by Justice Sandra Day O'Connor in *Lynch v. Donnelly* (1984).

Justice David H. Souter, concurring, also stressed the link between the requirement that the government must remain neutral in matters concerning religion and the principle that the establishment clause prohibits any endorsement of religion by the government. Souter emphasized that not only is official support for any one denomination prohibited, government support for religion generally is unconstitutional. This assertion was a direct response to arguments advanced in the past by those known as nonpreferentialists, including Chief Justice William H. Rehnquist.

Justice Antonin Scalia, writing in dissent, ridiculed the reference to "psychological coercion" that was included in Justice Kennedy's opinion by claiming that "interior decorating is a rock-hard science compared to psychology practiced by amateurs." Scalia defended the inclusion of invocations and benedictions in public school graduation exercises by highlighting the unifying role of prayer.

Why does Justice Kennedy contend that the inclusion of a nonsectarian prayer in a public school graduation ceremony would constitute subtle, indirect coercion on the part of the state? Why does Justice Blackmun maintain that the mixing of church and state would pose a threat to the survival of free, democratic government in the United States? What is the basis of Justice Souter's argument that it is not correct to interpret the establishment clause to allow nonpreferential government aid to religion? Why does Justice Scalia reject the contention that allowing a member of the clergy to offer a prayer at a public school graduation constitutes coercion by the government?

* * *

JUSTICE KENNEDY delivered the opinion of the Court.

* * *

The government involvement with religious activity in this case is pervasive, to the point of creating a state-sponsored and state-directed religious exercise in a public school. Conducting this formal religious observance conflicts with settled rules pertaining to prayer exercises for students, and that suffices to determine the question before us.

The principle that government may accommodate the free exercise of religion does not supersede the fundamental limitations imposed by the Establishment Clause. It is beyond dispute that, at a minimum, the Constitution guarantees that government may not coerce anyone to support or participate in religion or its exercise. . . . The State's involvement in the school prayers challenged today violates these central principles.

That involvement is as troubling as it is undenied. A school official, the principal, decided that an invocation and a benediction should be given; this is a choice attributable to the State, and from a constitutional perspective it is as if a state statute decreed that the prayers must occur. The principal chose the religious participant, here a rabbi, and that choice is also attributable to the State. The reason for the choice of a rabbi is not disclosed by the record, but the potential for divisiveness over the choice of a particular member of the clergy to conduct the ceremony is apparent.

Divisiveness, of course, can attend any state decision respecting religions, and neither its existence nor its potential necessarily invalidates the State's attempts to accommodate religion in all cases. The potential for divisiveness is of particular relevance here though, because it centers around an overt religious exercise in the secondary school environment where, as we discuss below, subtle coercive pressures exist and where the student had no real alternative which would have allowed her to avoid the fact or appearance of participation.

The State's role did not end with the decision to include a prayer and with the choice of clergyman. Principal Lee provided Rabbi Gutterman with a copy of the "Guidelines for Civic Occasions," and advised him that his prayers should be nonsectarian. Through these means the principal directed and controlled the content of the prayer. Even if the only sanction for ignoring the instructions were that the rabbi would not be invited back, we think no religious representative who valued his or her continued reputation and effectiveness in the community would incur the State's displeasure in this regard. It is a cornerstone principle of our Establishment Clause jurisprudence that "it is no part of the business of government to compose official prayers for any group of the American people to recite as a part of a religious program carried on by government," *Engel v. Vitale* (1962), and that is what the school officials attempted to do.

Petitioners argue, and we find nothing in the case to refute it, that the directions for the content of the prayers were a good-faith attempt by the school to ensure that the sectarianism which is so often the flashpoint for religious animosity be removed from the graduation ceremony. The concern is understandable, as a prayer which uses ideas or images identified with a particular religion may foster a different sort of sectarian rivalry than an invocation or benediction in terms more neutral. The school's explanation, however, does not resolve the dilemma caused by its participation. The question is not the good faith of the school in attempting to make the prayer acceptable to most persons, but the legitimacy of its undertaking that enterprise at all when the object is to produce a prayer to be used in a formal religious exercise which students, for all practical purposes, are obliged to attend. . . .

The lessons of the First Amendment are as urgent in the modern world as in the 18th Century when it was written. One timeless lesson is that if citizens are subjected to state-sponsored religious exercises, the State disavows its own duty to guard and respect that sphere of inviolable conscience and belief which is the mark of a free people. To compromise that principle today would be to deny our own tradition and forfeit our standing to urge others to secure the protections of that tradition for themselves.

As we have observed before, there are heightened concerns with protecting freedom of conscience from subtle coercive pressure in the elementary and secondary public schools. Our decisions in *Engel v. Vitale*, (1962) and *Abington School District* (1968) recognize, among other things, that prayer exercises in public schools carry a particular risk of indirect coercion. The concern may not be limited to the context of schools, but it is most pronounced there. What to most believers may seem nothing more than a reasonable request that the nonbeliever respect their religious practices, in a school context may appear to the nonbeliever or dissenter to be an attempt to employ the machinery of the State to enforce a religious orthodoxy. . . .

Inherent differences between the public school system and a session of a State Legislature distinguish this case from *Marsh v. Chambers* (1983). The considerations we have raised in objection to the invocation and benediction are in many respects similar to the arguments we considered in *Marsh*. But there are also obvious differences. The atmosphere at the opening of a session of a state legislature where adults are free to enter and leave with little comment and for any number of reasons cannot compare with the constraining potential of the one school event most important for the student to attend. The influence and force of a formal exercise in a school graduation are far greater than the prayer exercise we condoned in *Marsh*. The *Marsh* majority in fact gave specific recognition to this distinction and placed particular reliance on it in upholding the prayers at issue there. Today's case is different. At a high school graduation, teachers and principals must and do retain a high degree of control over the precise contents of the program, the speeches, the timing, the movements, the dress, and the decorum of the students. In this atmosphere the state-imposed character of an invocation and benediction by clergy selected by the school combine to make the prayer a state-sanctioned religious exercise in which the student was left with no alternative but to submit. This is different from *Marsh* and suffices to make the religious exercise a First Amendment violation. Our Establishment Clause jurisprudence remains a delicate and fact-sensitive one, and we cannot accept the parallel relied upon by petitioners and the United States between the facts of *Marsh* and the case now before us. . . .

Our society would be less than true to its heritage if it lacked abiding concern for the values of its young people, and we acknowledge the profound belief of adherents to many faiths that there must be a place in the student's life for precepts of a morality higher even than the law we today enforce. We express no hostility to those aspirations, nor would our oath permit us to do so. A relentless and all-pervasive attempt to exclude religion from every aspect of public life could itself become inconsistent with the Constitution. We recognize that, at graduation time and throughout the course of the educational process, there will be instances when religious values, religious practices, and religious persons will have some interaction with the public schools and their students. But these matters, often questions of accommodation of religion, are not before us. The sole question presented is whether a religious exercise may be conducted at a graduation ceremony in circumstances where, as we have found, young graduates who object are induced to conform. No holding by this Court suggests that a school can persuade or compel a student to participate in a religious exercise. That is being done here, and it is forbidden by the Establishment Clause of the First Amendment. . . .

JUSTICE BLACKMUN, concurring.

Nearly half a century of review and refinement of Establishment Clause jurisprudence has distilled one clear understanding: Government may neither promote nor affiliate itself with any religious doctrine or organization, nor may it obtrude itself in the internal affairs of any religious institution. The application of these principles to the present case mandates the decision reached today by the Court. . . .

I join the Court's opinion today because I find nothing in it inconsistent with the essential precepts of the Establishment Clause developed in our precedents. The Court holds that the graduation prayer is unconstitutional because the State "in effect required participation in a religious exercise." Although our precedents make clear that proof of government coercion is not necessary to prove an Establishment Clause violation, it is sufficient. Government pressure to participate in a religious activity is an obvious indication that the government is endorsing or promoting religion.

But it is not enough that the government restrain from compelling religious practices: it must not engage in them either. The Court repeatedly has recognized that a violation of the Establishment Clause is not predicated on coercion. . . .

The mixing of government and religion can be a threat to free government, even if no one is forced to participate. When the government puts its imprimatur on a particular religion, it conveys a message of exclusion to all those who do not adhere to the favored beliefs. A government cannot be premised on the belief that all persons are created equal when it asserts that God prefers some. . . .

When the government arrogates to itself a role in religious affairs, it abandons its obligation as guarantor of democracy. Democracy requires the nourishment of dialogue and dissent, while religious faith puts its trust in an ultimate divine authority above all human deliberation. . . .

It is these understandings and fears that underlie our Establishment Clause jurisprudence. We have believed that religious freedom cannot exist in the absence of a free democratic government, and that such a government cannot endure when there is fusion between religion and the political regime. We have believed that religious freedom cannot thrive in the absence of a vibrant religious community and that such a community cannot prosper when it is bound to the secular. And we have believed that these were the animating principles behind the adoption of the Establishment Clause. To that end, our cases have prohibited government endorsement of religion, its sponsorship, and active involvement in religion, whether or not citizens were coerced to conform. . . .

JUSTICE SOUTER, concurring.

I join the whole of the Court's opinion, and fully agree that prayers at public school graduation ceremonies indirectly coerce religious observance. I write separately nonetheless on two issues of Establishment Clause analysis that underlie my independent resolution of this case: whether the Clause applies to governmental practices that do not favor one religion or denomination over others, and whether state coercion of religious conformity, over and above state endorsement of religious exercise or belief, is a necessary element of an Establishment Clause violation.

Forty-five years ago, this Court announced a basic principle of constitutional law from which it has not strayed: the Establishment Clause forbids not only state practices that "aid one religion . . . or prefer one religion over another," but also those that "aid all religions." *Everson v. Board of Education of Ewing* (1947). Today we reaffirm that principle, holding that the Establishment Clause forbids state-sponsored prayers in public school settings no matter how nondenominational the prayers may be. In barring the State from sponsoring generically Theistic prayers where it could not sponsor sectarian ones, we hold true to a line of precedent from which there is no adequate historical case to depart. . . .

Some have challenged this precedent by reading the Establishment Clause to permit "nonpreferential" state promotion of religion. The challengers argue that, as originally understood by the Framers, "[t]he Establishment Clause did not require government neutrality between religion and irreligion nor did it prohibit the Federal Government from providing nondiscriminatory aid to religion." (*Wallace v. Jaffree*, 1985, REHNQUIST, J. dissenting). . . . While a case has been made for this position, it is not so convincing as to warrant reconsideration of our settled law; indeed, I find in the history of the Clause's textual development a more powerful argument supporting the Court's jurisprudence following *Everson*. . . .

That government must remain neutral in matters of religion does not foreclose it from ever taking religion into account. The State may "accommodate" the free exercise of religion by relieving people from generally applicable rules that interfere with their religious callings. Contrary to the views of some, such accommodation does not necessarily signify an official endorsement of religious observance over disbelief.

In everyday life, we routinely accommodate religious beliefs that we do not share. A Christian inviting an Orthodox Jew to lunch might take pains to choose a kosher restaurant; an atheist in a hurry might yield the right of way to an Amish man steering a horse-drawn carriage. In so acting, we express respect for, but not endorsement of, the fundamental values of others. We act without expressing a position on the theological merit of those values or of religious belief in general, and no one perceives us to have taken such a position.

The government may act likewise. Most religions encourage devotional practices that are at once crucial to the lives of believers and idiosyncratic in the eyes of nonadherents. By definition, secular rules of general application are drawn from the nonadherent's vantage and, consequently, fail to take such practices into account. Yet when enforcement of such rules cuts across religious sensibilities, as it often does, it puts those affected to the choice of taking sides between God and government. In such circumstances, accommodating religion reveals nothing beyond a recognition that general rules can unnecessarily offend the religious conscience when they offend the conscience of secular society not at all. Thus, in freeing the Native American Church from federal laws forbidding peyote use, see Drug Enforcement Administration Miscellaneous Exemptions (1991), the government conveys no endorsement of peyote rituals, the Church, or religion as such; it simply respects the centrality of peyote to the lives of certain Americans.

Whatever else may define the scope of accommodation permissible under the Establishment Clause, one requirement is clear: accommodation must lift a discernible burden on the free exercise of religion. Concern for the position of religious individuals in the modern regulatory state cannot justify official solicitude for a religious practice unburdened by general rules; such gratuitous largesse would effectively favor religion over disbelief. By these lights one easily sees that, in sponsoring the graduation prayers at issue here, the State has crossed the line from permissible accommodation to unconstitutional establishment.

Religious students cannot complain that omitting prayers from their graduation ceremony would, in any realistic sense, "burden" their spiritual callings. To be sure, many of them invest this rite of passage with spiritual significance, but they may express their religious feelings about it before and after the ceremony. They may even organize a privately sponsored baccalaureate if they desire the company of like-minded students. Because they accordingly have no need for the machinery of the State to affirm their beliefs, the government's sponsorship of prayer at the graduation ceremony is most reasonably understood as an official endorsement of religion and, in this instance, of Theistic religion. . . .

JUSTICE SCALIA, dissenting.

Three Terms ago, I joined an opinion recognizing that the Establishment Clause must be construed in light of the "[g]overnment policies of accommodation, acknowledgment, and support for religion [that] are an accepted part of our political and cultural heritage." That opinion affirmed that "the meaning of the Clause is to be determined by reference to historical practices and understandings." It said that "[a] test for implementing the protections of the Establishment Clause that, if applied with consistency, would invalidate long-standing traditions cannot be a proper reading of the Clause." *Allegheny County v. Greater Pittsburgh ACLU* (1989).

These views of course prevent me from joining today's opinion, which is conspicuously bereft of any reference to history. In holding that the Establishment Clause prohibits invocations and benedictions at public-school graduation ceremonies, the Court—with nary a mention that it is doing so—lays waste a tradition that is as old as public-school graduation ceremonies themselves, and that is a component of an even more long-standing American tradition of nonsectarian prayer to God at public celebrations generally. . . .

From our Nation's origin, prayer has been a prominent part of governmental ceremonies and proclamations. The Declaration of Independence, the document marking our birth as a separate people, "appeal[ed] to the Supreme Judge of the world for the rectitude of our intentions" and avowed "a firm reliance on the protection of divine Providence." In his first inaugural address, after swearing his oath of office on a Bible,

George Washington deliberately made a prayer a part of his first official act as President. . . .

The other two branches of the Federal Government also have a long-established practice of prayer at public events. As we detailed in *Marsh*, Congressional sessions have opened with a chaplain's prayer ever since the First Congress. And this Court's own sessions have opened with the invocation "God save the United States and this Honorable Court" since the days of Chief Justice Marshall.

In addition to this general tradition of prayer at public ceremonies, there exists a more specific tradition in invocations and benedictions at public-school graduation exercises. . . .

The Court presumably would separate graduation invocations and benedictions from other instances of public "preservation and transmission of religious beliefs" on the ground that they involve "psychological coercion." . . .

The deeper flaw in the Court's opinion does not lie in its wrong answer to the question whether there was state-induced "peer-pressure" coercion; it lies, rather, in the Court's making violation of the Establishment Clause hinge on such a precious question. The coercion that was a hallmark of historical establishments of religion was coercion of religious orthodoxy and of financial support by *force of law and threat of penalty*. Typically, attendance at the state church was required; only clergy of the official church could lawfully perform sacraments; and dissenters, if tolerated, faced an array of civil disabilities. Thus, for example, in the colony of Virginia, where the Church of England had been established, ministers were required by law to conform to the doctrine and rites of the Church of England; and all persons were required to attend church and observe the Sabbath, were tithed for the public support of Anglican ministers, and were taxed for the costs of building and repairing churches.

The Establishment Clause was adopted to prohibit such an establishment of religion at the federal level (and to protect state establishments of religion from federal interference). I will further acknowledge for the sake of argument that, as some scholars have argued, by 1790 the term "establishment" had acquired an additional meaning—"financial support of religion generally, by public taxation"—that reflected the development of "general or multiple" establishments, not limited to a single church. But that would still be an establishment coerced *by force of law*. And I will further concede that our constitutional tradition, from the Declaration of Independence and the first inaugural address of Washington, quoted earlier, down to the present day, has, with a few aberrations ruled out of order government-sponsored endorsement of religion—even when no legal coercion is present, and indeed even when no ersatz, "peer-pressure" psycho-coercion is present—where the endorsement is sectarian, in the sense of specifying details upon which men and women who believe in a benevolent, omnipotent Creator and Ruler of the world, are known to differ (for example, the divinity of Christ). But there is simply no support for the proposition that the officially sponsored nondenominational invocation and benediction read by Rabbi Gutterman—with no one legally coerced to recite them—violated the Constitution of the United States. To the contrary, they are so characteristically American they could have come from the pen of George Washington or Abraham Lincoln himself.

Thus, while I have no quarrel with the Court's general proposition that the Establishment Clause "guarantees that government may not coerce anyone to support or participate in religion or its exercise," I see no warrant for expanding the concept of coercion beyond acts backed by threat of penalty—a brand of coercion that, happily, is readily discernible to those of us who have made a career of reading the disciples of Blackstone rather than of Freud. . . .

Our religion-clause jurisprudence has become bedeviled (so to speak) by reliance on formulaic abstractions that are not derived from, but positively conflict with, our long-accepted constitutional traditions. Foremost among these has been the so-called *Lemon* test, see *Lemon v. Kurtzman* (1971), which has received well-earned criticism from many members of this Court. The Court today demonstrates the irrelevance of *Lemon* by essentially ignoring it, and the interment of that case may be the one happy byproduct of the Court's otherwise lamentable decision. Unfortunately, however, the Court has replaced *Lemon* with its psycho-coercion test, which suffers the double disability of having no roots whatever in our people's historic practice, and being as infinitely expandable as the reasons for psychotherapy itself. . . .

I must add one final observation: The founders of our Republic knew the fearsome potential of sectarian religious belief to generate civil dissension and civil strife. And they also knew that nothing, absolutely nothing, is so inclined to foster among religious believers of various faiths a toleration—no, an affection—for one another than voluntarily joining in prayer together, to the God whom they all worship and seek. Needless to say, no one should be compelled to do that, but it is a shame to deprive our public culture of the opportunity, and indeed the encouragement, for people to do it voluntarily. The Baptist or Catholic who heard and joined in the simple and inspiring prayers of Rabbi Gutterman on this official and patriotic occasion was inoculated from religious bigotry and prejudice in a manner that can not be replicated. To deprive our society of that important unifying mechanism, in order to spare the nonbeliever what seems to me the minimal inconvenience of standing or even sitting in respectful nonparticipation, is as senseless in policy as it is unsupported in law.

For the foregoing reasons, I dissent.

Source: Lee v. Weisman, 505 U.S. 577 (1992).

DOCUMENT 67: *Lamb's Chapel v. Center Moriches Union Free School District* (1993)

Section 414 of the New York Education Law authorized local school boards to adopt reasonable regulations to allow the use of public school facilities during noninstructional hours for ten specified purposes. Consistent with this state law the Center Moriches School District allowed the use of school facilities for social, civic, and recreational purposes (Rule 10), while prohibiting the use of the same facilities for religious purposes (Rule 7). In 1990 school officials cited these regulations when they rejected a request made by Lamb's Chapel, an evangelical Christian church. The religious group had hoped to use school facilities for the presentation of a film series on family values and child-rearing. The films advocated a return to "traditional, Christian family values."

Lamb's Chapel challenged this ruling in federal court. The argument was made that the school facilities, as a "public forum," should be open to all groups. Conversely, the school district maintained that it was precluded from opening its doors to religious groups by both state law and the First Amendment's establishment of religion clause, which applies to state and local authorities via the Fourteenth Amendment. The United States Court of Appeals for the Second Circuit, in affirmation of a lower court ruling, held that the school system had established a "limited public forum" and that it was reasonable to prohibit religious activities from such a forum.

In 1993 the U.S. Supreme Court reversed the court of appeals ruling in *Lamb's Chapel v. Center Moriches Union Free School District.* The decision was unanimous, and Justice Byron R. White, writing for the Court, reasoned that to deny religious groups equal access to public facilities would be to allow a discriminatory practice. In this respect White's opinion was consistent with previous Supreme Court rulings in *Widmar v. Vincent* (1981) and *Board of Education of Westside Community Schools v. Mergens* (1990). (See Document 65.)

Justice White rejected the school district's establishment clause claim by invoking the tripartite test enunciated by the Court in 1971 in *Lemon v. Kurtzman* (see Document 55). However, a concurring opinion by Justice Antonin Scalia criticized the continued use of this so-called *Lemon* test by proclaiming that the precedent stalks the Court's establishment clause jurisprudence like a "ghoul in a late-night horror movie."

Why does Justice White reject the contention that the establishment clause prohibits the use of public school facilities by religious groups during noninstructional hours? Why does Justice Scalia admonish his fellow Supreme Court justices for their continued reliance upon the *Lemon* test?

* * *

JUSTICE WHITE delivered the opinion of the Court.

There is no question that the District, like the private owner of property, may legally preserve the property under its control for the use to which it is dedicated. It is also common ground that the District need not have permitted after-hours use of its property for any of the uses permitted by the state education law. The District, however, did open its property for 2 of the 10 uses permitted by [the law]. The Church argued below that because under Rule 10 of the rules issued by the District, school property could be used for "social, civic, and recreational" purposes, the District had opened its property for such a wide variety of communicative purposes that restrictions on communicative uses of the property were subject to the same constitutional limitations as restrictions in traditional public fora such as parks and sidewalks. Hence, its view was the subject-matter or speaker exclusions on District property were required to be justified by a compelling state interest and to be narrowly drawn to achieve that end. Both the District Court and the Court of Appeals rejected this submission, which is also presented to this Court. The argument has considerable force, for the District's property is heavily used by a wide variety of private organizations, including some that presented a "close question," which the Court of Appeals resolved in the District's favor, as to whether the District had in fact already opened its property for religious uses. We need not rule on this issue, however, for even if the courts below were correct in this respect— and we shall assume for present purposes that they were—the judgment below must be reversed. . . .

There is no suggestion from the courts below or from the District or the State that a lecture or film about child-rearing and family values would not be a use for social or civic purposes otherwise permitted by Rule 10. That subject matter is not one that the District has placed off limits to any and all speakers. Nor is there any indication in the record before us that the application to exhibit the particular film involved here was or would have been denied for any reason other than the fact that the presentation would have been from a religious perspective. . . . The film involved here no doubt dealt with a subject otherwise permissible under Rule 10, and its exhibition was denied solely because the film dealt with the subject from a religious standpoint. The principle that has emerged from our cases "is that the First Amendment forbids the government to regulate speech in ways that favor some viewpoints or ideas at the expense of others." *City Council of Los Angeles v. Taxpayers for Vincent* (1984). . . .

The District, as a respondent, would save its judgment below on the ground that to permit its property to be used for religious purposes would be an establishment of religion forbidden by the First Amendment. This Court suggested in *Widmar v. Vincent* (1981) that the interest of the State in avoiding an Establishment Clause violation "may be [a] compelling" one justifying an abridgment of free speech otherwise protected by the First Amendment; but the Court went on to hold that permitting use of University property for religious purposes under the open access policy involved there would not be incompatible with the Court's Establishment Clause cases.

We have no more trouble than did the *Widmar* Court in disposing of the claimed defense on the ground that the posited fears of an Establishment Clause violation are unfounded. The showing of this film would not have been during school hours, would not have been sponsored by the school, and would have been open to the public, not just to church members. The District property had repeatedly been used by a wide variety of private organizations. Under these circumstances, as in *Widmar*, there would have been no realistic danger that the community would think that the District was endorsing religion or any particular creed, and any benefit to religion or to the Church would have been no more than incidental. As in *Widmar*, permitting District property to be used to exhibit the film involved in this case would not have been an establishment of religion under the three-part test articulated in *Lemon v. Kurtzman* (1971): The challenged governmental action has a secular purpose, does not have the principal or primary effect of advancing or inhibiting religion, and does not foster an excessive entanglement with religion.

The District also submits that it justifiably denied use of its property to a "radical" church for the purpose of proselytizing, since to do so would lead to threats of public unrest and even violence. There is nothing in the record to support such a justification, which in any event would be difficult to defend as a reason to deny the presentation of a religious point of view about a subject the District otherwise makes open to discussion on District property. . . .

JUSTICE SCALIA, concurring in the judgment.

I join the Court's conclusion that the District's refusal to allow use of school facilities for petitioners' film viewing, while generally opening the schools for community activities, violated petitioners' First Amendment free-speech rights. I also agree with the Court that allowing Lamb's Chapel to use school facilities poses "no realistic danger" of a violation of the Establishment Clause, but I cannot accept most of its reasoning in this regard. The Court explains that the showing of petitioners' film on school property after school hours would not cause the community to "think that the District was endorsing religion or any particular creed," and further notes that access to school property would not violate the three-part test articulated in *Lemon v. Kurtzman* (1971).

As to the Court's invocation of the *Lemon* test: Like some ghoul in a late-night horror movie that repeatedly sits up in its grave and shuffles abroad, after being repeatedly killed and buried, *Lemon* stalks our Establishment Clause jurisprudence once again, frightening the little children and school attorneys of Center Moriches Union Free School District. Its most recent burial, only last Term, was, to be sure, not fully six-feet under: our decision in *Lee v. Weisman* (1992) conspicuously avoided using the supposed "test" but also declined the invitation to repudiate it. Over the years, however, no fewer than five of the currently sitting Justices have, in their own opinions, personally driven pencils through the creature's heart (the author of today's opinion repeatedly), and a sixth has joined an opinion doing so. . . .

The secret of the *Lemon* test's survival, I think, is that it is so easy to kill. It is there to scare us (and our audience) when we wish it to do so, but we can command it to return to the tomb at will. When we wish to strike down a practice it forbids, we invoke it, see *Aguilar v. Felton* (1985) (striking down state remedial education program administered in part in parochial schools); when we wish to uphold a practice it forbids, we ignore it entirely, see *Marsh v. Chambers* (1983) (upholding state legislative chaplains). Sometimes, we take a middle course, calling its three prongs "no more than helpful signposts," *Hunt v. McNair* (1973). Such a docile and useful monster is worth keeping around, at least in a somnolent state; one never knows when one might need him.

For my part, I agree with the long list of constitutional scholars who have criticized *Lemon* and bemoaned the strange Establishment Clause geometry of crooked lines and wavering shapes its intermittent use has produced. I will decline to apply *Lemon*—whether it validates or invalidates the government action in question—and therefore cannot join the opinion of the Court today.

I cannot join for yet another reason: the Court's statement that the proposed use of the school's facilities is constitutional because (among other things) it would not signal endorsement of religion in general. What a strange notion, that a Constitution which *itself* gives "religion in general" preferential treatment (I refer to the Free Exercise Clause) forbids endorsement of religion in general. The Attorney General of New York not only agrees with that strange notion, he has an explanation for it: "Religious advocacy," he writes, "serves the community only in the eyes of its adherents and yields a benefit only to those who already believe." Brief for Respondent Attorney General 24. That was *not* the view of those who adopted our Constitution, who believed that the public virtues inculcated by religion are a public good. It suffices to point out that during the summer of 1789, when it was in the process of drafting the First Amendment, Congress enacted the famous Northwest Territory Ordinance of 1789, Article III of which provides, "Religion, morality, and knowledge, *being necessary to good government and the happiness of mankind*, schools and the means of education shall forever be encouraged." 1 Stat. 52 (emphasis added). Unsurprisingly, then, indifference to "religion in general" is *not* what our cases, both old and recent, demand. . . .

For the reasons given by the Court, I agree that the Free Speech Clause of the First Amendment forbids what respondents have done here. As for the asserted Establishment Clause justification, I would hold, simply and clearly, that giving Lamb's Chapel nondiscriminatory access to school facilities cannot violate that provision because it does not signify state or local embrace of a particular religious sect.

Source: Lamb's Chapel v. Center Moriches Union Free School District, 508 U.S. 384 (1993).

DOCUMENT 68: *Church of the Lukumi Babalu Aye, Inc. v. City of Hialeah* (1993)

In 1987 six ordinances were enacted in Hialeah, Florida that, collectively, prohibited the ritual sacrifice of an animal. The ordinances were essentially a legislative response to the public outcry that followed a successful attempt by practitioners of the Santeria religion to establish a place of worship in Hialeah. At the time it was estimated that approximately 50,000 followers of the faith lived in the southern part of Florida. The religion had originated in Cuba, and numerous Santeria rituals featured the ceremonial sacrifice of animals such as chickens, ducks, goats, sheep, and turtles.

The ordinances, which had virtually no effect on the killing of animals for nonreligious reasons, were challenged in federal court as violations of the First Amendment's free exercise of religion clause. The free exercise clause applies to state and local laws by way of the Fourteenth Amendment. The United States District Court for the Southern District of Florida, however, ruled that the ordinances were constitutional. The district court reasoned that there was a compelling governmental interest to protect animals from cruel and unnecessary killing and to protect the public from health risks related to the practice of animal sacrifice. In addition, the district court cited the need to protect children from emotional distress that could result from witnessing such a sacrifice. The compelling interest standard had been the ruling precedent in free exercise cases prior to the holding by the U.S. Supreme Court in 1990 in *Employment Division, Department of Human Resources of Oregon v. Smith* (see Document 47).

The district court ruling was affirmed by the Court of Appeals for the Eleventh Circuit in a one-paragraph per curium opinion. However, the Supreme Court concluded unanimously that the ordinances were unconstitutional in *Church of the Lukumi Babalu Aye, Inc. v. City of Hialeah* (1993). Justice Anthony M. Kennedy, who delivered the opinion of the Court, reiterated the standard introduced in *Smith* that the demonstration of a compelling state interest is not required when the law in question is neutral and of general applicability. However, since the Hialeah ordinances were viewed by Kennedy as being neither neutral nor generally applicable, he stipulated that the city was required to show that there was a compelling justification for the legislation and that this interest could not be satisfied by less restrictive means. Kennedy concluded that the city of Hialeah had failed to meet these standards.

There were no dissenting opinions, but there was disagreement over the application of the *Smith* precedent. In one concurring opinion Justice Antonin Scalia, the author of the *Smith* opinion, expressed his displeasure with the distinction made by Justice Kennedy between the terms "neutrality" and "general applicability." Justice Harry A. Blackmun was even more critical. As he had in his dissenting opinion in *Smith*, Blackmun stressed his fundamental objection to the general applicability standard. Blackmun continued to extol the virtues of the compelling interest and least restrictive means tests that had been enunciated in 1963 in *Sherbert v. Verner* (see Document 39). Justice David H. Souter, who had not been a member of the Supreme Court when *Smith* was argued, also identified flaws in the general applicability standard. For Souter, the rule announced in *Smith* simply did not exhibit "a comfortable fit with settled law."

According to Justice Kennedy, why did the ordinances in Hialeah fail to pass the neutrality test? Why did Justice Souter contend that the

constitutionality of the Hialeah ordinances could not accurately be
measured by the general applicability standard?

* * *

JUSTICE KENNEDY delivered the opinion of the Court.

* * *

In addressing the constitutional protection for free exercise of religion,
our cases establish the general proposition that a law that is neutral and
of general applicability need not be justified by a compelling governmental interest even if the law has the incidental effect of burdening a
particular religious practice. *Employment Div., Dept. of Human Resources
of Ore. v. Smith.* Neutrality and general applicability are interrelated, and,
as becomes apparent in this case, failure to satisfy one requirement is a
likely indication that the other has not been satisfied. A law failing to
satisfy these requirements must be justified by a compelling governmental interest and must be narrowly tailored to advance that interest.
These ordinances fail to satisfy the *Smith* requirements. We begin by
discussing neutrality. . . .

The record in this case compels the conclusion that suppression of the
central element of the Santeria worship service was the object of the
ordinances. First, though use of the words "sacrifice" and "ritual" does
not compel a finding of improper targeting of the Santeria religion, the
choice of these words is support for our conclusion. There are further
respects in which the text of the city council's enactments discloses the
improper attempt to target Santeria. . . .

In sum, the neutrality inquiry leads to one conclusion: The ordinances
had as their object the suppression of religion. The pattern we have recited discloses animosity to Santeria adherents and their religious practices; the ordinances by their own terms target this religious exercise; the
texts of the ordinances were gerrymandered with care to proscribe religious killings of animals but to exclude almost all secular killings; and
the ordinances suppress much more religious conduct than is necessary
in order to achieve the legitimate ends asserted in their defense. These
ordinances are not neutral, and the court below committed clear error in
failing to reach this conclusion.

We turn next to a second requirement of the Free Exercise Clause, the
rule that laws burdening religious practice must be of general applicability. All laws are selective to some extent, but categories of selection
are of paramount concern when a law has the incidental effect of burdening religious practice. . . .

We conclude, in sum, that each of Hialeah's ordinances pursues the city's governmental interests only against conduct motivated by religious belief. The ordinances "ha[ve] every appearance of a prohibition that society is prepared to impose upon [Santeria worshippers] but not upon itself." This precise evil is what the requirement of general applicability is designed to prevent.

A law burdening religious practice that is not neutral or not of general application must undergo the most rigorous of scrutiny. To satisfy the commands of the First Amendment, a law restrictive of religious practice must advance "interests of the highest order" and must be narrowly tailored in pursuit of those interests. The compelling interest standard that we apply once a law fails to meet the *Smith* requirements is not "water[ed] . . . down" but "really means what it says." *Employment Div., Dept. of Human Resources of Ore. v. Smith.* A law that targets religious conduct for distinctive treatment or advances legitimate governmental interests only against conduct with a religious motivation will survive strict scrutiny only in rare cases. It follows from what we have already said that these ordinances cannot withstand this scrutiny.

First, even were the governmental interests compelling, the ordinances are not drawn in narrow terms to accomplish those interests. As we have discussed, all four ordinances are overboard or underinclusive in substantial respects. The proffered objectives are not pursued with respect to analogous non-religious conduct, and those interests could be achieved by narrower ordinances that burdened religion to a far lesser degree. The absence of narrow tailoring suffices to establish the invalidity of the ordinances.

Respondent has not demonstrated, moreover, that, in the context of these ordinances, its governmental interests are compelling. Where government restricts only conduct protected by the First Amendment and fails to enact feasible measures to restrict other conduct producing substantial harm or alleged harm of the same sort, the interest given in justification of the restriction is not compelling. . . .

The Free Exercise Clause commits government itself to religious tolerance, and upon even slight suspicion that proposals for state intervention stem from animosity to religion or distrust of its practices, all officials must pause to remember their own high duty to the Constitution and to the rights it secures. Those in office must be resolute in resisting importunate demands and must ensure that the sole reasons for imposing the burdens of law and regulation are secular. Legislators may not devise mechanisms, overt or disguised, designed to persecute or oppress a religion or its practices. The laws here in question were enacted contrary to these constitutional principles, and they are void.

JUSTICE SOUTER, concurring in part and concurring in the judgment.

This case turns on a principle about which there is no disagreement, that the Free Exercise Clause bars government action aimed at suppressing religious belief or practice. The Court holds that Hialeah's animal-sacrifice laws violate that principle, and I concur in that holding without reservation.

Because prohibiting religious exercise is the object of the laws at hand, this case does not present the more difficult issue addressed in our last free-exercise case, *Employment Div., Dept. of Human Resources of Ore. v. Smith* (1990), which announced the rule that a "neutral, generally applicable" law does not run afoul of the Free Exercise Clause even when it prohibits religious exercise in effect. The Court today refers to that rule in dicta, and despite my general agreement with the Court's opinion I do not join Part II, where the dicta appear, for I have doubts about whether the *Smith* rule merits adherence. I write separately to explain why the *Smith* rule is not germane to this case and to express my view that, in a case presenting the issue, the Court should reexamine the rule *Smith* declared.

According to *Smith*, if prohibiting the exercise of religion results from enforcing a "neutral, generally applicable" law, the Free Exercise Clause has not been offended. I call this the *Smith* rule to distinguish it from the noncontroversial principle, also expressed in *Smith* though established long before, that the Free Exercise Clause is offended when prohibiting religious exercise results from a law that is not neutral or generally applicable. It is this noncontroversial principle, that the Free Exercise Clause requires neutrality and general applicability, that is at issue here. . . .

While general applicability is, for the most part, self-explanatory, free-exercise neutrality is not self-revealing. A law that is religion neutral on its face or in its purpose may lack neutrality in its effect by forbidding something that religion requires or requiring something that religion forbids. ("[A] regulation is not neutral in an economic sense if, whatever its normal scope or its intentions, it arbitrarily imposes greater costs on religious than on comparable nonreligious activities"). A secular law, applicable to all, that prohibits consumption of alcohol, for example, will affect members of religions that require the use of wine differently from members of other religions and nonbelievers, disproportionately burdening the practice of, say, Catholicism or Judaism. Without an exemption for sacramental wine, Prohibition may fail the test of religion neutrality.

It does not necessarily follow from that observation, of course, that the First Amendment requires an exemption from Prohibition; that depends on the meaning of neutrality as the Free Exercise Clause embraces it. The point here is the unremarkable one that our common notion of neutrality is broad enough to cover not merely what might be called formal neutrality, which as a free-exercise requirement would only bar laws with an object to discriminate against religion, but also what might be called substantive neutrality, which, in addition to demanding a secular object, would generally require government to accommodate religious differences by exempting religious practices from formally neutral laws. If the Free Exercise Clause secures only protection against deliberate discrimination, a formal requirement will exhaust the Clause's neutrality command; if the Free Exercise Clause, rather, safeguards a right to engage in religious activity free from unnecessary governmental interference, the Clause requires substantive, as well as formal, neutrality.

Though *Smith* used the term "neutrality" without a modifier, the rule it announced plainly assumes that free-exercise neutrality is of the formal sort. Distinguishing between laws whose "object" is to prohibit religious exercise and those that prohibit religious exercise as an "incidental effect," *Smith* placed only the former within the reaches of the Free Exercise Clause; the latter, laws that satisfy formal neutrality, *Smith* would subject to no free-exercise scrutiny at all, even when they prohibit religious exercise in application. . . .

The proposition for which the *Smith* rule stands, then, is that formal neutrality, along with general applicability, are sufficient conditions for constitutionality under the Free Exercise Clause. That proposition is not at issue in this case, however, for Hialeah's animal-sacrifice ordinances are not neutral under any definition, any more than they are generally applicable. This case, rather, involves the noncontroversial principle repeated in *Smith*, that formal neutrality and general applicability are necessary conditions for free-exercise constitutionality. . . .

Though *Smith* sought to distinguish the free-exercise cases in which the Court mandated exemptions from secular laws of general application, I am not persuaded. *Wisconsin v. Yoder*, and *Cantwell v. Connecticut*, according to *Smith*, were not true free-exercise cases but "hybrid[s]" involving "the Free Exercise Clause in conjunction with other constitutional protections, such as freedom of speech and of the press, or the right of parents . . . to direct the education of their children." Neither opinion, however, leaves any doubt that "fundamental claims of religious freedom (were) at stake." And the distinction *Smith* draws strikes me as ultimately untenable. If a hybrid claim is simply one in which another constitutional right is implicated, then the hybrid exception would probably be so vast as to swallow the *Smith* rule, and, indeed, the hybrid exception would cover the situation exemplified by *Smith*, since free speech and associational rights are certainly implicated in the peyote ritual. But if a hybrid claim is one in which a litigant would actually obtain an exemption from a formally neutral, generally applicable law under another constitutional provision, then there would have been no reason for the Court in what *Smith* calls the hybrid cases to have mentioned the Free Exercise Clause at all. . . .

Since holding in 1940 that the Free Exercise Clause applies to the

States, see *Cantwell v. Connecticut*, the Court repeatedly has stated that the Clause sets strict limits on the government's power to burden religious exercise, whether it is a law's object to do so or its unanticipated effect. *Smith* responded to these statements by suggesting that the Court did not really mean what it said, detecting in at least the most recent opinions a lack of commitment to the compelling-interest test in the context of formally neutral laws. But even if the Court's commitment were that pal[l]id, it would argue only for moderating the language of the test, not for eliminating constitutional scrutiny altogether. In any event, I would have trouble concluding that the Court has not meant what it has said in more than a dozen cases over several decades, particularly when in the same period it repeatedly applied the compelling-interest test to require exemptions, even in a case decided the year before *Smith*. In sum, it seems to me difficult to escape the conclusion that, whatever *Smith's* virtues, they do not include a comfortable fit with settled law. . . .

Source: Church of the Lukumi Babalu Aye, Inc. v. City of Hialeah, 508 U.S. 520 (1993).

DOCUMENT 69: *Zobrest v. Catalina Foothills School District* (1993)

When the parents of James Zobrest enrolled their son in Salpointe Catholic High School in Tucson, Arizona, they asked the Catalina Foothills School District to provide him with a sign language interpreter. The school district refused this request after stating that a public school system was precluded from providing a student in a sectarian school with such assistance by the establishment of religion clause contained in the First Amendment.

Subsequently, James, who had been deaf since birth, and his parents sought relief under the Individuals with Disabilities Act (IDEA) in the United States District Court for the District of Arizona. The district court, however, concluded that a sign language interpreter provided at the public's expense would serve as a "conduit for religious inculcation" and, thereby, promote the religious development of the student. This entanglement of church and state was ruled unconstitutional.

The Court of Appeals for the Ninth Circuit, citing *Lemon v. Kurtzman* (see Document 55), affirmed the district court holding. According to the court of appeals the primary effect of providing this type of public assistance to a student in a religious school would be an improper advancement of religion by the government. This ruling, however, was reversed by the Supreme Court in *Zobrest v. Catalina Foothills School District* (1993).

Chief Justice William H. Rehnquist wrote for the accommodationist majority in the 5–4 *Zobrest* decision. Rehnquist did not directly rely upon the tripartite *Lemon* test to resolve this dispute, but he did cite a pair of cases that had relied upon *Lemon* to settle establishment clause controversies: *Mueller v. Allen* (see Document 58) and *Witters v. Washington Department of Services for the Blind* (1986).

The key to Rehnquist's opinion was his conclusion that in this case the primary beneficiary of what he labeled a "neutral government program" was a handicapped child, not the sectarian school that he happened to attend. This principle, the child benefit theory, was introduced in 1930 in *Cochran v. Louisiana Board of Education* and later utilized in *Everson v. Board of Education of Ewing Township* (see Document 48). Signaling his displeasure with the Court's holding in *Aguilar v. Felton* (see Document 62), Rehnquist also asserted that the establishment clause does not contain an "absolute bar to the placing of a public employee in a sectarian school."

Justice Harry A. Blackmun, writing in dissent, admonished the majority for not remanding the dispute to a lower court for an examination of statutory and regulatory issues. Having offered this alternative, Blackmun did, however, present his own assessment of the constitutional matter at hand. He reasoned that the practical consequence of the majority's holding would be the placement of a public school employee in a sectarian school to participate directly in "religious indoctrination." Just as the district court objected to an interpreter serving as a "conduit" for religious instruction, Blackmun also saw this as a violation of the establishment clause.

According to Chief Justice Rehnquist, what distinguishes the circumstances of this case from prior "parochiaid" cases decided by the Supreme Court? Why does Justice Blackmun contend that the use of public funds to provide a sign language interpreter for a student in a sectarian school would violate the establishment clause?

* * *

CHIEF JUSTICE REHNQUIST delivered the opinion of the Court.

* * *

We have never said that "religious institutions are disabled by the First Amendment from participating in publicly sponsored social welfare programs." *Bowen v. Kendrick* (1988). For if the Establishment Clause did bar religious groups from receiving general government benefits, then "a church could not be protected by the police and fire departments, or have its public sidewalk kept in repair." *Widmar v. Vincent* (1981). Given that a contrary rule would lead to such absurd results, we have consistently held that government programs that neutrally provide benefits to a broad class of citizens defined without reference to religion are not readily subject to an Establishment Clause challenge just because sectarian institutions may also receive an attenuated financial benefit. Nowhere have we stated this principle more clearly than in *Mueller v. Allen* (1983) and *Witters v. Washington Dept. of Services for the Blind* (1986), two cases dealing specifically with government programs offering general educational assistance.

In *Mueller,* we rejected an Establishment Clause challenge to a Minnesota law allowing taxpayers to deduct certain educational expenses in computing their state income tax, even though the vast majority of those deductions (perhaps over 90%) went to parents whose children attended sectarian schools. . . .

Witters was premised on virtually identical reasoning. In that case, we upheld against an Establishment Clause challenge the State of Washington's extension of vocational assistance, as part of a general state program, to a blind person studying at a private Christian college to become a pastor, missionary, or youth director. . . .

That same reasoning applies with equal force here. The service at issue in this case is part of a general government program that distributes benefits neutrally to any child qualifying as "disabled" under the IDEA, without regard to the "sectarian-non-sectarian, or public-nonpublic nature" of the school the child attends. By according parents freedom to select a school of their choice, the statute ensures that a government-paid interpreter will be present in a sectarian school only as a result of the private decision of individual parents. In other words, because the IDEA creates no financial incentive for parents to choose a sectarian school, an interpreter's presence there cannot be attributed to state decision making. Viewed against the backdrop of *Mueller* and *Witters,* then, the Court of Appeals erred in its decision. When the government offers a neutral service on the premises of a sectarian school as part of a general program that "is in no way skewed towards religion," it follows under our prior decisions that provision of that service does not offend the Establishment Clause. Indeed, this is an even easier case than *Mueller* and *Witters* in the sense that, under the IDEA, no funds traceable to the government ever find their way into sectarian schools' coffers. The only indirect economic benefit a sectarian school might receive by dint of the IDEA is the disabled child's tuition—and that is of course, assuming that the school makes a profit on each student; that, without an IDEA interpreter, the child would have gone to school elsewhere; and that the school, then, would have been unable to fill that child's spot. . . .

The IDEA creates a neutral government program dispensing aid not to schools but to individual handicapped children. If a handicapped child chooses to enroll in a sectarian school we hold that the Establishment Clause does not prevent the school district from furnishing him with a sign-language interpreter there in order to facilitate his education. . . .

JUSTICE BLACKMUN, dissenting.

Today, the Court unnecessarily addresses an important constitutional issue, disregarding long-standing principles of constitutional adjudication. In so doing, the Court holds that placement in a parochial school classroom of a public employee whose duty consists of relaying religious messages does not violate the Establishment Clause of the First Amendment. I disagree both with the Court's decision to reach this question and with its disposition on the merits. I therefore dissent. . . .

Despite my disagreement with the majority's decision to reach the constitutional question, its arguments on the merits deserve a response. Until now, the Court never has authorized a public employee to participate directly in religious indoctrination. Yet that is the consequence of today's decision. . . .

At Salpointe, where the secular and the sectarian are "inextricably intertwined," governmental assistance to the educational function of the school necessarily entails governmental participation in the school's inculcation of religion. A state-employed sign-language interpreter would be required to communicate the material covered in religion class, the nominally secular subjects that are taught from a religious perspective, and the daily Masses at which Salpointe encourages attendance for Catholic students. In an environment so pervaded by discussions of the divine, the interpreter's every gesture would be infused with religious significance. Indeed, petitioners willingly concede this point: "That the interpreter conveys religious messages is a given in the case." By this concession, petitioners would seem to surrender their constitutional claim.

The majority attempts to elude the impact of the record by offering three reasons why this sort of aid to petitioners survives Establishment Clause scrutiny. First, the majority observes that provision of a sign-language interpreter occurs as "part of a general government program that distributed benefits neutrally to any child qualifying as 'disabled' under the IDEA, without regard to the "sectarian-nonsectarian, or public-nonpublic' nature of the school the child attends." Second, the majority finds significant the fact that aid is provided to pupils and their parents, rather than directly to sectarian schools. . . . And, finally, the majority opines that "the task of a sign-language interpreter seems to us quite different from that of a teacher or guidance counselor."

But the majority's arguments are unavailing. As to the first two, even a general welfare program may have specific applications that are constitutionally forbidden under the Establishment Clause. For example, a general program granting remedial assistance to disadvantaged school-children attending public and private, secular and sectarian schools alike would clearly offend the Establishment Clause insofar as it authorized the provision of teachers. Such a program would not be saved simply because it supplied teachers to secular as well as sectarian schools. Nor would the fact that teachers were furnished to pupils and their parents, rather than directly to sectarian schools, immunize such a program from Establishment Clause scrutiny. The majority's decision must turn, then, upon the distinction between a teacher and a sign-language inter-preter. . . .

. . . [O]ur cases consistently have rejected the provision by government of any resource capable of advancing a school's religious mission. . . .

. . . And our cases make clear that government crosses the boundary when it furnishes the medium for communication of a religious message. If petitioners receive the relief they seek, it is beyond question that a state-employed sign-language interpreter would serve as the conduit for James' religious education, thereby assisting Salpointe in its mission of religious indoctrination. But the Establishment Clause is violated when a sectarian school enlists "the machinery of the State to enforce a reli-gious orthodoxy." *Lee v. Weisman* (1992). . . .

. . . This case . . . involves ongoing, daily, and intimate governmental participation in the teaching and propagation of religious doctrine. When government dispenses public funds to individuals who employ them to finance private choices, it is difficult to argue that government is actually endorsing religion. But the graphic symbol of the concert of church and state that results when a public employee or instrumentality mouths a religious message is likely to "enlist—at least in the eyes of impression-able youngsters—the powers of government to the support of the reli-gious denomination operating the school." And the union of the church and state in pursuit of a common enterprise is likely to place the *impri-matur* of governmental approval upon the favored religion, conveying a message of exclusion to all those who do not adhere to its tenets. . . .

The Establishment Clause "rests upon the premise that both religion and government can best work to achieve their lofty aims if each is left free from the other within its respective sphere." *Illinois ex. rel. McCollum v. Board of Ed. of School Dist. No. 71, Champaign, Cty.* (1948). To this end, our cases have strived to "chart a course that preserve[s] the autonomy and freedom of religious bodies while avoiding any semblance of estab-lished religion." *Walz v. Tax Comm'n of New York City* (1970). I would not stray, as the Court does today, from the course set by nearly five decades of Establishment Clause jurisprudence. Accordingly, I dissent.

Source: Zobrest v. Catalina Foothills School District, 509 U.S. 1 (1993).

DOCUMENT 70: Religious Freedom Restoration Act (1993)

In 1963 the United States Supreme Court established a precedent that would guide its interpretation of the First Amendment's free exercise of religion clause for more than twenty-five years. Writing for the majority in *Sherbert v. Verner* (see Document 39), Justice William J. Brennan asserted that, to be upheld, an action by the government that infringes upon religious liberty must demonstrate a compelling public interest. In addition, whenever the free exercise of religion is limited by the government it should be by the least restrictive means possible.

In 1990 the Supreme Court explicitly rejected the *Sherbert* precedent in *Employment Division, Department of Human Resources of Oregon v. Smith* (see Document 47). Justice Antonin Scalia's majority opinion in *Smith* established that a compelling state interest is not required as long as the law in question is neutral and generally applicable.

The *Smith* decision generated a strong, adverse reaction across a wide spectrum of religious and public policy groups. Congress was lobbied for a restoration of the standards enunciated in *Sherbert v. Verner* by a coalition that included the National Association of Evangelicals, the Southern Baptist Convention, the American Jewish Congress, the National Conference of Catholic Bishops, the Mormon Church, the Traditional Values Coalition, the American Civil Liberties Union, and Americans United for Separation of Church and State.

Legislation was proposed in Congress to require the government, at all levels, to adhere to the compelling interest and least restrictive means tests. In the House of Representatives the bill was sponsored by Charles S. Schumer, a Democrat from New York, and Christopher C. Cox, a Republican from California. In the Senate it was sponsored by Edward M. Kennedy, a Democrat from Massachusetts, and Orrin G. Hatch, a Republican from Utah. In both houses the bill received overwhelming support. The House passed the proposal by a voice vote without objection, and in the Senate the bill was approved by a 97 to 3 margin.

The Religious Freedom Restoration Act, which Senator Kennedy called "one of the most significant pieces of legislation in support of religious freedom to ever come before Congress," was signed into law by President Clinton on November 16, 1993. Clinton praised the law, which, in his words, would hold the government "to a very high level of proof before it interferes with someone's free exercise of religion." The key portion of the act, Section 3, was designed to prevent the government from placing a burden on religious liberty unless it could, first, demonstrate the furtherance of a compelling governmental interest and, second, show that the law or action was the least restrictive means of furthering that compelling interest. In this regard the legislation echoed and restored the twofold test introduced thirty years earlier by Justice Brennan in *Sherbert v. Verner.*

According to Section 2 of the Religious Freedom Restoration Act, what were the objectives that the law was intended to achieve?

* * *

SECTION 1. SHORT TITLE.

This Act may be cited as the "Religious Freedom Restoration Act of 1993."

SEC. 2. CONGRESSIONAL FINDINGS AND DECLARATION OF PURPOSES.

(a) FINDINGS—The Congress finds that—

(1) the framers of the Constitution, recognizing free exercise of religion as an unalienable right, secured its protection in the First Amendment to the Constitution;

(2) laws "neutral" toward religion may burden religious exercise as surely as laws intended to interfere with religious exercise;

(3) governments should not substantially burden religious exercise without compelling justification;

(4) in Employment Division v. Smith, 494 U.S. 872 (1990) the Supreme Court virtually eliminated the requirements that the government justify burdens on religious exercise imposed by laws neutral toward religion; and

(5) the compelling interest test as set forth in prior Federal court rulings is a workable test for striking sensible balances between religious liberty and competing prior governmental interests.

(b) PURPOSES—The purposes of this Act are—

(1) to restore the compelling interest test as set forth in Sherbert v. Verner, 374 U.S. 398 (1963) and Wisconsin v. Yoder, 406 U.S. 205 (1972) and to guarantee its application in all cases where free exercise of religion is substantially burdened; and

(2) to provide a claim or defense to persons whose religious exercise is substantially burdened by government.

SEC. 3. FREE EXERCISE OF RELIGION PROTECTED.

(a) IN GENERAL—Government shall not substantially burden a person's exercise of religion even if the burden results from a rule of general applicability, except as provided in subsection (b).

(b) EXCEPTION—Government may substantially burden a person's exercise of religion only if it demonstrates that application of the burden to the person—

(1) is in furtherance of a compelling governmental interest; and

(2) is the least restrictive means of furthering that compelling governmental interest.

(c) JUDICIAL RELIEF—A person whose religious exercise has been burdened in violation of this section may assert that violation as a claim or defense in a judicial proceeding and obtain appropriate relief against a government. Standing to assert a claim or defense under this section shall be governed by the general rules of standing under article III of the Constitution.

SEC. 4. ATTORNEYS FEES.

(a) JUDICIAL PROCEEDINGS—Section 722 of the Revised Statutes (42 U.S.C. 1988) is amended by inserting "the Religious Freedom Restoration Act of 1993," before "or title VI of the Civil Rights Act of 1964."

(b) ADMINISTRATIVE PROCEEDINGS—Section 504(b)(1)(C) of title 5, United States Code, is amended—

(1) by striking "and" at the end of clause (ii);

(2) by striking the semicolon at the end of clause (iii) and inserting ", and"; and

(3) by inserting "(iv) the Religious Freedom Restoration Act of 1993;" after clause (iii).

SEC. 5. DEFINITIONS.

As used in this Act—

(1) the term "government" includes a branch, department, agency, instrumentality, and official (or other person acting under color of law) of the United States, a State, or a subdivision of a State;

(2) the term "State" includes the District of Columbia, the Commonwealth of Puerto Rico, and each territory and possession of the United States;

(3) the term "demonstrates" means meets the burdens of going forward with the evidence and of persuasion; and

(4) the term "exercise of religion" means the exercise of religion under the First Amendment to the Constitution.

SEC. 6. APPLICABILITY.

(a) IN GENERAL—This Act applies to all Federal and State law, and the implementation of that law, whether statutory or otherwise, and whether adopted before or after the enactment of this Act.

(b) RULE OF CONSTRUCTION—Federal statutory law adopted after the date of the enactment of this Act is subject to this Act unless such law explicitly excludes such application by reference to this Act.

(c) RELIGIOUS BELIEF UNAFFECTED—Nothing in this Act shall be construed to authorize any government to burden any religious belief.

SEC. 7. ESTABLISHMENT CLAUSE UNAFFECTED.

Nothing in this Act shall be construed to affect, interpret, or in any way address that portion of the First Amendment prohibiting laws respecting the establishment of religion (referred to in this section as the "Establishment Clause"). Granting government funding, benefits, or exemptions, to the extent permissible under the Establishment Clause, shall not constitute a violation of this Act. As used in this section, the term "granting," used with respect to government funding, benefits, or exemptions, does not include the denial of government funding, benefits, or exemptions.

Speaker of the House of Representatives.
Vice President of the United States and
President of the Senate.

Source: Congressional Record (Washington, D.C., 1993); 42 U.S.C. 2000; 107 Stat. 1488; see also the following World Wide Web site: http://thomas.loc.gov/

DOCUMENT 71: *Board of Education of Kiryas Joel Village School District v. Grumet* (1994)

In 1994 the United States Supreme Court decided a case that originated in Kiryas Joel, New York. The village, located approximately forty miles northwest of New York City, had a population of about 8,500 people at the time. All of the residents of Kiryas Joel were members of the Satmar Hasidic sect. Practitioners of this form of Judaism interpret the Torah strictly, and they generally reject assimilation into the modern world. They speak Yiddish as their primary language, eschew television and radio, and segregate the sexes outside of the home. Children wear distinctive yet simple clothing which includes head coverings for boys and modest dresses for girls.

Parents in Kiryas Joel preferred to send their children to religious schools in the village rather than nearby public schools maintained by the Monroe-Woodbury Central School District. Prior to 1985 the public school system did provide special services for the disabled children in Kiryas Joel in an annex adjacent to one of the religious schools. However, following the Supreme Court decision in *Aguilar v. Felton* (Document 62), those children who suffered from physical, mental, and emotional disorders were required to attend a public school outside of Kiryas Joel for the special services. Parents complained that this experience left their children traumatized, and by 1989 only one child from the village was attending a neighboring public school.

The New York legislature responded in 1989 by passing a statute, known as Chapter 748 of the state's code of laws, which designated the village of Kiryas Joel as a separate school district. Subsequently a public school solely for children with special needs was established in the community. No other public school was needed in the village because all of the other students continued to attend religious schools.

The statute was challenged in state court by the New York State School Boards Association, whose executive director was Louis Grumet. It was alleged that the statute was a violation of the First Amendment's establishment of religion clause, which applied to the states by way of the Fourteenth Amendment. The state court pronounced the law unconstitutional after invoking the three-pronged test articulated in 1971 in *Lemon v. Kurtzman* (see Document 55). This ruling was affirmed by an intermediate appellate court and the New York Court of Appeals prior to being appealed to the U.S. Supreme Court.

In *Board of Education of Kiryas Joel Village School District v. Grumet* (1994), the Supreme Court also concluded that the New York statute was an unconstitutional violation of the establishment clause. Without relying upon the *Lemon* test, Justice David H. Souter delivered the opinion for a splintered Court. Souter reasoned that the action by the state legislature was one of religious favoritism since it had placed the power over public education in the hands of an electorate defined by a common religious belief. The statute, therefore, contravened the principle of neutrality.

Souter's opinion was joined in full by three members of the Court: Harry A. Blackmun, John Paul Stevens, and Ruth Bader Ginsburg. Justices Blackmun and Stevens both wrote brief concurring opinions. Blackmun wrote to neutralize any suggestion that the Court's decision was a departure from the principles established in *Lemon v. Kurtzman*. Stevens expressed his objection to a law that he argued would only continue the segregation of the children residing in Kiryas Joel from the inhabitants of neighboring communities.

The key votes were cast by Justices Sandra Day O'Connor and Anthony M. Kennedy. O'Connor, concurring in part and concurring in the judgment, wrote an opinion that was noteworthy for at least two reasons. First, she related that in her opinion it would be constitutional for a state to enact neutral criteria that would provide all villages with the opportunity to operate their own school districts. Second, Justice O'Connor observed that in this case, as in *Lee v. Weisman* (see Document 66) and *Zobrest v. Catalina Foothills School District* (see Document 69), the Court had resolved an establishment clause controversy without resorting to the tripartite *Lemon* test. She then speculated that no single test could stand as a "grand unified theory" to settle myriad disputes that arise under the clause.

Justice Kennedy wrote separately, concurring in the judgment. He argued that the New York statute should have been invalidated on the narrow ground that the First Amendment prohibits political boundaries from being drawn on the basis of religion. Kennedy termed this violation "religious gerrymandering." In addition, both O'Connor and Kennedy urged the Court to reconsider the *Aguilar* precedent.

Justice Antonin Scalia, joined by two other members of the Court, saw the New York law as a neutral accommodation of a group's unique culture, not their religious beliefs. As in a number of his written opinions prior to this case, Scalia once again employed sarcasm to ridicule the Court's holding.

What reasons did Justice Souter list in support of his contention that the New York statute violated the principle of neutrality that is required by the establishment clause? What arguments were advanced by Justice Scalia to counter Souter's analysis of the dispute?

* * *

JUSTICE SOUTER delivered the opinion of the Court.

* * *

It is, first, not dispositive that the recipients of state power in this case are a group of religious individuals united by common doctrine, not the group's leaders or officers. Although some school district franchise is common to all voters, the State's manipulation of the franchise for this district limited it to Satmars, giving the sect exclusive control of the political subdivision. . . .

It is undisputed that those who negotiated the village boundaries when applying the general village incorporation statute drew them so as to exclude all but Satmars, and that the New York Legislature was well aware that the village remained exclusively Satmar in 1989. . . . The significance of this fact to the state legislature is indicated by the further fact that carving out the village school district ran counter to customary districting practices in the State. Indeed, the trend in New York is not toward dividing school districts but toward consolidating them. The thousands of small common school districts laid out in the early 19th century have been combined and recombined, first into union free school districts and then into larger central school districts, until only a tenth as many remain today. Most of these cover several towns, many of them cross country boundaries, and only one remains precisely coterminous with an incorporated village. The object of the State's practice of consolidation is the creation of districts large enough to provide a comprehensive education at affordable cost, which is thought to require at least 500 pupils for a combined junior-senior high school. The Kiryas Joel Village School District, in contrast, has only 13 local, full-time students in all (even including out-of-area and part-time students leaves the number under 200), and in offering only special education and remedial programs it makes no pretense to be a full-service district. . . .

Because the district's creation ran uniquely counter to state practice, following the lines of a religious community where the customary and neutral principles would not have dictated the same result, we have good reasons to treat this district as the reflection of a religious criterion for identifying the recipients of civil authority. Not even the special needs of the children in this community can explain the legislature's unusual Act, for the State could have responded to the concerns of the Satmar parents without implicating the Establishment Clause, as we explain in some detail further on. We therefore find the legislature's Act to be substantially equivalent to defining a political subdivision and hence the qualification for its franchise by a religious test, resulting in a purposeful and forbidden "fusion of governmental and religious functions."

The fact that this school district was created by a special and unusual Act of the legislature also gives reason for concern whether the benefit received by the Satmar community is one that the legislature will provide equally to other religious (and nonreligious) groups. . . .

The fundamental source of constitutional concern here is that the legislature itself may fail to exercise governmental authority in a religiously neutral way. The anomalously case-specific nature of the legislature's exercise of state authority in creating this district for a religious community leaves the Court without any direct way to review such state action for the purpose of safeguarding a principle at the heart of the Establishment Clause, that government should not prefer one religion to another, or religion to irreligion. Because the religious community of Kiryas Joel did not receive its new governmental authority simply as one of many communities eligible for equal treatment under a general law, we have no assurance that the next similarly situated group seeking a school district of its own will receive one. . . . Nor can the historical context in this case furnish us with any reason to suppose that the Satmars are merely one in a series of communities receiving the benefit of special school district laws. Early on in the development of public education in New York, the State rejected highly localized school districts for New York City when they were promoted as a way to allow separate schooling for Roman Catholic children. And in more recent history, the special Act in this case stands alone.

In finding that Chapter 748 [the statute at issue] violates the requirement of governmental neutrality by extending the benefit of a special franchise, we do not deny that the Constitution allows the state to accommodate religious needs by alleviating special burdens. Our cases leave no doubt that in commanding neutrality the Religion Clauses do not require the government to be oblivious to impositions that legitimate exercises of state power may place on religious belief and practice. . . .

But accommodation is not a principle without limits, and what petitioners seek is an adjustment to the Satmars' religiously grounded preferences that our cases do not countenance. Prior decisions have allowed religious communities and institutions to pursue their own interests free from governmental interference . . . but we have never hinted that an otherwise unconstitutional delegation of political power to a religious group could be saved as a religious accommodation. Petitioners' proposed accommodation singles out a particular religious sect for special treatment, and whatever the limits of permissible legislative accommodations may be . . . it is clear that neutrality as among religions must be honored.

In this case we are clearly constrained to conclude that the statute before us fails the test of neutrality. It delegates a power this Court has said "ranks at the very apex of the function of a State," *Wisconsin v. Yoder* (1972), to an electorate defined by common religious belief and practice, in a manner that fails to foreclose religious favoritism. It therefore crosses the line from permissible accommodation to impermissible establishment. . . .

JUSTICE SCALIA, dissenting.

The Court today finds that the Powers That Be, up in Albany, have conspired to effect an establishment of the Satmar Hasidim. I do not know who would be more surprised at this discovery: the Founders of our Nation or Grand Rebbe Joel Teitelbaum, founder of the Satmar. The Grand Rebbe would be astounded to learn that after escaping brutal persecution and coming to America with the modest hope of religious toleration for their ascetic form of Judaism, the Satmar had become so powerful, so closely allied with Mammon, as to have become an "establishment" of the Empire State. And the Founding Fathers would be astonished to find that the Establishment Clause—which they designed "to insure that no one powerful sect or combination of sects could use political or governmental power to punish dissenters," *Zorach v. Clauson* (1952), has been employed to prohibit characteristically and admirably American accommodation of the religious practices (or more precisely, cultural peculiarities) of a tiny minority sect. I, however, am *not* surprised. Once this Court has abandoned text and history as guides, nothing prevents it from calling religious toleration the establishment of religion.

Unlike most of our Establishment Clause cases involving education, these cases involve no public funding, however slight or indirect, to private religious schools. They do not involve private schools at all. The school under scrutiny is a public school specifically designed to provide a public secular education to handicapped students. The superintendent of the school, who is not Hasidic, is a 20-year veteran of the New York City public school system, with expertise in the area of bilingual, bicultural, special education. The teachers and therapists at the school all live outside the village of Kiryas Joel. While the village's private schools are profoundly religious and strictly segregated by sex, classes at the public school are coed and the curriculum secular. The school building has the bland appearance of a public school, unadorned by religious symbols or markings; and the school complies with the laws and regulations governing all other New York State public schools. There is no suggestion, moreover, that this public school has gone too far in making special adjustments to the religious needs of its students. In sum, these cases involve only public aid to a school that is public as can be. The only thing distinctive about the school is that all the students share the same religion.

None of our cases has ever suggested that there is anything wrong with that. In fact, the Court has specifically *approved* the education of students of a single religion on a neutral site adjacent to a private religious school. . . . If a State can furnish services to a group of sectarian students on a neutral site adjacent to a private religious school, or even *within* such a school, how can there be any defect in educating those same students in a public school? . . . There is no danger in educating religious students in a public school.

For these very good reasons, JUSTICE SOUTER's opinion does not focus upon the school, but rather upon the school district and the New York Legislature that created it. His arguments, though sometimes intermingled, are two: that reposing governmental power in the Kiryas Joel School District is the same as reposing governmental power in a religious group; and that in enacting the statute creating the district, the New York State Legislature was discriminating on the basis of religion, *i.e.*, favoring the Satmar Hasidim over others. . . .

JUSTICE SOUTER's position boils down to the quite novel proposition that any group of citizens (say, the residents of Kiryas Joel) can be invested with political power, but not if they all belong to the same religion. Of course such *disfavoring* of religion is positively antagonistic to the purposes of the Religion Clauses, and we have rejected it before. . . .

I turn, next, to JUSTICE SOUTER's second justification for finding an establishment of religion: his facile conclusion that the New York Legislature's creation of the Kiryas Joel School District was religiously motivated. But in the Land of the Free, democratically adopted laws are not so easily impeached by unelected judges. . . .

There is of course no possible doubt of a secular basis here. The New York Legislature faced a unique problem in Kiryas Joel: a community in which all the non-handicapped children attend private schools, and the physically and mentally disabled children who attend public school suffer the additional handicap of cultural distinctiveness. It would be troublesome enough if these peculiarly dressed, handicapped students were sent to the next town, accompanied by their similarly clad but unimpaired classmates. But all the unimpaired children of Kiryas Joel attend private school. The handicapped children suffered sufficient emotional trauma from their predicament that their parents kept them home from school. Surely the legislature could target this problem, and provide a public education for these students, in the same way it addressed, *by a similar law*, the unique needs of children institutionalized in a hospital.

Since the obvious presence of a neutral, secular basis renders the asserted preferential effect of this law inadequate to invalidate it, JUSTICE SOUTER is required to come forward with direct evidence that religious preference was the objective. His case could scarcely be weaker. In consists, briefly, of this: The People of New York created the Kiryas Joel Village School District in order to further the Satmar religion, rather than for any proper secular purpose, because (1) they created the district in an extraordinary manner—by special Act of the legislature, rather than under the State's general laws governing school-district reorganization; (2) the creation of the district ran counter to a State trend towards consolidation of school districts; and (3) the District includes only adherents of the Satmar religion. On this indictment, no jury would convict.

One difficulty with the first point is that it is not true. There was really nothing so "special" about the formation of a school district by an Act of the New York Legislature. The State has created both large school districts . . . and small specialized school districts for institutionalized children, through these special Acts. But in any event all that the first point proves, and the second point as well (countering the trend toward consolidation), is that New York regarded Kiryas Joel as a special case, requiring special measures. I should think it *obvious* that it did, and obvious that it *should have*. But even if the New York Legislature had never before created a school district by special statute (which is not true), how could the departure from those past practices possibly demonstrate that the legislature had religious favoritism in mind? It could not. To be sure, when there is no special treatment there is no possibility of religious favoritism; but it is not logical to suggest that when there *is* special treatment there is *proof* of religious favoritism.

JUSTICE SOUTER's case against the statute comes down to nothing more, therefore, than . . . the fact that all the residents of the Kiryas Joel Village School District are Satmars. But all its residents also wear unusual dress, have unusual civic customs, and have not much to do with people who are culturally different from them. (The Court recognizes that "the Satmars prefer to live together to facilitate individual religious observance and maintain social, cultural and religious values, but that it is not 'against their religion' to interact with others.'') On what basis does JUS-TICE SOUTER conclude that it is the theological distinctiveness rather than the cultural distinctiveness that was the basis for New York State's decision? The normal assumption would be that it was the latter, since it was not theology but dress, language, and cultural alienation that posed the educational problem for the children. JUSTICE SOUTER not only does not adopt the logical assumption, he does not even give the New York Legislature the benefit of the doubt. . . .

I have little doubt that JUSTICE SOUTER would laud this humanitarian legislation if all of the distinctiveness of the students of Kiryas Joel were attributable to the fact that their parents were nonreligious commune-dwellers, or American Indians, or gypsies. The creation of a special, one-culture school district for the benefit of those children would pose no problem. The neutrality demanded by the Religion Clauses requires the same indulgence towards cultural characteristics that *are* accompanied by religious belief. . . .

The Court's decision today is astounding. Chapter 748 involves no public aid to private schools and does not mention religion. In order to invalidate it, the Court casts aside, on the flimsiest of evidence, the strong presumption of validity that attaches to facially neutral laws, and invalidates the present accommodation because it does not trust New York to be as accommodating toward other religions (presumably those less powerful than the Satmar Hasidim) in the future. This is unprecedented—except that it continues, and takes to new extremes, a recent tendency in the opinions of this Court to turn the Establishment Clause into a repealer of our Nation's tradition of religious toleration. I dissent.

Source: Board of Education of Kiryas Joel Village School District v. Grumet, 512 U.S. 687 (1994).

DOCUMENT 72: *Rosenberger v. University of Virginia* (1995)

The First Amendment to the United States Constitution prohibits laws respecting an establishment of religion. It also prohibits laws that abridge freedom of speech. In 1990 a controversy began on the campus of the University of Virginia that would eventually require the U.S. Supreme Court to examine the intersection of these two fundamental rights.

The University of Virginia was founded in 1819 by Thomas Jefferson, the primary author of the 1786 Virginia Statute for Religious Freedom (see Document 23). In addition, a letter written by Jefferson in 1802 included the now famous metaphor of a wall of separation between church and state. In 1990 the university established by Jefferson, similar to most state universities, maintained a fund to underwrite extracurricular student activities. At the University of Virginia each full-time student was assessed a mandatory fee of $14 per semester. The resulting Student Activities Fund (SAF) was designed to support a wide range of activities related to the university's educational mission.

Student groups known as Contracted Independent Organizations (CIOs) that published newspapers could request funding from the activities fund to reimburse outside companies for printing costs. In 1990, however, the University of Virginia refused to authorize the payment of $5,862 to the printer of the first edition of a student newspaper titled *Wide Awake: A Christian Perspective at the University of Virginia*. University officials reasoned that even though the newspaper was produced by a bona fide CIO, Wide Awake Productions (WAP), SAF guidelines stated that funding could not be used to cover costs associated with the publication of a student newspaper that "primarily promotes or manifests a particular belief in or about a deity or an ultimate reality."

Wide Awake Productions, founded by Ronald Rosenberger and other students, filed a lawsuit in the U.S. District Court for the Western District of Virginia alleging that the action taken by the University of Virginia had abridged their freedom of speech. The district court, however, ruled in favor of the university. This holding was affirmed by the U.S. Court of Appeals for the Fourth Circuit, which stated that compliance with the establishment clause in this instance required the violation of freedom of speech.

Before the Supreme Court the conflict between the student group and the university was framed as a dispute over equal access to public funds. Prior to deciding *Rosenberger v. University of Virginia* in 1995 the Court had rendered accommodationist holdings in three cases that raised the issue of equal access to public facilities: *Widmar v. Vincent* (1981), *Board of Education of the Westside Community Schools v. Mergens* (1990) (see Document 65), and *Lamb's Chapel v. Center Moriches Union Free School District* (1993) (see Document 67). In *Rosenberger* the Supreme Court agreed with the court of appeals that by refusing to cover the cost of printing the Christian newspaper *Wide Awake* the University of Virginia had violated the guarantee of freedom of speech. Unlike the court of appeals, however, the Supreme Court concluded that this limitation on student expression was not justified.

Justice Anthony M. Kennedy, writing for the majority in this 5–4 decision, argued that the establishment clause requires neutrality toward religion and, to the contrary, the path followed by the officials at the University of Virginia constituted viewpoint discrimination. By relying primarily upon the *Lamb's Chapel* precedent, and by emphasizing freedom of speech rather than the establishment clause, Kennedy avoided a reconsideration of the vitality of the three-part test enunciated in *Lemon v. Kurtzman* (1971). (See Document 55.)

The dissent by Justice David H. Souter in *Rosenberger* made only a passing reference to *Lemon*, but his focus was nonetheless squarely on the establishment clause. Souter viewed the majority's position as an approval of direct government funding for core religious activities. His stated concern was that the Court's initial move in this direction would gain momentum, creating a trend that would be difficult to either retard or stop.

Why did Justice Kennedy reject the position that the University of Virginia could not cover the cost of printing a religious newspaper due to the establishment clause? What were the main points of Justice Souter's dissenting opinion?

*   *   *

JUSTICE KENNEDY delivered the opinion of the Court.

*   *   *

It is axiomatic that the government may not regulate speech based on its substantive content or the message it conveys. Other principles follow from this precept. In the realm of private speech or expression, government regulation may not favor one speaker over another. Discrimination against speech because of its message is presumed to be unconstitutional. These rules informed our determination that the government offends the First Amendment when it imposes financial burdens on certain speakers based on the content of their expression. When the government targets not subject matter but particular views taken by speakers on a subject, the violation of the First Amendment is all the more blatant. Viewpoint discrimination is thus an egregious form of content discrimination. The government must abstain from regulating speech when the specific motivating ideology or the opinion or perspective of the speaker is the rationale for the restriction.

These principles provide the framework forbidding the State from exercising viewpoint discrimination, even when the limited public forum is one of its own creation. . . . Once it has opened a limited forum, however, the State must respect the lawful boundaries it has itself set. . . . Thus, in determining whether the State is acting to preserve the limits of the forum it has created so that the exclusion of a class of speech is legitimate, we have observed a distinction between, on the one hand, content discrimination, which may be permissible if it preserves the purposes of that limited forum, and, on the other hand, viewpoint discrimination, which is presumed impermissible when directed against speech otherwise within the forum's limitations. . . .

Vital First Amendment speech principles are at stake here. The first danger to liberty lies in granting the State the power to examine publications to determine whether or not they are based on some ultimate idea and if so for the State to classify them. The second, and corollary, danger is to speech from the chilling of individual thought and expression. That danger is especially real in the University setting, where the State acts against a background and tradition of thought and experiment that is at the center of our intellectual and philosophic tradition. . . .

Based on the principles we have discussed, we hold that the regulation invoked to deny SAF support, both in its terms and in its application to these petitioners, is a denial of their right of free speech guaranteed by the First Amendment. It remains to be considered whether the violation following from the University's action is excused by the necessity of complying with the Constitution's prohibition against state establishment of religion. We turn to that question. . . .

If there is to be assurance that the Establishment Clause retains its force in guarding against those governmental actions it was intended to prohibit, we must in each case inquire first into the purpose and object of the governmental action in question and then into the practical details of the program's operation. Before turning to these matters, however, we can set forth certain general principles that must bear upon our determination.

A central lesson of our decisions is that a significant factor in upholding governmental programs in the fact of Establishment Clause attack is their neutrality towards religion. We have decided a series of cases addressing the receipt of government benefits where religion or religious views are implicated in some degree. The first case in our modern Establishment Clause jurisprudence was *Everson v. Board of Ed. of Ewing* (1947). They were cautioned that in enforcing the prohibition against laws respecting establishment of religion, we must "be sure that we do not inadvertently prohibit [the government] from extending its general state law benefits to all its citizens without regard to their religious belief." We have held that the guarantee of neutrality is respected, not offended, when the government, following neutral criteria and evenhanded policies, extends benefits to recipients whose ideologies and viewpoints, including religious ones, are broad and diverse. . . .

The governmental program here is neutral toward religion. There is no suggestion that the University created it to advance religion or adopted some ingenious device with the purpose of aiding a religious cause. The object of the SAF is to open a forum for speech and to support various student enterprises, including the publication of newspapers, in recognition of the diversity and creativity of student life. The University's SAF Guidelines have a separate classification for, and do not make third-party payments on behalf of, "religious organizations," which are those "whose purpose is to practice a devotion to an acknowledged ultimate reality or deity." The category of support here is for "student news, information, opinion, entertainment, or academic communications media groups," of which Wide Awake was 1 of 15 in the 1990 school year. WAP did not seek a subsidy because of its Christian editorial viewpoint; it sought funding as a student journal, which it was.

The neutrality of the program distinguished the student fees from a tax levied for the direct support of a church or group of churches. A tax of that sort, of course, would run contrary to Establishment Clause concerns dating from the earliest days of the Republic. The apprehensions of our predecessors involved the levying of taxes upon the public for the sole and exclusive purpose of establishing and supporting specific sects. The exaction here, by contrast, is a student activity fee designed to reflect the reality that student life in its many dimensions includes the necessity of wide-ranging speech and inquiry and that student expression is an integral part of the University's educational mission. . . .

It does not violate the Establishment Clause for a public university to grant access to its facilities on a religion-neutral basis to a wide spectrum of student groups, including groups which use meeting rooms for sectarian activities, accompanied by some devotional exercises. This is so even where the upkeep, maintenance, and repair of the facilities attributed to those uses is paid from a student activities fund to which students are required to contribute. The government usually acts by spending money. Even the provision of a meeting room, as in *Mergens* and *Widmar*, involved governmental expenditure, if only in the form of electricity and heating or cooling costs. The error made by the Court of Appeals, as well as by the dissent, lies in focusing on the money that is undoubtedly expended by the government, rather than on the nature of the benefits received by the recipient. If the expenditure of governmental funds is prohibited whenever those funds pay for a service that is, pursuant to a religion-neutral program, used by a group for sectarian purposes, then *Widmar*, *Mergens*, and *Lamb's Chapel* would have to be overruled. Given our holdings in these cases, it follows that the public university may maintain its own computer facility and give student groups access to that facility, including the use of the printers, on a religion neutral, say first-come-first-served basis. If a religious student organization obtained access on that religion-neutral basis and used a computer to compose or a printer or copy machine to print speech with a religious content or viewpoint, the State's action in providing the group with access would no more violate the Establishment Clause than would giving those groups access to an assembly hall. There is no difference in

logic or principle, and no difference of constitutional significance, between a school using its funds to operate a facility to which students
have access, and a school paying a third-party contractor to operate the
facility on its behalf. The latter occurs here. The University provides
printing services to a broad spectrum of student newspapers qualified
as CIOs by reason of their officers and membership. Any benefit to religion is incidental to the government's provision of secular services for
secular purposes on a religion-neutral basis. Printing is a routine, secular,
and recurring attribute of student life.

By paying outside printers, the University in fact attains a further degree of separation from the student publication, for it avoids the duties of
supervision, escapes the costs of upkeep, repair, and replacement attributable to student use, and has a clear record of costs. As a result, and as in
Widmar, the University can charge the SAF, and not the taxpayers as a
whole, for the discrete activity in question. It would be formalistic for us to
say that the University must forfeit these advantages and provide the
services itself in order to comply with the Establishment Clause. It is, of
course, true that if the State pays a church's bills it is subsidizing it, and we
must guard against this abuse. That is not a danger here, based on the considerations we have advanced and for the additional reason that the student publication is not a religious institution, at least in the usual sense of
that term as used in our case law, and it is not a religious organization as
used in the University's own regulations. It is instead a publication involved in a pure forum for the expression of ideas, ideas that would be
both incomplete and chilled were the Constitution to be interpreted to require that state officials and courts scan the publication to ferret out views
that principally manifest a belief in a divine being. . . .

To obey the Establishment Clause, it was not necessary for the University to deny eligibility to student publications because of their viewpoint. The neutrality commanded of the State by the separate Clauses of
the First Amendment was compromised by the University's course of
action. The viewpoint discrimination inherent in the University's regulation required public officials to scan and interpret student publications
to discern their underlying philosophic assumptions respecting religious
theory and belief. That course of action was a denial of the right of free
speech and would risk fostering a pervasive bias or hostility to religion,
which could undermine the very neutrality the Establishment Clause
requires. There is no Establishment Clause violation in the University's
honoring its duties under the Free Speech Clause.

The judgment of the Court of Appeals must be, and is, reversed.

JUSTICE SOUTER, dissenting.

* * *

The central question in this case is whether a grant from the Student Activities Fund to pay Wide Awake's printing expenses would violate the Establishment Clause. Although the Court does not dwell on the details of Wide Awake's message, it recognizes something sufficiently religious in the publication to demand Establishment Clause scrutiny. Although the Court places great stress on the eligibility of secular as well as religious activities for grants from the Student Activities Fund, it recognizes that such evenhanded availability is not by itself enough to satisfy constitutional requirements for any scheme that results in a benefit to religion. Something more is necessary to justify any religious aid. Some members of the Court, at least, may think the funding permissible on a view that it is indirect, since the money goes to Wide Awake's printer, not through Wide Awake's own checking account. The Court's principal reliance, however, is on an argument that providing religion with economically valuable services is permissible on the theory that services are economically indistinguishable from religious access to governmental speech forums, which sometimes is permissible. But this reasoning would commit the Court to approving direct religious aid beyond anything justifiable for the sake of access to speaking forums. The Court implicitly recognizes this in its further attempt to circumvent the clear bar to direct governmental aid to religion. Different members of the Court seek to avoid this bar in different ways. The opinion of the Court makes the novel assumption that only direct aid financed with tax revenue is barred, and draws the erroneous conclusion that the involuntary Student Activities Fee is not a tax. . . .

The Court's difficulties will be all the more clear after a closer look at Wide Awake than the majority opinion affords. The character of the magazine is candidly disclosed on the opening page of the first issue, where the editor-in-chief announces Wide Awake's mission in a letter to the readership signed, "Love in Christ": it is "to challenge Christians to live, in word and deed, according to the faith they proclaim and to encourage students to consider what a personal relationship with Jesus Christ means." The masthead of every issue bears St. Paul's exhortation, that "[t]he hour has come for you to awake from your slumber, because our salvation is nearer now than when we first believed. Romans 13:11." . . .

This writing is no merely descriptive examination of religious doctrine or even of ideal Christian practice in confronting life's social and personal problems. Nor is it merely the expression of editorial opinion that incidentally coincides with Christian ethics and reflects a Christian view of human obligation. It is straightforward exhortation to enter into a relationship with God as revealed in Jesus Christ, and to satisfy a series of moral obligations derived from the teachings of Jesus Christ. . . .

Using public funds for the direct subsidization of preaching the word is categorically forbidden under the Establishment Clause, and if the

Clause was meant to accomplish nothing else, it was meant to bar this use of public money. Evidence on the subject antedates even the Bill of Rights itself, as may be seen in the writings of Madison, whose authority on questions about the meaning of the Establishment Clause is well settled. . . . Four years before the First Congress proposed the First Amendment, Madison gave his opinion on the legitimacy of using public funds for religious purposes, in the Memorial and Remonstrance Against Religious Assessments, which played the central role in ensuring the defeat of the Virginia tax assessment bill in 1786 and framed the debate upon which the Religion Clauses stand. . . .

The principle against direct funding with public money is patently violated by the contested use of today's student activity fee. . . . The University exercises the power of the State to compel a student to pay it . . . and the use of any part of it for the direct support of religious activity thus strikes at what we have repeatedly held to be the heart of the prohibition on establishment. . . .

Why does the Court not apply this clear law to these clear facts and conclude, as I do, that the funding scheme here is a clear constitutional violation? The answer must be in part that the Court fails to confront the evidence set out in the preceding section. . . .

Since I cannot see the future I cannot tell whether today's decision portends much more than making a shambles out of student activity fees in public colleges. Still, my apprehension is whetted by Chief Justice Burger's warning in *Lemon v. Kurtzman* (1971): "in constitutional adjudication some steps, which when taken were thought to approach 'the verge,' have become the platform for yet further steps. A certain momentum develops in constitutional theory and it can be a 'downhill thrust' easily set in motion but difficult to retard or stop."

I respectfully dissent.

Source: Rosenberger v. University of Virginia, 515 U.S. 819 (1995).

DOCUMENT 73: *Capitol Square Review and Advisory Board v. Pinette* (1995)

The Statehouse in Columbus, Ohio, is surrounded by a ten-acre, state-owned plaza known as Capitol Square. The plaza was designated a forum for public events and the discussion of public issues. Responsibility for requesting access to the square was held by the Capitol Square Review and Advisory Board.

On November 18, 1993, the board voted to prohibit all unattended displays in the plaza. Five days later the board nullified this action after being pressured to do so by the governor; as a result, the state was authorized to erect its annual Christmas tree display in the square. Subsequently, on the same day that a rabbi's request to display a menorah was approved, the board rejected an application submitted by the Ohio branch of the Ku Klux Klan. The Klan had hoped to erect a large wooden cross in the plaza.

A burning cross, as used by the Klan for decades, has generally been regarded as a symbol of racial hatred and intimidation. Nonetheless, in its application Klan officials proclaimed that the purpose of placing their nonincendiary Latin cross in Capitol Square was to "assert the right of all religious views to be expressed on an equal basis on public property." The board defended its rejection of the Klan's application by stating that it was simply complying with the First Amendment's establishment of religion clause.

The Ohio Klan, through its leader, Vincent Pinette, sought relief in the United States District Court for the Southern District of Ohio. The district court rejected the contention that the cross could reasonably be construed to be an endorsement of Christianity by the state of Ohio. As a result, an injunction was issued that required the board to allow the Klan to erect its display in the plaza. Once erected the display did include a cardboard sign that stated that the cross was "erected by private individuals without government support." The cross was soon destroyed by vandals, and the board later allowed local church groups to erect about a dozen crosses in the square.

Following the holiday season the district court's ruling was appealed to the U.S. Court of Appeals for the Sixth Circuit, and the earlier decision was affirmed. When the Supreme Court agreed to review the dispute many observers hoped that the case would produce a definitive statement on the erection of religious displays on public property. In 1984, in *Lynch v. Donnelly*, the Court voted to allow the inclusion of a nativity scene in a larger display that featured other traditional Christmas symbols. Five years later, in *Allegheny County v. American Civil Liberties Union* (see Document 64), however, the Court held that a nativity scene standing alone in a courthouse was not permissible.

In *Capitol Square Review and Advisory Board v. Pinette* (1995), the Supreme Court concluded that the Klan's cross in Capitol Square constituted private religious speech in a public forum. The Klan's right to display this cross, according to the Court, was protected by the free speech clause in the First Amendment.

A plurality of four justices, headed by Antonin Scalia, who delivered the opinion of the Court, reasoned that since this case concerned private speech rather than government speech, the endorsement test was simply inapplicable. Instead, Justice Scalia relied upon the equal access doctrine that had been introduced in *Widmar v. Vincent* (1981). Conversely, Justice David H. Souter, and two other members of the Court who concurred in the judgment, regarded the endorsement standard as the appropriate standard to resolve this controversy.

Justice John Paul Stevens, one of two justices who dissented, expressed his fear that the general public would invariably perceive the placement of a religious display on public property as an endorsement by the government. He therefore issued a call for a reconstruction of Thomas Jefferson's wall of separation between church and state.

Why did Justice Scalia rely upon the *Widmar* and *Lamb's Chapel* precedents rather than the *Allegheny County* and *Lynch* decisions? Why did Justice Souter insist that the endorsement test was the proper standard to evaluate the facts in this case? What is the inherent danger that Justice Stevens claims accompanies the placement of a religious display on public property?

* * *

JUSTICE SCALIA announced the judgment of the Court.

* * *

There is no doubt that compliance with the Establishment Clause is a state interest sufficiently compelling to justify content-based restrictions on speech. Whether that interest is implicated here, however, is a different question. And we do not write on a blank slate in answering it. We have twice-previously addressed the combination of private religious expression, a forum available for public use, content-based regulation, and a State's interest in complying with the Establishment Clause. Both times, we have struck down the restriction on religious content.

In *Lamb's Chapel*, a school district allowed private groups to use school facilities during off-hours for a variety of civic, social and recreational purposes, excluding, however, religious purposes. We held that even if school property during off-hours was not a public forum, the school district violated an applicant's free-speech rights by denying it use of the facilities solely because of the religious viewpoint of the program it wished to present. We rejected the district's compelling-state-interest Establishment Clause defense (the same made here) because the school property was open to a wide variety of uses, the district was not directly sponsoring the religious group's activity, and "any benefit to religion or to the Church would have been no more than incidental." The *Lamb's Chapel* reasoning applies *a fortiori* here, where the property at issue is not a school but a full-fledged public forum.

Lamb's Chapel followed naturally from our decision in *Widmar*, in which we examined a public university's exclusion of student religious groups from facilities available to other student groups. There also we addressed official discrimination against groups who wished to use a "generally open forum" for religious speech. And there also the State claimed that its compelling interest in complying with the Establishment Clause justified the content-based restriction. We rejected the defense because the forum created by the State was open to a broad spectrum of groups and would provide only incidental benefit to religion. We stated categorically that "an open forum in a public university does not confer an imprimatur of state approval on religious sects or practices."

Quite obviously, the factors that we considered determinative in *Lamb's Chapel* and *Widmar* exist here as well. The State did not sponsor respondents' expression, the expression was made on government property that had been opened to the public for speech, and permission was requested through the same application process and on the same terms required of other private groups. . . .

Of course, giving sectarian religious speech preferential access to a forum close to the seat of government (or anywhere else for that matter) would violate the Establishment Clause (as well as the Free Speech Clause, since it would involve content discrimination). And one can conceive of a case in which a governmental entity manipulates its administration of a public forum close to the seat of government (or within a government building) in such a manner that only certain religious groups take advantage of it, creating an impression of endorsement *that is in fact accurate*. But those situations, which involve governmental *favoritism*, do not exist here. Capitol Square is a genuinely public forum, is known to be a public forum, and has been widely used as a public forum for many, many years. Private religious speech cannot be subject to veto by those who see favoritism where there is none. . . .

If Ohio is concerned about misperceptions, nothing prevents it from requiring all private displays in the Square to be identified as such. That would be a content-neutral "manner" restriction which is assuredly constitutional. But the State may not, on the claim of misperception of official endorsement, ban all private religious speech from the public square, or discriminate against it by requiring religious speech alone to disclaim public sponsorship.

Religious expression cannot violate the Establishment Clause where it (1) is purely private and (2) occurs in a traditional or designated public forum, publicly announced and open to all on equal terms. Those conditions are satisfied here, and therefore the State may not bar respondents' cross from Capitol Square. . . .

JUSTICE SOUTER, concurring in part and concurring in the judgment.

Although I agree in the end that, in the circumstances of this case, petitioners erred in denying the Klan's application for a permit to erect a cross on Capitol Square, my analysis of the Establishment Clause issue differs from JUSTICE SCALIA's, and I vote to affirm in large part because of the possibility of affixing a sign to the cross adequately disclaiming any government sponsorship or endorsement of it.

The plurality's opinion declines to apply the endorsement test to the Board's action, in favor of a *per se* rule: religious expression cannot violate the Establishment Clause where it (1) is private and (2) occurs in a public forum, even if a reasonable observer would see the expression as indicating state endorsement. This *per se* rule would be an exception to the endorsement test, not previously recognized and out of square with our precedents. . . .

Even if precedent and practice were otherwise, however, and there were an open question about applying the endorsement test to private speech in public forums, I would apply it in preference to the plurality's view, which creates a serious loophole in the protection provided by the endorsement test. In JUSTICE SCALIA's view, as I understand it, the Establishment Clause is violated in a public forum only when the government itself intentionally endorses religion or willfully "foster[s]" a misperception of endorsement in the forum, or when it "manipulates" the public forum "in such a manner that only certain religious groups take advantage of it." If the list of forbidden acts is truly this short, then governmental bodies and officials are left with generous scope to encourage a multiplicity of religious speakers to erect displays in public forums. As long as the governmental entity does not "manipulat[e]" the forum in such a way as to exclude all other speech, the plurality's opinion would seem to invite such government encouragement, even when the result will be the domination of the forum by religious displays and religious speakers. By allowing government to encourage what it can not do on its own, the proposed *per se* rule would tempt a public body to contract out its establishment of religion, by encouraging the private enterprise of the religious to exhibit what the government could not display itself.

Something of the sort, in fact, may have happened here. Immediately after the District Court issued the injunction ordering petitioners to grant the Klan's permit, a local church council applied for a permit, apparently for the purpose of overwhelming the Klan's cross with other crosses. The council proposed to invite all local churches to erect crosses, and the Board granted "blanket permission" for "all churches friendly to or affiliated with" the council to do so. The end result was that a part of the square was strewn with crosses, and while the effect in this case may have provided more embarrassment than suspicion of endorsement, the opportunity for the latter is clear. . . .

JUSTICE STEVENS, dissenting.

The Establishment Clause should be construed to create a strong presumption against the installation of unattended religious symbols on public property. Although the State of Ohio has allowed Capitol Square, the area around the seat of its government, to be used as a public forum, and although it has occasionally allowed private groups to erect other sectarian displays there, neither fact provides a sufficient basis for rebutting that presumption. On the contrary, the sequence of sectarian displays disclosed by the record in this case illustrates the importance of rebuilding the "wall of separation between church and State" that Jefferson envisioned. . . .

The plurality does not disagree with the proposition that the State may not espouse a religious message. It concludes, however, that the State has not sent such a message; it has merely allowed others to do so on its property. Thus, the State has provided an "incidental benefit" to religion by allowing private parties access to a traditional public forum. In my judgment, neither precedent nor respect for the values protected by the Establishment Clause justifies that conclusion. . . .

The Establishment Clause, "at the very least, prohibits government from appearing to take a position on questions of religious belief or from 'making adherence to a religion relevant in any way to a person's standing in the political community.'" *County of Allegheny v. American Civil Liberties Union, Greater Pittsburgh Chapter* (1989), quoting *Lynch v. Donnelly* (1984) (O'CONNOR, J., concurring). At least when religious symbols are involved, the question of whether the state is "appearing to take a position" is best judged from the standpoint of a "reasonable observer." It is especially important to take account of the perspective of a reasonable observer who may not share the particular religious belief it expresses. A paramount purpose of the Establishment Clause is to protect such a person from being made to feel like an outsider in matters of faith, and a stranger in the political community. If a reasonable person could perceive a government endorsement of religion from a private display, then the State may not allow its property to be used as a forum for that display. No less stringent rule can adequately protect nonadherents from a well-grounded perception that their sovereign supports a faith to which they do not subscribe.

In determining whether the State's maintenance of the Klan's cross in front of the Statehouse conveyed a forbidden message of endorsement, we should be mindful of the power of a symbol standing alone and unexplained. Even on private property, signs and symbols are generally understood to express the owner's views. The location of the sign is a significant component of the message it conveys. . . .

So it is with signs and symbols left to speak for themselves on public property. The very fact that a sign is installed on public property implies official recognition and reinforcement of its message. That implication is especially strong when the sign stands in front of the seat of the government itself. The "reasonable observer" of any symbol placed unattended in front of any capitol in the world will normally assume that the sovereign—which is not only the owner of that parcel of real estate but also the lawgiver for the surrounding territory—has sponsored and facilitated its message.

That the State may have granted a variety of groups permission to engage in uncensored expressive activities in front of the capitol building does not, in my opinion, qualify or contradict the normal inference of endorsement that the reasonable observer would draw from the unattended, freestanding sign or symbol. Indeed, parades and demonstrations at or near the seat of government are often exercises of the right of the people to petition their government for a redress of grievances—exercises in which the government is the recipient of the message rather than the messenger. Even when a demonstration or parade is not directed against government policy, but merely has made use of a particularly visible forum in order to reach as wide an audience as possible, there usually can be no mistake about the identity of the messengers as persons other than the State. But when a statue or some other freestanding, silent, unattended, immovable structure—regardless of its particular message—appears on the lawn of the Capitol building, the reasonable observer must identify the State either as the messenger, or at the very least, as one who has endorsed the message. . . .

The State's general power to restrict the types of unattended displays does not alone suffice to decide this case, because Ohio did not profess to be exercising any such authority. Instead, the Capitol Square Review Board denied a permit for the cross because it believed the Establishment Clause required as much, and we cannot know whether the Board would have denied the permit on other grounds. Accordingly, we must evaluate the State's rationale on its own terms. But in this case, the endorsement inquiry under the Establishment Clause follows from the State's power to exclude unattended private displays from public property. Just as the Constitution recognizes the State's interest in preventing its property from being used as a conduit for ideas it does not wish to give the appearance of ratifying, the Establishment Clause prohibits government from allowing, and thus endorsing, unattended displays that take a position on a religious issue. If the State allows such stationary displays in front of its seat of government, viewers will reasonably assume that it approves of them. As the picture appended to this opinion demonstrates, a reasonable observer would likely infer endorsement from the location of the cross erected by the Klan in this case. Even if the disclaimer at the foot of the cross (which stated that the cross was placed there by a private organization) were legible, that inference would remain, because a property owner's decision to allow a third party to place a sign on her property conveys the same message of endorsement as if she had erected it herself.

When the message is religious in character, it is a message the state can neither send nor reinforce without violating the Establishment Clause. Accordingly, I would hold that the Constitution generally forbids the placement of a symbol of a religious character in, on, or before a seat of government. . . .

Source: Capitol Square Review and Advisory Board v. Pinette, 515 U.S. 753 (1995).

DOCUMENT 74: President Clinton's Statement on Religious Expression in Public Schools (July 13, 1995)

In July of 1995 President William Jefferson Clinton issued a statement on religious expression in the nation's public schools. The President covered topics such as private religious speech, graduation prayers, teaching values, and the observation of religious holidays.

President Clinton proclaimed that the First Amendment contains the "twin pillars of religious liberty: the constitutional protection for the free exercise of religion, and the constitutional prohibition on the establishment of religion by the state." Clinton then proceeded to seek a middle ground by announcing that the First Amendment protects "a greater degree of religious expression in public schools than many Americans may now understand." The establishment clause does not prohibit purely private religious speech by students, Clinton stated, but it does limit the government. Specifically, public schools cannot legitimately coerce the conscience of a student or convey an official endorsement of religion.

To supplement his defense of private religious expression in an environment that is required to be free of coercion and endorsement, President Clinton relied upon both the Equal Access Act (Document 60) and the Religious Freedom Restoration Act (Document 70). At the end of his address Clinton directed the Secretary of Education, in consultation with the Attorney General, to convey the principles in his statement to public school officials across the nation.

According to President Clinton, what activities are permissible in public schools due to the free exercise of religion clause? What limitations does the establishment clause place on religious expression in the public school environment?

* * *

Religious freedom is perhaps the most precious of all American liberties—called by many our "first freedom." Many of the first European settlers in North America sought refuge from religious persecution in their native countries. Since that time, people of faith and religious institutions have played a central role in the history of this nation. In the First Amendment, our Bill of Rights recognizes the twin pillars of religious liberty: the constitutional protection for the free exercise of religion, and the constitutional prohibition on the establishment of religion by the state. Our nation's founders knew that religion helps to give our people the character without which a democracy can not survive. Our founders also recognized the need for a space of freedom between government and the people—that the government must not be permitted to coerce the conscience of any individual or group.

In the over 200 years since the First Amendment was included in our Constitution, religion and religious institutions have thrived throughout the United States. In 1993, I was proud to reaffirm the historic place of religion when I signed the Religious Freedom Restoration Act, which restores a high legal standard to protect the exercise of religion from being inappropriately burdened by government action. In the greatest traditions of American citizenship, a broad coalition of individuals and organizations came together to support the fullest protection for religious practice and expression.

Religious Expression in Public Schools

I share the concern and frustration that many Americans feel about situations where the protections accorded by the First Amendment are not recognized or understood. This problem has manifested itself in our nation's public schools. It appears that some school officials, teachers and parents have assumed that religious expression of any type is either inappropriate, or forbidden altogether, in public schools.

As our courts have reaffirmed, however, nothing in the First Amendment converts our public schools into religion-free zones or requires all religious expression to be left behind at the school house door. While the government may not use schools to coerce the conscience of our students or to convey official endorsement of religion, the government's schools also may not discriminate against private religious expression during the school day.

I have been advised by the Department of Justice and the Department of Education that the First Amendment permits—and protects—a greater degree of religious expression in public schools than many Americans may now understand. The Departments of Justice and Education have advised me that, while application may depend upon specific factual contexts and will require careful consideration in particular cases, the following principles are among those that apply to religious expression in our schools:

Student prayer and religious discussion: The Establishment Clause of the First Amendment does not prohibit purely private religious speech by students. Students therefore have the same right to engage in individual or group prayer and religious discussion during the school day as they do to engage in other comparable activity. For example, students may read their Bibles or other scriptures, say grace before meals, and pray before tests to the same extent they may engage in comparable nondisruptive activities. Local school authorities possess substantial discretion to impose rules of order and other pedagogical restrictions on student activities, but they may not discriminate against religious activity or speech.

Generally, students may pray in a nondisruptive manner when not engaged in school activities or instruction, and subject to the rules that normally pertain in the applicable setting. Specifically, students in informal settings, such as cafeterias and hallways, may pray and discuss their religious views with each other, subject to the same rules of order as apply to other student activities and speech. Students may also speak to and attempt to persuade their peers about religious topics just as they do with regard to political topics. School officials, however, should intercede to stop student speech that constitutes harassment aimed at a student or a group of students.

Students may also participate in before- or after-school events with religious content, such as "see you at the flag pole" gatherings, on the same terms as they may participate in other noncurriculum activities on school premises. School officials may neither discourage nor encourage participation in such an event.

The right to engage in voluntary prayer or religious discussion free from discrimination does not include the right to have a captive audience listen or to compel other students to participate. Teachers and school administrators should ensure that no student is in any way coerced to participate in religious activity.

Graduation prayer and baccalaureates: Under current Supreme Court decisions, school officials may not mandate or organize prayer at graduation nor organize religious baccalaureate ceremonies. If a school generally opens its facilities to private groups, it must make its facilities available on the same terms to organizers of privately sponsored religious baccalaureate services. A school may not extend preferential treatment to baccalaureate ceremonies and may in some instances be obliged to disclaim official endorsement of such ceremonies.

Official neutrality regarding religious activity: Teachers and school administrators, when acting in those capacities, are representatives of the state and are prohibited by the Establishment Clause from soliciting or encouraging religious activity and from participating in such activity with students. Teachers and administrators also are prohibited from discouraging activity because of its religious content and from soliciting or encouraging antireligious activity.

Teaching about religion: Public schools may not provide religious instruction, but they may teach about religion, including the Bible or other scripture: the history of religion, comparative religion, the Bible (or other scripture)-as-literature, and the role of religion in the history of the United States and other countries all are permissible public school subjects. Similarly, it is permissible to consider religious influences on art, music, literature and social-studies. Although public schools may teach about religious holidays, including their religious aspects, and may celebrate the secular aspects of holidays, schools may not observe holidays as religious events or promote such observance by students.

Student assignments: Students may express their beliefs about religion in the form of homework, artwork, and other written and oral assignments free of discrimination based on the religious content of their submissions. Such home and classroom work should be judged by ordinary academic standards of substance and relevance, and against other legitimate pedagogical concerns identified by the school.

Religious literature: Students have a right to distribute religious literature to their schoolmates on the same terms as they are permitted to distribute other literature that is unrelated to school curriculum or activities. Schools may impose the same reasonable time, place and manner or other constitutional restrictions on distribution of religious literature as they do on nonschool literature generally, but they may not single out religious literature for special regulation.

Religious excusals: Subject to applicable state laws, schools enjoy substantial discretion to excuse individual students from lessons that are objectionable to the student or the student's parents on religious or other conscientious grounds. School officials may neither encourage nor discourage students from availing themselves of an excusal option. Under the Religious Freedom Restoration Act, if it is proved that particular lessons substantially burden a student's free exercise of religion and if the school cannot prove a compelling interest in requiring attendance, the school would be legally required to excuse the student.

Released time: Subject to applicable state laws, schools have the discretion to dismiss students to off-premises religious instruction, provided that schools do not encourage or discourage participation or penalize those who do not attend. Schools may not allow religious instruction by outsiders on school premises during the school day.

Teaching values: Though schools must be neutral with respect to religion, they may play an active role with respect to teaching civic values and virtue, and the moral code that holds us together as a community. The fact that some of these values are held also by religions does not make it unlawful to teach them in school.

Student garb: Students may display religious messages on items of clothing to the same extent that they are permitted to display other comparable messages. Religious messages may not be singled out for suppression, but rather are subject to the same rules as generally apply to comparable messages. When wearing particular attire, such as yarmulkes and head scarves, during the school day is part of students' religious practice, under the Religious Freedom Restoration Act schools generally may not prohibit the wearing of such items.

I hereby direct the Secretary of Education, in consultation with the Attorney General, to use appropriate means to ensure that public school districts and school officials in the United States are informed, by the start of the coming school year, of the principles set forth above.

Equal Access Act

The Equal Access Act is designed to insure that, consistent with the First Amendment, student religious activities are accorded the same access to public school facilities as are student secular activities. Based on decisions of the Federal courts, as well as its interpretations of the act, the Department of Justice has advised me of its position that the act should be interpreted as providing, among other things, that:

General provisions: Student religious groups at public secondary schools have the same right of access to school facilities as is enjoyed by other comparable student groups. Under the Equal Access Act, a school receiving Federal funds that allows one or more student noncurriculum-related clubs to meet on its premises during noninstructional time may not refuse access to student religious groups.

Prayer services and worship exercises covered: A meeting, as defined and protected by the Equal Access Act, may include a prayer service, Bible reading, or other worship exercise.

Equal access to means of publicizing meetings: A school receiving Federal funds must allow student groups meeting under the Act to use the school media—including the public address system, the school newspaper and the school bulletin board—to announce their meetings on the same terms as other noncurriculum-related student groups in a nondiscriminatory matter. Schools, however, may inform students that certain groups are not school sponsored.

Lunch-time and recess covered: A school creates a limited open forum under the Equal Access Act, triggering equal access rights for religious groups, when it allows students to meet during their lunch periods or other noninstructional time during the school day, as well as when it allows students to meet before and after the school day.

I hereby direct the Secretary of Education, in consultation with the Attorney General, to use appropriate means to insure that public school districts and school officials in the United States are informed by the start of the coming school year of these interpretations of the Equal Access Act.

Source: New York Times, July 13, 1995, Section B, p. 10.

DOCUMENT 75: *Agostini v. Felton* (1997)

In 1985, in *Aguilar v. Felton* (see Document 62), the United States Supreme Court ruled that a program conducted in New York City which sent public school teachers into parochial schools to provide remedial education to disadvantaged children was unconstitutional. This program, authorized by Title I of the Elementary and Secondary Education Act of 1965, was seen as a violation of the First Amendment's establishment clause because it necessitated an excessive entanglement between church and state.

Approximately ten years later the district court injunction that made the *Aguilar* decision binding upon the New York City school system was challenged under Federal Rule of Civil Procedure 60(b)(5). The petitioners emphasized three points in their complaint. First, it was argued, a modification of the injunction was warranted due to the exorbitant cost of complying with the court order. Second, in 1994, in *Board of Education of Kiryas Joel Village School District v. Grumet* (see Document 71), five Supreme Court justices had asserted that the *Aguilar* decision should be reconsidered. Third, it was alleged, subsequent holdings in cases concerning the establishment clause had undermined the *Aguilar* decision to the point that it was no longer good law. The U.S. District Court for the Eastern District of New York denied the motion, and the Court of Appeals for the Second Circuit affirmed this ruling.

The U.S. Supreme Court, however, reversed the *Aguilar* decision in *Agostini v. Felton* (1997) by a 5–4 margin. Justice Sandra Day O'Connor wrote the majority opinion. O'Connor reasoned that neither the burden incurred by compliance with *Aguilar* nor statements made by members of the Court in *Kiryas Joel* were sufficient to mandate a reversal of the *Aguilar* precedent under Rule 60(b)(5). However, O'Connor asserted that *Aguilar* was no longer good law due to Supreme Court holdings in cases such as *Witters v. Washington Department of Services for the Blind* (1986) and *Zobrest v. Catalina Foothills School District* (1993) (see Document 69).

It is worth noting that Justice O'Connor relied upon the three-part test originally advanced in *Lemon v. Kurtzman* (see Document 55) as a vehicle to resolve conflicts concerning the establishment clause. *Agostini* not only affirmed the continued vitality of the *Lemon* test, it confirmed once again that the often maligned standard could be used to produce an accommodationist conclusion.

Justice David H. Souter, writing in dissent, criticized the majority for its willingness to abandon what he regarded as a sensible precedent rendered only twelve years earlier. He warned that as a result of the *Agostini* decision public funds could be used to underwrite "the entire cost of instruction provided in any ostensibly secular subject in any religious school."

According to Justice O'Connor, what modification took place in the Supreme Court's evaluation of the constitutionality of government aid to religious schools after the *Aguilar* decision in 1985? How did this change in the Court's position affect the Court's decision in *Agostini*? Why does Justice Souter object to the use of the *Zobrest* decision as a precedent to overturn the Court's holding in *Aguilar*?

* * *

JUSTICE O'CONNOR delivered the opinion of the Court.

In *Aguilar v. Felton* (1985), this Court held that the Establishment Clause of the First Amendment barred the city of New York from sending public school teachers into parochial schools to provide remedial education to disadvantaged children pursuant to a congressionally mandated program. On remand, the District Court for the Eastern District of New York entered a permanent injunction reflecting our ruling. Twelve years later, petitioners—the parties bound by that injunction—seek relief from its operation. Petitioners maintain that *Aguilar* cannot be squared with our intervening Establishment Clause jurisprudence and ask that we explicitly recognize what our more recent cases already dictate: *Aguilar* is no longer good law. We agree with petitioners that *Aguilar* is not consistent with our subsequent Establishment Clause decisions and further conclude that, on the facts presented here, petitioners are entitled under Federal Rule of Civil Procedure 60(b)(5) to relief from the operation of the District Court's prospective injunction. . . .

The question we must answer is a simple one: Are petitioners entitled to relief from the District Court's permanent injunction under Rule 60(b)? Rule 60(b)(5), the subsection under which petitioners proceeded below, states:

"On motion and upon such terms as are just, the court may relieve a party . . . from a final judgment [or] order . . . [when] it is no longer equitable that the judgment should have prospective application." . . .

Petitioners point to three changes in the factual and legal landscape that they believe justify their claim for relief under Rule 60(b)(5). They first contend that the exorbitant costs of complying with the District Court's injunction constitute a significant factual development warranting modification of injunction. Petitioners also argue that there have been two significant legal developments since *Aguilar* was decided: a majority of Justices have expressed their views that *Aguilar* should be reconsidered or overruled, and *Aguilar* has in any event been undermined by subsequent Establishment Clause decisions. . . .

What is most fatal to the argument that New York City's Title I program directly subsidizes religion is that it applies with equal force when those services are provided off-campus, and *Aguilar* implied that providing the services off-campus is entirely consistent with the Establishment Clause. Justice SOUTER resists the impulse to upset this implication, contending that it can be justified on the ground that Title I services are "less likely to supplant some of what would otherwise go on inside [the sectarian schools] and to subsidize what remains" when those services are offered off-campus. But Justice SOUTER does not explain why a sectarian school would not have the same incentive to "make patently significant cut-backs" in its curriculum no matter where Title I services are offered, since the school would ostensibly be excused from having to provide the Title I-type services itself. Because the incentive is the same either way, we find no logical basis upon which to conclude that Title I services are an impermissible subsidy of religion when offered on-campus, but not when offered off-campus. Accordingly, contrary to our conclusion in *Aguilar*, placing full-time employees on parochial school campuses does not as a matter of law have the impermissible effect of advancing religion through indoctrination.

Although we examined in *Witters* and *Zobrest* the criteria by which an aid program identifies its beneficiaries, we did so solely to assess whether any use of that aid to indoctrinate religion could be attributed to the State. A number of our Establishment Clause cases have found that the criteria used for identifying beneficiaries are relevant in a second respect, apart from enabling a court to evaluate whether the program subsidizes religion. Specifically, the criteria might themselves have the effect of advancing religion by creating a financial incentive to undertake religious indoctrination. This incentive is not present, however, where the aid is allocated on the basis of neutral, secular criteria that neither favor nor disfavor religion, and is made available to both religious and secular beneficiaries on a nondiscriminatory basis. Under such circumstances, the aid is less likely to have the effect of advancing religion. . . .

Applying this reasoning to New York City's Title I program, it is clear that Title I services are allocated on the basis of criteria that neither favor nor disfavor religion. The services are available to all children who meet the Act's eligibility requirements, no matter what their religious beliefs or where they go to school. The Board's program does not, therefore, give aid recipients any incentive to modify their religious beliefs or practices in order to obtain those services.

We turn now to *Aguilar's* conclusion that New York City's Title I program resulted in an excessive entanglement between church and state. Whether a government aid program results in such an entanglement has consistently been an aspect of our Establishment Clause analysis. We have considered entanglement both in the course of assessing whether an aid program has an impermissible effect of advancing religion, *Walz v. Tax Comm'n of City of New York* (1970), and as a factor separate and apart from "effect," *Lemon v. Kurtzman* (1971). Regardless of how we have characterized the issue, however, the factors we use to assess whether an entanglement is "excessive" are similar to the factors we use to examine "effect." That is, to assess entanglement, we have looked to "the character and purposes of the institutions that are benefited, the nature of the aid that the State provides, and the resulting relationship between the government and religious authority." Similarly, we have assessed a law's "effect" by examining the character of institutions benefited and the nature of the aid that the State provided. Indeed, in *Lemon* itself, the entanglement that the Court found "independently" to necessitate the program's invalidation also was found to have the effect of inhibiting religion. Thus, it is simplest to recognize why entanglement is significant and treat it—as we did in *Waltz*—as an aspect of the inquiry into a statute's effect.

Not all entanglements, of course, have the effect of advancing or inhibiting religion. Interaction between church and state is inevitable, and we have always tolerated some level of involvement between the two. Entanglement must be "excessive" before it runs afoul of the Establishment Clause. . . .

The pre-*Aguilar* Title I program does not result in an "excessive" entanglement that advances or inhibits religion. As discussed previously, the Court's finding of "excessive" entanglement in *Aguilar* rested on three grounds: (i) the program would require "pervasive monitoring by public authorities" to ensure that Title I employees did not inculcate religion; (ii) the program required "administrative cooperation" between the Board and parochial schools; and (iii) the program might increase the dangers of "political divisiveness." Under the current understanding of the Establishment Clause, the last two considerations are insufficient by themselves to create an "excessive" entanglement. They are present no matter where Title I services are offered, and no court has held that Title I services cannot be offered off-campus. Further, the assumption underlying the first consideration has been undermined. In *Aguilar*, the Court presumed that full-time public employees on parochial school grounds would be tempted to inculcate religion, despite the ethical standards they were required to uphold. Because of this risk *pervasive* monitoring would be required. But after *Zobrest* we no longer presume that public employees will inculcate religion simply because they happen to be in a sectarian environment. Since we have abandoned the assumption that *pervasive* monitoring of Title I teachers is required. There is no suggestion in the record before us that unannounced monthly visits of public supervisors are insufficient to prevent or to detect inculcation of religion by public employees. Moreover, we have not found excessive entanglement in cases in which States imposed far more onerous burdens on religious institutions than the monitoring system at issue here.

To summarize, New York City's Title I program does not run afoul of any of three primary criteria we currently use to evaluate whether government aid has the effect of advancing religion: it does not result in governmental indoctrination; define its recipients by reference to religion; or create an excessive entanglement. We therefore hold that a federally funded program providing supplemental, remedial instruction to disadvantaged children on a neutral basis is not invalid under the Establishment Clause when such instruction is given on the premises of sectarian schools by government employees pursuant to a program containing safeguards such as those present here. The same considerations that justify this holding require us to conclude that this carefully constrained program also cannot reasonably be viewed as an endorsement of religion. Accordingly, we must acknowledge that *Aguilar*, as well as the portion of *Ball* addressing Grand Rapids' Shared Time program, are no longer good law. . . .

JUSTICE SOUTER, dissenting.

In this novel proceeding, petitioners seek relief from an injunction the District Court entered 12 years ago to implement our decision in *Aguilar v. Felton* (1985). . . . [T]he Court's holding that petitioners are entitled to relief under Rule 60(b) is seriously mistaken. The Court's misapplication of the rule is tied to its equally erroneous reading of our more recent Establishment Clause cases, which the Court describes as having rejected the underpinnings of *Aguilar's* companion case, *School Dist. of Grand Rapids v. Ball* (1985). The result is to repudiate the very reasonable line drawn in *Aguilar* and *Ball*, and to authorize direct state aid to religious institutions on an unparalleled scale, in violation of the Establishment Clause's central prohibition against religious subsidies by the government.

I respectfully dissent. . . .

. . . I believe *Aguilar* was a correct and sensible decision, and my only reservation about its opinion is that the emphasis on the excessive entanglement produced by monitoring religious instructional content obscured those facts that independently called for the application of two central tenets of Establishment Clause jurisprudence. The State is forbidden to subsidize religion directly and is just as surely forbidden to act in any way that could reasonably be viewed as religious endorsement. . . .

As is explained elsewhere, the flat ban on subsidization antedates the Bill of Rights and has been an unwavering rule in Establishment Clause cases, qualified only by the conclusion two Terms ago that state exactions from college students are not the sort of public revenues subject to the ban. The rule expressed the hard lesson learned over and over again in the American past and in the experiences of the countries from which we have come, that religions supported by governments are compromised just as surely as the religious freedom of dissenters is burdened when the government supports religion. The ban against state endorsement of religion addresses the same historical lessons. Governmental approval of religion tends to reinforce the religious message (at least in the short run) and, by the same token, to carry a message of exclusion to those of less favored views. The human tendency, of course, is to forget the hard lessons, and to overlook the history of governmental partnership with religion when a cause is worthy, and bureaucrats have programs. That tendency to forget is the reason for having the Establishment Clause (along with the Constitution's other structural and libertarian guarantees), in the hope of stopping the corrosion before it starts.

These principles were violated by the programs at issue in *Aguilar* and *Ball*, as a consequence of several significant features common to both Title I, as implemented in New York City before *Aguilar*, and the Grand Rapids Shared Time program: each provided classes on the premises of the religious schools, covering a wide range of subjects including some at the core of primary and secondary education, like reading and mathematics; while their services were termed "supplemental," the programs and their instructors necessarily assumed responsibility for teaching subjects that the religious schools would otherwise have been obligated to provide, the public employees carrying out the programs had broad responsibilities involving the exercise of considerable discretion, while the programs offered aid to nonpublic school students generally (and Title I went to public school students as well), participation by religious school students in each program was extensive, and, finally, aid under Title I and Shared Time flowed directly to the schools in the form of classes and programs, as distinct from indirect aid that reaches schools only as a result of independent private choice. . . .

What, therefore, was significant in *Aguilar* and *Ball*, about the placement of state-paid teachers into the physical and social settings of the religious schools was not only the consequent temptation of some of those teachers to reflect the schools' religious missions in the rhetoric of their instruction, with a resulting need for monitoring and the certainty of entanglement. What was so remarkable was that the schemes in issue assumed a teaching responsibility indistinguishable from the responsibility of the schools themselves. The obligation of primary and secondary schools to teach reading necessarily extends to teaching those who are having a hard time at it, and the same is true of math. Calling some classes remedial does not distinguish their subjects from the schools' basic subjects, however inadequately the schools may have been addressing them.

What was true of the Title I scheme as struck down in *Aguilar* will be just as true when New York reverts to the old practices with the Court's approval after today. There is simply no line that can be drawn between the instruction paid for at taxpayers' expense and the instruction in any subject that is not identified as formally religious. While it would be an obvious sham, say, to channel cash to religious schools to be credited only against the expense of "secular" instruction, the line between "supplemental" and general education is likewise impossible to draw. If a State may constitutionally enter the schools to teach in the manner in question, it must in constitutional principle be free to assume, or assume payment for, the entire cost of instruction provided in any ostensibly secular subject in any religious school. . . .

In sum, if a line is to be drawn short of barring all state aid to religious schools for teaching standard subjects, the *Aguilar-Ball* line was a sensible one capable of principled adherence. It is no less sound, and no less necessary, today.

The Court today ignores this doctrine and claims that recent cases rejected the elemental assumptions underlying *Aguilar* and much of *Ball*. But the Court errs. Its holding that *Aguilar* and the portion of *Ball* addressing the Shared Time program are "no longer good law," rests on mistaken reading. . . .

Source: Agostini v. Felton, 117 S. Ct. (1997).

DOCUMENT 76: *City of Boerne v. Flores* (1997)

In 1963, in *Sherbert v. Verner* (see Document 39), the United States Supreme Court ruled that to survive judicial scrutiny a law that restricts the free exercise of religion must be intended to advance a compelling governmental interest in the least restrictive manner possible. This twofold standard stood until 1990, when it was rejected by the Supreme Court in *Employment Division, Department of Human Resources of Oregon v. Smith* (see Document 47).

Congress, in direct response to the *Smith* decision, enacted the Religious Freedom Restoration Act of 1993 (see Document 70). The act, which restored the "compelling interest" and "least restrictive means" standards, had the support of major religious groups and was passed in both houses of Congress by overwhelming majorities.

Subsequently, a dispute that originated in Boerne, Texas, required the Supreme Court to consider the constitutionality of the Religious Freedom Restoration Act (RFRA). The Catholic Archbishop of San Antonio had applied for a building permit to enlarge a church located in Boerne, twenty-eight miles northwest of San Antonio. Citing an ordinance passed by the Boerne City Council which had been intended to preserve historic districts in the city, local officials denied the Archbishop's request. The Archbishop challenged the denial of his application for a building permit in the U.S. District Court for the Western District of Texas. This complaint alleged that the denial was a violation of the Religious Freedom Restoration Act, but the district court concluded that Congress had exceeded its authority when it enacted the legislation.

Congress had relied upon the Fourteenth Amendment when it enacted the Religious Freedom Restoration Act. Section 1 of the amendment guarantees that a state cannot deprive a person of life, liberty, or property without due process of law, or deny any person the equal protection of the laws. Section 5 of the amendment empowers Congress to enforce these guarantees with appropriate legislation. The Court of Appeals for the Fifth Circuit ruled that the act was constitutional, thereby reversing the district court decision.

The Supreme Court, in *City of Boerne v. Flores* (1997), held that the Religious Freedom Restoration Act was not a proper exercise of the enforcement power conferred upon Congress by Section 5 of the Fourteenth Amendment. Justice Anthony M. Kennedy, writing for the majority in this 6–3 decision, concluded that the act was a contradiction of two of the basic principles of American government: separation of powers and federalism.

Justice Sandra Day O'Connor, writing in dissent, agreed with the majority that Congress lacks the authority to define or expand the scope of constitutional rights by the enactment of a statute. However, O'Connor objected to the majority's use of the *Smith* holding as the ruling precedent because, in her opinion, *Smith* had been wrongly decided. O'Connor, therefore, called for re-examination of *Smith* to correct the misrepresentation of the free exercise clause that it had initiated. O'Connor fortified her view of the meaning of the free exercise clause with a detailed historical analysis of religious liberty.

Why does Justice Kennedy contend that the Religious Freedom Restoration Act, as enacted by Congress, was an infringement upon the authority of the states by the national government? Why does Justice O'Connor call upon the Court to reevaluate its decision in the *Smith* case?

* * *

JUSTICE KENNEDY delivered the opinion of the Court.

A decision by local zoning authorities to deny a church a building permit was challenged under the Religious Freedom Restoration Act of 1993 (RFRA). The case calls into question the authority of Congress to enact RFRA. We conclude the statute exceeds Congress' power....

Congress enacted RFRA in direct response to the Court's decision in *Employment Div., Dept. of Human Resources of Oregon v. Smith* (1990). There we considered a Free Exercise Clause claim brought by members of the Native American Church who were denied unemployment benefits when they lost their jobs because they had used peyote. Their practice was to ingest peyote for sacramental purposes, and they challenged an Oregon statute of general applicability which made use of the drug criminal. In evaluating the claim, we declined to apply the balancing test set forth in *Sherbert v. Verner* (1963), under which we would have asked whether Oregon's prohibition substantially burdened a religious practice and, if it did, whether the burden was justified by a compelling government interest: The application of the *Sherbert* test, the *Smith* decision explained, would have produced an anomaly in the law, a constitutional right to ignore neutral laws of general applicability. The anomaly would have been accentuated, the Court reasoned, by the difficulty of determining whether a particular practice was central to an individual's religion. We explained, moreover, that it "is not within the judicial ken to question the centrality of particular beliefs or practices to a faith, or the validity of particular litigants' interpretations of those creeds." . . .

RFRA prohibits "[g]overnment" from "substantially burden[ing]" a person's exercise of religion even if the burden results from a rule of general applicability unless the government can demonstrate the burden "(1) is in furtherance of a compelling governmental interest; and (2) is the least restrictive means of furthering that compelling governmental interest." The Act's mandate applies to any "branch, department, agency, instrumentality, and official (or other person acting under color of law) of the United States," as well as to any "State, or . . . subdivision of a State." The Act's universal coverage . . . "applies to all Federal and State law, and the implementation of that law, whether statutory or otherwise, and whether adopted before or after [RFRA's enactment]." In accordance with RFRA's usage of the term, we shall use "state law" to include local and municipal ordinances. . . .

Congress relied on its Fourteenth Amendment enforcement power in enacting the most far reaching and substantial of RFRA's provisions, those which impose its requirements on the States. The Fourteenth Amendment provides, in relevant part:

"Section 1. . . . No State shall make or enforce any law which shall abridge the privileges or immunities of citizens of the United States; nor shall any State deprive any person of life, liberty, or property, without due process of law; nor deny to any person within its jurisdiction the equal protection of the laws.

* * *

"Section 5. The Congress shall have power to enforce, by appropriate legislation, the provisions of this article."

The parties disagree over whether RFRA is a proper exercise of Congress' power "to enforce" by "appropriate legislation" the constitutional guarantee that no State shall deprive any person of "life, liberty, or property, without due process of law" nor deny any person "equal protection of the laws." . . .

Any suggestion that Congress has a substantive, non-remedial power under the Fourteenth Amendment is not supported by our case law. In *Oregon v. Mitchell* (1970), a majority of the Court concluded Congress had exceeded its enforcement powers by enacting legislation lowering the minimum age of voters from 21 to 18 in state and local elections. The five Members of the Court who reached this conclusion explained that the legislation intruded into an area reserved by the Constitution to the States. . . .

If Congress could define its own powers by altering the Fourteenth Amendment's meaning, no longer would the Constitution be "superior paramount law, unchangeable by ordinary means." It would be "on a level with ordinary legislative acts, and, like other acts . . . alterable when the legislature shall please to alter it." (*Marbury v. Madison*, 1803) Under this approach, it is difficult to conceive of a principle that would limit congressional power. Shifting legislative majorities could change the Constitution and effectively circumvent the difficult and detailed amendment process contained in Article V.

We now turn to consider whether RFRA can be considered enforcement legislation under the Fourteenth Amendment.

Respondent contends that RFRA is a proper exercise of Congress' remedial or preventive power. The Act, it is said, is a reasonable means of protecting the free exercise of religion as defined by *Smith*. It prevents and remedies laws which are enacted with the unconstitutional object of targeting religious beliefs and practices. To avoid the difficulty of proving such violations, it is said, Congress can simply invalidate any law which imposes a substantial burden on a religious practice unless it is justified by a compelling interest and is the least restrictive means of accomplishing that interest. If Congress can prohibit laws with discriminatory effects in order to prevent racial discrimination in violation of the Equal Protection Clause, then it can do the same, respondent argues, to promote religious liberty.

While preventive rules are sometimes appropriate remedial measures, there must be a congruence between the means used and the ends to be achieved. The appropriateness of remedial measures must be considered in light of the evil presented. Strong measures appropriate to address one harm may be an unwarranted response to another, lesser one.

A comparison between RFRA and the Voting Rights Act is instructive. In contrast to the record which confronted Congress and the judiciary in the voting rights cases, RFRA's legislative record lacks examples of modern instances of generally applicable laws passed because of religious bigotry. The history of persecution in this country detailed in the hearings mentions no episodes occurring in the past 40 years. . . .

Regardless of the state of the legislative record, RFRA cannot be considered remedial, preventive legislation, if those terms are to have any meaning. RFRA is so out of proportion to a supposed remedial or preventive object that it cannot be understood as responsive to, or designed to prevent, unconstitutional behavior. It appears, instead, to attempt a substantive change in constitutional protections. Preventive measures prohibiting certain types of laws may be appropriate when there is reason to believe that many of the laws affected by the congressional enactment have a significant likelihood of being unconstitutional. . . .

RFRA is not so confined. Sweeping coverage ensures its intrusion at every level of government, displacing laws and prohibiting official actions of almost every description and regardless of subject matter. RFRA's restrictions apply to every agency and official of the Federal, State, and local Governments. RFRA applies to all federal and state law, statutory or otherwise, whether adopted before or after its enactment. RFRA has no termination date or termination mechanism. Any law is subject to challenge at any time by any individual who alleges a substantial burden on his or her free exercise of religion. . . .

The stringent test RFRA demands of state laws reflects a lack of proportionality or congruence between the means adopted and the legitimate end to be achieved. If an objector can show a substantial burden on his free exercise, the State must demonstrate a compelling governmental interest and show that the law is the least restrictive means of furthering its interest. Claims that a law substantially burdens someone's exercise of religion will often be difficult to contest. Requiring a State to demonstrate a compelling interest and show that it has adopted the least restrictive means of achieving that interest is the most demanding test known to constitutional law. . . . Laws valid under *Smith* would fall under RFRA without regard to whether they had the object of stifling or punishing free exercise. We make these observations not to reargue the position of the majority in *Smith* but to illustrate the substantive alteration of its holding attempted by RFRA. Even assuming RFRA would be interpreted in effect to mandate some lesser test, say one equivalent to intermediate scrutiny, the statute nevertheless would require searching judicial scrutiny of state law with the attendant likelihood of invalidation. This is a considerable congressional intrusion into the States' traditional prerogatives and general authority to regulate the health and welfare of their citizens.

The substantial costs RFRA exacts, both in practical terms of imposing a heavy litigation burden on the States and in terms of curtailing their traditional general regulatory power, far exceed any pattern or practice of unconstitutional conduct under the Free Exercise Clause as interpreted in *Smith*. Simply put, RFRA is not designed to identify and counteract state laws likely to be unconstitutional because of their treatment of religion. In most cases, the state laws to which RFRA applies are not ones which will have been motivated by religious bigotry. If a state law disproportionately burdened a particular class of religious observers, this circumstance might be evidence of an impermissible legislative motive. RFRA's substantial burden test, however, is not even a discriminatory effects or disparate impact test. It is a reality of the modern regulatory state that numerous state laws, such as the zoning regulations at issue here, impose a substantial burden on a large class of individuals. When the exercise of religion has been burdened in an incidental way by a law of general application, it does not follow that the persons affected have been burdened any more than other citizens, let alone burdened because of their religious beliefs. In addition, the Act imposes in every case a least restrictive means requirement—a requirement that was not used in the pre-*Smith* jurisprudence RFRA purported to codify—which also indicates that the legislation is broader than is appropriate if the goal is to prevent and remedy constitutional violations.

When Congress acts within its sphere of power and responsibilities, it has not just the right but the duty to make its own informed judgment on the meaning and force of the Constitution. This has been clear from the early days of the Republic. In 1789, when a Member of the House of Representatives objected to a debate on the constitutionality of legislation based on the theory that "it would be officious" to consider the constitutionality of a measure that did not affect the House, James Madison explained that "it is incontrovertibly of as much importance to this branch of the Government as to any other, that the constitution should be preserved entire. It is our duty." 1 Annals of Congress 500 (1789). Were it otherwise, we would not afford Congress the presumption of validity its enactments now enjoy.

Our national experience teaches that the Constitution is preserved best when each part of the government respects both the Constitution and the proper actions and determinations of the other branches. When the Court has interpreted the Constitution, it has acted within the province of the Judicial Branch, which embraces the duty to say what the law is. (*Marbury v. Madison*, 1803). When the political branches of the Government act against the background of a judicial interpretation of the Constitution already issued, it must be understood that in later cases and controversies the Court will treat its precedents with the respect due them under settled principles, including *stare decisis*, and contrary expectations must be disappointed. RFRA was designed to control cases and controversies, such as the one before us; but as the provisions of the federal statute here invoked are beyond congressional authority, it is this Court's precedent, not RFRA, which must control. . . .

It is for Congress in the first instance to "determin[e] whether and what legislation is needed to secure the guarantees of the Fourteenth Amendment," and its conclusions are entitled to much deference. Congress' discretion is not unlimited, however, and the courts retain the power, as they have since *Marbury v. Madison*, to determine if Congress has exceeded its authority under the Constitution. Broad as the power of Congress is under the Enforcement Clause of the Fourteenth Amendment, RFRA contradicts vital principles necessary to maintain separation of powers and the federal balance. The judgment of the Court of Appeals sustaining the Act's constitutionality is reversed.

JUSTICE O'CONNOR, dissenting.

I dissent from the Court's disposition of this case. I agree with the Court that the issue before us is whether the Religious Freedom Restoration Act (RFRA) is a proper exercise of Congress' power to enforce Section 5 of the Fourteenth Amendment. But as a yardstick for measuring the constitutionality of RFRA, the court uses its holding in *Employment Div., Dept. of Human Resources of Oregon v. Smith* (1990), the decision that prompted Congress to enact RFRA as a means of more rigorously enforcing the Free Exercise Clause. I remain of the view that *Smith* was wrongly decided, and I would use this case to reexamine the Court's holding there. Therefore, I would direct the parties to brief the question whether *Smith* represents the correct understanding of the Free Exercise Clause and set the case for reargument. If the Court were to correct the misinterpretation of the Free Exercise Clause set forth in *Smith*, it would simultaneously put our First Amendment jurisprudence back on course and allay the legitimate concerns of a majority in Congress who believed that *Smith* improperly restricted religious liberty. We would then be in a position to review RFRA in light of a proper interpretation of the Free Exercise Clause.

I agree with much of the reasoning set forth in the Court's opinion. Indeed, if I agreed with the Court's standard in *Smith*, I would join the opinion. As the Court's careful and thorough historical analysis shows, Congress lacks the "power to decree the *substance* of the Fourteenth Amendment's restrictions on the States." Rather, its power under Section 5 of the Fourteenth Amendment extends only to *enforcing* the Amendment's provisions. In short, Congress lacks the ability independently to define or expand the scope of constitutional rights by statute. Congress, no less than this Court, is called upon to consider the requirements of the Constitution and to act in accordance with its dictates. But when it enacts legislation in furtherance of its delegated powers, Congress must make its judgments consistent with this Court's exposition of the Constitution and with the limits placed on its legislative authority by provisions such as the Fourteenth Amendment.

The Court's analysis of whether RFRA is a constitutional exercise of Congress' power . . . is premised on the assumption that *Smith* correctly interprets the Free Exercise Clause. This is an assumption that I do not accept. I continue to believe that *Smith* adopted an improper standard for deciding free exercise claims. In *Smith*, five Members of this Court—without briefing or argument on the issue—interpreted the Free Exercise Clause to permit the government to prohibit, without justification, conduct mandated by an individual's religious beliefs, so long as the prohibition is generally applicable. Contrary to the Court's holding in that case, however, the Free Exercise Clause is not simply an antidiscrimination principle that protects only against those laws that single out religious practice for unfavorable treatment. Rather, the Clause is best understood as an affirmative guarantee of the right to participate in religious practices and conduct without impermissible governmental interference, even when such conduct conflicts with a neutral, generally applicable law. Before *Smith*, our free exercise cases were generally in keeping with this idea: where a law substantially burdened religiously motivated conduct—regardless whether it was specifically targeted at religion or applied generally—we required government to justify that law with a compelling state interest and to use means narrowly tailored to achieve that interest. . . .

The Court's rejection of this principle in *Smith* is supported neither by precedent nor, as discussed below, by history. The decision has harmed religious liberty. . . . I believe that, in light of both our precedent and our Nation's tradition of religious liberty, *Smith* is demonstrably wrong. Moreover, it is a recent decision. As such, it has not engendered the kind of reliance on its continued application that would militate against overruling it.

Accordingly, I believe that we should reexamine our holding in *Smith*, and do so in this very case. In its place, I would return to a rule that requires government to justify any substantial burden on religiously motivated conduct by a compelling state interest and to impose that burden only by means narrowly tailored to achieve that interest. . . .

The historical evidence casts doubt on the Court's current interpretation of the Free Exercise Clause. The record instead reveals that its drafters and ratifiers more likely viewed the Free Exercise Clause as a guarantee that government may not unnecessarily hinder believers from freely practicing their religion, a position consistent with our pre-*Smith* jurisprudence. . . .

The original Constitution, drafted in 1787 and ratified by the States in 1788, had no provisions safeguarding individual liberties, such as freedom of speech or religion. Federalists, the chief supporters of the new Constitution, took the view that amending the Constitution to explicitly protect individual freedoms was superfluous, since the rights that the amendments would protect were already completely secure. Moreover, they feared that guaranteeing certain civil liberties might backfire, since the express mention of some freedoms might imply that others were not protected. According to Alexander Hamilton, a Bill of Rights would even be dangerous, in that by specifying "various exceptions to powers" not granted, it "would afford a colorable pretext to claim more than were granted." *The Federalist No. 84*, p. 513 (C. Rossiter ed. 1961). Anti-Federalists, however, insisted on more definite guarantees. Apprehensive that the newly established federal government would overwhelm the rights of States and individuals, they wanted explicit assurances that the federal government had no power in matters of personal liberty. Additionally, Baptists and other Protestant dissenters feared for their religious liberty under the new Federal Government and called for an amendment guaranteeing religious freedom.

In the end, legislators acceded to these demands. By December 1791, the Bill of Rights had been added to the Constitution. With respect to religious liberty, the First Amendment provided: "Congress shall make no law respecting an establishment of religion, or prohibiting the free exercise thereof." U.S. Const., Amdt. 1. Neither the First Congress nor the ratifying state legislatures debated the question of religious freedom in much detail, nor did they directly consider the scope of the First Amendment's free exercise protection. It would be disingenuous to say that the Framers neglected to define precisely the scope of the Free Exercise Clause because the words "free exercise" had a precise meaning. As is the case for a number of the terms used in the Bill of Rights, it is not exactly clear what the Framers thought the phrase signified.

. . . [T]he Framers did not intend simply to prevent the Government from adopting laws that discriminated against religion. Although the Framers may not have asked precisely the questions about religious liberty that we do today, the historical record indicates that they believed that the Constitution affirmatively protects religious free exercise and that it limits the government's ability to intrude on religious practice.

The principle of religious "free exercise" and the notion that religious liberty deserved legal protection were by no means new concepts in 1791, when the Bill of Rights was ratified. To the contrary, these principles were first articulated in this country in the colonies of Maryland, Rhode Island, Pennsylvania, Delaware, and Carolina, in the mid-1600's. These colonies, though established as sanctuaries for particular groups of religious dissenters, extended freedom of religion to groups—although often limited to Christian groups—beyond their own. Thus, they encountered early on the conflicts that may arise in a society made up of a plurality of faiths.

The term "free exercise" appeared in an American legal document as early as 1648, when Lord Baltimore extracted from the new Protestant governor of Maryland and his councilors a promise not to disturb Christians, particularly Roman Catholics, in the "free exercise" of their religion. Soon after, in 1649, the Maryland Assembly enacted the first free exercise clause by passing the Act Concerning Religion. . . . Various agreements between prospective settlers and the proprietors of Carolina, New York, and New Jersey similarly guaranteed religious freedom, using language that paralleled that of the Rhode Island Charter of 1663. . . .

These documents suggest that, early in our country's history, several colonies acknowledged that freedom to pursue one's chosen religious beliefs was an essential liberty. Moreover, these colonies appeared to recognize that government should interfere in religious matters only when necessary to protect the civil peace or to prevent "licentiousness." In other words, when religious beliefs conflicted with civil law, religion prevailed unless important state interests militated otherwise. Such notions parallel the ideas expressed in our pre-*Smith* cases—that government may not hinder believers from freely exercising their religion, unless necessary to further a significant state interest.

The principles expounded in these early charters re-emerged over a century later in state constitutions that were adopted in the flurry of constitution-drafting that followed the American Revolution. By 1789, every State but Connecticut had incorporated some version of a free exercise clause into its constitution. These state provisions, which were typically longer and more detailed than the federal Free Exercise Clause, are perhaps the best evidence of the original understanding of the Constitution's protection of religious liberty. After all, it is reasonable to think that the States that ratified the First Amendment assumed that the meaning of the federal free exercise provision corresponded to that of their existing state clauses. The precise language of these state precursors to the Free Exercise Clause varied, but most guaranteed free exercise of religion or liberty of conscience, limited by particular, defined state interests. . . .

In addition to these state provisions, the Northwest Ordinance of 1787—which was enacted contemporaneously with the drafting of the Constitution and re-enacted by the First Congress—established a bill of rights for a territory that included what is now Ohio, Indiana, Michigan, Wisconsin, and part of Minnesota. Article I of the Ordinance declared:

"No person, *demeaning himself in a peaceable and orderly manner*, shall ever be molested on account of his mode of worship or religious sentiments, in the said territory."

The language used in these state constitutional provisions and the Northwest Ordinance strongly suggests that, around the time of the drafting of the Bill of Rights, it was generally accepted that the right to "free exercise" required, where possible, accommodation of religious practice. If not—and if the Court was correct in *Smith* that generally applicable laws are enforceable regardless of religious conscience—there would have been no need for these documents to specify, as the New York Constitution did, that rights of conscience should not be "construed as to excuse acts of licentiousness, or justify practices inconsistent with the peace or safety of [the] State." Such a proviso would have been superfluous. Instead, these documents make sense only if the right to free exercise was viewed as generally superior to ordinary legislation, to be overridden only when necessary to secure important government purposes. . . .

The practice of the colonies and early States bears out the conclusion that, at the time the Bill of Rights was ratified, it was accepted that government should, when possible, accommodate religious practice. Unsurprisingly, of course, even in the American colonies inhabited by people of religious persuasions, religious conscience and civil law rarely conflicted. Most 17th and 18th century Americans belonged to denominations of Protestant Christianity whose religious practices were generally harmonious with colonial law. Moreover, governments then were far smaller and less intrusive than they are today, which made conflict between civil law and religion unusual.

Nevertheless, tension between religious conscience and generally applicable laws, though rare, was not unknown in pre-Constitutional America. Most commonly, such conflicts arose from oath requirements, military, conscription, and religious assessments. The ways in which these conflicts were resolved suggest that Americans in the colonies and early States thought that, if an individual's religious scruples prevented him from complying with a generally applicable law, the government should, if possible, excuse the person from the law's coverage. . . .

The Religion Clauses of the Constitution represent a profound commitment to religious liberty. Our Nation's Founders conceived of a Republic receptive to voluntary religious expression, not of a secular society in which religious expression is tolerated only when it does not conflict with a generally applicable law. As the historical sources discussed above show, the Free Exercise Clause is properly understood as an affirmative guarantee of the right to participate in religious activities without impermissible governmental interference, even where a believer's conduct is in tension with a law of general application. Certainly, it is in no way anomalous to accord heightened protection to a right identified in the text of the First Amendment. For example, it has long been the Court's position that freedom of speech—a right enumerated only a few words after the right to free exercise—has special constitutional status. Given the centrality of freedom of speech and religion to the American concept of personal liberty, it is altogether reasonable to conclude that both should be treated with the highest degree of respect.

Although it may provide a bright line, the rule the Court declared in *Smith* does not faithfully serve the purpose of the Constitution. Accordingly, I believe that it is essential for the Court to reconsider its holding in *Smith*—and to do so in this very case. I would therefore direct the parties to brief this issue and set the case for reargument.

I respectfully dissent from the Court's disposition of this case.

Source: City of Boerne v. Flores, 117 S. Ct. 2157 (1997).

DOCUMENT 77: Religious Diversity in the United States of America (1998)

Religious liberty, anchored in the Constitution's First and Fourteenth Amendments, has flourished in the United States of America. And this freedom of conscience has brought about an extraordinary diversity of religions among the American people. The variety of religious denominations and sects in America is greater than in any place on earth.

Every major world religion is vibrantly practiced in the United States. For example, there are numerous practitioners of the Baha'i faith, Buddhism, Christianity, Hinduism, Islam, and Judaism. During the colonial and founding eras, various Protestant denominations of Christianity were the prevalent religions. There also were Jews and Roman Catholics, but not many.

During the nineteenth and twentieth centuries, immigrants from all regions of the world came to the United States. And they brought various religions of the world to America.

By the end of the twentieth century Christians were still the majority among religious practitioners in the United States. The largest Christian denomination in the United States of America was the Roman Catholic Church, with more than 61 million members. There were more than 90 million members of various Protestant Christian churches. But no single Protestant church was as large as the Roman Catholic Church in the United States. There also were more than 40 million Americans who identified themselves as Christians but were not members of any Christian church.

At the end of the twentieth century, the United States included many non-Christians. There were more than 3.5 million Jews, more than 3 million Muslims, more than 1 million Hindus, and nearly 1 million Buddhists.

More than 50 million Americans did not identify with any religion. They were either nonbelievers or believers with no particular religious identity.

Freedom of choice in religion is a distinguishing characteristic of the United States of America. This freedom is legally guaranteed by the U.S. Constitution and the fifty state constitutions. Further, it is culturally reinforced through the long-standing and pervasive tradition of religious toleration. This freedom of choice in religion has yielded extraordinary religious diversity.

What are the largest groups of Protestant Christians? What are the main non-Christian religious groups in the United States?

* * *

Religious Groups (More than 50,000 members)	Members
Adventist Churches	840,777
Baha'i Faith	133,000
Baptist Churches	33,209,484
Brethren (German Baptists)	195,680
Buddhists of America	780,000
Christian and Missionary Alliance	311,612
Christian Brethren	100,000
Christian Congregation	114,685
Churches of Christ	2,250,000
Churches of God	281,673
Church of the Nazarene	608,008
Community Churches	250,000
Congregational Churches	107,653

Religious Groups (More than 50,000 members)	Members
Disciples of Christ	910,297
Eastern Orthodox Churches	4,013,821
Episcopal Church	2,536,550
Evangelical Covenant Church	93,136
Evangelical Free Church	242,619
Friends (Quakers)	188,466
Full Gospel Fellowship	195,000
Grace Gospel Fellowship	60,000
Hindu	1,285,000
Independent Fundamental Churches	69,857
Islam	3,332,000
Jehovah's Witnesses	975,829
Jewish (Orthodox, Conservative, Reform)	3,500,000
Latter-Day Saints (Mormon)	4,977,779
Lutheran Churches	8,302,594
Mennonite Churches (including Old Order Amish)	350,547
Methodist Churches	13,483,130
Pentecostal Churches	10,122,982
Presbyterian Churches	4,160,154
Reformed Churches	1,570,718
Roman Catholic Church	61,207,914
Salvation Army	453,150
Unitarian-Universalist Association	215,000

Source: Adapted from *World Almanac and Book of Facts 1999* (Mahwah, N.J., 1998), pp. 684–685.

FURTHER READING

Gaddy, Barbara, T. William Hall, and Robert J. Marzano. *School Wars: Resolving Our Conflict over Religion and Values*. San Francisco: Jossey-Bass, 1996.

Hall, Kermit L., ed. *Major Problems in American Constitutional History: From 1870 to the Present*. Lexington, Mass.: D.C. Heath, 1992, pp. 462–506.

Jelen, Ted G., and Clyde Wilcox. *Public Attitudes Toward Church and State*. Armonk, N.Y.: M. E. Sharpe, 1995.

Kramnick, Isaac, and R. Laurence Moore. *The Godless Constitution: The Case Against Religious Correctness*. New York: W. W. Norton, 1997.

Nord, William A. *Religion and American Education: Rethinking a National Dilemma*. Chapel Hill: University of North Carolina Press, 1995.

Seegers, Mary C., and Ted G. Jelen. *A Wall of Separation? Defining the Public Role of Religion*. Lanham, Md.: Rowman and Littlefield, 1998.

Appendix: Categorical Listings of U.S. Supreme Court Cases Treated in This Volume

A. Equal Access to Public Facilities

B. Free Speech, Fund Raising, and Religion

C. Government Support for Religious Schools

I. Sunday Closing Laws

J. Tax Exemptions for Religious Institutions

Glossary

Appeal. A request to a higher court to review the decision of a lower court.

Appellant. The person who appeals to a higher court to review the decision of a lower court.

Circuit court of appeals. In the judicial system of the United States, there is a court of appeals between the federal district court and the Supreme Court. This typically is the court to which one might appeal to review a decision of the district court.

Civil law. The category of law pertaining to private rights and remedies. In a civil law court case, one person brings suit against another person.

Concurring opinion. An opinion that agrees with the court's decision in a case but disagrees with the reasoning that led to this decision. A justice of the Supreme Court, for example, may write a concurring opinion which offers her or his own reasons that differ from those of the Court's decision.

Criminal law. The type of law that pertains to offenses against the government. In a criminal law court case, the government claims that a person has violated a state or federal law and should be punished.

Defendant. The person defending herself or himself in a civil law case. In a criminal law case, the person accused of committing a crime.

Dissenting opinion. An opinion that disagrees with the decision of the court in a case. A justice, for example, may write a dissenting opinion to explain why he or she disagrees with the majority's opinion. The dissenter may hope to influence public opinion or a future decision of the court.

District court. The court of original jurisdiction in the federal judicial system. A case decided at this lower level of the judicial system may be appealed to the circuit court of appeals and from there to the U.S. Supreme Court.

Due process of law. Certain established rules and procedures must be followed in order that the rights of individuals are fairly protected in legal proceedings. The

Fifth and Fourteenth Amendments of the U.S. Constitution each include a due process clause.

Equal protection of the laws. A guarantee of the Fourteenth Amendment of the U.S. Constitution that no person or category of persons shall be denied the same protection of the laws enjoyed by others.

Establishment clause. One of two religion clauses of the First Amendment of the U.S. Constitution; it prohibits the federal government from making any law to establish a national religion or to otherwise promote or become preferentially involved with religion.

Free exercise clause. One of two religion clauses of the First Amendment of the U.S. Constitution; it prohibits the federal government from acting to prevent a person's freedom to practice his or her religion.

Holding. The court's decision and its reasons in support of the decision in a particular case.

Injunction. A court order that prohibits a person from doing something.

Judicial review. The power of courts of law to review acts by government and to decide whether or not they are in agreement with the Constitution. If not, such acts are declared void or unconstitutional.

Jurisdiction. The authority of a court to hear and decide a case.

Majority opinion. The written explanation of the court's decision in a case to which more than half of the court's members have agreed.

Plaintiff. The person who brings a lawsuit to court.

Plurality opinion. When a sufficient number of justices issue concurring opinions, rather than agreeing fully with the court's primary opinion, the decision is made by a plurality, not a clear-cut majority.

Precedent. A judicial decision in a court case that may be used in deciding subsequent similar cases.

Religious test clause. A clause in Article VI of the U.S. Constitution that prohibits any religious test or oath as a qualification for holding any public office.

Remand. To send back a case from a higher court, such as the U.S. Supreme Court, to the court from which it came for further action.

Stare decisis. Latin words that mean "Let the decision stand." The expectation that principles of law established in earlier judicial decisions will be followed in similar subsequent cases.

Statute. A written law made by a legislature, such as the U.S. Congress.

Index

About the Editors

JOHN J. PATRICK is Director of the Social Studies Development Center and Professor of Education at Indiana University, Bloomington. He is the editor of *Founding the Republic: A Documentary History* (Greenwood, 1995) and the author of *How to Teach the Bill of Rights*.

GERALD P. LONG is a teacher of history and government at Brown County High School in Nashville, IN. He is the author of *Constitutional Rights of Juveniles and Students: Lessons on Sixteen Supreme Court Cases*.

Primary Documents in American History and Contemporary Issues

The Abortion Controversy
Eva R. Rubin, editor

The AIDS Crisis
Douglas A. Feldman and Julia Wang Miller, editors

Capital Punishment in the United States
Bryan Vila and Cynthia Morris, editors

Founding the Republic
John J. Patrick, editor

Free Expression in America
Sheila Suess Kennedy, editor

Genetic Engineering
Thomas A. Shannon, editor

The Gun Control Debate
Marjolijn Bijlefeld, editor

Major Crises in Contemporary American Foreign Policy
Russell D. Buhite, editor

The Right to Die Debate
Marjorie B. Zucker, editor

The Role of Police in American Society
Bryan Vila and Cynthia Morris, editors

Sexual Harassment in America
Laura W. Stein

States' Rights and American Federalism
Frederick D. Drake and Lynn R. Nelson, editors

U.S. Immigration and Naturalization Laws and Issues
Michael LeMay and Elliott Robert Barkan, editors

Women's Rights in the United States
Winston E. Langley and Vivian C. Fox, editors